Hans Christian Andersen in American Literary Criticism of the Nineteenth Century

Hans Christian Andersen in American Literary Criticism of the Nineteenth Century

Herbert Rowland

FAIRLEIGH DICKINSON UNIVERSITY PRESS
Vancouver • Madison • Teaneck • Wroxton

Published by Fairleigh Dickinson University Press
Copublished by The Rowman & Littlefield Publishing Group, Inc.
4501 Forbes Boulevard, Suite 200, Lanham, Maryland 20706
www.rowman.com

6 Tinworth Street, London SE11 5AL, United Kingdom

*Fairleigh Dickinson University Press gratefully acknowledges the support received for
scholarly publishing from the Friends of FDU Press.*

British Library Cataloguing in Publication Information Available

Library of Congress Cataloging-in-Publication Data Available

Names: Rowland, Herbert, author.
Title: Hans Christian Andersen in American literary criticism of the
    nineteenth-century / Herbert Rowland.
Description: Vancouver ; Madison [NJ] : Fairleigh Dickinson University
    Press ; Lanham : Copublished by Rowman & Littlefield Publishing Group,
    Inc., [2020] | Sequel to: More Than Meets the Eye. | Includes
    bibliographical references and index.
Identifiers: LCCN 2020033413 (print) | LCCN 2020033414 (ebook) | ISBN
    9781683932666 (cloth ; alk. paper) | ISBN 9781683932673 (electronic)
Subjects: LCSH: Andersen, H. C. (Hans Christian), 1805-1875—Criticism and
    interpretation. | Andersen, H. C. (Hans Christian),
    1805-1875—Appreciation—United States.
Classification: LCC PT8120 .R64 2020 (print) | LCC PT8120 (ebook) | DDC
    398.8--dc23
LC record available at https://lccn.loc.gov/2020033413

Contents

Acknowledgments

I would like to thank the staff of the Interlibrary Loan Office of Purdue University, especially Cheryl A. Sagendorf and Connie Richards, for their patience in handling my endless requests for publications that were often rare, difficult to locate, and—heavy. Special thanks go to electronic resources librarian Anna Seiffert and Dr. Robert Freeman, associate professor, bibliographer, and reference librarian, both of Purdue, for providing me with extended temporary access to parts of a database not held at the university that were critical to my work. A number of librarians around the country graciously furnished me with various kinds of information: Autumn L. Mather, of the Newberry Library in Chicago; Michele McNabb, of the Danish Immigrant Museum in Elk Horn, Iowa; Jamie Kingman Rice, of the Maine Historical Society in Portland; and Deborah Thomas, of the National Digital Newspaper Program at the Library of Congress. I would also like to express my gratitude to James Gifford, director of Fairleigh Dickinson University Press, as well as to the editorial committee of the press for their interest in the study and to James in particular for his helpful suggestions for its improvement. Thanks also go to the anonymous reader, who read the manuscript with exceptional care and made many valuable comments. My thanks and apologies to any other individuals whose good services should be recognized here.

Preface

In the preface to a study published in 2006 under the title *More Than Meets the Eye: Hans Christian Andersen and Nineteenth-Century American Criticism* I wrote the following:

> The title of the present volume probably contains a couple of surprises for the vast majority of readers, even the literary scholars among them. Longer than anyone can remember, Americans and other English speakers have associated the name of Hans Christian Andersen almost exclusively with fairy tales for children. Yet the title of this book indicates that critical study of Andersen, like that of Emerson or any other literary figure, is both possible and has actually been practiced in the United States. In Denmark and other parts of Scandinavia, indeed, there exists a long tradition of Andersen scholarship that continues to thrive to this day. In histories of Danish and Scandinavian literature Andersen occupies a position reserved for major writers. . . . This recognition derives in part from the knowledge that Andersen's fairy tales are only a portion of a lifework that also includes several novels and travel books, many plays, a substantial body of poetry, and an autobiography.[1]

With respect to those who have not read *More Than Meets the Eye*, the surprise value of these words must still hold. For those who *have* read it, a volume of 274 pages, another surprise must lie in the publication of the present book, which is the sequel to it. *Hans Christian Andersen in American Literary Criticism of the Nineteenth Century* owes its existence to the fact that the digitization of older American periodicals has meanwhile proceeded apace, adding rich sources to those available for the earlier study.[2] Among these resources, newspapers figured prominently, only three of which featured in *More Than Meets the Eye*. Contemporary newspapers indeed proved to have devoted considerable space to book reviews, many of which were of perhaps surprisingly high quality. This is also true of many notices published in magazines that did not enjoy the same repute as, for example, the *Atlantic Monthly*, *Harper's New Monthly*, or *Putnam's Magazine.*

The plethora of "new" notices and articles gleaned from these sites—some three and a half times as many as were formerly available—reveals, among many other things, that the American Andersen-reception was more rapidly responsive to newly published works and, on the whole, far more penetrating than appeared to be the case during the preparation of *More Than Meets the Eye.* It also sheds light on American critics' then apparent neglect of Andersen's fairy tales, which, according to numerous reviews of other writings by the Dane, became his most popular works soon after making their debut in 1846: there was no such neglect after all. The writings by Hjalmar Hjorth Boyesen, William Dean Howells, and Horace E. Scudder examined in the first book may be the most perceptive individual American commentaries on Andersen made during the time under consideration. However, many of those scrutinized in the following pages are themselves highly percipient, corroborating, amplifying, and augmenting previously discussed insights. In aggregate, they constitute an even more imposing body of work than that investigated in the earlier study, one which includes additional contributions by the writers just named that heretofore escaped detection. *More Than Meets the Eye* went a long way toward rectifying the prevailing image of Andersen in the United States and remains profitable reading for the valuable material it covers. However, *Hans Christian Andersen in American Literary Criticism of the Nineteenth Century* goes well beyond it, updating it in certain respects. Surely, additional reviews and articles will eventually emerge from their present obscurity, but the number and provenance of those that have already come to light suggest that further finds will not significantly alter the portrait finished here.

NOTES

1. Herbert Rowland, *More Than Meets the Eye: Hans Christian Andersen and Nineteenth-Century American Criticism* (Madison and Teaneck, NJ: Fairleigh Dickinson University Press, 2006), 7.

2. Newly accessible to me were the "American Antiquarian Society Historical Periodicals" (more than 6,500 and increasing as of this writing); the "American Periodical Series" (1,240 magazines and journals); "America's Historical Newspapers" (more than 2,000 titles and still growing); "Chronicling America: Historic American Newspapers" (11,505,288 selected pages); Newspapers.com (more than 4,500 and still adding); "Nineteenth-Century U.S. Newspapers" (500); "ProQuest Historical Papers" (52 from the United States); and "Small Town Newspapers" (more than 250) as well as sites sponsored by individual periodicals such as "HarpWeek Archives" (*Harper's Weekly*) and "The Nation Digital Archive."

Introduction

One of the major themes in Andersen scholarship over the past twenty-five years or so has been the response to the poet and his work outside of Denmark. A survey of relevant books and bibliographies reveals that during this period no less than some sixty studies have been devoted to Andersen's reception in nearly thirty countries, ranging from most of the nations of Europe to ones as far-flung as China, Japan, Vietnam, Mexico, and South Africa.[1] An even greater number, some seventy books and articles, have dealt with various aspects of translating Andersen into the languages of these countries as well as Arabic. As demonstrated more extensively in the conclusion, the present volume takes its place within this current of research as the major full-scale examination of the response to Andersen in the United States.[2] American commentators focused their attention on Andersen's works per se. However, we shall see that questions of translation also occupied several of them, especially toward the end of the nineteenth century, when the fairy tales and stories had already attained the status of classics.

It should be noted that a large number of reviews published in American periodicals originated in Great Britain and that many of these publications were themselves either shipped to, or reprinted in the United States. This means, of course, that British critics played a role in shaping Americans' understanding of Andersen. Nonetheless, I have limited myself to the work of American commentators, for the study attempts to determine express critical opinion rather than the, in any event, elusive influence of reviewers on readers or on each other. Taking into account the broad similarities between American and British critics' responses to Andersen, moreover, it would be of little profit to subject their relationship to scrutiny. More practically, finally, Elias Bredsdorff long ago published an extensive investigation of

British reviews of Andersen's writings, and it would make little sense to repeat his work.[3]

Hans Christian Andersen in American Literary Criticism of the Nineteenth Century can offer, at best, conjectural generalization about the impact Andersen's critics had on the American reading public. However, it is certainly reasonable to assume that they exerted an influence of varying kind, breadth, and degree and that the evidence examined can therefore be considered symptomatic of broader opinion.[4] The earlier reference to Boyesen indicates that my use of the term "American commentator" is not absolute. While the Norwegian and a few others came to the United States from abroad, however, they published their work in American periodicals for American readers, and, if often enjoying certain advantages over their native-born counterparts, did so for the most part quite matter-of-factly.

In order to create an aggregate profile of American review criticism of Andersen, I have sought to identify as many of his reviewers as possible and to characterize their critical programs, where practicable. The sketches of significant figures such as William Gilmore Simms and John Neal, about whom substantial information is available, naturally tend toward detail. Unfortunately, the policy of anonymous reviewing, which remained in place throughout most of the nineteenth century, conceals the identity of the majority of Andersen's reviewers, whose work must therefore speak entirely for itself. I have also endeavored to provide as much data about the periodicals as possible—their editors, editorial policy, target readership, and circulation. Such factors complement the critical writings by suggesting both the nature and the reach of Andersen criticism.

Hans Christian Andersen in American Literary Criticism of the Nineteenth Century proceeds in the mode of straightforward historical-analytical scholarship and is arranged according to genre and chronology. Chapter 1 presents a statistical overview of the material examined in the following chapters, and it is here that most of the corrections of *More Than Meets the Eye* are made. Andersen's six novels and most of his several travel books and sketches are the subjects of chapters 2 and 3, respectively. A comparatively brief chapter on his poetry and plays (chapter 4) provides information about his work in genres underrepresented in American criticism. By way of a preview, two of the poems became part of church services and Sunday School classes in America beginning in 1869, and one of the plays figured importantly in, and in connection with a treatise on a prominent motif in Western literature. Chapter 5 deals with Andersen's autobiography, which received more critical attention than any other single work by the author, while chapter 6 treats the fairy tales and stories, for which he presently, though not immediately, became best known. The final chapter (chapter 7) scrutinizes an assortment of critical general interest articles, which include writings by some of Andersen's most distinguished American commentators. Each chapter begins with an overview of its contents, together with plot summaries and information on the contemporary reception in Denmark and other countries, where applicable, and closes with a summary of its findings. The conclusion draws together the major strands of earlier discussion and addresses the place of the American reception within the international response to Andersen. In each chapter, discussion proceeds chronologically in the main, and the list of primary sources is arranged in chronological order.

Neither length nor originality influenced the inclusion of the reviews and articles examined in the study. Many cover from one to several columns on the typically densely printed pages of the periodicals, but perhaps the majority are brief, especially when compared to notices published in English and German journals. However, even some of these possess an integrity, a wholeness of vision that make them illuminating. A goodly number of the writings are truly unique in opinion, viewpoint, expression, and/or contextualization, but others are more pedestrian in nature. Some of the latter have been included for consideration nonetheless, for they are instructive in their own way, and the aim of the book remains to assemble a composite picture of Andersen's critical reception in the United States, utilizing as many available resources as recommend themselves, whatever the reasons may be. Certain pieces that are not particularly useful or repeat insights formulated more perceptively or in broader contexts elsewhere have been excluded from discussion, though all are entered in the "Chronological List of Primary Sources" at the end of the book. A few reviews and articles deal with more than one work or aspect of Andersen's oeuvre and are thus discussed in the appropriate chapters and counted as separate writings. An even smaller number treat Andersen in broader contexts and/or together with other figures.

Given the lack of ready access to the reviews and articles, I have quoted copiously from them, using run-in quotations except for lengthy passages for aesthetic purposes, and I am confident that I have either reproduced or paraphrased the most telling portions from each. When listing or discussing Andersen's fairy tales as printed in nineteenth-century collections, I have retained the often varying titles used by the contemporary translators. Otherwise, I have employed the translations by Jean Hersholt, the Danish American actor and collector of Anderseniana whose edition is considered by perhaps the leading expert in the field to be the best in English.[5] Danish titles of the tales as well as the other works appear as found in *Andersen: H. C. Andersens Samlede Værker* (*Andersen: Hans Christian Andersen's Collected Works*), issued by the Danske Sprog- og Litteraturselskab (Danish Society for Language and Literature) and the most recent and complete edition of the writings.[6] In general, I have used both the English and Danish titles in first references to works, the latter in parentheses, and the English titles alone in subsequent references. I am responsible for the translations from secondary sources.

Hans Christian Andersen in American Literary Criticism of the Nineteenth Century is addressed principally to Andersen scholars and other Scandinavianists as well as to Americanists, both in the United States and abroad. Modern theory contends that works of literature, as found on the printed page, represent so many sets of potential meanings that come into existence only through the act of reading. If this is true, then nineteenth-century American critics' readings of Andersen's writings perforce constitute them in part, realizing them in often new and unique ways conditioned by, among other things, their tradition(s) of reading. They thereby complement the "co-creation" of the works by other Andersen readers of all times and places, including those currently active in Scandinavian studies, with their peculiar traditions of reading and literary-historical interests. For this reason, if for no other, they should engage the attention of these individuals.

Those who study the literature of another country, no matter what their nationality, generally seek recognition through their contributions to the literary scholarship of that nation, which is natural and proper. However, such individuals can play another important and unique role as, for example, *American* Scandinavianists or *American* Germanists by also contextualizing the objects and results of their research in the experience of their home country. With respect to Andersen's reception in the United States, the fundamental question should be how his coeval American critics did so, either overtly or by implication. That is, how did they "naturalize" a respected contemporary author from abroad in their own culture and public and private spheres? In other words, to what "uses" did they put him while pursuing their own ends?

These questions should surely also, or perhaps primarily, arouse the interest of purveyors of American culture. For their forebears—whose trade they might well have plied had they lived before the institutionalization of English literary study beginning around the last quarter of the nineteenth century[7]— assigned Andersen distinctive roles in various American "dramas" of the time. They made him a supporting character in the closet piece featuring the lengthy conflict between the romance and the novel and chose him as an adjudicator in the decades-long tragi-comedy created by literary and journalistic sensationalism. Most significantly, perhaps, they cast him as a leading figure in the national tragedy surrounding slavery, the Civil War, and Reconstruction. Andersen's much admired poetic style, in turn, apparently inspired a substantial number of his American critics to dip their pens in similar ink. For many, some of whom were accomplished authors in their own right, rendered commentaries in lyrical locutions that retain a distinctive, if often quaint, appeal even today. A few of them, animated by other qualities of Andersen's writing, delivered themselves of what amount to independent works.

Scandinavianists and Americanists may or may not have expert knowledge of each other's fields. I have therefore included a large amount of information for purposes of perspective and clarity that will be self-evident to one or the other of the groups, and for this I ask their forbearance.

NOTES

1. Many of these contributions are found in the proceedings of the four international Hans Christian Andersen conferences held during this time: *Andersen og verden: Indlæg fra den Første Internationale H. C. Andersen-Konference 25.–31. august 1991,* ed. Johan de Mylius, Aage Jørgensen, and Viggo Hjørnager Pedersen (Odense: Odense Universitetsforlag, 1993); *Hans Christian Andersen, a Poet in Time: Papers from the Second International Hans Christian Andersen Conference 29 July to 2 August 1996,* ed. Johan de Mylius, Aage Jørgensen, and Viggo Hjørnager Pedersen (Odense: Odense University Press, 1999); *H. C. Andersen: Old Problems and New Readings*, ed. Steven P. Sondrup (Odense and Provo: Hans Christian Andersen Center, University of Southern Denmark Press, and Brigham Young University, 2004); and *Hans Christian Andersen: Between Children's Literature and Adult Literature: Papers from the Fourth International Hans Christian Andersen Conference 1 August to 5 August 2005*, ed. Johan de Mylius, Aage Jørgensen, and Viggo Hjørnager Pedersen (Odense: Hans Christian Andersen Center, University of Southern Denmark, 2005). Also see the names of countries in the indices to Aage Jørgensen, *H. C. Andersen—Litteraturen 1875–1968: En Bibliografi* (Aarhus: Akademisk Boghandel, 1970); *H. C. Andersen—Litteraturen 1969–1994: En Bibliografi* (Odense: H. C. Andersens Hus, 1995); *H. C. Andersen—Litteraturen 1995–2006: En Bibliografi* (Odense: Odense Bys Museer, 2006); and the periodical bibliographies in *Anderseniana* for 1997, 1998, 2008, 2010, 2013, and 2018.

2. Brief treatments of the subject are found in Aage Jørgensen, "H. C. Andersen i Europas spejl," *Anderseniana,* 1995, 22–24, and Herbert Rowland, "The Image of H. C. Andersen in American Magazines during the Author's Lifetime," in Sondrup, *H. C. Andersen: Old Problems and New Readings*, 175–98.

3. Elias Bredsdorff, *H. C. Andersen og England* (Copenhagen: Rosenkilde og Baggers Forlag, 1954), 428–88. A search of modern electronic resources would doubtless reveal additional reviews, but given Bredsdorff's coverage of the major British journals and the other factors cited earlier, the decision to exclude analysis of English notices seems reasonable.

4. What Nina Baym writes about the reviewing of novels applies to other genres as well: "But novel reviewing . . . was directed toward readers, was conducted in constant awareness of what people were reading, and was always trying to understand their reasons for public preferences. The reviews offer guidance and correction in a

way that enables us to see what they thought they were guiding and correcting"; Nina Baym, *Novels, Readers and Reviewers: Responses to Fiction in Antebellum America* (Ithaca, NY: Cornell University Press, 1984), 19.

5. See *The Complete Andersen: All of the 168 Stories by Hans Christian Andersen*, trans. Jean Hersholt (New York: Heritage Press, 1942–1947) and Viggo Hjørnager Pedersen, *Ugly Ducklings? Studies in the English Translations of Hans Christian Andersen's Tales and Stories* (Odense: University Press of Southern Denmark, 2004), 277.

6. See Hans Christian Andersen, *Andersen: H. C. Andersens Samlede Værker*, ed. Klaus P. Mortensen et al., 18 vols. (Copenhagen: Danske Sprog- og Litteraturselskab/ Gyldendal, 2003–2007). With certain exceptions, future references to this edition are to *Samlede Værker*.

7. See Gerald Graff, *Professing Literature: An Institutional History* (Chicago and London: University of Chicago Press, 1987), 55.

Chapter One

The American Reception of Andersen in Statistical Overview

Statistics provide little insight into critical opinion of an author's work per se. However, they can play an important ancillary role in its study by reflecting matters such as the course of its history; the preferences of publishers, critics, and readers; and the geographical, social, and cultural horizons of the writer's readership in the broadest sense. The information and figures in the present chapter offer such a multidimensional overview of Andersen's critical reception in the United States during roughly the second half of the nineteenth century. The survey takes the form of introductory comments and six tables, each of which is followed by discussion of the most important findings.

The American response to Andersen explored in the subsequent chapters emerged primarily from an examination of 223 notices and fifteen general interest articles that came out between 1845 and the final year of the century. These publications form the basis of the present study. However, they are complemented by another 109 reviews, (pre-)publication announcements, and advertisements as well as ten general interest articles and nineteen other pieces of various kinds. While mostly brief and of minor overall import, these writings often offer illuminating or useful individual insights. The figures in the tables below represent only the principal critical writings, but the deliberations in the succeeding chapters draw on the additional material as well, and, as mentioned earlier, all relevant titles are included in the "Chronological List of Primary Sources" at the end of the book.

Research for this study has shown that the works discussed in notices and other writings were not the only avenue to Andersen that reviewers and the general public alike enjoyed. Certain poems and numerous individual tales as well as excerpts from longer works were issued in a large number of magazines and newspapers. Indeed, 535 occurrences of such printings surfaced during the preliminary work for this book, and evidence exists that many

more remain to be discovered.[1] One must assume that they furthered professional (and general) readers' acquaintance with Andersen and influenced their
opinion(s) of him. Though subjected to minimal examination in this volume,
they form a significant part of the context in which Andersen's commentators
wrote. Together with the writings referenced in the preceding paragraph, they
attest to what can only be described as an exceedingly high degree of awareness of the poet in the American public during the period in question.

As indicated in the introduction, Americans' access to Andersen's poetry
and plays is discussed in chapter 4. They received their greatest exposure to
his extensive prose through the many editions published in England and the
United States. Bredsdorff's bibliography lists more than 180 collections of
the fairy tales and stories, sixteen editions of the novels, nine of the travel
books, and four of the autobiographies that appeared from 1846 to 1899;
many of these were issued in later, often multiple printings.[2] However, at
least seventy-eight individual fairy tales and stories, exactly half of the total
156, attained an even higher profile through their publication, in some 270
individual occurrences, in a wide assortment of magazines, newspapers,
and books.[3] It is impossible to conclusively identify the influences that determined the selection of the tales. However, the relatively numerous printings of "The Angel" ("The Dead Child and the Angel," etc.; "Engelen";
18), "Grandmother" ("En Historie" ["Bedstemoder"]; 13), and "The Daisy"
("Gaaseurten"; 11), among others, suggest that the sentiment and religiosity also found in the poetry, together with an admixture of commentary on
class and the social role of the poet as the voice of nature, were decisive or
contributing factors. Humorous and/or satiric tales such as "The Emperor's
New Clothes" ("Keiserens nye Klæder"; 22) and "What the Old Man Does Is
Always Right" ("Hvad Fatter gjør, det er altid det Rigtige"; 11) also gained
favor with editors and, apparently, the general public as well.

During the nineteenth century, novels and other long prose works were
commonly issued serially in periodicals before being published in book form.
The reverse, however, was rare, so it is no surprise that American magazines
and newspapers generally carried only excerpts from Andersen's novels,
travel books, and autobiographies. If there is some surprise, it is that the
novel(ette) *Lucky Peer* (*Lykke-Peer*) and *A Visit to Charles Dickens's House*
(*Et Besøg hos Charles Dickens i Sommeren 1857*) both appeared at least once
in their entirety in periodicals.[4] All the same, the comparatively large number
of excerpts, particularly from *A Poet's Bazaar* (*En Digters Bazar*, 1842) and
the autobiographies, supports the notion of Andersen's high visibility and
popularity in the United States. It also invites the conjecture that the apparent failure of the ten-volume Author's Edition of 1869–1871 was due not to
indifference on the part of the American public, but rather to circumstantial

factors such as the coincidental depression in the book publishing industry from 1860 to 1880; exacerbated by the economic panic of 1873 and the ensuing national depression, this downturn occurred at a time when the normally profit-yielding printings of the books were likely issued.[5] The great popularity of Charles Dickens in America, as in all of Europe, suffices to explain the appeal of *A Visit*, while Andersen's own powers of description doubtless drew publishers and readers alike to the *Bazaar*. Almost one-third of the excerpts from the autobiographies revolve around the Dane's friendship with everybody's darling, Swedish singer Jenny Lind, and somewhat more than one-fourth convey his reminiscences of the highly esteemed Alexandre Dumas (père). Several recount how Andersen, as a child, rebuked a man about to strike him by asking how he dare do so before the eyes of God. This and the many other anecdotes frequently found under headings such as "Literary News" and "Foreign Items," not least of all those revealing Andersen's many eccentricities, indicate a wide interest among Americans in the man as well as the author.

Table 1.1 registers all the publications of Andersen's works discussed in the reviews and critical general interest articles. They are listed according to genre, year(s) of appearance, and the number of commentaries each received, together with the respective years of issuance. The last column combines these totals with those found in *More Than Meets the Eye*, numerically illustrating the entirety of the American critical reception of Andersen during the nineteenth century.

Table 1.1.   English-Language Editions of Andersen's Works Discussed in Reviews and General Interest Articles

This table shows all English-language editions of Andersen's works discussed in reviews and general interest articles published in American periodicals during the nineteenth century, together with related figures. Compiled by the author.

Autobiographies		
The [True] Story of My Life (Mit eget Eventyr uden Digtning / Mit Livs Eventyr; 1847, 1871	29 reviews, 1847–1871	44 reviews, 1847–1875
Fairy Tales and Stories	81 reviews, 1846–1899	97 reviews, 1846–1899
General		3 reviews, 1854, 1861, 1875
The Nightingale, and Other Stories (1846)	1 review, 1846	1 review, 1846
Wonderful Stories for Children (1846)	5 reviews, 1846–1847	5 reviews, 1846–1847

(continued)

Table 1.1. *(continued)*

Fairy Tales and Stories (cont.)		
A Christmas Greeting (1847)	2 reviews, 1848	3 reviews, 1848
The Shoes of Fortune, and Other Tales (1847)	2 reviews, 1848	2 reviews, 1848
A Danish Story Book (1848)	3 reviews, 1848, 1864	4 reviews, 1848, 1864
The Dream of Little Tuk, and Other Tales (1848)	5 reviews, 1848	5 reviews, 1848
Hans Andersen's Story Book (1849)[a]	2 reviews, 1848	4 reviews, 1848–1849, 1852
The Story Teller (1850)	1 review, 1851	1 review, 1851
The Ugly Duck, and Other Tales (1850)		1 review, 1850
Little Ellie, and Other Tales		
The Story Teller		
Wonderful Tales from Denmark (1850)	2 reviews, 1850–1851	2 reviews, 1850–1851
Hans Andersen's Wonderful Tales (1851)		1 review, 1851
A Poet's Day Dreams (1853)	1 review, 1853	1 review, 1853
The Sand-Hills of Jutland (1860)	16 reviews, 1860	18 reviews, 1860
The Ice-Maiden, and Other Tales (1863)	7 reviews, 1863–1864	9 reviews, 1863–1864
The Mud King's Daughter, and Other Tales (1864?)	1 review, 1864	1 review, 1864
The Will-o'-the-Wisps Are in Town (1867)	1 review, 1867	1 review, 1867
Wonder Stories Told for Children (1870)	10 reviews, 1870	12 reviews, 1870
Fairy Tales and Sketches (1871)		1 review, 1871
Stories and Tales (1871)	10 reviews, 1871	10 reviews, 1871
Hans Andersen's Good Wishes for the Children (1873)	1 review, 1873	1 review, 1873
Fairy Tales and Stories (1887)	1 review, 1887	1 review, 1887
The Little Mermaid, and Other Stories (1893)	4 reviews, 1893	4 reviews, 1893
Tales from Hans Andersen (Lippincott; 1893)	1 review, 1893	1 review, 1893
Fairy Tales (1894)	1 review, 1894	1 review, 1894
Tales from Hans Andersen (T. Y. Crowell; 1893)	3 reviews, 1892, 1894, 1898	3 reviews, 1892, 1894, 1898
Fairy Tales from Hans Christian Andersen (1899)	1 review, 1899	1 review, 1899
Novels	66 reviews, 1845–1892	74 reviews, 1845–1892
The Improvisatore: or, Life in Italy (*Improvisatoren*; 1845, 1870)	22 reviews, 1845–1892	25 reviews, 1845–1892
O. T. (*O. T.*; 1845, 1870)	14 reviews, 1845–1871	15 reviews, 1845–1871

Novels (cont.)

Only a Fiddler (*Kun en Spillemand*; 1845, 1870)	15 reviews, 1845–1870	18 reviews, 1845–1870
The Two Baronesses (*De to Baronesser*; 1869)	14 reviews, 1869–1870	15 reviews, 1869–1870
To Be, or Not to Be? (*"At være eller ikke være"*)	1 review, 1857	1 review, 1857

Prose Poem

Picture Book without Pictures (*Billedbog uden Billeder*; 1847)	4 reviews, 1848–1849	6 reviews, 1847–1852

Travel Books	43 reviews, 1846–1872	51 reviews, 1846–1872
A Poet's Bazaar (*En Digters Bazar*; 1846)	16 reviews, 1846–1871	18 reviews, 1846–1872
In Spain and A Visit to Portugal (*I Spanien, Et Besøg i Portugal 1866*; 1870)	16 reviews, 1870	19 reviews, 1870
Pictures of Travel (*Skyggebilleder* et al.; 1871)[b]	11 reviews, 1871–1872	14 reviews, 1851–1872

Critical General Interest Articles	15, 1854–1896	38, 1854–1896

a The volume bears the publication year of 1849, but either it was released the preceding year or the reviews, which appeared in December 1848, were based on advance copies.

b This is the title of a volume in the Author's Edition that contains *Rambles in the Hartz Mountains* (*Skyggebilleder af en Reise til Harzen, det sachsiske Schweiz etc. etc., i Sommeren 1831*, literally, *Silhouettes of a Trip to the Hartz Mountains, Saxon Switzerland, etc., etc., in the Summer of 1831*); *Pictures of Sweden* (*I Sverrig*); *In Switzerland* (*Brudstykke af en Reise i Schweitz*, literally, *Fragments of a Trip to Switzerland*, which includes the individually published travel sketches "Ragatz" ["Ragaz (Bad-Pfäffers)"], "The Lion at Lucerne" ["Løven ved Luzern"], and "The Celebration at Oberammergau" ["Passionsskuespillet i Oberammergau i 1860"]); and *A Visit at Charles Dickens's House* (*Et Besøg hos Charles Dickens i Sommeren 1857*). The figure in the final column includes the reviews of *Pictures of Sweden* counted in 2006.

Table 1.1 confirms that Andersen's memoirs attracted more critical commentary than any other single work. If one considers the autobiographical nature of the travel books, indeed, then commentators' interest in Andersen as a person appears even more, substantially more marked. All the same, the novels, taken together (i.e., as a genre) exceed both the autobiography and the travelogues, individually, in number of reviews and approach their total when combined. Not surprisingly, the fairy tales and stories far outstripped all of the other kinds, especially when one includes *Picture Book without Pictures* (*Billedbog uden Billeder*), which was often published together with them, in their number; three of the collections approximate or surpass certain of the novels and travel books in cumulative number of reviews. Thus, American critics accorded Andersen's imaginative work substantially more scrutiny than to his writing about his life, as one would expect. It bears stating here that a couple of them made noteworthy remarks on two of his plays, if not in dedicated reviews. However, there is no evidence that any of them took more than a cursory look at the novels *To Be, or Not to Be?* (*"At være eller ikke være"*) and *Lucky Peer*, though both were available in English translation soon after their appearance in Denmark.[6] And the poetry apparently elicited no critical reaction at all. Nonetheless, the 272 reviews and thirty-eight critical general interest articles, 310 writings in all, represent an abundance of interest in Andersen among American critics.

Table 1.2 shows the chronological distribution of the reviews and general interest articles, including all but four, which were published in 1857 and 1858 and thus fall outside of the groupings that emerge.[7]

Table 1.2.   Chronological Groupings of Commentaries on Andersen's Work

This table indicates the chronological groupings into which the commentaries on Andersen's works fall. Compiled by the author.

	1845–1853	*1860–1867*	*1869–1871*	*1872–1899*
Fairy Tales and Stories	22	26	21	12
The [True] Story of My Life	9	0	20	0
The Improvisatore	5	0	15	2
O. T.	5	0	11	0
Only a Fiddler	5	0	9	0
The Two Baronesses	0	0	14	0
Picture Book without Pictures	4	0	0	0
In Spain and A Visit to Portugal	0	0	16	0
Pictures of Travel	0	0	11	1
A Poet's Bazaar	1	0	15	0
General Interest Articles	0	4	1	8
Totals	51	30	133	23

Table 1.2 reveals a chronological pattern of critical commentary similar to that of its predecessor of 2006, the largest clusters occurring from the mid-1840s to the early 1850s and from the late 1860s to the early 1870s. The first and third clusters reflect, respectively, Andersen's initial entry into the English-speaking world and the American consciousness as well as the wave of attention he received upon the issuance of the Author's Edition. At the same time, certain noteworthy differences are apparent. While the 1850s remain a comparatively barren decade, the period from 1860 to 1867, though a high point only with respect to the stories and tales, produced a number of writings nearly quadruple that recorded in the earlier study. Most of these pieces are accounted for by the responses to Anne S. Bushby's collection *The*

Sand-Hills of Jutland and Fanny Fuller's American translation of *The Ice-Maiden* and other stories, which were concentrated just before and during the Civil War, 1860 and 1863, respectively. These commentaries were followed by a mere sprinkling leading up to the publication of the first volumes of the Author's Edition in 1869. Then, it is not too much to say, the dam broke and the floodwaters surged. Between 1869 and 1871, 133 writings appeared in American periodicals, almost all of them reviews that followed the volumes of the Author's Edition as they were issued. They comprise roughly 56 percent of all the newly discovered notices and articles.

The total of publications that came out between 1872 and 1899 amounts to an average of somewhat less than one per year and is thus anything but impressive. Together with the numerous, varied kinds of noncritical general interest articles that appeared over the same time span, however, it bespeaks a sustained, in part evaluative interest in Andersen that lasted well beyond his death in 1875.[8]

The mistaken notion that Andersen wrote his fairy tales and stories primarily or exclusively for children grew more firmly entrenched in the United States over the later decades of the nineteenth century. It was during this time that his novels and other works fell increasingly into neglect. Both developments may be traced at least in part to the fact that around one-quarter of his more realistic *stories*, which are devoid of the preternatural or the supernatural characteristic of the *fairy tales* and were mostly written during the later stages of his career, were reviewed in either none or in only one or two of the collections critiqued in American periodicals.[9] Those that entirely escaped reviewers' ken include "The Gardener and the Noble Family" ("Gartneren og Herskabet"), "The Great Sea Serpent" ("Den store Søslange"), and "The New Century's Goddess" ("Det nye Aarhundredes Musa"), which rank among Andersen's classic works and/or reflect his interest in social issues and science and technology. Such "non-reception" would clearly not have sharpened the critical eye for the prominence of the "story" in his oeuvre or of Andersen as a social commentator or proponent of technological progress. A lack of familiarity with them during the dozen years of Americans' greatest exposure to the stories and tales may also have dulled their awareness of the novels and other works that were clearly written for adults.

As indicated earlier, American critics devoted significantly less attention to Andersen following his death in 1875 than during the preceding period. However, journalists and, consequently, the American public continued to embrace him, as the chronological distribution of noncritical general interest articles reveals.

The shape of the distribution shown in table 1.3 resembles that of the critical writings. The many articles that came out in the 1870s obviously bespeak a writer at the peak of his popularity. The lion's share appeared from 1869 to the mid-1870s and thus can be attributed largely to the issuance of the Author's Edition and Andersen's death. However, these general interest pieces continued to appear in significant numbers throughout the final quarter of the century. The 1880s, while representing a comparative lull, still produced a sum approaching 86 percent of the total of the two and a half decades extending from the mid-1840s through the 1860s, and the 1890s witnessed a surge of writing substantially greater than all the other decades combined, with the exception of the 1870s. A similar but even more imposing picture emerges when one considers the distribution of all the publications relating to Andersen during the relevant period—reviews and critical general interest articles, both major and minor, articles with significant commentary, noncritical writings, and texts.

Table 1.3.   Distribution of Critical Writings by Decade

This table registers the distribution of reviews and general interest articles related to Andersen's work by decade. Compiled by the author.

1840s	1850s	1860s	1870s	1880s	1890s
3	19	49	314	61	157

Table 1.4 reveals the 1860s to have been a peak in Americans' broader interest in Andersen. Seventy-two of the publications issued during the decade, almost two-thirds of them composed of reviews, critical general interest articles, and individual texts, appeared in 1869, in the course of which the first volumes of the Author's Edition came out. Thirty-seven others, more than half of them texts, were published in 1868, perhaps owing in part to the debut of Andersen's tales in the *Riverside Magazine for Young People*, which was edited by Horace Scudder.[10] However, the remaining 132 publications were spread over all the preceding years of the decade, with thirty-nine, twenty-three, fourteen, and twenty clustered in 1860, 1861, 1864, and 1867, respectively. Sixty-seven of them were critical commentaries of various kinds, while 125 were texts. All of this is to say that interest in Andersen was not only growing but also was already substantial even in the years leading up to the apogee of his presence in the American press. The steep decline in that interest apparent in the 1880s began during the second half of the preceding decade, when only fifty-four of the total 715 publications appeared, a mere 7.5 percent, which may have been a natural reaction to the intensity of the attention paid Andersen during the preceding years. In any case, the significant upswing of the 1890s suggests that he had found a permanent home in the American consciousness, not least of all because the vast majority of the publications that created it were of a popular, general interest nature.

Table 1.4.   Distribution of American Publications Related to Andersen

This table shows the decade-wise distribution of all relevant American publications related to Andersen. Compiled by the author.

1840s	1850s	1860s	1870s	1880s	1890s
147	93	241	715	100	239

Total: 1,535[a]

a The 1,535 publications, combined with the seventy-two available for *More Than Meets the Eye*, brings the total for the American reception of Andersen in the nineteenth century to 1,607.

Tables 1.5 and 1.6 register all of the periodicals containing substantial critical commentary about Andersen and his work that were uncovered during research for this book. Magazines and newspapers are listed and discussed separately, compiled with the knowledge that it is often hard to distinguish between the two.[11] They are entered alphabetically, together with the number of writings each published and the years they appeared.

Table 1.5.   Magazines Containing Commentaries on Andersen

This table lists the magazines in which the most important discussions of Andersen appeared, together with the number of commentaries and the years of their appearance. Compiled by the author.

Advance	2; 1869, 1870
Albion	1; 1869
Aldine	1; 1871
American Literary Gazette and Publishers' Circular (Philadelphia)	3; 1863, 1864, 1869
American Literary Magazine	1; 1848
American Presbyterian Review	1; 1870
American Quarterly Church Review	1; 1870
Anglo American	2; 1845, 1846
Ballou's Pictorial Drawing-Room Companion	2; 1857, 1858
Broadway Journal	1; 1845
Catholic World	1; 1870
Chautauquan	1; 1888
Christian Advocate	1; 1869
Christian Inquirer	4; 1847 (1), 1848 (3)
Christian Parlor Book	1; 1849
Christian Register	2; 1848, 1849
Christian Review	1; 1848
Christian Standard	2; 1870, 1871
Christian Union	7; 1870 (3), 1871 (4)
Christian World	3; 1847 (1), 1848 (2)
Churchman	4; 1846 (1), 1870 (1), 1871 (2)
College Courant	3; 1871
Congregational Review	2; 1870, 1871
Congregationalist and Boston Recorder	1; 1870

(continued)

Table 1.5. *(continued)*

Crayon	1; 1860
Critic	3; 1886, 1887, 1895
Dial	2; 1893, 1894
Eclectic Magazine	5; 1860 (1), 1869 (1),1870 (3)
Evangelical Quarterly	1; 1870
Farmers' Home Journal	1; 1876
Golden Hours	1; 1870
Hall's Journal of Health	1; 1871
Harper's New Monthly Magazine	2; 1869, 1871
Harper's Weekly	1; 1875
Harvard Advocate	1; 1871
(Holden's) Dollar Magazine	3; 1848, 1849, 1851
Hours at Home	1; 1870
Independent	5; 1860, 1861, 1863, 1870, 1871
International Magazine	1; 1852
Ladies' National Magazine	1; 1845
Ladies' Repository (Boston)	3; 1845, 1847, 1860
Ladies' Repository (Cincinnati)	1; 1871
Lady's Home Magazine	1; 1860
Land We Love	1; 1868
Liberal Christian	1; 1870
Lippincott's Monthly Magazine	1; 1893
Literary World	4; 1848
Littell's Living Age	1; 1848
Maine Farmer	1; 1869
Merchants' Magazine and Commercial Review	1; 1860
Methodist Quarterly Review	2; 1860, 1882
Monthly Journal of the American Unitarian Association	1; 1860
Monthly Religious Magazine and Independent Journal	1; 1860
Moore's Rural New-Yorker	2; 1871
Mothers' Journal and Family Visitant	1; 1847
Nation	2; 1869, 1893
National Sunday School Teacher	1; 1871
New York Evangelist	4; 1848 (1), 1869 (1), 1870 (2)
Outlook	1; 1895
Overland Monthly	1; 1871
Peterson's Magazine	4; 1860, 1863, 1864, 1871
Phrenological Journal	4; 1870 (1), 1871 (2), 1875 (1)
Presbyterian	4; 1846, 1848, 1869, 1870
Putnam's Magazine	1; 1857
Riverside Bulletin	2; 1871
Round Table	2; 1865, 1867
Scribner's Monthly	1; 1872
Southern and Western Magazine and Review	1; 1845

Southern Review	1; 1880
St. Nicholas	1; 1875
Trumpet and Universalist Magazine	1; 1848
Una	1; 1853
Universe	1; 1869
Wide Awake	1; 1888
Wood's Household Magazine	1; 1871
Young American's Magazine of Self-Improvement	1; 1847
Zion's Herald	3; 1869 (1), 1870 (2)

On perusing table 1.5, one is struck by the sheer number of magazines that published criticism on Andersen, seventy-seven in all. Perhaps even more striking is the diversity of the periodicals, which accommodate every level of the brow, from farmers, businessmen, and the health conscious, both physical (*Hall's Journal of Health*) and "psychological" (the *Phrenological Journal*); to the general reader and women, for example, *Ballou's Pictorial Drawing-Room Companion* and the five nominally women's magazines; on to the art devotee, for example, the *Aldine* and the *Crayon*; and to those that fall under the rubrics of "literary" and "religious," which, as one might expect, form the majority. There may be some surprise in the fact that the list includes only four publications for children.

Great variety also prevails within the individual types of publications. Among the religious periodicals, organs of assorted Protestant denominations such as the *Congregationalist and Boston Recorder*, the Methodist *Christian Advocate*, and the Baptist *Christian Union / Outlook* accompany the *Catholic World*. While the *Riverside Bulletin* was little more than the advertising arm of a publishing firm, the *Critic*, the *Literary World*, and similar journals offered capable to high-quality writing and reviewing. One should bear in mind that the vast majority of the magazines under discussion were very "literary" when compared to their modern counterparts. Indeed, the religious magazines printed more notices than did the literary periodicals (27 vis-à-vis 25), more, in fact, than any other magazine type, though in the course of their runs many abandoned or drifted away from their original theological orientation, evolving into general family publications with a moral-religious ethos. Also, the sophistication of the magazines' offerings varied substantially from one class of publication to the other, and the quality of perhaps most ebbed and flowed, sometimes considerably, depending on editorial predilection, ability, and luck, over their often lengthy lives. Upward of thirty of the magazines are included in those that Mott designates as "important" or "more important," though his comments on many others suggest that the lists are representative rather than exhaustive.[12] Certainly, *Harper's New Monthly Magazine*,

Harper's Weekly, *Lippincott's Monthly*, the *Nation*, *Putnam's Magazine*, and *Scribner's Monthly* rank among the best the country had to offer at the time.

Reliable circulation figures for historical magazines (and newspapers) are often difficult or impossible to come by, especially for the time leading up to 1869, when *Rowell's American Newspaper Directory* began its annual appearance.[13] And even *Rowell's* has its limitations, for some editors refused to reveal their (likely paltry) numbers, and others puffed or otherwise misstated theirs. What is clear from table 1.5 is that the great majority of the magazines, whatever the extent of their subscription list, did little, individually, to spread critical awareness of Andersen's writing in the general public, for more than 60 percent of them published only one notice of his works, and nearly 16 percent only two. Even some of those that printed more, often in close proximity to each other, had comparatively few paying customers. Among the literary magazines, for example, the *American Literary Gazette and Publishers' Circular*, which published three relevant pieces from the late 1850s to the mid-1860s, had an annual circulation of less than 2,000, and the *Literary World*, which printed four in 1848 alone, never rose above 3,500.[14] When evaluating such numbers, however, one should remember that then, as now, magazines and newspapers were often read by more than one person. More important, review critics and other literati read each other's work, thus forming a small but consequential coterie within the periodical readership that, through their own writing, could exert an influence on critical and public opinion which was disproportionately greater than the figures in their individual ledgers might suggest. Moreover, certain literary magazines could boast impressive to, for the time, exorbitant numbers. *Lippincott's Monthly*, for instance, had some 75,000 subscribers during the year its review of a collection of tales came out, and the highly successful *Harper's New Monthly* had lists of 112,000 and 120,000 during the relevant years. Some of the religious publications also suffered from poor sales: the *American Presbyterian Review* circulated only 1,500 copies, and the *Congregational Review* a mere 1,000. However, most of those for which figures were available enjoyed better fortune, ranging between 8,000 and 33,600. And the *Independent* and the *Christian Union*, the latter of which published more reviews of Andersen's works than any other magazine in the country, recorded some 75,000 and almost 140,000, respectively, during his heyday in the 1860s and 1870s.

As table 1.6 indicates, the newspapers bear comparison with the magazines, if not in number, then certainly in terms of variety. The fifty-six papers range in location from Bangor, Maine, to San Francisco and from Chicago to Galveston, Texas. Some 67 percent of them were based in the eastern part of the country, particularly the Northeast, consistent with the development of the country at the time. Slightly more than 14 percent were clustered in urban

Table 1.6. Newspapers Containing Commentaries on Andersen

This table records the newspapers in which the most important commentaries on Andersen came out, together with their numbers and years of publication. Compiled by the author.

Ægis and Gazette (Worcester, Massachusetts)	1; 1872
Albany Argus (New York)	1; 1869
Albany Evening Journal (New York)	1; 1870
Bangor Daily Whig and Courier (Maine)	2; 1869, 1871
Boston Daily Advertiser	1; 1873
Boston Evening Transcript	3; 1848, 1860, 1865
Boston Herald	1; 1891
Boston Olive Branch	1; 1848
Boston Weekly Messenger	1; 1847
Brooklyn Daily Eagle (New York)	2; 1869, 1870
Capital (Washington, DC)	1; 1871
Chicago Daily Tribune	1; 1899
Cincinnati Daily Gazette	1; 1874
Cleveland Morning Herald	1; 1871
Daily Evening Bulletin (San Francisco)	5; 1861 (1), 1869 (1), 1870 (1), 1871 (2)
Daily National Intelligencer (Washington, DC)	1; 1845
Daily Ohio State Journal (Columbus)	1; 1860
Daily Picayune (New Orleans)	3; 1870, 1871, 1878
Democrat and Chronicle (Rochester, New York)	1; 1871
Detroit Free Press	3; 1869, 1871, 1893
Evening Post (New York)	3; 1860, 1870, 1871
Evening Telegraph (Philadelphia)	3; 1869 (2), 1870 (1)
Fayetteville News (North Carolina)	1; 1868
Galveston Daily News	1; 1869
Georgia Weekly Telegraph and Georgia Journal & Messenger (Macon)	1; 1871
Hartford Daily Courant (Connecticut)	2; 1869, 1871
Indiana Progress (Pennsylvania)	1; 1872
Indianapolis News	1; 1871
Inter Ocean (Chicago)	2; 1894, 1896
Kansas City Journal (Missouri)	1; 1897
Lebanon Courier and Semi-Weekly Report (Pennsylvania)	1; 1892
Lowell Daily Citizen and News (Massachusetts)	1; 1870
New Hampshire Sentinel (Keene)	1; 1872
Newport Mercury (Rhode Island)	1; 1871
New-York Commercial Advertiser	2; 1850, 1860
New-York Tribune	4; 1871 (1), 1893 (1), 1895 (2)
North American (Philadelphia)	1; 1845
North American and United States Gazette (Philadelphia)	8; 1864 (1), 1869 (1), 1870 (4), 1871 (2)
Norwich Morning Bulletin (Connecticut)	1; 1870
Pittsburgh Daily Commercial (Pennsylvania)	1; 1869

(continued)

Table 1.6. *(continued)*

Pittsburgh Weekly Gazette (Pennsylvania)	2; 1870, 1871
Portland Daily Press (Maine)	2; 1870, 1871
Portland Transcript (Maine)	11; 1860 (1), 1869 (2), 1870 (4), 1871 (4)
Press (Philadelphia)	2; 1863, 1871
Providence Evening Press (Rhode Island)	7; 1860 (1), 1869 (1), 1870 (2), 1871 (3)
Raleigh Register (North Carolina)	1; 1851
Sacramento Daily Union	2; 1861, 1869
Salem Observer (Massachusetts)	1; 1849
Southern Patriot (Charleston, South Carolina)	1; 1845
Spirit of the Times (New York)	2; 1846
Sunday-School Times (Philadelphia)	4; 1870 (2), 1871 (2)
Tarboro Southerner (North Carolina)	1; 1868
Tennessean (Nashville)	1; 1871
Trenton State Gazette (New Jersey)	1; 1871
Vermont Watchman & State Journal (Montpelier)	3; 1870 (1), 1871 (2)
World (New York)	1; 1863

centers of the present Midwest, while, perhaps surprisingly, an identical percentage were spread across the South, the West bringing up the rear with between 3 percent and 4 percent. More than two-thirds were dailies, most emanating from large population centers. The substantial remainder were published weekly (and, in a couple of instances, semiweekly), characteristically in villages or towns, and mainly, or strictly, for local consumption.[15] The names of the majority suggest that they were primarily *news*papers, but titles such as the *Bangor Daily Whig and Courier* of Maine and the *Democrat and Chronicle* of Rochester, New York, signal the various political angles from which the news was self-evidently presented and which are concealed by more conventional names like the *Albany Evening Journal* (New York) and the *Pittsburgh Gazette* (Pennsylvania), which were Democratic and Republican, respectively.[16] Similarly, the *Tarboro Southerner* of North Carolina proclaims its telling regional allegiance on its masthead, whereas the name of the Worcester, Massachusetts, *Ægis and Gazette* discloses nothing (specific) of its strong abolitionist ethos. In addition to expressing opinion and reporting current events, local and/or national, many papers were comparatively heavily invested in literature and literary criticism, publishing poetry, short stories, serialized novels, and reviews. The issue of the weekly *Portland Transcript* of Maine for May 12, 1860, to cite a random example, includes five poems, two stories, and a section of book notices among the eclectic contents of its eight pages.

Many if not most Americans will recognize the names of the *Boston Herald*, the *Chicago Tribune*, and, perhaps, the *Tennessean*, which were founded in the early to mid-nineteenth century and remain in publication today. Surely, many graybeards will be familiar with those of the *Boston Evening Transcript*, the New York *World*, and the *New-York (Herald) Tribune*, which originated around mid-century and survived until 1931, 1941, and 1966, respectively; the latter lives on after a fashion as the *International New York Times*, which until 2013 was called the *International Herald Tribune*. The papers brought Andersen to the attention of Americans after much the same pattern as the magazines. Indeed, the percentage of those that issued only one or two notices of his works is identical to that of their journalistic rivals. At the opposite extreme, a few of the papers exceeded the magazines in developing what one might call an Andersen tradition. The *Providence Evening Press* (Rhode Island) and the *North American and United States Gazette* of Philadelphia published seven and eight reviews, respectively, and the *Portland Transcript* issued a total of eleven, all but one from 1869 through 1871. These twenty-six notices represent more than 23 percent of the total. As with the magazines, however, even certain "single" writings, such as those found in the *Ægis and Gazette* and the *Fayetteville News* (and the *Tarboro Southerner*), rank among the most instructive of all.[17] And like the *Harper's* publications and other comparable magazines mentioned earlier, the *Boston Evening Transcript*, the *Chicago Tribune*, and New York's *Evening Post*, *Tribune*, and *World* number among the highest-quality and most successful papers of the era.

In the second half of the nineteenth century, American magazines generally had larger circulations than their competitors in newsprint.[18] *Peterson's*, for example, which published commentary on Andersen between 1861 and 1871, recorded a subscription of about 140,000 during the three years for which *Rowell's* is available. By contrast, Horace Greeley's very successful *New-York Tribune* claimed only 45,000 in 1871, when one of its reviews of Andersen came out. Most periodicals of both kinds, however, had much shorter subscriber lists. Papers in many important cities sold no more than 20,000, with dailies averaging from 3,820 in the 1860s to 4,532 in the 1970s and 5,200 by 1890; thousands of weeklies had sales of from a few hundred to around a thousand.[19] Some of the papers in which Andersen figured fell within or even below these averages. The Andersen-friendly *North American and United States Gazette* of Philadelphia stated its circulation at only 5,200 in one of the relevant years and refused to reveal its numbers for the other two; the almost equally sympathetic *Providence Evening Press* declined to release its figure for one year and claimed only 4,000 for the remaining ones. On the other hand, the New York *World*, and the *Boston Herald* had

circulations of 26,000 and 82,323, respectively, and even the seemingly local weekly *Portland Transcript* sold some 18,000 copies throughout New
England, New York, and parts of Canada. No less than the magazines, the
newspapers gave thousands upon thousands of Americans the opportunity to
gain knowledge and an appreciation of Andersen's writing.[20]

The 238 major critical writings devoted to Andersen in nineteenth-century
America compares quite favorably with the numbers recorded contemporane-
ously in other countries, which we shall see in some detail in the conclusion
to this study. Americans' critical interest in and exposure to the author's work
becomes even more impressive when one considers the dozens of additional
commentaries that appeared over the same time period. The stories and tales
received the most reviews owing to their great popularity and the resulting
publication of a large number of collections. All the same, the novels, travel
books, and autobiographies attracted the attention of scores of reviewers.

Many Americans owed their familiarity with Andersen to the numerous
individual tales and excerpts from longer texts that appeared in magazines
and newspapers. Later chapters will confirm that editorial choices reflect
the American predilection for, among other things, sentiment, religion, humor, and travel literature, with its depictions of foreign scenery and cultural
luminaries.

Tables 1.2–1.4 demonstrate in different ways that the American Andersen
reception unfolded in several waves, two of the later ones being the largest
and most comprehensive, rather than in response to the works as they first appeared in English translation, as one might anticipate. They also show that for
varying reasons and in varying degrees Andersen was a significant presence
in the United States for most of the second half of the nineteenth century.

Tables 1.5 and 1.6 reveal a certain universality in the American response
to Andersen. The periodicals in which the relevant reviews and articles appeared were distributed across all the settled regions of the United States,
reflecting the contemporary state of the country's expansion. They represent
all levels of society and cultural pretension. The one factor that provides the
American reception with definition is the types of magazines and newspapers
that published the largest number of writings on the poet. Andersen received
his greatest coverage in general magazines and religious publications (23
percent), most of which gradually lost their original spiritual orientation, and
urban daily newspapers (21.6 percent). These were followed at a considerable distance by literary magazines (6 percent) and regional weeklies (1.3
percent). Whatever the type, the periodicals in aggregate provided many
thousands of Americans with the possibility of familiarizing themselves with
Andersen's writing.

NOTES

1. I have not included a dedicated list of these printings in the volume in order to conserve space, but one is available upon request to the author at the Department of German and Russian, Stanley Coulter Hall, Purdue University, West Lafayette, IN 47907.

2. Elias Bredsdorff, *Danish Literature in English Translation, with a Special Hans Christian Andersen Supplement: A Bibliography* (Copenhagen: Ejnar Munksgaard, 1950), 121–38, 173–75, 177–78, 181–82.

3. See note 1 above.

4. *Lucky Peer*, *Scribner's Monthly Magazine*, January 1871, 270–76; February 1871, 391–98; March 1871, 505–16; April 1871, 625–39; *A Visit to Charles Dickens's House*, *Eclectic Magazine*, February 1871, 183–96. In the early 1840s, so-called mammoth weeklies made a practice of publishing entire novels in their (many oversized) pages, but increased postage rates led to their demise by around mid-decade; see Frank Luther Mott, *A History of American Magazines 1741–1850* (1930; repr., Cambridge, MA: Harvard University Press, 1957), 358–63.

5. See Herbert Rowland, "The Author's Edition of H. C. Andersen's Works: An American-Danish Collaboration," *Orbis Litterarum* 60 (2005): especially 465–66.

6. *To Be, or Not to Be? A Novel*, trans. Mrs. [Anne S.] Bushby (London: Richard Bentley, 1857). A rather unusual but meaningful judgment of the novel is discussed in chapter 2. As indicated in note 4, *Lucky Peer* was published in *Scribner's Monthly* from January to April 1871.

7. I have made additional adjustments in the several tables that cause the numbers to vary slightly. As stated in the introduction, a couple of reviews deal with more than one work or collection, and I have generally treated each discussion as a discrete commentary. Moreover, another couple of writings were reprinted in other publications, and I have counted each separately based on the conviction that the number of occurrences is more telling of Americans' exposure to critical opinion of Andersen than that of individual pieces.

8. For the number of noncritical general interest articles see table 1.4.

9. In the "Advertisement," or introduction, to one of the two volumes of tales in the Author's Edition, Horace Scudder writes,

It was found impossible to bring all of his [Andersen's] shorter stories and fancies within the compass of a single volume, and in making the division some regard was had to that which he has himself several times pointed out—that his stories are sometimes pure inventions of fancy and sometimes have their root in historic incidents or events, and scenes of which he has been cognizant. At the same time, anyone who made the attempt to separate these writings exactly upon such a line would find, as Andersen himself has said, that after all one must accept the undiscriminating term of popular usage and call them all *stories*. Thus the companion volume [*Wonder Stories Told for Children*] is not all fancy, and this is not all fact; the elements are mingled. . . . Still, in a rough way, the two volumes do each represent strongly one and the other of these elements. (Horace E. Scudder, "Advertisement," in *Stories and Tales*, by Hans Christian Andersen, author's ed., ed. Horace E. Scudder [Boston and New York: Hurd and Houghton, 1871], vii).

10. Eleven of the works were eventually published in the magazine—for the first time anywhere; see Erik Dal, "Hans Christian Andersen's Tales and America," *Scandinavian Studies* 40 (1968): 11–13.

11. Mott comments on the difficulty in differentiating between nineteenth-century magazines and newspapers in *American Journalism, a History: 1690 to 1960*, 3rd ed. (New York: Macmillan, 1962), viii.

12. For these lists, see Mott, *A History of American Magazines 1741–1850*, 214 and 528; *A History of American Magazines, 1850–1865* (1938; repr., Cambridge, MA: Harvard University Press, 1966), 218; *A History of American Magazines 1865–1885* (1938; repr., Cambridge, MA: Harvard University Press, 1966), 318; and *A History of American Magazines 1885–1905* (Cambridge, MA: Harvard University Press, 1957), xvi.

13. George P. Rowell, *George P. Rowell & Co.'s American Newspaper Directory* (New York: Rowell, 1869–1909). Henceforth, references to this title will be cited as *Rowell's* for the year in question plus relevant page numbers. The *Directory* included figures for magazines as well as newspapers.

14. See Mott, *A History of American Magazines 1865–1885*, 551 and 456, respectively. The number of a periodical's subscribers varied over time, of course. For this reason, circulation figures, where known, are generally given in the sketches of individual publications or in the discussions of specific notices and articles.

15. Mott discusses various aspects of the weeklies in *American Journalism*, 295, 296; 396–97; 478–80; and 589.

16. Michael Schudson examines the history of the notion of objectivity in newspaper journalism in *Discovering the News: A Social History of American Newspapers* (New York: Basic Books, 1978).

17. The *Fayetteville News* and the *Tarboro Southerner* published the same review.

18. Much of the information in this paragraph is drawn from Mott, *American Journalism*, 506–7.

19. Mott, *American Journalism*, 303, 402.

20. A handful of critical general interest articles appeared in books and "libraries" of literature, rather than in magazines or newspapers, and will be introduced at the appropriate points in the study.

Chapter Two

The Novels

Over the course of his life, Hans Christian Andersen wrote a total of six novels. Indeed, he aspired to be Denmark's foremost novelist and was best known for his work in the genre for some time, especially outside of Denmark.[1] Three of the works appeared in relatively rapid succession, from 1835 to 1837, during the first decade of his career, while the others came out in 1848, 1857, and 1870, respectively. The early novels and the final one all reflect Andersen's lifelong preoccupation with the nature of the artist and his place in life. These themes are also present in the other two works, but they are secondary in the one to Andersen's picture of society and in the other to his views on religion and philosophy. The novels have long trailed far behind the fairy tales and stories in popularity and scholarly interest, which is true, of course, of Andersen's other works as well. However, one need only glance at the Andersen scholarship of the past some two to three decades to recognize that they have not been forgotten.[2] And between 1984 and 2001, all six were republished in Denmark, three of them enjoying second editions after the turn of the century. Like most of Andersen's works, they were also included in the *Samlede Værker* of 2003–2007, and one was issued in a new American translation in 2018.[3]

The chapter deals with the novels in chronological order and in sections dedicated to each, with the exception of the last two works, which are treated in a single section due to the paucity of commentary on them. Each section proceeds chronologically in order to show both the continuities and discontinuities in reviewer concerns over the different phases of the Andersen reception. All but the last one begin with a brief plot summary to provide context for the reviews and the accompanying commentary. Several themes in addition to those mentioned above emerge from the critics' remarks. They

will be identified as such in the course of the discussion and recapitulated in
the summary at the end of the chapter.

THE IMPROVISATORE

Andersen made his entrance into the English-speaking world in British
literata Mary Howitt's translation of his first novel, *Improvisatoren*, as *The
Improvisatore; or, Life in Italy*, which was published in London in February
1845 and issued soon afterward in an American edition titled *Life in Italy:
The Improvisatore* by Harper & Brothers in New York and B. B. Mussey in
Boston.[4] The novel tells the story of a poor Roman boy named Antonio who,
by virtue of his gift for improvising lyrics and melodies to songs suggested
by his listeners, rises to social prominence, wealth, and personal happiness.
Along the way, however, he experiences many highs and lows of various
kinds, including his love for the famous Spanish singer Annunziata and his
seemingly unsuccessful rivalry with his friend Bernardo for her affection. He
accidentally shoots Bernardo and flees to Naples, after which he meets the
blind Maria/Lara in Paestum and then again, following an accident at sea,
in the Blue Grotto of Capri, where he cures her blindness with herbs. He
subsequently returns to Rome and the Borghese family, which had taken him
in as a boy for schooling and now supports him as he completes his higher
education. Having lost his dearest friend, Flaminia, to the convent, he sets out
on a journey that takes him to Venice, where he encounters both Annunziata,
now broken and mortally ill, who reveals that she had in truth preferred him
to Bernardo, and Lara, whom he marries and takes to an estate in southern
Italy. The novel closes with the couple's nostalgic return to the Blue Grotto.

   The Improvisatore helped establish the modern novel in Denmark and is
generally considered either a precursor or the first example of the bildungsroman in Danish literature.[5] It thus participates in a type of novelistic literature
that has its roots in European Romanticism, going back at least as far as
Goethe's *Wilhelm Meisters Lehrjahre* (*Wilhelm Meister's Apprenticeship*;
1796). Despite what has been called a "tortuous" plot with a "vast number"
of characters and incidents, the thematic center of the work indeed lies in
Antonio's formation as an individual and an artist, largely in response to
the cultural artifacts and values of his environment.[6] The novel received a
comparatively extensive and generally positive reception by Danish critics
on its publication in 1835 and was a resounding success with the public both
in Denmark and abroad.[7] Like the other novels, but to a greater degree than
most, it continues to attract the attention of scholars.

The first American response to *The Improvisatore* came out in the *Broadway Journal* on April 12, 1845.[8] The magazine was the brainchild of Charles F. Briggs (1804–1877), a New York novelist, critic, journalist, and editor who cultivated an urbane, humorous-satiric style in numerous contributions to the city's *Knickerbocker Magazine*.[9] The *Journal* failed to survive its first year of existence, but during that short time, Briggs succeeded in assembling an impressive group of contributors and/or coeditors that included Richard Henry Dana, Margaret Fuller, James Russell Lowell, and Edgar Allen Poe.[10] The magazine published poetry and commentary on music, theater, and politics, but its forte was review criticism. Briggs wrote many of the notices himself and thus perhaps that of Andersen's *Improvisatore*.

However, the review does more credit to the publishing firm of Harper & Brothers than to Andersen and his novel, perhaps more than to the reviewer himself:

> This is No. 49 of the "Library of Select Novels," and embraces 125 closely printed octavo pages, in minion, double columns—yet is sold for a shilling—a thing difficult to understand. It can scarcely be expected that this state of affairs can last; and we advise all to secure a complete set of the "Library of Select Novels." We doubt if *in the world* there exists in the same compass, for anything like the same price, the same amount of excellent light reading as will be found in the 49 numbers of this series.[11]

Unless he is speaking with tongue in cheek, a possibility which, given the predominant tone in literary New York at the time, cannot at all be excluded, the reviewer differs from many of his contemporaries in his view of the Harpers' assault on the book market with cheap reprints of novels by foreign authors. Of Andersen's novel he writes only, "The Improvisatore is a peculiar work, and affects the reader with a singular sense of the new in letters:—this feeling results from our want of acquaintance with the Danish turn of thought and expression." Thus, the review says less about the work per se—only, by implication, that it is an example of "light reading," no insignificant comment in itself—than about Americans' current knowledge of the typical stylistic and reflective bent of Denmark, which stood pars pro toto for all of Scandinavia. Andersen was indeed one of the first Scandinavian writers to be introduced to the country, and the very first Dane to be introduced on a large scale.[12] At the same time, the notice reveals the critic's sense of the novel's originality, which was shared by numerous other writers.

The second reviewer had more of substance to say about *The Improvisatore* and its author than his predecessor. His notice appeared in the Boston *Ladies' Repository*, which at the time of publication bore the subtitle *A Universalist Monthly Magazine for the Home Circle* and ran under different titles for more than forty years (1832–1874), possessing a reach that extended beyond church membership and the two thousand subscribers it apparently never exceeded.[13] The editor at the time was Universalist pastor and journalist Henry Bacon (1813–1856), who largely abandoned the original feminist impulse of the magazine in favor of a policy which, while continuing to acknowledge the fundamental importance of women, aimed principally at their moral-religious development. The review leaves no doubt about the writer's opinion of Andersen's work: "This is No. 49 of the Library of Select Novels, and opens to us a new vein of gold in the mountain of literature." All the same, the reviewer speaks more of the "gold" in the author's heart than in the novel itself:

> If the story is as interesting as Mrs. Howitt's sketch of the Author, it must be full of interest. We cannot read the productions of such a heroic man, the conqueror of circumstances, without discerning himself in his writings; and the reflections, the noble and affectionate suggestions, in which he indulges appeal to us, not as mere episodes in his narrative, but the utterance of the heart. Let him who is easily inclined to be discouraged by opposing circumstances, read the sketch of Andersen, with which this volume opens, and he will be ashamed of his want of heroism.

Having commented on the recognition the novel brought Andersen, even from his critics, the reviewer continues, "How we do love to read the works of such spirits! Spirits who hear divine songs in their childhood and never forget them through all after life, but labor and struggle to give utterance to the high themes and grand thoughts which they suggest." The novel per se inspires the reviewer to write, "'The Improvisatore' is full of the most absorbing interest, and our readers cannot but be gratified with it. It reflects to us the impressions which a rare poetic and thoughtful spirit received from sojourning amid the glories of nature and art in the fine country of Italy."

The notice bears witness, first and foremost, to the quite personal impact the biographical sketch of Andersen had on the writer, who proved to be one of numerous critics and myriads of other nineteenth-century Americans so affected. Of course, the reviewer and his (or her) countrymen had no way of knowing that the sketch was based largely on an essay written by the Frenchman Xavier Marmier, which in turn was greatly influenced by the inveterate self-promoter Andersen himself, who approached Marmier with his well-rehearsed life story during the latter's stay in Copenhagen in 1837–1838.[14] There is much in Andersen's portrayal of himself, in his autobiographies and elsewhere, that is more mythical than factual. However, the true course of his life and the substance of his character, to the extent they are known, certainly suffice to justify a good deal of the admiration he received as a man, especially in a country where Horatio Alger turned thirteen the year *The Improvisatore* with its biographical overview was published.[15] Not surprisingly, given the periodical's orientation as a religious family magazine, the content and near rhapsodic diction in portions of the review show that its author was indebted to both the moralist-biographicist notion of literature and literary study inherited from the eighteenth century and the sensibilist concept prevalent in Romanticism.

One detects a similar spirit in a review that appeared in the *Ladies' National Magazine* in July 1845.[16] The periodical was the fruit of an attempt by one of the principals of the *Saturday Evening Post* and *Graham's Magazine* to capitalize on the great success of *Godey's Lady's Book* by creating a less expensive competitor in the field of fashion and light literature.[17] Within a decade of its founding, owner and editor Charles J. Peterson gave the publication his own name, which as *Peterson's Magazine* became one of the most successful periodicals of the century, reaching a circulation of 140,000 by 1869. His main contributor was Ann S. Stephens (1810–1886), who later gained recognition and popularity as a magazine editor in her own right and as an author of short stories and so-called dime novels.[18] She also worked for the *Ladies' National* as an associate or contributing editor and wrote editorials and perhaps reviews as well.

The notice exudes the air of Romantic sentimentality that pervaded magazines of this kind and many others of the day: "This is a story of Italian life, giving the reader beautiful glimpses of a poet's soul in all its struggles with poverty and dependence. The book is full of fine descriptions of scenery, persons and events. The visit to Vesuvius is terribly grand in description—and there is one picture of a cave half submerged in water surpassingly beautiful."[19] The reviewer is one of many who acknowledge Andersen's treatment of the inner life and outward trials of the artist as well as his exceptional descriptive ability, themes that recur in other reviews, but one of few who offer specific details of the novel's settings and plot. S/he responds almost viscerally to the fall of the Spanish prima donna from her lofty position: "The connection of Annunziata with the story is like a sable thread woven with some rich fabric. A fate like hers touches the heart more deeply even than *scenes of horror*. To feel beauty and all those powers that have enchanted the multitude, pass from one while still in youth must be terrible" [emphasis added]. The "scenes of horror" which Annunziata's sad lot allegedly surpasses in affective force likely represent an oblique reference to—and perhaps a comment on—a significant phenomenon in contemporary American fiction that will be discussed in some detail shortly.

Less sentimental but equally positive is a review that appeared in the *Daily National Intelligencer*, the first important newspaper in Washington, DC, and in some respects, according to Mott, the greatest of all the papers ever published in the nation's capital.[20] Founded in 1800, the *Intelligencer* soon became the authoritative voice of the executive branch of the federal government, and its reports were for twenty-five years the semiofficial source of information about the proceedings of Congress, for its own readers and all other papers as well. Beginning with Andrew Jackson's presidency, the paper's fortunes shifted with those of the political parties, but it was an official government organ under William Henry Harrison and John Tyler (i.e., through the early months of 1845), and then again under Millard Fillmore. Judging by the notice of *The Improvisatore*, its review criticism at that time was quite respectable.

The writer is as aware as his cohorts of the novelty of Andersen's work: "The success which has attended Mrs. Howitt's translations from the Swedish has induced her to break new grounds, and she has here given us a very exquisite specimen of the recent literature of Denmark."[21] He, too, responds to the struggle of genius with adversity but even more so to the phenomenon of genius itself and its creations: "With a mind sensitively alive to poetic impressions, he [Andersen] visited Italy, and the enthusiasm generated by his residence in that land of history, poetry, and art, has found vent in the work before us, the most popular and successful of Andersen's productions. The interest lies in the development of an individual mind, the Improvisatore, and in the glowing descriptions of Italian scenery." More succinctly and straightforwardly than his colleague at the *Ladies' National*, the reviewer identifies the elements of *Bildung* and painterliness as central to the novel.

He somehow finds the plot simple, but "we are carried along by a current of thought and feeling which has always the appear[ance] of springing from a real and natural source. It is like an autobiography; and it is scarcely possible to doubt that the Danish poet and novelist has embodied his own feelings and experience of life in the character of *Antonio*." In view of the aforementioned phenomenon to be discussed presently, it is significant that the notice continues, "[t]here is a simplicity and apparently unlabored ease about the narrative which are very attractive, and even in the delineations of passion, which are least within the range of common sympathies, we are not offended by *straining or extravagance*" [emphasis added].

The reviewer is more favorably disposed to Howitt's English style than Danish critics have been to her rendering of Andersen's novel as such, but he nonetheless recognizes features in it that are indeed present in the original itself: "It is spirited and beautiful English, and yet contains internal evidence of faithfulness, from the felicity with which it conveys shades of thought and feeling which are evidently foreign. This preservation, if we may so speak, of the flavor of an original work, without a too literal observance of the original idiom, is the highest merit of a translation." Citing the impossibility of conveying a valid impression of such a work through isolated extracts, the writer offers an extended passage from the end of part 1, chapter 11 ("The Last Day of the Carnival"; "Den sidste Carnivalsdag") in order to at least "show the author's manner of depicting the externals of Italian life."

The issue of the *Southern and Western Magazine and Review* for September 1845 contains a notice of *The Improvisatore* that is important in its implications for central issues of American literary life in the nineteenth century.[22] The magazine was edited by Charleston poet, novelist, and historian William Gilmore Simms (1806–1870) and was generally called simply "Simms's Magazine."[23] Beginning his literary career writing Romantic poetry in emulation of Byron, Simms soon turned his attention to prose and, between 1833 and 1869, penned twenty-four novels and more than a hundred stories dealing primarily with the history of the South and the frontier.[24] Though best known today for his fiction, he also wrote biographies, essays, and much else, assembling a body of work that filled more than eighty volumes, not to mention unpublished writing probably sufficient to fill twenty more. This oeuvre earned him a significant role in the contemporary world of letters, both in and outside the South, and, in recent years, has led to his designation as the "South's chief literary spokesman" and the "Old South's foremost public intellectual."[25] Simms had already edited a newspaper and several short-lived magazines before founding the *Southern and Western* and allowed it to be merged with the far more renowned *Southern Literary Messenger* within a year due to unprofitability—its circulation never rose above two thousand.[26] He returned to magazine editing and writing with greater success in the *Southern Quarterly Review*, making it, according to Mott, the finest antebellum journal in the South and one of the best American quarterlies overall.[27]

In the *Southern and Western*, meanwhile, Simms raised a platform for the Young America movement, a loosely organized current in sociopolitical and cultural thought of mid-century. On the one hand, figures such as Senator Stephen A. Douglas of Illinois and editor John L. O'Sullivan of New York sought to reshape the antebellum Democratic party by making it more progressive and adaptive, for example, by moving it away from Jacksonian agrarian populism and closer to Whig notions of a market economy and nationalism.[28] On the other hand, litterateurs like Evert Duyckinck aimed to free themselves from the British literary-cultural traditions represented by the urbane, cosmopolitan coterie around Lewis Gaylord Clark and the *Knickerbocker Magazine* and to win recognition for the excellence and exceptional character of America's own literature.[29] For Simms, the latter aim entailed in particular acknowledgment of the contributions made by the regional literatures of the pluralistic democracy, for example, those of the South and

West.[30] To these ends, he created a distinctive hybrid periodical, part serious literary review and part entertaining magazine miscellany, in which most of the poetry, stories, and articles flowed from his own prolific pen. In his review criticism, he demonstrated what has been called a "rare understanding of literature and the literary world"; though a staunch supporter of the South and its "peculiar institution," he was objective in his treatment of Northern writers, who, of course, published the majority of the books he reviewed.[31] He alone was responsible for the "Editorial Bureau," the substantial review department at the end of each issue, and thus for the notice of Andersen's *Improvisatore*.[32]

In a section of the "Bureau" titled "Popular Fiction. Harpers' Publications," Simms opens with the words, "There would seem to be some improvement in the demand for works of fiction, in due degree with the diminution of that flood of cheap publications by which the popular swallow was choked rather than pacified. We suspect that most of the publishers of cheap books have burnt their fingers. It is certain that their number is very much diminished."[33] Simms may well have had reference here in part to mammoth weeklies such as *Brother Jonathan* and the *New World*, which offered entire novels, mostly English reprints, at prices substantially lower than those of bound books.[34] In summer 1842, a representative of the *New World* stole a copy of a novel soon to be released by Harpers and set fire to the building, which led to Fletcher Harper's lobbying the Post Office to require that the mammoths pay postage at book rates and, ultimately, to the end of competition from that quarter— perhaps an explanation for Simms's use of the expression "to burn one's fingers."[35] In the words that follow, however, Simms makes it clear that he was no admirer of the Harpers either, who were reviled by many for their own publication of pirated English novels in inexpensive editions and long neglect of American writers: "It is almost only from the press of Harper & Brothers, that these works now issue; and the supply from their immense manufactory, for the last three months, has been equally various and large."[36]

At the same time, Simms's reviews of the Harpers' publications are quite evenhanded, as his treatment of Andersen's *Improvisatore* shows: "It is a story of deep interest, and superior merit—not a collection of commonplaces—of 'hair-breadth escapes,' and horror-rousing incidents, clumsily huddled together; but an artistical composition, unique in its arrangements, and with a strong air of originality." The works with which Simms contrasts Andersen's novel here formed a main current in the flood of cheap books mentioned at the outset—namely, the sensationalist publications that followed the rise of the penny press in the 1830s and the appearance of Eugène Sue's *Les mystères de Paris* (1842–1843), which came out in two American translations in 1843 and 1844.[37] Made possible by technological advances wrought by the Industrial Revolution, advances that enabled faster and less expensive printing processes, the advent of penny dailies such as the New York *Sun* and *Herald*, the *Public Ledger* of Philadelphia, and the Baltimore *Sun* introduced the habit of newspaper reading to a working-class public that had largely been neglected by more expensive publications addressed to the mercantile and educated classes.[38] The penny papers naturally tailored their content to the real or perceived interests of their target readership, at their worst indulging in crudeness and indecency that could sink to the level of sensationalized crime and sex.[39] In his *Mysteries of Paris*, Sue brought together characters from various social classes, but his realistic depiction of life among the urban poor struck a new note in fiction, inviting a reading of the novel as a socialist critique of conditions in France. It also inspired a wave of, often, far more lurid and less engaged than self-referential "city mysteries" that swept across the Western world, including the United States.[40]

Major American cities and small towns alike served as settings for such imitations, but the most popular of all was perhaps George Lippard's *The Quaker City, or The Monks of Monk Hall: A Romance of Philadelphia Life* (1844–1845), whose success induced the author to found a weekly paper called the *Quaker City* as an outlet for similar writing.[41] According to Reynolds, novels like Lippard's "forged a new irrational style aimed at reproducing the rebellious, savage forces of American culture; and its unmasking of the social elite was enforced through extreme violence, sexual scenes ranging from the suggestive to the disgustingly perverse. . . . This kind of fiction often featured excessive gore and mass chicanery, conveyed in an intentionally disruptive, quirky style designed to outrage the genteel reader."[42] In addition to such novels and the penny papers, "sensational literature" included "seamy social texts such as . . . trial reports[,] and crime pamphlets . . . erotic and pornographic writings."[43] Yet it was the "Yellow Jacket" literature of the day of which the author of *Confessions and Experience of a Novel Reader* wrote in 1855, "If any one has doubts as to the fearfully rapid increase of this public poison—a demoralizing literature, the real 'Pandora's box of evil passions'— the flood-gate, from beneath whose slimy jaws run a stream of pollution, sending forth its pestilential branches to one great ocean of immorality, let such a one take a trip with me through the length and breadth of our land."[44]

Like the originator of these words, William Gilmore Simms was one of many figures in the contemporary literary world who condemned such sensationalism in journalism and fiction. He himself cultivated a prose style that has earned his inclusion in recent studies of the phenomenon, to be sure.[45] However, his review of *The Improvisatore* suggests that he was nonetheless indebted to the prevailing bourgeois notion of (high) culture inherited from Europe, though he attempted to break free from it or, better, to establish a differentiated American variation on it. He was clearly wrong in his assessment of the stage the flood of sensationalist writing had reached—Lippard's *Quaker City* sold sixty thousand copies in the year of its publication and continued to sell at least ten thousand annually over the next decade.[46] Furthermore, George Thompson, who, according to Reynolds, "has the dubious distinction of having written the most purely disgusting novels in pre-Civil War America," did not publish his best-known work, *Venus in Boston*, until 1849, and the anonymous novel reader cited earlier wrote his *Confessions* only in 1855.[47]

For present purposes, however, it is noteworthy that Simms presents Andersen's *Improvisatore* as an antidote to sensationalism, much like other reviewers of this and some of the later novels, as we shall see. In addition to the excellences already mentioned—the deep interest and superior merit of the story, the novel's artistic composition, and "strong air of originality"—he notes that "[t]he author's taste is delicate, his fancy lively, and his genius of graceful manner and structure, if not distinguished by great boldness and power."[48] As an advocate of a vigorous American national literature, Simms prized daring and forcefulness in an author, but here he clearly places more emphasis on matters of form. The looseness of the plot (i.e., the uniqueness of its "arrangements"), which frequently elicited criticism after about 1860, appeals to the advocate of Young America and the critic of the allegedly epigonic, even un-American *Knickerbocker* circle as evidence of artistic originality. Simms does not use the word "romance" in his evaluation of Andersen's work, but his approval of its distinctive story line suggests that he viewed it as such within the context of the ongoing theoretical discussion about the relation between the romance and the novel, to which we shall have reason to recur over the course of the present chapter. While Simms valued a rich, expansive plot and a lively "fancy," or imagination, he also placed a high premium on an organizing consciousness and saw one displayed in the delicate taste and graceful manner and structure of the genius, or spirit, exhibited in the novel.[49]

Simms opines additionally, "His [Andersen's] life is one that will instruct and encourage the young beginner, of humble fortunes, and good natural endowments. No life could have been more humble and adverse at the beginning—no career more discouraging or, finally, more triumphant." It is an open question whether or to what extent an apparent literal reading of Mary Howitt's biographical sketch of Andersen favorably predisposed Simms to the novel, and one may reasonably say the same of the many other commentators who made comparable statements. In view of the similar trajectory of his own life, the notion is certainly plausible.[50] At all events, central features of the work sympathetic to the romancer and member of Young America surely sufficed of themselves to elicit his warm reception of Andersen's novel.

Although several editions of *The Improvisatore* appeared from 1847 to 1863, the next reviews of the work came out only in 1869 in response to its issuance in the Author's Edition. In the meantime, a commentary published in 1853 may well have rested on a reading of the original edition. It was not a review per se, though it might easily have been, but rather a segment of a book titled *Six Months in Italy* that was written by attorney and prolific author and review critic George Stillman Hillard (1808–1879).[51] Hillard long shared an extensive law practice with famed abolitionist Charles Sumner in Boston and, for many years, served in city political offices as well as in both houses of the Massachusetts legislature and as United States attorney for the District of Massachusetts.[52] His law office was a gathering place for local politicians and literary figures, including Henry Wadsworth Longfellow and Nathaniel Hawthorne, who numbered among his friends as well as his clients. He contributed numerous articles and reviews on a wide variety of subjects to important magazines such as the *North American Review*, the *Christian Examiner*, and the *New England Magazine*, and he edited the *Christian Register* and the Boston *Courier* for periods of time. In addition to magazine writing, his literary activity consisted principally in biographical and varied editorial work that produced, for example, books on Captain John Smith and George McClellan, editions of Spenser and Walter Savage Landor, and a series of school readers—as a young man he had taught at George Bancroft's experimental Round Hill School. *Six Months in Italy* was the product of a stay in the country from fall 1847 to winter 1848. Well received on its appearance, the book was later called "probably the most popular book about Italy by an American" and had the distinction of being republished in England.[53]

In a chapter devoted to notable visitors to Italy, Hillard begins the section on Andersen by rehearsing the strong attraction the country had long exerted on men of imagination from Northern Europe. While correct in this observation, he soon skates on increasingly slick ice. First, he asserts that the power of Italy over Northern Europeans "would seem to justify the theory that all knowledge is but recognition; and that these ardent Scandinavians, *who feel and express the spirit of the country more than its own people* were natives of some pre-adamite Italy, and find themselves in their first home only when south of the Alps" [emphasis added].[54] Farther along, he writes of Andersen's "northern imagination—dreamy, spiritual, and fantastic—without the passion and intensity which, in the South, usually accompany poetical genius like his. It would be difficult for any Italian to produce a book so redolent of Italy as 'The Improvisatore'; because he would not feel, to the same extent as a susceptible stranger, the peculiar character of objects and scenes which to him had become dulled by long familiarity."[55] If the notion of a foreigner's heightened sensitivity to a new culture is certainly discussible, despite its lack of differentiation here, Hillard unquestionably falls victim to the romanticized view of the North popularized by Longfellow in his essay on Swede Esaias Tegnér's *Frithiof's Saga* (1837) and his anthology *The Poetry and Poets of Europe* (1844), a view that had more to do with the American's own predilections than with the living reality of Scandinavia in either the past or the present. Nevertheless, his notion of "Northernness" influenced that of many of the reviewers treated in these pages.[56]

Incorrect in his statement that Andersen never lived in Italy for any length of time—the Dane actually spent several extended periods in the country—Hillard is close to the truth when he opines that "no one has ever made better use of his opportunities for studying and observing the country" and that "[n]o book brings back the externals of Italy more distinctly and vividly to the eye of the mind than this novel of the Danish poet's."[57] One may well share his view that the novel's "chief literary merit resides in its descriptions, which are correct in substance and animated with the most sincere poetical enthusiasm"; and one may find him absolutely accurate in his assessment that "Andersen has a large share of that happy faculty which may be called pictorial memory—the power of preserving, in all their original freshness, the impressions made by the sight upon the mind. In his thoughts, Italian pictures dwell like flowers in a conservatory, and not like dried plants in an herbarium," which he demonstrates with a number of examples drawn from the text.[58]

Hillard couches his brief criticism of the novel in terms that appear less severe than they in fact are in substance: "The story is improbable, the characters are not drawn with a very firm or discriminating touch, and the sentiment is sometimes a little lackadaisical."[59] However, he is so taken with Andersen's descriptive power—and in this he is far from alone—that he can conclude, "but all who love Italy, and wish to have it recalled to their thoughts, will pardon these defects in consideration of its pictures and its descriptions, which commend themselves to the memory by their truth, and to the imagination by their beauty."[60] Hillard's appreciation for Andersen's descriptive faculty and ready willingness to overlook his perceived flaws both likely stem from an implicit adherence to the notion prominent in the later eighteenth and nineteenth centuries that the development of mankind and human cultures have a parallel in that of the individual human being from childhood to adulthood, an idea associated with the theory of recapitulation, or biogenetic law. In his *The Relation of the Poet to His Age*, an address delivered to the Phi Beta Kappa chapter at Harvard in 1843, he writes the following:

> All early poetry is essentially picturesque. It is written at a time when the eye is the chief instrument of knowledge. Everything is seen clearly and presented in the vertical light and sharply-defined shadows of noon-day. . . . The crowd of impressions comes in too thick and fast to admit of discrimination and analysis.

. . . The poet is too full of his matter to think of his style. He cannot pause in his rush of feeling to select his word with the care with which the worker in mosaic does his color. Homely images are saved from being vulgar, and minute details from being tedious, by their vividness and truth. Poetry is a record of sensations, not reflections.[61]

Thus, it would appear that Hillard, much like Friedrich Schiller and the many adherents of his concept of naïve and sentimental poetry, saw in the Northern child of nature and his *Improvisatore* something akin to the freshness of the origin found in the literature of Greek antiquity, a reflection of the "epic" stage of man's development, as Goethe and others might have said. In the complex modern world, the "sentimental" or "dramatic" stage of human evolution, by contrast, "The writer of fiction must analyze motives, and lay bare the secret springs of action with metaphysical acuteness and discrimination. It is not enough to see the movement of the hands upon the dial-plate, we must also watch the play of the inner machinery, by which that movement is created and transmitted."[62] Accordingly, the novel's "improbable" plot, its lack of distinct characterization, and its "lackadaisical" sentiment, whatever the author may have meant by that term, are corollaries of Andersen's artistic sensibility. Thus, Hillard can pardon them, calling them "defects," rather inconsistently, in deference to a general shift in sensibility observable even in the late antebellum period.[63] Other commentators were less willing to follow suit.

Editions of *The Improvisatore* appeared in either London or New York in the years 1847, 1857, 1861, and 1863; between 1845 and 1864 a total of sixteen editions of the other novels and the travel books came out, not to mention the four editions of the autobiographies.[64] One may therefore be forgiven for being perplexed that in 1869 a reviewer could state matter-of-factly, "We are happy to find that Messrs. Hurd & Houghton have undertaken to give the public a complete edition of this writer's [Andersen's] works, which only require to be better known to be appreciated as they deserve."[65] One's puzzlement only grows on noting that the review appeared in the *American Literary Gazette and Publishers' Circular*, a forerunner of today's *Publishers Weekly*, which until 1863 had been principally a bibliography for the publishing industry.[66] Past editors of the *Circular* had been Irish-born author, editor, and critic Robert Shelton Mackenzie, who was among Simms's correspondents, and Charles Rudolph Rode, who came to the magazine in 1856 when it absorbed the *Criterion*, a short-lived but high-caliber critical weekly on which he had served in a similar capacity, and who edited and wrote reviews for the publication until his death in 1865.[67] It is unclear who replaced Rode and who wrote the notice of *The Improvisatore*, but the individual was likely cut from similar cloth, that is to say, a then well-known member of the literary circles of New York and/or Philadelphia. According to Mott, the paper had a subscription list of less than two thousand at the time the review appeared.[68]

Like Simms and others, the reviewer is deeply impressed by Andersen's life, so much so, indeed, that he devotes more space to it than to the novel ostensibly under consideration. All the same, he, like Hillard, expresses his admiration for the great painterly gift displayed in the novel:

> The glowing warmth of his descriptions seem to partake of the sunny land of which he writes, and it needs but little imagination on the part of the reader to fancy himself wandering amidst the ruins of imperial Rome, or watching a band of merry dark-eyed peasant girls dancing gayly to the music of their tambourines, among the vine-clad hills of Naples. However much the beauty of the work may have lost by translation, enough remains to place it among the very highest of its class, and gives evidence of the able way in which that duty has been performed.[69]

One may well wonder how Andersen was able to survive the linguistic journey from the original Danish of his novel through the German translation used by Howitt to her English rendering and to arrive there sufficiently hale (if not hearty) to receive such a greeting, which was common enough in critical responses to her translations of his novels.[70] Considering the limits of her eventual command of Danish, the wonder is even greater with regard to the warm reception given her collections of the stories and tales.[71] The critical, and popular, response to Andersen in the United States surely stemmed mostly from the nature of the works themselves, but it quite possibly derived in part from the contemporary popularity of Howitt's own original writing and the resulting credibility she enjoyed in the country. Carl Woodring writes, "As a living foreign poet second in popularity only to Mrs. Hemans by 1835, and to none by 1845, Mary Howitt continuously enlarged her audience in the United States until the decade of the Civil War."[72]

As an interesting aside, the critic for the *Circular* makes a point to mention "The Dying Child" ("Det döende Barn") as being "among the most celebrated" of the "many poems and tales of great beauty and merit" the author has written, perhaps having come across the piece in *Graham's Magazine* or one of the numerous other publications in which it appeared.[73] Thus, while Andersen's poetry was never reviewed in the United States, chiefly because so little of it was translated into English, it did not entirely escape the notice of American commentators, as chapter 4 makes even clearer.

The review in the *Circular* was the first response to the publication of *The Improvisatore* in the Author's Edition on August 28, 1869.[74] Eleven others followed over the course of the next few months, the first two appearing on the same day, September 11, in the Philadelphia *Evening Telegraph* and the

Portland Transcript of Portland, Maine.[75] The *Telegraph* was only four years old when the notice was published, but it had already gained recognition for innovations such as utilizing its namesake in transmitting dispatches and reprinting editorials from papers in New York and other American cities as well as, by the 1870s, major cities in Europe and other parts of the world; it had also reached a very respectable circulation of twenty-six thousand.[76] According to contemporary local historians, the *Telegraph* had "always preserved a high literary character," presenting the "choicest extracts from current publications in every branch of knowledge;" venturing into the field of fiction, for example, publishing Victor Hugo's last novel, *Ninety-Three* (*Quatrevingt-treize*), in daily installments; and paying "special attention to elaborate criticism in all departments of literature and art, including music and the drama."[77] The editor in charge of the "special departments of literary, art, musical, and dramatic criticism" was William J. Clark Jr. (1839–1889), who came to the *Telegraph* from a similar position on Philadelphia's *Sunday Dispatch*.[78] He studied art at the Pennsylvania Academy under Thomas Eakins, becoming an accomplished amateur painter himself, and championed the now famed realist's unconventional work in his review criticism. As a longtime member and sometime president of the Philadelphia Sketch Club, he induced his former teacher to serve as an instructor for the organization.

It is clear from the beginning of the review that Clark is well disposed to Andersen, for he opens with the words, "By undertaking the issue of a complete series of Hans Christian Andersen's writings, the publishers of this volume are doing a genuine service to the reading public of America. There is no living writer who better deserves a hearty and emphatic welcome than the delightful Danish prose poet, and there is none who is more likely to be received into the households of the land as a familiar friend."[79] After devoting a portion of the notice to the stories and tales, the Philadelphian diplomatically takes up a strain of thought central to Simms's review: "It is pleasant to believe that the taste for Andersen's writing is increasing, for it is a pure and wholesome taste, and there are no better books than his to place in the hands of children of all ages to cultivate in them an appreciation of good literature, and a complete set of his works will be an invaluable addition to any library." By this point in time, the heyday of Lippard and Thompson was past, but sensationalist writing had become part of the (sub)literary landscape of the United States, and in the intervening period the so-called sensation novel of Wilkie Collins, Charles Reade, Elizabeth Bradden, and others had sprung forth from native English sources and attracted a readership in this country.[80]

As his opening sentence suggests, Clark was one of many reviewers of the novel who sensed poetry in Andersen's prose: "This work is a prose poem, and while it is difficult to pronounce in favor of any one of Andersen's stories, there are few who will not be disposed to consider it the most charming of his numerous writings." Perhaps owing to his strong bent toward pictorial art, Clark recognizes a sympathetic spirit in Andersen's verbal brushwork: "The story itself is attractive, and a deep interest is maintained from first to last in the fortunes of the hero, but the chief value of the book is in the graceful and poetical descriptions of Italian life, scenery, and art." Nonetheless, he summarizes his overall impression of the book as one of a "combination of humor, pathos, and poetry that few persons upon reading once will omit to read again."

The *Portland Transcript* was a popular literary and news weekly that ran for more than seventy years between 1837 and 1910.[81] Although based in Maine, where it reportedly went to every town in the state, it was also widely distributed in the rest of New England as well as in New York and the Maritime provinces of Canada, circulating around eighteen thousand copies all together, a considerable sum for such a paper.[82] The *Transcript* was long published and edited by editor, author, and historian E. H. Elwell and S. T. Pickard, who was married to a niece of John Greenleaf Whittier and became the poet's literary executor and biographer.[83] The identity of the reviewer is uncertain.

The critic confirms Americans' current lack of familiarity with Andersen's longer prose: "Hans Christian Andersen has heretofore been chiefly known to the American public as a writer of stories for children. No complete edition of his works ever having appeared in English dress, his eminence as a novelist, traveller and poet, is but little appreciated on this side of the water."[84] Like the reviewer for the *Ladies' National*, he accompanies his approval of Andersen's depiction of Italy with concrete examples:

> It is a novel of Italian life, full of poetry and passion. The career of Antonio, the little Improvisatore, is told from his childhood, with charming simplicity, and great fidelity to local coloring. The fete days of Rome, her monks and her beggars; the life of the peasant on the campagna, and of the nobles in their palaces; the Jesuits' school, the Jews' quarter, and the wild, rollicking life of the young officers of the Papal Guards, are al [*sic*] graphically described.

Although the review contains no explicit criticism of the novel, the closing comment suggests a possible reservation expressed unambiguously in notices to be discussed shortly: "The volume will be read with pleasure *by all admirers of Andersen*" [emphasis added].

Two of the critiques expressed opposing views on the choice of *The Improvisatore* as the first volume of the Author's Edition, that of the *Christian Advocate* (pro) and that of *Harper's New Monthly Magazine* (con); a third, which appeared in the *Albion*, hints at a possible reason for the negative opinion.[85] The *Christian Advocate* of New York, one of a number of regional magazines of the same name, was the leading weekly of the Methodist Episcopal Church and enjoyed a run of well over a hundred years.[86] By 1879, it had a subscription list of 70,000, though claiming "only" 30,000 in 1869.[87] Originally a religious newspaper, it evolved into a quality family magazine of spiritual character that contained numerous departments, such as the one for book reviews. *Harper's New Monthly Magazine*, the progenitor of today's *Harper's*, was one of the leading general literary publications in the country and by far the most successful, among the few to attract a national and even international readership. When the Civil War broke out, it had an unparalleled circulation of 200,000, and, though suffering losses for some time thereafter, still listed 112,000 in 1869 and 120,000 two years later.[88] The *Albion* was essentially an eclectic weekly based in New York, which, like other periodicals of its kind, specialized in reprinting material originally published in British journals, claiming 15,000 subscribers in 1870.[89]

The anonymous reviewer for the *Advocate* writes, "'The Improvisatore' is a kind of general introduction to the whole of the author's collected works; giving some account of his life, but in a way the least stiff and formal. . . . This specimen volume promises well for the execution of the whole series."[90] The unidentified individual responsible for the "Editor's Book Table" in *Harper's* welcomes the Author's Edition per se but qualifies his greeting by opining that "[t]he choice of this volume was not really a happy one . . . for its excellences are not such as will induce strangers to this author to seek his further acquaintance; it is a book rather for the friends of Andersen than for those who are unacquainted with him."[91] Most of the rather lengthy notice in the *Albion* is composed of a detailed description of the plot, following its many twists and turns all the way to the fourth chapter of part 2, where Antonio appears in the theater in San Carlo. Here, the reviewer writes, perhaps with a smile, "The story *now* becomes involved, and borders on the marvelous" [emphasis added], at which point he relates how Antonio is shipwrecked, discovers Lara in the haunted blue grotto, and cures her blindness with the red flowers, and such.[92] It was quite possibly the "involved," "marvelous" nature of the story line that ill disposed the *Harper's* editor toward the *The Improvisatore* as the first volume of the Author's Edition. Of the novel's style, the critic for the *Albion* writes only that the work "is marked by the same simplicity . . . that distinguishes the author's less pretentious works." Like others, he remarks on the descriptiveness of the novel, though appearing to be less impressed by it than most: "Much of *The Improvisatore* is occupied with descriptions of Italian life and scenery, and, judging from the copious footnotes, is designed to give Herr Andersen's northern fellow-countrymen an idea of that sunny clime. The story is a very pleasing and harmless one, and will give to younger readers, especially, a tolerably accurate conception of southern Italy." The writer provides no explanation of why the book should be especially instructive to younger readers, but similar statements about this and other works suggest that the notion is rooted in the increasingly prevalent association of Andersen with children's literature.

The author of the review published in the *Nation* minces no words in expressing his dissatisfaction with the novel's form.[93] Stringent literary criticism, however, was quite characteristic of the magazine, which was founded in 1865 and, of course, continues in publication today. While most contemporary American journals practiced what was called "genial" criticism—that is, gentle, if not laudatory treatment of everything that was not conspicuously flawed or immoral—the *Nation* strove for rigor and objectivity, which was frequently tantamount to severity.[94] This editorial policy earned the magazine the enmity of many but also, twenty years later, the anonymous observation that review criticism in American periodicals had almost become a new art owing to its example.[95] Another reason for the less than genial nature of the review may lie in the fact that in the years following its establishment the magazine had little good to say about fiction in general, perhaps a remnant of moral reservation toward the form. During this time, its circulation never rose above six thousand, but, as Mott writes, "the power of the *Nation* came not from the number of its readers, but from their station and influence and from the frequency with which it was quoted. And a power it rapidly became, indubitably, in both politics and letters."[96] The identity of Andersen's reviewer is uncertain—the *Nation*'s corps of review critics was as extensive as it was of great distinction.[97] However, it is known that novelist and journalist William Dean Howells wrote reviews for the magazine in the late 1860s, and, given the tenor of his notices of other works by Andersen, he would seem to be as likely a possibility as any.[98]

The review deals with both *The Improvisatore* and *The Two Baronesses* (*De to Baronesser*), Andersen's fourth novel, which came out in the Author's Edition in late 1869. It is somewhat curious that Scudder issued the latter before the second and third novels, *O. T.* (*O. T.*) and *Only a Fiddler* (*Kun en Spillemand*), which, together with *The Improvisatore*, originally appeared within a period of two years (1835–1837) and are more closely related to each other than to their successor. A possible explanation may lie in a desire for variety on the part of the editor. In any case, the reviewer finds that the novels themselves

are perhaps curious rather than anything else; though of course he [Andersen] is a man who could not write seven or eight hundred pages without saying much that one would gladly read. But we think they will be found chiefly interesting for the light they throw upon the author himself rather than for anything they are in themselves. They make it evident, for one thing, that great as he is in short stories, a long one is too much for him. Everywhere in these novels there are weaknesses. Effects without good cause; causes that produce no effects; personages that are of no use; wild improbabilities side by side with the most threadbare incidents; borrowings from others, and repetitions of himself. . . . Of plot he seems never to have had any conception; and the short flights of his little prose poems for children must have further weakened his constructive abilities.[99]

Considerations of form and overall conception determine much of the reviewer's response to the novels. However, he also reacts to other, more fundamental concepts of poetics he sees at work in them, "these two jumbles of prose and poetry": "As for Italy's influence upon [Andersen], we imagine that a chief effect which it had upon his genius was to confirm him in the notion which he seems to hold, in common perhaps with most northern poets of modern times, that profuse pouring out of poetical impressions is poetry truly so called. 'Improvisatore' is made rather tedious by rhapsodies of this kind." One assumes that the writer was equally impatient with the Longfellow of *Hyperion*, the Poe of "Ligeia" and "The Fall of the House of Usher," and the Thoreau of *Walden.* One also suspects that he was similarly dismissive of the Heinrich Heine of books one through three of the *Pictures of Travel (Reisebilder)*, the Joseph von Eichendorff of *Premonition and Present (Ahnung und Gegenwart)*, and the novels of Andersen's countryman Bernhard Severin Ingemann, or that he would have been, had he read them. For all were in varying degrees directly or indirectly beholden to, or in sympathy with Friedrich Schlegel's notion of the novel as the ideal literary means of both reflecting and partaking of the "harmonious organism and chaotic plenitude of life," precepts central to his view of Romantic poetry as a "progressive universal poetry."[100]

Writing some sixteen years after Hillard, the reviewer for the *Nation* is far more specific and expansive in his criticism of Andersen's handling of plot, characterization, and the expression of sentiment and much more laconic and vague with regard to his redeeming qualities. In a paper addressed to J. Henry Harper in connection with the latter's history of Harper Brothers, Howells wrote, probably around 1910,

I detested the sentimental and the romantic in fiction, and I began at once [upon assuming responsibility for the "Editor's Study" in *Harper's New Monthly Magazine* around 1866] to free my mind concerning the romanticists, as well dead as alive . . . and since then one of the bitterest of my English enemies has generously written me that I was quite right in what I was always saying about romanticism, if not the romanticists. I am not sure that I was, now; but I was sure then. . . . The worst of it I did not then perceive, or know that my long fight had been a losing fight; I perceive now that the monstrous rag-baby of romanticism is as firmly in the saddle as it was before the joust began, and that it always will be, as long as the children of men are childish.[101]

Despite his expressed doubt regarding his earlier thinking, the older Howells still cannot abide Romanticism and, by extension, the romance associated with it. In his lecture on "Novel-Writing and Novel-Reading" of 1899, he clearly places higher value on the (realistic) novel than on the romance, not to mention what he calls the "romanticist novel," a sort of romance in a novel's clothing.[102] Whether Andersen's reviewer was Howells or someone else, he obviously shared the novelist's realist sympathies and unequivocally articulated the likely opinions of his colleagues at *Harper's* and the *Albion* as well as all those critics who took umbrage at the Dane's formal and notional sentimental Romanticism.

Judging by its article on the Author's Edition, the *Eclectic Magazine of Foreign Literature* was no more given to genial criticism than the *Nation*.[103] However, its objections only partially overlap with those of the relative newcomer, and it also has quite positive things to say, things that reveal a divergent understanding of the novel as a genre. The *Eclectic* enjoyed a long life, running from 1844 to 1907, though it listed only ten thousand subscribers in 1870.[104] It was one of many contemporary magazines that filled their pages with material culled from foreign, chiefly British, journals, at this time mainly serial fiction by writers such as Bulwer-Lytton, Dickens, Charles Reade, and Thackeray. It also reprinted book reviews from the major British periodicals, but the present one lacks the attribution given those notices and offers other evidence of an American origin.[105]

A healthy portion of the densely printed, two-column review is taken up by a discussion of children's literature to which we shall return in chapter 6. The greater part is again devoted to both *The Improvisatore* and *The Two Baronesses*, which, the reviewer writes,

> are remarkable for the freshness, delicacy of imagination, and poetic sympathy with Nature in all her moods and aspects, which characterize even the simplest of Andersen's tales. Like the novels of Bjornson [*sic*], they are essentially idyllic— delicious prose-poems, in which the tragedy, comedy, and commonplace of life are transmuted into a world of idealities, appealing strongly to the imagination, but seldom dramatically to our sentiments.[106]

Perhaps surprisingly, however, such virtues ultimately prove to be failings: "Herein lies their weakness as novels. They lack action, and the dramatic vigor of movement so essential where a dozen or more lives are concentrated into a few hours' reading, and the possession of which has given popular fame to the works of writers who are infinitely inferior to Andersen in poetic ability, and far narrower in their range of sympathies."[107] The reviewer continues along a by now equally familiar line:

> Notwithstanding some most excellent pieces of characterization, the author's personages, with a few exceptions, leave upon us the impression of impersonality; like his fairies, they are perfectly natural. If not human, they are wondrously like humanity, but they lack the one vital element of individuality. For this reason we think that Andersen will never rank so high as a novelist as he does as a poet and story-teller. The very merits of his novels (and they are many and eminent) are of that subtle, refined kind which, to be recognized, require a nature kindred to the author's own, or an artistic sense which only comes of high cultivation.[108]

The reviewer for the *Eclectic* joins other writers in his criticism of Andersen's handling of plot and character, offering greater detail than most. However, he has unusually high regard for the imaginative and poetic qualities of the works, implicitly criticizing the vast majority of readers for their inability to perceive such sophistication. On balance, he evinces a notion of the novel that requires a tight and spirited line of action and clearly differentiated characters anchored in lived experience, but one that also admits of those refinements at which Andersen excels. He thus achieves a certain compromise between the novel and the romance, something like the "Romanticist novel" that Howells despised and the "neutral ground" of which Thompson and Link have written.[109]

The reviewer's comments on *The Improvisatore* follow from his general reflections on Andersen's novels:

> "*The Improvisatore*," which is much the better of the two [novels], is a story of Italian life; and while in comparison with the noble comprehensiveness and intellectual grandeur of George Eliot's "Romola," it seems thin, illusive, and colorless, there is no other novel in our language written at such a sustained, imaginative level, with so true an insight into Italian character on its better and more poetic side, and with such brilliant powers of scenic description. The story, though pathetic and pleasing, is but the medium for the study of national character and for recording a traveller's impressions; but to those who would make acquaintance with modern Italy and Italian life, with Rome and the Campagna, and Venice and Naples, and all the scenery which has long become classic, in the most pleasing manner, we cannot do better than commend them to "*The Improvisatore*." For Andersen, while possessing the enthusiasm and sensibility of a genuine poet, is also a shrewd, accurate, and thoughtful observer.[110]

One may find that the reviewer's representation of the novel as a study of national character and as a travelogue does a disservice to Andersen's treatment of the problematic nature of artistic sensibility. However, he does credit the author for his power of imagination, scenic description, and reflective observation.

One might expect a similarly "un-genial" attitude from the *Catholic World*, a general family magazine with a distinctly religious perspective that was begun by Isaac T. Hecker, founder of the Community of Paulist Fathers, in 1865, the same year the *Nation* came into being.[111] At that point in time, the "culture wars" led by the idealist convert and former member of Brook Farm and Fruitlands against secularism, Protestantism, and the Catholic Church itself still lay in the future, but the *Catholic World* was already no stranger to controversy.[112] The crosstown *Nation* was a continual and severe critic of the journal but nonetheless conceded it a "more masculine tone than any of the other magazines," no mean praise from a paper that prided itself in its own stridency.[113] Though it struggled to attract subscribers, registering around ten thousand in 1870, the *World* maintained a high standard in its literary tone and editorial practice.[114] Andersen's reviewer may have been one-time Transcendentalist and socialist Orestes Brownson, who also converted to Catholicism and wrote reviews and much else for the journal.[115]

In any event, the reviewer acknowledges *The Improvisatore* (and *The Two Baronesses*) "as old friends in new garments, and hasten[s] to bid them welcome."[116] Not surprisingly, he is captivated by Andersen's faculties of observation and depiction:

> His powers of description are surpassed by few writers in any language, and the places he has visited, Rome, Naples, Vesuvius, Venice, Copenhagen, with the islands nestling about Denmark, stand before the reader in living colors, glowing with light and truth. One feels that these graphic representations are not drawn from a highly-wrought imagination, but that they are living realities. The narratives of the ascent of Vesuvius, the *Infiorata*, the first impressions of Venice, are wonderful samples of this power of delineation.

In contrast to his colleague at the *Nation* he can write, "High-toned morals and an utter freedom from maudlin sentimentality mark both these volumes; the tales are told with vigor, and the interest sustained to the end." To be sure, he senses in the author a son of the "beery monk of Wittenberg":[117]

> The *Improvisatore*, who is born and passes most of his years in Italy, tells his own story, and claims, as do most of the characters introduced, to belong to the Catholic Church; but we think a true Catholic would detect the fact that the kind-hearted, genial man who wrote the tale had not the happiness of being in the faith: though there is nothing harsh or unkind, or perhaps no intentional injustice, toward the church, yet there is here and there the slight touch of sarcasm concerning what the writer supposes to be a dogma of the faith, or a hit at some

local Catholic custom, which would not have come from the pen of a loyal son of our holy Mother.[118]

Like both Hecker and Brownson, the reviewer is clearly sensitive to criticism of the Catholic Church. However, he is nonetheless objective enough to give Andersen a reception he most certainly would have appreciated, one quite probably owing to the morality and humanity the writer saw in the novel as well, perhaps, as to a set of poetic assumptions on his part that was more retrospective than prospective in nature.

The author of the review published in the *Advance* saw Andersen's portrayal of the Catholic Church in a different light.[119] The *Advance* was an avowedly Congregationalist weekly that was founded in Chicago in 1867 out of dissatisfaction with the originally Congregationalist *Independent*'s gradual turn from religious to social issues.[120] It soon became the leading organ of the denomination in the western part of the country, claiming in 1869 that its circulation of twenty thousand was the largest of any religious paper west of New York, and had a run of fifty years.[121] The writer uses the review as an opportunity to take a shot over the bow of the Catholic Church: "One senses in it [the book] . . . the attractive side of Romanism, and also the idolatry, triviality and empty ritualism of much of its alleged piety," words that must surely have rankled Hecker and his associates if they had the misfortune to read them.[122]

Otherwise, however, the review is more objective and quite positive, sounding notes both familiar and unwonted:

> The present [volume of the Author's Edition] . . . recounts, as self-told, the experience from childhood of one of the peculiar productions of Italy, a poet gifted with the power of improvising upon any given theme. The story is surcharged with Italian life, and will have a special charm for those familiar with the people and scenery of that beautiful country, where artistic genius is hereditary and the atmosphere is filled with sentiment. The book itself is a prose poem, and, except that it ends happily, has a tone of sadness throughout. It is a tale of art and religion, of society and education, of passion and purity.

The reviewer concludes with the words, "There is also a touching moral in the career of the beautiful prima donna Annunziata, from the hour of her triumph to that of her death in obscurity, poverty and sorrow." Without going into the specifics of plot and character, the reviewer highlights certain important aspects of the novel, not least of all its undeniable darker side.

The final major review of *The Improvisatore* to be discussed here appeared in the *Universe*, a weekly miscellany that was established in 1868 as the *Chicagoan* and claimed a circulation of five thousand for 1869.[123] Despite absorbing two other weeklies and changing its name to broaden its appeal, the paper failed to survive its first year. During that brief space, however, it succeeded in publishing one of the most positive of all the notices of the novel, indeed, of all American commentaries on the author and his work. The review begins as follows:

> There is a world of tender pathetic thought in Hans Christian Andersen, and his stories read like the rippling of spring-waters. If he who has power to awaken in the heart its best and purest feelings, to kindle fires of thought sacred as those that burn upon celestial altars, to quicken all noble purpose of the soul and genialize and expand the whole nature, be a great man—then is the author we speak of the greatest. Upon every page we find thoughts that sink deep and stir the still currents of our interior life.[124]

The reviewer then quotes and comments upon a passage from chapter 2 of the novel as an example:

> "There is a song about the nightingale, which, when it was quite young, sat in the nest and picked the green leaves of the rose, without being aware of the buds which were just [beginning] to form; months afterwards, the rose unfolded itself, the nightingale sang only of it, flew among the thorns, and wounded itself." This instance of the delicate touch of a master of poetry, is but one among a thousand, in this beautiful volume. Its story is, as all the author's stories are, finished, pure, daintily-expressed, and admirably calculated to charm both young and old.

The reviewer's highly emotive and image-rich language both reflects and highlights the affective and poetic power he finds in Andersen's writing, in *The Improvisatore*, as the example indicates, and in general. Significantly, and uniquely, he experiences in the novel a union of feeling and thought, or thought borne on feeling, of the most profound kind, a fusion capable of forming and enlarging the mind, soul, and character and elevating the individual to greatness. Like the reviewer for the *Advance*, he is sensitive to the melancholy of the work, for example, to the pain depicted as intimately involved with the creative sensibility and the artistic life and exemplified by the passage from chapter 2. He also views the novel as the creation of a consummate artist, one who draws on the inspiration of nature, as evoked by the images of rippling spring water and the rosebuds and rose—perhaps an echo of Longfellow's understanding of Nordic culture. His observation that the novel is appropriate for young and old alike may have been made with a view to the many Americans who, like the authors of other reviews discussed in this and later chapters, associated Andersen primarily or entirely with his fairy tales and the nursery. In one of the last notices of the novel to appear in our period, indeed, the reviewer confirms this state of affairs, writing, "The world half forgets that Hans Christian Andersen does not belong exclusively to the children, but the new paper-covered edition [of the novel] . . . will probably undeceive some readers of light literature this summer."[125] Despite, or because of his Romantic sensibility and what many modern readers may dismiss as mere hyperbole, in any case, the reviewer for the *Universe* comes close to some fundamental truths about Andersen and his work.

O. T.

Like *The Improvisatore*, Andersen's second novel, *O. T.*, was released in both English and American editions in 1845 in Mary Howitt's translation. The initials in the title refer in part to the protagonist, Otto Thostrup, who, following his youth on a plantation in western Jutland, pursues university study in Copenhagen. There, he becomes friends with Vilhelm, a young baron from the island of Fyn, who invites him to visit him at his family's estate, where he falls in love with Vilhelm's sister Sophie. From this point, the novel unfolds along the trajectories of the relationships between Otto and Vilhelm, Otto and Sophie, and Otto and his nemesis, Heinrich. The two students appear to be polar opposites: Otto, a proud, introverted intellectual, and Vilhelm, a somewhat superficial, artistically inclined extrovert. However, they prove to be complementary natures, remaining close despite occasional differences all the way through a two-year-long tour abroad to the end. Otto loses Sophie to a friend of her family but ultimately recognizes her shallowness and wins the affection of her more thoughtful sister, Louise.

Early in the novel, Otto discloses the secret that has haunted him ever since it was revealed to him by Heinrich: The initials "O. T." tattooed on his shoulder stand not only for his name but also for his birthplace, Odense Prison, in Danish "Odense Tugthus." Heinrich crops up periodically to taunt Otto with this knowledge, ultimately threatening to proclaim Sidsel, in reality his own daughter, as Otto's long-lost sister. In the end, it comes to light that Otto's sister is in fact the ethereal servant-girl Eva, who dies before Vilhelm can convince her that his love for her can overcome the prevailing social barriers, and that the siblings' mother was imprisoned for noble reasons.

Much like its predecessor, *O. T.* is a coming-of-age novel in the tradition of the *Entwicklungsroman* (novel of development), or bildungsroman.[126] Otto's growth as an individual occurs less in reflex to his cultural environment than in inner and outer dialogue with friends and acquaintances and the varying landscapes of Jutland, Zealand, particularly Copenhagen, and Fyn. The novel received a warm welcome from the Danish public and was translated into several European languages, but it found less favor with critics and has remained in the background of the scholarly discussion of Andersen's novels.[127]

O. T. drew little attention from American reviewers on its initial publication in English together with *Only a Fiddler.* Indeed, an announcement of
its issuance in the Author's Edition states that the well-known children's
writer "is now introduced to many readers in this country for the first time
in connection with stories for a mature constituency."[128] However, several
advertisements and publication announcements that came out in 1845 and
1846 provide evidence that critics and the general public at least had the
opportunity to read the novel when it was originally published. New York's
Evening Post and *Commercial Advertiser*, for instance, carried the following
ad in several issues: "The style and arrangement of these pictures of Danish
life, differing from the ordinary routine of fiction, contain some exquisite
drawings of children's characters, and the patriarchal, together with some
touches of truth, sense and feeling, highly original and captivating. They will
unquestionably take rank with the best of the productions of Miss Bremer."[129]
These ads and announcements offered contemporary readers a preview of the
novel and give us a modest foretaste of its eventual critical reception in the
United States.

At the time under discussion, *O. T.* received only one true review, which
appeared in the *Southern Patriot.*[130] Published in Charleston, South Carolina,
the paper apparently failed to distinguish itself in any substantial way, for
Mott's astonishingly comprehensive work contains not one word about it.
And a nineteenth-century history of the press in Charleston says little of its
content and character other than to remark on a passing editorial conten-
tiousness.[131] All the same, the *Patriot* must have been a financial success,
for in its two instantiations it enjoyed a run of thirty-four years, from 1814
to 1848, and thus outstripped virtually all of its geographic cohorts, including the much acclaimed *Southern Quarterly Review* and *Southern Literary
Messenger.* In a rarity for the day, the review under consideration is signed,
by one "*S. Hart, sen.*," most likely Samuel Nathan Hart Sr. (1808–1880), a
Charleston book publisher and seller and leader of the local Reform Jewish
community.[132]

Hart deems *O. T.* of "higher interest, though of less impressive moral" than
Only a Fiddler, though, as we shall see, commentary on the latter generally
takes, or implies an opposing view.[133] He adopts what rapidly became a leit-
motiv in Andersen criticism, writing, somewhat inconsistently, that the novel
is "chiefly attractive by its piquant varieties, and happy sketchiness, rather
than by the concentration of the author's genius upon the delineation of any
one history or character. . . . The author's defect is his wandering, and the lack
of that intensity of mood and purpose, which compels, rather than persuades,
the reader." At the same time, Hart is favorably impressed that, "[s]prinkled
over the narrative, is a great deal of æsthetical philosophy, and much of the

more graceful surfaces of poetry." While many critics observe the poetic qualities of Andersen's longer prose, Hart is one of very few who appreciate the aesthetic reflection that forms a major part of its intellectual substructure. Although he does not elaborate on his insight, he may well have been thinking of passages such as the one in part 2, chapter 3, where the narrator delivers himself of what amounts to a theory of poetic realism in nuce. Following the examples set by Sir Walter Scott and Danes Poul Martin Møller and Steen Steensen Blicher, it was indeed Andersen's aim, and achievement, to found the realistic Danish novel, never mind that the fruits of his labors strike the modern sensibility as "romances" rather than "novels," in Howells's understanding of the terms.[134]

In contrast to its early fate, *O. T.* garnered several notices on its appearance in the Author's Edition on June 18, 1870, though these were generally briefer and less "engaged" than those of *The Improvisatore*, and less welcoming besides.[135] In the Philadelphia *Evening Telegraph*, William J. Clark Jr. writes that the novel is "interesting as a description of *a* class of Danish society and a certain style of scenery," notwithstanding the fact that it moves largely in both good bourgeois and lower aristocratic society and from remote West Jutland to urban Copenhagen to the manors on the island of Fyn [emphasis added].[136] Clark continues, "Andersen is at his best in his short stories and sketches, but his longer romances, although they will never rival these in popularity, are nevertheless entertaining on account of the charming grace of the author's style and the poetical atmosphere with which he invests the commonest affairs of life." In a sense, Clark takes from the novels in order to give to the tales, and all that is left—a "charming grace" of style and a "poetical atmosphere," bereft of accompanying examples—is so vague as to be almost meaningless: he does not so much as allude to any specific details of the volume under scrutiny. However, his expressed sense of an everyday world imbued with poetry implies recognition of the poetic-realist nature of the works. Indeed, it is perhaps not unimportant that he calls them "romances" rather than "novels." Whether he attached significantly different genre associations to the terms or simply used them interchangeably is unclear, but in view of the ongoing discussion mentioned earlier, one suspects that the former was the case.[137]

Most of the reviews of *O. T.* were published in July 1870, including the one that appeared in the *Telegraph* and one that was issued in another Philadelphia newspaper, the *North American and United States Gazette*.[138] This paper traced its lineage back to the eighteenth century but began publication in its current form in 1847 and then ran until 1925, recording a circulation of fifty-two hundred for the year in question.[139] The publisher and editor of the paper at the time was Morton McMichael. Though trained in the law, he early pursued literary interests, earning Poe's commendation for both his prose and poetry, and became a leading figure in the journalistic and public life of his adopted hometown.[140] It is doubtful that he wrote the notice himself, as the *North American* had a large cadre of staff and contributors. However, he or his associates evidently chose reviewers well, for the assessment of *O. T.* is one of the better of all the American critiques of Andersen's works.

Like Clark and certain of his other colleagues, the critic finds the plot per se less integral to the novel than, one suspects, the author did himself: "So far as the narrative goes it relates the loves of a young man and woman that were unfortunate and tragic. But this is merely a thread, shot occasionally into sight, and never of much importance."[141] The writer thus disregards the love of Otto and Louise as well as the social-psychological relationship between Otto and his friend Vilhelm, which more truly drives the plot. It is the vicarious traveler through Denmark and Danish society who finds the novel worthwhile:

> The material portion consists in the description of Danish life at Copenhagen, but particularly in the wilder region of Jutland. The common people furnish the characters. The events are tame but national; and much may be acquired of Danish life, manners, religion and superstition, that could not be gleaned from any work of history or morals. It is the small pictures raised at various times, and of no great importance, that give value to the whole.

The reviewer is plainly aware of the power of literature to go beyond historiography and formalized morality to paint a picture of national life and, by extension, life in general. Indeed, modern readers of the novel may well agree with his sense of what is important in the work.

However, his ultimate verdict on the work is severe, if not harsh: "The distinguished reputation of the author, acquired through his short compositions, will float this [work] more than its own merits. It lacks concentration, consistency and culmination; and the failure in these particulars is hardly compensated by the exquisite pictures that make oases in its progress. As a teller of tales Andersen is almost peerless; but as a writer of sustained fiction he has many superiors." In contrast to some reviewers of *The Improvisatore*, this commentator's dissatisfaction with the formal aspects of *O. T.* is not counterbalanced, or even blunted, by the admittedly "exquisite pictures" drawn by Andersen's pen, which are reduced to forming "oases" in an otherwise implicitly arid imaginative landscape. *O. T.* is not a great novel, and neither is it a great romance. However, it is better as the latter than as the former; indeed, it is an example of the latter. The reviewer uses neither term to classify the work, but he surely understood the expression "sustained fiction" in the contemporary sense of "novel," and his judgment of the text most likely stemmed from a Howellsian impatience with the romance.

A notice of similar gist appeared toward the end of July in the *Independent*.[142] Originally an organ of Congregationalism, this weekly made a name for itself particularly under the influence and sometime editorship of Henry Ward Beecher (1813–1887), an exceptionally popular clergyman, social reformer, journalist, and speaker who made the periodical a vehicle for his decided antislavery stance.[143] Later, under the editorship of his former assistant editor, Theodore Tilton, it became a pillar of support for women's suffrage. The magazine long enjoyed notoriety for the caliber of its literary contributors, which was not the least of the reasons that it reached a circulation of around sixty-eight thousand the year its review of *O. T.* was published.[144]

The author of the notice has much in common with his colleague at the *North American and United States Gazette*. Though more discreet in formulating his appraisal of *O. T.*, he makes his relevant notions of genre even more apparent:

> With the strongest prejudice in favor of the dear Danish story-teller, Hans Andersen, we cannot but wish that he had stuck to his stories of the wild, weird kind. We do not altogether like his *O. T., A Romance*. It is strange enough, and has a Norseland charm about it; but the habits of a teller of marvelous tales are not wholly favorable to romance writing. As a story-teller, Andersen makes a world of improbabilities; and, as improbability is the law of his world, his fancy is without fetters. But a romance owes something (not much, maybe; but something, at least) to the ordinary sequence of events in this everyday sphere. Under these limitations we think good Hans chafes a bit, and through them we think he breaks quite unlawfully now and then.[145]

This reviewer, like others already and yet to be noted, demonstrates that the concept of typecasting existed long before the advent of film and television. Such was the success of Andersen's stories and tales that all of his other works, including his highly popular autobiography, stood in their shadow. His "unlawful" breaches of verisimilitude in *O. T.* presumably refer, for instance, to the villainous deeds of the unsavory Heinrich. The reviewer could not have been aware of the autobiographical resonance of these features or how deeply their parallels in Andersen's life troubled him, nor, however, might he ultimately have cared. These aspects of the work are more melodramatic than contrary to experience—some unfortunates do have skeletons in their closets and mean-spirited acquaintances quite prepared to open the doors and let them out. However, their theatricality as well as the reviewer's transparent reservations toward the romance, doubtless reflecting a preference for the modern novel, suffice to explain his judgment of the work. Despite his verdict, he is kind enough to conclude, somewhat self-contradictorily, "But this story is beautiful, if it is a little disjointed; touching and sweet, if it is somewhat improbable."

Other reviewers had unprejudiced, either objective or purely positive responses to the novel. The author of the notice in the *Portland Transcript* was not only not repelled by the intrigue surrounding Otto's tattoo but appears to have indeed been drawn to it:

> It is a story of a high spirited and sensitive Jutlander, Otto Thostrup, who in his youth had his initials tattooed upon his shoulder, and was afterwards taunted with them by one who knew some circumstances of his birth of which he was ignorant, and which gave a disgraceful significance to the letters. Hence the title of the book. The sting of the taunt rankled in his soul till he had unravelled [*sic*] the whole mystery of his origin.[146]

Interestingly, the reviewer finds a parallel between this work and one that has since become an American classic: "The story of his [Otto's] mother's life reminds one of the principal incident in Hawthorne's *Scarlet Letter*. She suffers the disgrace of punishment as a thief, to shield her lover who is a scamp." The similarity between the two novels does not run deep—the mother's action is of secondary importance to Andersen's work, and its impact is in any case more social than moral or psychological, though it certainly affects Otto's sense of self. However, the fact that the reviewer recognizes it shows that he is reading more closely, and thinking more broadly, than many of his cohorts. Still, he closes in a familiar fashion: "The story is told in the author's charmingly simple style, and abounds in lively sketches of Danish life, manners, and legends."

Yet another July review appeared in the *Churchman*, an Episcopalian weekly of Hartford, Connecticut, and, later, New York that ran from 1867 to 1980.[147] In the year in question, the publication's editor(s) claimed that its circulation of eight thousand made it the *"largest paper with the largest circulation in the Protestant Episcopal Church."*[148] The reviewer sounds notes both familiar and unfamiliar:

> Probably to some readers this is not new. This edition, however, is the author's edition with quite a number of his own notes. It is a purely Danish story, and, like his other novels, is written in the pleasant and peculiar style which is so unlike every other. It is a tale of no great variety of incident or novelty of character, but homelike, hearty, and pure. One cannot but be struck by the strong nationality of its tone, and the sketches of Danish moral life are very fresh and attractive. The meaning of the mystical initials of the title makes part of the interest of the story, and therefore we shall not reveal it.

The writer gives a credible indication that *O. T.* had in fact been read in the United States in earlier editions, perhaps suggesting that he was an older individual or at least one with a better memory or one of wider reading. He perceives in the novel a wholesome quality that he associates with moral character. Like his colleague at the *Portland Transcript*, he finds the circumstances and events surrounding the "mystical initials" appealing, from which one may infer an openness to the romance in both reviewers. He joins a number of commentators who emphasize the pronounced Danish-national character of the work, and they were right to do so. Johan de Mylius asserts that Andersen indeed sought in the novel to provide a broad and colorful picture of contemporary Denmark for a foreign readership, though it is very likely that Americans contextualized the picture differently than Denmark's European neighbors.[149]

ONLY A FIDDLER

Andersen's third effort in long prose and the last translated by Mary Howitt was *Only a Fiddler*, which was issued together with *O. T.* in London and New York in 1845. The novel follows the fortunes of two childhood sweethearts, Christian and Naomi, whose dissimilar natures and surroundings lead them to take very different paths through life. Christian is a poor but talented boy from Svendborg on the island of Fyn who aspires to become a famous violinist. However, his retiring, dreamy personality and a lack of encouragement and support from others prevent him from realizing his potential and hopes. Instead, he becomes a poor music teacher in Copenhagen and finally a village "fiddler" who has resigned from life, never having relinquished his unrequited love for Naomi, but enjoys the solace of friends and children and the consolation of religion. In stark contrast to Christian, Naomi is a strong-willed, vital Jewish girl who as the adopted daughter of a noble family experiences a youth of privilege. Growing bored with her life, however, she runs off with a circus rider named Ladislaus, who proves to be a woman-beater, driving her to flee to Rome and then Paris. There, she marries a marquis and lives a life of luxurious dissipation, and growing restlessness, until the ever vengeful Ladislaus turns up to reveal his former relationship with her to her husband, himself noble in name only, after which she remains outwardly proud but inwardly broken. While on a journey through Fyn, her coach interrupts a funeral procession in which, unbeknownst to her, Christian is being borne to the cemetery, and with this, the novel closes.

Only a Fiddler has been called both a bildungsroman and an anti-bildungsroman, and Christian's failure to achieve the wholeness of personality

associated with the Goethean form certainly lends credibility to the latter designation.[150] The novel was Andersen's most successful work to date, regarding both sales and critical reception, and provided his entrée to Germany and
the rest of Europe.[151] Although posterity has generally been less charitable,
one recent scholar has called the novel both original and of the first rank.[152]

Much as was the case with *O. T.*, only two American reviewers appear to
have commented on *Only a Fiddler* on its initial publication in the United
States. One of the individuals was of course the author of the joint notice
of the two novels in the *Southern Patriot* discussed in part earlier, in all
likelihood Samuel Nathan Hart Sr.[153] Many of Hart's remarks apply in equal
measure to both works: "The 'Improvisatore' was a very striking romance.
These before us are distinguished by similar characteristics. They exhibit a
nice blending of the details of domestic life, with some of the more imposing attributes of fiction,—are, at once simple, and ambitious, and betray all
those irregularities of mood and art which denote the eccentric temper, and
the irregular education." Hart's sense of the irregular in the novels may well
derive from his reading of the biographical sketch of Andersen that introduces Howitt's translation of *The Improvisatore*, which he mentions at the
beginning of his review. And he fails to enlarge on what he understands as
the "more imposing attributes of fiction." However, his comparison of the
two works to *The Improvisatore* as a romance intimates a certain concept
of the genre, and the tone in which he makes it implies a favorable attitude
toward the form.

Nonetheless, Hart's perception of irregularity in the texts suggests a theoretical reservation, certainly toward the unapologetic wild-and-wooliness of
Simms's and others' practice of the romance (see the discussion of John Neal
in chapter 6). With respect to *Only a Fiddler*, however, he is willing to pardon
departures from his structural ideal in view of other virtues: "But the very
inequalities with which the critic finds fault, are the sources of the author's
success with the reader. These inequalities keep him from drowsing over
the pages as he turns them. 'Only a Fiddler,' embodies the life and the life-
struggle of a musical genius, who, after all, comes to nothing; and is so full
of lively picture and piquant sketch, that we forgive readily a hundred defects
in the plan and arrangement of the story." Hart's comments foreshadow both
positive and negative aspects of later reviews.

The only other early notice of *Only a Fiddler* came out in Philadelphia's
North American, a precursor to the *North American and United States Gazette*, introduced earlier in this chapter.[154] The paper was published by George
R. Graham, who for a time made the concurrently running magazine that bore
his name one of the most preeminent and financially successful periodicals
of the first half of the nineteenth century.[155] However, he withdrew from the

comparatively prosperous *North American* a year or so after partner Morton McMichael and others merged it with the *United States Gazette* in 1847.[156]

The reviewer was obviously familiar with the biographical sketch of Andersen that had accompanied *The Improvisatore* into the literary arena only some six months earlier, for he sees *Only a Fiddler* as a kind of sublimated autobiography:

> The miseries and struggles of a musical genius under disadvantages of the most trying and hopeless character, are described with an earnestness[,] a simplicity, and a depth of feeling, which show, at once, that the author has made his own trials the staple of his narrative but embellished with the accessories which his imagination readily suggested, as necessary to relieve it from having too much the appearance of a piece of autobiography.[157]

However, a more interesting comment relates to a theme taken up with varying emphasis by later reviewers: "The moral tone of the work, as was the case with the *Improvisatore*[,] would sometimes call for reprehension, were it not apparent that the writer adopts it for working out a moral theory of his own, or rather, of the present age, a theory which goes to extenuate, almost to overlook, the vices of the lower orders upon the plea that society has not performed its duty towards them." Critics of the novel twenty-five years hence also raise the question of morality, but none does so within the context of societal inequity. It is quite likely that the reviewer of the Philadelphia *North American* read the work with an eye on related conditions in the United States, not to mention his own hometown, seeing in it the aims, if not the methods, of a George Lippard.

On its appearance in the Author's Edition, probably sometime in August 1870, *Only a Fiddler* engaged the attention of American critics more forcefully than any of Andersen's other novels.[158] The earliest of the responses, which came out in the *North American and United States Gazette* late in the month, bears little resemblance to the notice that appeared in the paper's forerunner in 1845, focusing initially on the "Danishness" of the novel:

> The sixth volume in the republication of Anderson [*sic*] is purely Danish in its cast and character. As it is in his home stories that the writer excels, and in which he has laid his distinguished reputation, the "Fiddler" will continue to be shelved by the side of the Improvisatore and the Harz Mountains—with the best. The old Norse flavor penetrates the whole, and real Danish life is the material. There are Scandinavian episodes that reach to Sweden and Norway, just as there are side winds blowing in from Paris and Germany; but the tale is substantially one of Denmark; its people, scenery, lands, customs and faith. The nautical element is pronounced, as must be the case in any satisfactory Danish story, and the religion of the country is brought out vividly.[159]

Though his likening of *The Improvisatore* and the "Harz Mountains" (see chapter 3) to "home stories" such as *O. T.* and *Only a Fiddler* is puzzling, the reviewer's apparent understanding of the expression reveals true insight into *Fiddler* and most of Andersen's other novels. For it implies a kinship between these works and the so-called everyday stories (*hverdagshistorier*) of contemporary Dane Thomasine Gyllembourg and Fredrika Bremer.[160]

The reviewer does not waste many words on the plot: "The fiddler, Christian, loves a beautiful girl who prefers to marry a French Marquis, and her loss leads to his death. The story is not intricate, nor is it handled in any original manner."[161] With these few broad strokes and comments, which condense a wide-ranging story line to virtual nothingness, the writer turns to what is truly one of the key features of the novel: "The interest concentrates in the Flemish nicety of details, the pre-Raphaelite fidelity of narrative that distinguishes it, and by which a most thorough insight is obtained to the subjective side of Danish character, while all of its objective features are vividly described." It would come as no great surprise if the reviewer proved to have been William J. Clark Jr. or another member of the Philadelphia Sketch Club. For he not only has a painter's eye but also employs an artist's terminology to characterize Andersen's descriptive narrative style, comparing it to the precise detail and vitality of the Flemish School and the faithfulness to nature that members of the Pre-Raphaelite Brotherhood saw in the roughly contemporaneous religious art of Italy.[162] It would have been appropriate, and perhaps highly instructive, if the individual had elaborated on his notion of Andersen's peculiar narrative mode as a means of revealing Danish interiority. As it stands, however, the idea is unique in American Andersen criticism and uncommonly thought provoking. The critic concludes with a seeming reservation followed by high praise: "The apparent simplicity of the style may check appreciation at first, but its masterly touches will command perusal when that has been begun. There are no better books of their class."

A review of a different stripe appeared in the *Christian Union*.[163] Established under a different name in 1867 as a Baptist weekly, the periodical gradually transitioned into a general family magazine that ran under different titles and with changes of focus until 1935.[164] Chief editor at the time was Henry Ward Beecher, whose great popularity and suggestions regarding editorial staffing contributed to the immediate success of the paper, which may have reached a circulation of thirty-five thousand by the time the notice appeared and triple that number within two years.[165] Its list of contributors contains familiar names such as Beecher's sister Harriet Beecher Stowe, Louisa May Alcott, Edward Everett Hale, Helen Hunt Jackson, Charles Dudley Warner, John Greenleaf Whittier, and others. The literary editor was Dorsey

Gardner, a seasoned journalist and author who, if he did not write the review himself, presided over its publication.[166]

The reviewer is another who experienced disappointment on his first encounter with Andersen's long fiction, and his chief reason for doing so strikes a by now familiar chord:

> It is the first time we have met the author in sustained fiction, and we must confess that he disappoints us. There is, to be sure, the Andersen style, quaint and simple, and with the subdued undervein of poetry. Still, something of the naïve, the infantile shrewdness, has been sacrificed to the thread of the narrative, and that is not strong enough to hold us. The hero, the person, that is, who is "only a fiddler," is a very poor creature, who remains to the end only a fiddler, and an obscure and mediocre one, merely by reason of his entire lack of force of character, his superabundance of that kind of vapid goodness which the Sunday-school-book heroes have made so nauseously familiar.[167]

The writer much prefers the darker shades of the novel to the lighter: "Far more interesting is she who comes nearest to being the heroine—a Jewess, beautiful, brilliant, abounding in character, in genius, in self-will, but who allows herself, unconverted, to be confirmed, resigns herself to a life of disreputable and impure adventure, marries without clearing her conscience—goes through life, in a word, in quest of vicious self-indulgence, all from sheer lack of heart or of purpose." If at this point the reader thinks that the critic is done with poor Christian, he is soon disabused of the notion:

> Nor, except that the hero subsides out of life—dying is too sharply pronounced a thing to apply to anything he is capable of doing—is there any definite result to anything. Through a constant succession of incidents—pleasing or striking enough of themselves, though without enduring impression—we come at last to the end of the book, having never found the something in the nature of substance we have constantly expected to present itself on the next page.

Based on the reviewer's predilection for Naomi and her story line, one cannot help but speculate that he was at least susceptible to, and perhaps an admirer of, sensational fiction. However that may have been, he was one of many who at times roundly criticized the compositional style of *Only a Fiddler* and Andersen's other novels, both in the Dane's own time and, later, at home and abroad. For some, as Iben Holk writes, a novel was supposed to be structured in a systematic way to reflect the author's view of life; for others, it was to be designed so as to mirror everyday existence in one or more social classes, often with the end of improving social-political conditions.[168] According to the motto "the novel is the field of possibility," however, Holk finds that Andersen's works in the genre are well structured, each according to its own purpose. In *Only a Fiddler*, he asserts, that purpose is to contrast Christian and Naomi as representatives of personal freedom and emancipation, or, as de Mylius writes, of art and life, respectively.[169] With regard to nineteenth-century America, one might consider the romance the true field of possibility, but our reviewer, the same as many or most writing in 1869 and later, had more restrictive ideas of the possibilities of long fiction. Again like others, however, he is able to find redeeming qualities in the work of a favored author: "In spite of all this, there is enough fineness of fancy and beauty of thought to make the book worth reading; and there are few, who know Andersen at all, who do not desire to know all of him that is possible."[170]

An obvious proponent of the romance, and an exception to the growing rule, was the originator of a review that came out in the *Portland Daily Press* of Portland, Maine.[171] He writes that the book

> is a romance in the true sense of the term, and is quite different in cast and character from the modern novel. The romantic history of Christian, the hero, and Naomi, the heroine, commences with their childhood, and is carried through many vicissitudes and adventures with never failing interest, to a touching close.—One cannot but wonder, not only at the fullness of the gifted author's imagination, but at the stories of little interesting facts and incidents which his mind has gathered, and which . . .

Unfortunately, the review apparently fell victim to a printer's error, for it was left in this state of incompletion, thereby shortchanging readers, and Andersen, of a spirited apologia of the romance and of *Only a Fiddler* as an exemplar of it.[172]

A more extensive review of the work appeared in San Francisco's *Daily Evening Bulletin*.[173] Relevant information about the paper is scarce, limited essentially to the following facts.[174] First editor James King launched a crusade against local public abuses and thereby made the *Bulletin* a force in the city and state, reportedly achieving, for the time and place, an unheard of circulation of seven thousand. For his trouble, he was gunned down on a street in broad daylight by one of the men he had attacked editorially, who was then lynched. Beyond these both heartening and lurid details it is certain only that King or one of his successors was wise in his choice of reviewers, for the notice of *Only a Fiddler* is perhaps as expert and revealing as any that Andersen received in the United States.

The writer begins his commentary on the novel, the work of "one of the living classics of Scandinavian literature," as follows:

> This is one of the most lengthy and elaborate of Andersen's works. With much of the quaint fancy, naïve simplicity of sentiment, and fine bits of description

which characterize the author's short tales, it has a more ambitious aim. The whole plot turns on the hard career of a poor musical genius, highly sensitive, romantic and unpractical, contrasted with the easy life of a wealthy young beauty, intellectual, wilful and eccentric, with the stain of an illicit origin and a secret *liason* [*sic*] on her soul. The youth is pure, gentle, pious, unselfish, a victim of poverty and caste, who never realizes his ambition, and dies lonely of a broken heart. The girl, whom he loved despairingly, and who was once his playmate, marries a Marquis, leads a life of luxury amid a large circle of admirers, and returns to her native spot just as the funeral cortege of the poor fiddler passes to the grave. These two characters, and others in the book, are strongly individualized, and the scenes through which they are led to the sequel of the drama in which they play a part are sketched with much animation and truth.[175]

The reviewer recognizes the distinct contrast between Christian and Naomi and implies recognition of that contrast as the structural principle of the novel. He is not at all put off by the compositional technique of the work. However, he does voice a reservation toward one aspect of it: "Yet there is something unhealthy [sensationalist?] in the conception of the character and career of the heroine, in her strange predisposition to moral outlawry, her premature cynicism and bitterness. One's sense of poetical justice is shocked that she encounters no retribution but the concealed unrest of a mind that despises the hollow shams of life and a heart that frets over the lack of happiness for itself which it fails to confer on another." For this reviewer, as for most mid-Victorian critics, poetic justice in fiction was an imperative of Christian morality.[176] At the same time, he is realist enough to be able to write that "one is also obliged to confess that things often go that way in the world, and that it is really common for genius and virtue to go unrewarded and unhappy to the grave." And he also sees a moral principle at work in the novel: "The author suggests one moral of a practical kind, which he puts in the mouth of the dying fiddler: 'Here is it still good in the world, and the people are also good. I am now quite convinced of that which thou [Luzie] saidst to me many years ago: 'the common gifts to man are so great, that it is sinful to desire uncommon abilities from the Divinity. He who is placed aloft is exposed to the sharp winds; we who stand lowly feel them not.'"

While accepting the plot and characters of the novel on their own terms, the writer prefers other aspects of the work:

More than in the plot of this tale have we found pleasure in its happy sketches of Danish character and scenery, which are like photography and Dutch painting combined, and in its bits of strange tradition and superstition, which seem like remnants, as they are, of the old Norse times and myths. Indeed, throughout the whole story there is a breezy freshness which speaks of the morning of

Scandinavian literature, and in the plot itself there is a tinge of that fatalism which the rude sagas had in common with the refined drama of the Greeks.

The true "remnants" may be of Longfellow's mythical Scandinavia rather than of Norse mythology, and the fatalism may owe more to the Romantic notion of the artist's problematic relationship to life, or society, than to Greek tragedy.[177] However, the appreciation expressed in these comparisons rests on solid ground, on Andersen's very real descriptive gifts and portrayal of the artist as unfit for life. In type, if not necessarily in literary stature, Christian is indeed a descendent of Goethe's Tasso, a rough contemporary of Hawthorne's Owen Warland, and a precursor of Herman Bang's William Høg and Thomas Mann's Hanno Buddenbrook, Gustav Aschenbach, and other related characters. And the reviewer is right to point out the poetic quality of Andersen's prose, which, unlike most commentators, he exemplifies with a passage from the text, specifically from chapter 6 of part 1:

> There is a crispness and simplicity in Andersen's style which is lost only when he moralizes, or sentimentalizes, more like a a [sic] Frenchman than a Dane, suggesting that Frenchified Goth Heinrich Heine. His poetical quality is purer, and reveals itself in such bits as this, which are not rare in the book: "Not a single cloud showed itself in the whole sky. A bird of prey flew up, and with the many strokes of his wings directed his course toward the near wood. *The whole heat of the day seemed to rest upon the back of this bird.*" Nothing can be finer than that in its way. Those who have not read Anderson [sic] will find that his books open a new world to them.[178]

Reading these lines, one may wince on thinking of the not yet, or perhaps only inwardly "Frenchified" Heine of the *Journey to the Harz Mountains* (*Die Harzreise*) and other works, of, for example, the lyrical description of the valley of the river Ilse in the Harz and the personification of the Ilse as a young girl, which then melts into a ballad-like poem. However, the reviewer is right to say that Andersen's prose is purer than Heine's in the sense that it does not exhibit the frequent sarcastic, often cynical tonal shifts for which Heine is famous and which indeed characterize the narrative style of *Journey to the Harz Mountains*. Sarcasm and cynicism, Andersen reserved largely for the character of Naomi.

The notice published in the *Portland Transcript* is similar in structure and assessment to the one just discussed.[179] The reviewer contrasts Christian and the "little flirt of a Jewess" at some length and then reflects on the vast difference between their fates, captured most graphically at the conclusion of the novel, where the coach bearing Naomi and her aristocrat husband crosses paths with Christian's simple funeral procession: "The book dramatically ends with this curious reversal of the demands of 'poetic justice.' Still, we are made to see the gilded misery of Naomi's lot, and the substantial happiness of Christian's, and all this without one word of moralizing. It is the perfection of the art of story-telling." This writer is less troubled by the inequitable fortunes of Christian and Naomi than his counterpart at the *Daily Evening Bulletin* and is quite favorably impressed by Andersen's avoidance of moral "preaching." Indeed, he finds that the author deals tactfully with his sensitive subject matter: "As in most of Andersen's works, the author often steps on what English and American writers avoid as 'delicate' ground. He is never indelicate in his allusions, and yet he does not shrink from showing the gay mockeries and the dark despairs that are the accompaniments and the fruits of illicit love." In other words, he presents the concomitants and consequences of immoral behavior without sensationalizing them.

Interestingly, the questions of poetic justice and delicate subjects are never raised in the review published in *Zion's Herald*, the oldest of the Methodist weeklies, which was established in 1823 and continued under a series of different titles until 2011, claiming a subscription list of sixteen thousand in 1870.[180] Indeed, the five main reviews of *Only a Fiddler* discussed in these pages offer evidence that moral-religious concerns were not the monolithic force in American letters that they are widely thought to have been, especially abroad, and reviews of the other novels bear this out. Alternatively, the notices suggest that such issues had become far less decisive in the formation of aesthetic judgment than in the period leading up to around the middle of the nineteenth century, during which, however, a Samuel Hart could already ignore moral-religious questions in favor of ones of an aesthetic nature.

Anyone who believes or assumes that British reviewers were less morally judgmental in their attitude toward literature than their American brethren should read the notice of *Only a Fiddler* published in London's *Gentleman's Magazine* in 1845, during the heyday of the English reception of Andersen, which is quoted here in its entirety.[181] The writer first expresses serious general reservations toward the translation of fiction from abroad:

We cannot say we consider the present taste for translating foreign works of fiction at all a good sign of the times. There are doubtless here and there some of these works which may be read with amusement and information, but the greater portion, it is to be feared, are unhappily distinguished by very lax views of morality, and a very latitudinarian tone of religious opinion. What renders both these defects still more dangerous is, the manner in which they display themselves; they do not occur now and then as exceptions to the general tone of sentiment, but they run through the whole work, so as to form a continual undercurrent of unwholesome and pernicious sentiment. We are confident that many of these books, if they had appeared as original works instead of as translations, would have met with general reprobation.

The reviewer then turns to Andersen's novel: "The work before us may be very clever in its way, and it contains many brilliant passages, many pleasing and simple pictures of Danish life, but still there is a freedom of thought on matters of morality, a lax and wild mode of expression, if not worse, on religious subjects, which are earnestly to be deprecated, and which cannot fail to excite very painful feelings in every well-regulated mind, and to the young and the inexperienced must be full of danger."

Significantly, the *Gentleman's Magazine* was a popular general periodical rather than a religious publication, one, incidentally, that went all the way back to 1731 and was the first to bear the designation "magazine."[182] Under its current publisher, to be sure, it devoted more space to religious subjects than under previous regimes, and its present editor, John Mitford, was an Anglican clergyman. However, these circumstances may or may not have influenced the choice of reviewers, for Mitford's inclinations would appear to have been far more literary than clerical in nature.[183] His extensive literary activities included, for example, not only editions of Milton and Cowper but also of Swift and Prior.[184] In any case, both the *Christian Union* and *Zion's Herald* were not only nominally religious in origin and orientation, and yet their reviews of *Only a Fiddler* are far more "latitudinarian," in a positive sense, than that of the *Gentleman's Magazine.*[185]

Initially, the reviewer for *Zion's Herald* makes some observations common to other American notices of the novel, opining that the work is "full of local color. Denmark's history, geography, manners and customs, low and high, are well illustrated."[186] However, his comments are largely and more specifically literary in nature, for example, "It [the novel] has many pretty sentiments, neat fancies, and striking expressions. Thus the opening describes the return of spring and the stork in Denmark," at which point passages drawn from the first chapter of the novel follow at length. His only criticism relates to the English rendering of a poem from part 1, chapter 14, of which he writes, "The pretty poetry of Andersen is horribly rendered. How doggrelish are these verses, undoubtedly neat and sad in their original." His lone comment of a religious nature is one of approval: "He [Christian] is also a Christian of the Danish type, and in the last page dies with this for his last word: 'When I am dead, give my Bible to thy [Luzie's] children. There lives within it a treasure that can be corrupted neither by moth nor rust.'"

In September 1876, an article titled "Hans Christian Andersen—'Only a Fiddler'" appeared in the *Farmers' Home Journal.*[187] Founded in 1867 in Lexington, Kentucky, the weekly had since moved across state to Louisville, where it now had an estimated circulation of forty-five hundred and continued in publication until 1932.[188] The piece is in essence a general interest article that takes a brief look at the author's life and work. The reason for the title, and the main motive for the article as well, is the announcement in the first paragraph that the paper will commence publication of the novel in the next issue. Attempts to confirm whether this in fact happened have failed, but the sentences that follow the announcement contain a couple of opinions of interest: "Only a Fiddler is marked by a naive simplicity, a singular absence of sensationalism, quiet purity, and poetic treatment, and we feel sure that it will please our readers." This writer, like others who commented on *Only a Fiddler* as well as *The Improvisatore*, considers the novels a welcome alternative to the sensationalism that they all apparently abhorred.

THE TWO BARONESSES

Charles Beckwith Lohmeyer's translation of *The Two Baronesses*, Andersen's fourth novel, appeared in London in 1848, about a month before the original was released in Denmark. At the beginning of the work, three students of noble birth and their tutor take shelter from stormy seas at a run-down property on the coast of Fyn, where they discover a baby girl together with her dying mother and decide to make her their "daughter." They place Elisabeth, as they name her, in the care of Baron Herman's widowed grand-mother, Baroness Dorothea, where she remains for five years. Originally a commoner, Dorothea had wed the son of a landowner who had cruelly punished her father, but she is nevertheless susceptible to the flaws of the class into which she married, high-handedly expelling Elisabeth from her home for breaking one of her rules. Elisabeth is then taken in by the tutor, Moritz, who becomes a clergyman on one of the Hallig Islands off the coast of Schleswig, where she grows up. While in Copenhagen as a young woman, she meets Herman again, and a bond begins to develop which, years later and following numerous complications, leads to their marriage and move as baron and baroness to the now restored estate where Elisabeth was born.

In *The Two Baronesses*, Andersen abandoned the bildungsroman form of his first three novels, although the work contains much talk about art and Elisabeth is a budding writer. At its core, it is a novel of Denmark, its landscapes, its people, and its social relations, this at a time when the country was involved in the bloody Three Years' War with German forces over Schleswig and Holstein. The novel received a mixed but generally positive welcome by critics, though it sold poorly, and is now considered by many to be Andersen's best effort in the genre.[189]

Little more than a week after its publication in London, the novel met with the first of at least ten, in part substantial and generally quite positive English reviews, which Bredsdorff attributes in large measure to the recent success of *The Improvisatore* and the autobiography.[190] For uncertain reasons, the comparable reception of those books in the United States apparently inspired no native sons to take pen in hand when the new novel came out, perhaps because no American edition followed the British one, as had been the case with the previous works, though many English publications were read and reviewed on this side of the Atlantic at the time. The novel may have profited from its proximity to *The Improvisatore* when it was issued in the Author's Edition in October 1869.[191] At any rate, several reviews ensued in relatively short order, and while most were welcoming, some were less than hospitable.

One of the first appeared in the *Portland Transcript*, whose notice of *The Improvisatore* had come out only a little over a month earlier.[192] The review consists almost entirely of a plot summary, but it nonetheless follows virtually as published. The characters and events chosen for inclusion suggest recognition of a central aspect of the work, one that reflects an underappreciated element of Andersen's writing in general.

> In the romance of *The Two Baronesses* Hans Christian Andersen draws an interesting picture of the social life of Denmark, and particularly of the relation formerly existing between the nobles and the peasants, or serfs. The principal characters are the old Baroness and the young Baroness—the former the daughter of a peasant, the latter a foundling adopted by a company of young nobles at the moment of her birth and the death of her mother, whom they discover in an old ruined castle, where, like them, she has taken refuge from a storm. The child, christened Elisabeth, is taken in charge by the old Baroness, grandmother of one of the young nobles, whose wife she ultimately becomes. The character of the old Baroness, eccentric and whimsical, yet marked by originality, and full of strong sense and soft humanities, is a natural development of the conditions from which she has sprung. She plants flowers on the spot where stood the wooden horse on which her father suffered at the command of the brutal old Count, her husband's father, and presents to her grandson, on his marriage with Elisabeth, a wooden spoon cut out of a plank from the wooden horse, that it may tell their child from whence he comes, and "teach him that we are all and every one poor men's children before the Lord." There is a simple pathos in the death scene of the old Baroness, betraying the hand of the true artist.

The reviewer's diction, especially in his characterization of the old baroness and closing sentences, suggests a quite sympathetic, even empathetic, and socially and politically resonant reading of the novel, in which he was not at all alone. The work contains numerous figures and subplots and covers 261 compactly printed pages in the Author's Edition. However, the critic fixes his attention squarely on the broader relationships represented particularly by the two title characters and devotes a large portion of his plot summary to a description of the indignity and death the elder baroness's peasant father suffered at the behest of his aristocrat landlord and its impact on her. This, she now turns to the benefit of her loved ones—and, potentially, the reader—as a lesson in the equality of all men as human beings.

The social element of Andersen's novel also takes center stage in the *Presbyterian*, a leading church weekly founded in Philadelphia in 1831 that claimed a circulation of twenty-three thousand in 1870.[193] The reviewer first addresses Andersen's stature in Denmark:

> Recent Copenhagen journals give very full accounts of a festival held in honor of the fiftieth anniversary of Andersen's first arrival in that city. A native of the island of Funen, he went, a poor boy, to Copenhagen, in September, 1819. He has always been distinguished by royal patronage in each succeeding reign, during his fifty years of residence in that city. Denmark feels a great and just pride in him, not only for his acknowledged genius and power as an author, but because the whole tendency of his writings has been in the cause of right and truth.

The writer then turns to Andersen's feeling for the common people: "Moreover, he has always been the poor man's and the working man's friend. The secret of his popularity is that which makes Dickens to-day the most popular writer in England—his sympathy with the masses. This tale, 'The Two Baronesses,' has the same key-note. It is written in Andersen's agreeable but peculiar style, and the German flavor is well preserved in the translation." Even twenty-four years after his debut in English and English-speaking countries there remained ignorance or uncertainty among some Americans regarding Andersen's nationality and mother tongue, and perhaps about conditions in Europe as well. He is a native of Fyn (Funen) and the pride of Denmark but writes in German—though, in fairness, German-writing Danes did exist, and, as we have seen, some of Andersen's early works, including his widely read autobiography, were indeed rendered into English from German translations, which may have created long-lingering and generalized false impressions.[194]

Andersen was by no means a specifically political writer or an overt critic of existing conditions.[195] A shoemaker's son who forged his way gradually, but persistently into upper-middle-class and aristocratic circles, indeed, he was criticized in his own time for sycophancy toward the nobility, and not without some justification. Beyond mere ego-caressing flattery, however, it was the objective recognition and friendly support of certain noble families, first in Germany and later in Denmark, that largely determined his attitude toward the aristocracy. Moreover, he was quite aware and, in fact, a member of the *åndelige Adel*, the so-called nobility of the mind, whose members attained their high rank through natural gifts, self-cultivation, and achievement rather than through birth, which knew no boundaries of class. And from stories and tales such as "The Little Match Girl" ("Den lille Pige med Svovl-stikkerne") and "The Bell" ("Klokken") to plays like *The Mulatto* (*Mulat-ten*) and some of the poems written during the two wars over Schleswig and Holstein (1848–1851, 1864), not to mention the novels and autobiography, his work attests implicitly or explicitly to a keen consciousness of the deep inequities in society and solidarity with the common people as well as to an at times overwhelming sense of the depths of human suffering—this, at a time when Denmark, like much of Europe, was wending a very wayward way toward egalitarianism in society and government.

Thus, the reviewers for the *Portland Transcript* and the *Presbyterian* were quite on the mark in focusing on the sociopolitical relationships depicted in *The Two Baronesses*. It is entirely understandable that they did so as Ameri-cans, citizens of a young republic intensely proud of its ideals and institutions of government, one, moreover, that had only recently salvaged the form in which these ideals and institutions had originated from a savage civil war. Interestingly, only one of the ten British reviews of the work did so, and the writer actually criticizes Andersen for his expressed sympathy:

> Andersen is a class writer. He knows his own origin. He sympathizes with his order. It is observable in all his writings. His heroes and heroines are from be-low; even when they bear the external marks of rank we discover some strong link which associates them with the people; there is a bar sinister in all their escutcheons. Of the two Baronesses the one is the daughter of an ill-used serf, the other of a strolling organ-player; and, that there should be no disparity of condition, to give rise to bitter reflections in after-life, the Baron himself who gives rank to the latter, is really the son of an Italian bandit. This part of the story is disagreeable and objectionable, and also, as it seems to us, useless to the narrative. Andersen occasionally introduces scenes and persons in his stories, which, though drawn from real life and his own observation, are better avoided. We know not whether English manners are more straitlaced than Danish, but books which are intended for large circulation should be studiously free from every offence to propriety.[196]

At least one English reviewer of Andersen's novel would indeed appear to have been more straitlaced with regard to social and political "propriety" than either Andersen or his American contemporaries.

Some reviewers uniformly underscored the Danishness of *The Two Baron-esses* without referring specifically to the social conditions depicted in the novel. One such issued a notice of the work in the *Connecticut Courant* of Hartford, which, founded in 1764, continues to appear today as the oldest US newspaper in continuous publication.[197] The editor in chief and joint publisher at the time was Joseph R. Hawley (1826–1905), who served as a major gen-eral in the Union army and as a leader in the organization of the Republican

Party in Connecticut, founding a newspaper to espouse his political views.[198] Trained as a lawyer, he served part of a term as governor of Connecticut and then several terms in Congress, during which he delegated most of his editorial duties to others.[199] Hawley's assistant editor was Charles Dudley Warner, the soon-to-become popular novelist and essayist now best known for his collaboration with Mark Twain on *The Gilded Age.*[200] It may well have been to his influence that the *Courant* owed its pronounced literary character. In 1869, the paper had a daily circulation of four thousand.[201]

Although the Danish original of the novel bore no genre designation in its title, Beckwith Lohmeyer added "A Romance" to it in his translation, and the reviewer for the *Courant* apparently let himself be guided by the addition:

[The book] is a romance of Denmark, the story being chiefly interesting from the fresh characters in it, men[,] women, and children, whose traits are all peculiar to the country, whose habits of life and way of talking, whose love of home, strong affection, indifference to peril and love of wrestling with nature mark a northern people, unsophisticated and uncontaminated. The scene of the story is largely upon the Hallige[r] and other islands, lone sand hills which are almost as much the sport of the ocean as the floating ships. The inhabitants are as familiar with the sea as the wild ducks; there is a domestic wildness and picturesqueness in their lives unmatched by any other European people. They are true descendants of the old Northm[e]n and inherit their love for legends and mythic stories. In the long winter nights the firesides are enlivened by the old sagas and the relation of Frisian legends. This novel, which is bright and sparkling with the peculiar genius of the author, is full of the most admirable sketches of nature, not in weary descriptions, but done in a dash, and is uncommonly interesting as a sketch of the home life and domestic customs of a people *sui generis.*[202]

This reviewer offers one more demonstration of the impact Longfellow's view of Scandinavia had on American literati. His lettered contemporaries in Denmark and other countries of the North would likely have been surprised, and perhaps bemused or even annoyed, on discovering themselves described as unsophisticated. However, he displays a sensitive and appreciative organ for Andersen's truly minute portrayal of men and manners in a corner of Denmark that was surely as unfamiliar to most readers in the nation's capital as it was to American coevals, who may well have responded more positively to it than they. Despite the relative youth of domestic intellectual and artistic expression, Americans in fact existed in a Euro-American cultural continuum, and more than a few of them had a sense of living in a *Spätzeit*, a late stage of cultural development tending toward decline, for which the North appeared to offer a rejuvenating remedy. At least for some, the cure assumed the very appealing form of romance.[203]

Another review of *The Two Baronesses* appeared in the New York *Evangelist*, a Presbyterian weekly founded in 1832 expressly as an instrument of social reform that enjoyed a comparatively large circulation of sixteen thousand in 1869.[204] Its first editor, Joshua Leavitt, was an abolitionist who later edited both the *Emancipator*, the publication of the American Anti-Slavery Society, and the *Independent*, itself, we recall, an abolitionist and suffragist paper. In addition to advocating for abolition, temperance, and other reforms, the paper published articles on subjects as diverse as farming, science, bills in Congress, and foreign religious news as well as reviews of a wide variety of books and magazines.

Despite the *Evangelist*'s editorial focus, Andersen's reviewer was concerned with *The Two Baronesses* strictly as art. Following introductory remarks, he writes, "[Andersen] has an ideal of what should be aspired to by the writer of fiction, far above the common level of attainment. In this work we meet a passage which he puts in the mouth of one of his characters, which doubtless reflects his own views."[205] The passage is drawn from a conversation between Herman and a friend ironically called the *Kammerjunker*, or Chamberlain. The latter has just expressed his objection to any literary work that contains no new idea, to which Herman responds,

> In novels and romances . . . I would not have events alone, but characters and poetry. A novel that contains only events is read but once; the unexpected, the surprising, which was the life and soul of it, is departed, dead after perusal. On the contrary, where the human character appears forcibly and naturally drawn; where thoughts exist in living words; where poetry has its imperishable growth, to such a work we return again and again; that book is read and re-read; one comes from it refreshed, as from a ramble in the woods in the Spring.[206]

By this time, Hawthorne and Melville had written their novels, Poe his one, and Eliot most of hers, creating variously proportioned blends of incident, psychological study, and imagination—as well as social observation and commentary. Nonetheless, Herman's succinct poetic-realist manifesto, a poetics of the novel that was indeed Andersen's own, clearly resonated with this reviewer. A possible explanation lies in the continuation of the conversation between Herman and the Chamberlain, which the reviewer relates and comments upon as follows: "A combination of Jean Paul and Walter Scott would serve as a standard of highest attainment,—so it is here suggested. To this Andersen has evidently aspired. We meet in his writings not a little which reminds us at once of the gifted German and the Northern Wizard."[207] Perhaps the reviewer missed in contemporary fiction the arabesque quality so integral to Jean Paul's style, though the modern reader may discern little of it in *The*

Two Baronesses and, certainly, almost none of the verse strewn throughout the earlier novels.

The writer takes a broader look at the work toward the end of the review, making observations that perhaps most would consider as valid today as they were at the time they were written:

> [Andersen's] story carries us back two generations—to Denmark at the close of the last century. It brings before us genial pictures of nature, and quaint sketches of present life. The characters, distinctly drawn, are sufficiently varied. Some of them are of the lettered class, and can discuss in Andersen's own way questions of literary taste and ethics. One charm of the book is the variety thus afforded, and if the reader is not disposed to re-read, he will pleasantly and distinctly recall much which he has perused.

Andersen indeed introduces and follows a large number and wide variety of characters, none more "distinctly drawn" than the old baroness, which enables him to present a panoramic view of Danish society, at the close of the eighteenth century *and* in his own time—a kind of "charm," if charm it truly be, that has meaning.[208] Moreover, characters such as Herman, the Chamberlain, and Elisabeth are indeed capable of speaking on matters of "literary taste and ethics."

Not all American commentators were entirely pleased with *The Two Baronesses.* The reviewer for the *North American and United States Gazette*, for example, having presented an overview of Andersen's "conquest" of Europe, writes,

> The Two Baronesses is located at and near Copenhagen. It moves along the coast, to the interior and to sea. It deals with all grades of society, but principally with the middle and lower classes, and particularly with their children. There is marriage and death, and the usual incident of life, with a greater infusion of mystery and supernaturalism than are permitted to literature in general. The story is just strong enough to hold the sketches that are strung upon it, and the whole will make as delightful an entertainment for the young as they can have; and one that is without a fault.[209]

Despite the quite positive tenor of the last phrases, the body of the review, including the references to the novel's variety and social dimension, is largely descriptive and unenthusiastic in tone; the story line, for instance, is "just" strong enough to connect the events. Indeed, one senses some contradiction between the final verdict and what precedes it. On the other hand, the only true criticism relates to a perceived excess of "mystery and supernaturalism," which perhaps refers to the element of superstition and the important role of religion in the novel. Why the book should be delightful entertainment for the young is, again, explicable only in light of the growing understanding of Andersen as a children's author.

The review of *The Improvisatore* and *The Two Baronesses* that appeared in the *Eclectic Magazine* is also mixed:

> "*The Two Baronesses*" is scarcely so careful a story as "*The Improvisatore*," and, unless very badly written, has been unskilfully [*sic*] translated. It is a simple tale of life in the author's native Denmark, depicting very clearly the character, customs, and peculiarities of the people, and, as might have been expected, giving some excellent sketches of local scenery. We get a glimpse of what the land of the old Vikings has become in the nineteenth century, such as cannot be easily obtained elsewhere.[210]

The reviewer was obviously pleased with the "Danishness" of the novel, but it is unclear what he meant by the term "careful" and which aspects of the work he had in mind when using it. It cannot refer to plot or character, perhaps the most likely possibilities, for those elements of *The Improvisatore* are criticized earlier in the review. Maybe the writer missed in *The Two Baronesses* the "sustained, imaginative level" he found in *The Improvisatore*, which compensated for the flawed structure and characterization that it shares with the later work.

Briefer but similarly mixed reviews came out in Philadelphia's *Evening Telegraph* and yet another Presbyterian publication, the *American Presbyterian Review*.[211] The critic for the *Telegraph* agrees with others that Andersen "seems to lack the ability to handle a large subject with the necessary skill, and his novels have consequently done but little for his reputation. . . . There are good bits of scenery and character [in *The Two Baronesses*], but the story is rather disconnected and unsatisfactory." In contrast to *The Improvisatore*, the critic avers, *The Two Baronesses* gives a description of Andersen's native Denmark, "but, strange to say, he appears to lack the hearty sympathy with his subject that makes 'The Improvisatore' such a delightful book to read." Andersen's perceived lack of commitment to his subject matter may derive simply from the critic's sense of the differences between Italy and Denmark.

The *American Presbyterian Review* was a heavy, almost entirely theological quarterly edited by Henry B. Smith of Union Theological Seminary, which reported a circulation of about fifteen hundred in 1870.[212] The writer begins on a positive note, observing that *The Two Baronesses* is a novel, "the scene of which is laid in Denmark, and [which] contains descriptions of northern life, picturesque and dramatic in character."[213] "And yet," he continues, "we are disappointed in the book. Either it does him [Andersen] great injustice, or else the reputation he has achieved rests on no solid foundation. The book is tame, and almost puerile, compared with a thousand works of its class which it were easy to name." "Tameness" and "puerility" possess little expressive power as critical categories beyond their negativity, but at least the latter has the (questionable) distinction of having been applied to Andersen and his works with some frequency, perhaps under the influence of the fairy tales and the autobiography.

The most substantial negative review of the novel came out in the *Detroit Free Press*, which originated in 1831 and remains in publication today.[214] The paper was an advocate of the Democratic Party from the beginning and, during the Civil War, became a leading voice of self-styled Peace Democrats, opponents of the war in the North who were reviled by Republicans as "Copperheads."[215] After the war, the *Free Press* gained a national reputation for wit and humor largely due to the writing of Charles B. Lewis, who, signing as "M. Quad," satirized the middle-class American family, parodied the "extravagances" of Western newspapers, and, still in the spirit of Copperheadism, had fun at the expense of blacks.[216] In 1869, the year the review appeared, the paper had a daily subscription list of nineteen thousand.[217]

The reviewer was clearly predisposed to react favorably to *The Two Baronesses*, out of deference to the fairy tales and stories, one suspects:

> In a recent notice of "The Improvisatore," by this author, attention was called to the fact that it was one of a series of his romances now in course of publication in this country, and the hope was expressed that the "Danish Story-Teller" would prove as successful in writing for grown people as he had in his books for children. The volume before us adds little to that hope, if it does not positively weaken it. It may be that the translator has failed to do the author justice, or perhaps the frigid climate of Denmark, where the scene of the present story is laid, may have had a chilling effect upon the author's imagination.[218]

However, the writer renders an unambiguous verdict on the novel: "But whatever the cause, as a *romance* it is certainly inferior to the 'Improvisatore,' and the publishers would have done better by commencing their series with this book, unless—which is hardly probable—they intend to issue the books comprising it in the inverse order of their merit." He offers the following in support of his conclusion:

> The Old Baroness is a grandmother, with an unnatural spite against the upper class, into which she was married; and the young one is a foundling without anything particular about her; while the barons who personate nearly all the other characters in the book, are a well dressed set of lay-figures, whose motives—where they seem to have any—are as difficult to understand as the Schleswig-Holstein unpleasantness used to be. Whatever features of interest the characters and incident might have in the Danish costume, they seem remarkably commonplace in English dress.

Such evidence may strike the reader as questionable or outright unfounded. If anyone had a *natural* spite, or justified antagonism toward the nobility, it was the elder baroness. Although characterization was not one of Andersen's strengths, he outdid himself in creating her and the Chamberlain. And the other major figures, Elisabeth chief among them, are sufficiently individualized to play their roles in what is essentially a social, or class drama of everyday life in the landed gentry, which in rural Denmark could certainly be modest, if not necessarily "commonplace." In keeping with the social-political bias of the *Free Press*, indeed, the reviewer seems unhappy with the novel principally because he finds it insufficiently aristocratic! His meiotic and history-challenged allusion to the "unpleasantness" during the wars over Schleswig and Holstein calls to mind a contemporary "genteel" way of referring to the Civil War and Reconstruction in the South.

Several other periodicals issued brief commentaries on *The Two Baronesses*, but most amount to little more than publication announcements. A short announcement-like notice that appeared in the *Independent* includes the words, "Andersen's writing is the furthest possible remove from sensationalism. We should be glad of any evidence of its popularity among the romance readers of America."[219] A brief review that came out in the *Providence Evening Press* sounds a similar note: "If there were no worse novels than Christian Andersen gives to the public the moral sentiment of the novel reading public would not be poisoned or vitiated. He is one among the few novelists whose works obtain an unalloyed favorable criticism at our hands."[220] These otherwise unremarkable glances at Andersen's work have the virtue of taking up the theme of sensationalism found in even the earliest reviews of *The Improvisatore* and *Only a Fiddler* and thus provide a fitting conclusion to a survey of the American reception of his novels.

TO BE, OR NOT TO BE? AND *LUCKY PEER*

The survey cannot include Andersen's two other novels, *To Be, or Not to Be?* (1857) and *Lucky Peer* (1870), for, as mentioned in chapter 1, neither appears to have received full review treatment in the United States. Indeed, *Lucky Peer* suffered the same fate in England, and *To Be, or Not to Be?* got only four notices there.[221] This, however, is not to say that American periodicals completely ignored the novels. The *American Publishers' Circular and Literary Gazette* published an advertisement and four announcements of *To Be, or Not to Be?* beginning early in the year of its issuance, which provides strong evidence that the novel was sold and read, if not professionally critiqued.[222]

And *Putnam's Magazine* reprinted briefly commented portions of two of the English reviews.[223]

With respect to theme, *To Be, or Not to Be?* is Andersen's most ambitious novel. In it, he attempts to reconcile faith and reason, religion and science, concluding that they are not antithetical to each other, indeed, that reason and its products are extensions of divinity in the material world which bear, or should bear, the stamp of their origin in the form of ethics. Andersen intended the novel as a response to the materialism of German philosophers Ludwig Feuerbach, David Friedrich Strauß, and others, assuming a position similar to that of liberal Protestant theologians of the eighteenth century and their progeny, who emphasized moral-ethical behavior over dogma and the role traditionally ascribed to Christ. He gave shape to these ideas in a bildungsroman similar, as such, to his first three novels, in which the main character, Niels Bryde, proceeds from unreflective faith to doubt to informed belief.

The writer for *Putnam's* begins with the words, "Hans Christian Andersen's new book is not a success. The fairy story-teller makes a poor theologian," whereupon he cites the better part of a review published in the *Athenæum* and a paragraph from one that appeared in the *Examiner.*[224] In the portions quoted, the former objects at once to a perceived sectarian-formalist bias and failure to support faith, while the latter censures treatment of such a weighty subject as the immortality of the soul in what he terms a short novel. The reviewer for the *Literary Gazette* combines features of both.[225] However, he also has some quite positive things to say about the strictly literary, or storytelling side of the novel, as does the reviewer for the *Athenæum*, and the notice in *Lloyd's Weekly London Newspaper* is entirely affirmative.[226] Ignoring the relation of faith and reason altogether, the writer for *Lloyd's* discusses the novel as an introduction to contemporary life in Denmark, much like *The Two Baronesses*. Now, from the standpoint of inclusivity and objectivity, not to mention accuracy respecting Andersen's "thesis," one may well be inclined to fault all four reviewers, specifically for overemphasizing and/or neglecting significant aspects of the novel. For instance, by far the greatest part of it consists of mimetic fiction rather than religious-theological speculation, though the not insubstantial discursive portions go beyond even the most liberal notions of verisimilitude.[227] Moreover, *To Be, or Not to Be?* is about the same length as *The Two Baronesses*, and, of the earlier novels, only *The Improvisatore* is substantially longer. For present purposes, however, it is more important that the reviewer for *Putnam's*—for such he was by implication—chose to totally disregard the friendly notice as well as virtually all the favorable comments in the others—that is, to present an almost exclusively antipathetic view of the novel.[228] Why might that have been?

It is possible, of course, that the writer had no access to, or for other unknown reasons did not read the reviews in the *Literary Gazette* and *Lloyd's
Weekly*. As mentioned earlier, however, all the major British literary journals and newspapers were regularly reprinted in, or shipped to the United
States throughout most of the nineteenth century, and the *Literary Gazette*
and *Lloyd's Weekly* belong to that number.[229] *Putnam's* was a high-quality
magazine both as a literary journal and as a review organ, publishing the best
writing that New York and New England had to offer. Mott states that "the
first series of *Putnam's* [1853–1857], or at least the first half of that series,
maintained consistently about the highest level which an American magazine had reached up to that time," and that "there was some good reviewing
[in American magazines]. *Putnam's*, the *Atlantic Monthly*, and the *Literary
World* did some really excellent work in that kind."[230] In view of the magazine's distinction, one would expect the writer to have been familiar with the
relevant reviews in the important British periodicals.

One can only speculate why the reviewer proceeded as he did, but *Putnam's*
self-understanding may offer a clue. The leading lights of the magazine during its early phase were editor Charles F. Briggs and associate editors George
William Curtis and Parke Godwin.[231] Briggs enjoyed early success as a satirist
and humorist with his novel *The Adventures of Harry Franco* (1839), which
became a model for Melville, and mined a similar vein in spoofs of life in his
adopted hometown until the late 1840s, when he turned more to newspaper editorial work. Curtis cultivated social satire with a lighter touch in writings such
as *The Potiphar Papers* (1853) and then for years as the occupant of the "Easy
Chair" in *Harper's New Monthly Magazine*. Godwin was principally a sharp-
penned political writer and journalist who wrote books on, among other things,
Fourierism and democracy as well as a volume of influential political essays.

All three men were Republican in their politics, sympathizers of the
merchant class, and genuinely Christian in their views on religion and/
or morality, tending toward high Episcopalianism. Briggs and Curtis were
New Englanders, Godwin from New Jersey, but they all spent most of their
professional lives in New York City and had a distinct sense of themselves
as Gothamites, harboring an animus toward Transcendentalism and Boston
"snobbery." That is to say, they were metropolitan in their outlook and tastes,
entertaining, for example, a decided preference for the emerging realist novel
over the romance. When planning *Putnam's*, the trio may have had *Harper's
New Monthly* in their sights, determining to publish and pay American authors well for their work instead of plundering English periodicals for unpaid
serials in the absence of international copyright laws. In terms of urban ca-
chet, however, it was the *Knickerbocker* that *Putnam's* competed with and
surpassed for the important first four years of its existence.

To Be, or Not to Be? has its humorous and whimsical moments in its drawing of character and depiction of incident, from Pastor Mollerop of provincial
Jutland, who finds the narrow streets of Copenhagen and their tall dwellings,
with families living across from each other, upstairs and downstairs, a little
too much like Noah's ark; to Mister Svane, a sort of genius who, it is said,
was intended by nature to be a patron of the arts and to live for the beautiful
but who found that no one can live from the beautiful, that it sooner eats one
up itself, whose many inventions come to naught, and whose traffic with the
beautiful consists of proofreading manuscripts and buying valuable books
and engravings at auctions to sell to collectors; to Poul, Niels's father, who
is killed when a maid working on an upper floor of a building in one of the
narrow streets of the capital drops a window on his head. However, such
descriptions serve to make the characters sympathetic or interesting rather
than the butts of humor. As its allusive title suggests, *To Be, or Not to Be?* is
fundamentally a serious piece of fiction, certainly not one to be mistaken for
the lighter or heavier satire preferred by *Putnam's* editors.

The work also has distinctly realistic elements, for example, the depictions
of Niels's experiences as a soldier during the Three Years' War. However,
his pronounced representational character as the archetypal young man, proceeding along the path of formation and development according to a scheme
newly realized in Denmark by Meïr Aron Goldschmidt in *Homeless* (*Hjem-
løs*, 1853–57), would alone surely qualify the work as a romance rather than a
novel from the perspective of *Putnam's*, not to mention the markedly idealist
treatment of the relationship between religion and science and the question
of life after death. As represented in the English reviews, finally, Andersen's
supposed heterodoxy and conclusion that faith is a gift rather than an acquisition, though the purest Martin Luther, must have somehow offended the
religious sensibility of *Putnam's* reviewer.[232]

Lucky Peer, Andersen's sixth and final novel, appeared in *Scribner's
Monthly* in four installments from January through April of 1871.[233] Written
in only three weeks, it is Andersen's shortest novel, covering only eighty-two
pages in the *Samlede Værker* and displaying a single, linear plot. It thus qualifies more as a long story or novelette than as a novel, as which it is nonetheless
generally designated. In the work, Andersen reprises his favored novel type,
following his protagonist from his childhood as the sensitive, talented son
of a warehouse worker to his blossoming as a musical artist and his ultimate
triumph in his art (though he dies in his triumphal moment). However, to all
appearances, as stated before, the novel received no hearing among American
review critics—this, despite at least ten advertisements and publication announcements that were printed in seven different magazines, some of which
accompanied the installments of the novel with short general comments as

they appeared in *Scribner's*.[234] Collectively, the five general magazines among the seven had a circulation of 79,300; the two trade publications, for which figures were unavailable in 1871, must have increased this number by a few thousand.[235] *Scribner's* itself had 55,000 subscribers at this point in time, which means that at least 134,000 Americans read, or had the opportunity to read or to know of *Lucky Peer* on its appearance in the United States.[236]

One of them did in fact quote from the novel. In an article titled "New Departures and Old Ways," which was published in Cincinnati's *Ladies' Repository* in 1874, E. S. Martin recommends that Americans maintain both due respect for the past and openness toward the future.[237] To emphasize the point, she writes, "It is a mere croaking cynicism that is always prating about the old days being better than the new. That beautiful creation of Hans Andersen, the grandmother of Lucky Peer, exclaims, 'One hour here, is a hundred years in the past!'"[238] Martin's quotation indicates that the novel was indeed read, and one is surely permitted to surmise that she was no isolated instance. Considering Andersen's great contemporary popularity and the renewed awareness of his novel writing due to the publication of the Author's Edition, however, the citation and the positive nature of its usage also entitle one to wonder why no reviewers took note of the work.

The first American notices of *The Improvisatore* came out only a couple of months after the British edition of the book, six months earlier and in greater numbers than was previously thought. Reviews of the novels in general, as of Andersen's other works for that matter, appeared in a broad variety of magazines and newspapers of equally varying success and reach. The *Christian Union*, *Harper's New Monthly Magazine*, the *Independent*, and the *National Intelligencer* were among the most important and widely circulated periodicals of the day. Another sizeable number of notices appeared in class periodicals, ones that address specific constituencies within the general readership, that ranged from respectable to excellent in quality. Both the *Christian Advocate* and the *Churchman* played prominent roles in the religious press, and the two magazines titled the *Ladies' Repository* were noted women's journals.[239] Andersen's reviewers included individuals of national and regional repute such as George Stillman Hillard, William Gilmore Simms, and perhaps Charles F. Briggs and William Dean Howells. Several of the anonymous commentators, for example, those writing for the *Eclectic*, the San Francisco *Daily Evening Bulletin*, and the *Universe*, who demonstrate variously high degrees of competence in their métier, might also be recognizable were their identities known.

Several early critics express a distinct sense of the "newness" and "freshness" (i.e., the novelty and originality) of *The Improvisatore*, and members of a later generation still have the same experience on reading *O. T.* Reviewers also note the imaginativeness of the works. Such responses emanate in part from a sense of the "Northernness" of the novels largely attributable to Longfellow, in part from the role that "*Bildung*" and art play in them, though the writers may not have been familiar with the term "bildungsroman" and its referent.[240] Though not entirely escaping criticism, *The Improvisatore* is generally deemed the best of the novels, while *O. T.* receives the fewest accolades. The responses to *Only a Fiddler* and *The Two Baronesses* are decidedly mixed but, whatever their verdict, carry all the more weight because they are generally longer and engage the works more incisively than the critiques of the earlier novels. Critical opinion of *To Be, or Not to Be?* and *Lucky Peer* is limited to a satiric hitched ride on condemnatory English reviews and a positive but isolated quotation and application, respectively.

The most common criticisms of Andersen as a novelist are directed at his handling of plot and character. Both early and late, some reviewers declare him guilty of poorly constructed, improbable story lines and ill-defined, colorless, and thus unbelievable figures, for which the notice of *The Improvisatore* and *The Two Baronesses* in the *Nation* and that of the latter in the *Detroit Free Press* are representative.[241] On the other hand, no few critics find these weaknesses mitigated or counterbalanced by certain redeeming qualities, and others react in a purely affirmative fashion. For Hillard, Andersen's plot construction and characterization in *The Improvisatore* are consequences of his artistic sensibility and can therefore be pardoned, whereas the San Francisco *Daily Evening Bulletin* sees precisely these aspects of *Only a Fiddler* as strengths rather than weaknesses.[242]

Numerous critics affirm the poetic nature of Andersen's novelistic prose. The writer for the *Eclectic* holds that in *The Improvisatore* and *The Two Baronesses* such poetry was purchased at the price of vigorous action, and the prosaic reviewer for the *Nation* complains that the novels are "jumbles" of poetry and prose.[243] For the great majority of commentators, however, the lyricism of Andersen's novels lies entirely on the credit side of the ledger. Here, too, lie the many asseverations of Andersen's exceptional descriptive ability, which represents perhaps the only element of his artistry that remained entirely untouched by criticism. With respect to *O. T.*, *Only a Fiddler*, and *The Two Baronesses*, many writers would have agreed with the colleague who spoke of a "Flemish," or "pre-Raphaelite," distinctiveness of detail that serves to delineate Denmark and Danish society, that in *Only a Fiddler*, indeed, serves to highlight the inequities of society.[244]

The positive as well as the negative criticism—of the novels as of the works treated in later chapters—reflects varying assumptions about the nature and imperatives of literary art. A couple of the reviews bear witness to a moralist-biographicist notion of literature that both hearkens back to the thinking of the eighteenth century and anticipates the positivism of the later nineteenth. Hillard likely saw in *The Improvisatore* a reflection of his and others' understanding of literature as an emanation of biogenetic law. However, the vast majority of reviews disclose premises that lie at various points along the differentiated continuum uniting the Romanticism that largely distinguished the greater part of the century in the United States and the realism which gradually emerged after the Civil War. The Howellsian impatience with *The Improvisatore* and *The Two Baronesses* found in the *Nation*, which may have originated with Howells himself, is the most striking example of the realist impulse, while the idealist tendency and poetic diction of the *Universe*'s appraisal of the former epitomize the Romantic spirit that dominated reviewers' responses to the works. The two currents conjoin in the *Eclectic*'s review of these first two volumes of the Author's Edition.

Of particular interest is the fact that a goodly number of reviewers contextualized the novels explicitly or implicitly within contemporary currents in American culture. Many reviewers, early and late, took their notices as occasions to criticize the sensationalist writing of the era by holding the novels up as exemplars of "good" writing. Those influenced by Longfellow idealized the novels in their "purity" as lodestars for the development of a specifically American literature. Moral-religious considerations entered into the thinking of some, but, on the whole, it is unclear whether the writers were motivated by strictly moral impulses or rather by a secularized sense of offended decency and taste. The question of morality comes to the fore particularly in reviews of *Only a Fiddler*. A couple of critics are taken aback by the unequal lots of Christian and Naomi, especially by the fact that Naomi suffers no poetic retribution for her transgressions. At the same time, they recognize that such injustice is not contrary to experience and that Naomi must endure a "gilded misery" of her own. One reviewer, indeed, appreciates the absence of explicit moralizing in the novel.[245] And even in these reviews questions of art counterbalance or outweigh the issue of morality.

Several critics exhibit a keen awareness—one is tempted to say a typically American awareness—of the social-political relationships displayed in *O. T.* and *The Two Baronesses*. None of them expresses this perception more pointedly than the writer for the *Presbyterian*, who sees in *The Two Baronesses* a reflection of Andersen as a friend of the poor man and the working man.[246]

William Gilmore Simms responds to the loose (i.e., "original") plot construction of *The Improvisatore* with the enthusiasm of a "Young American." In so doing, he champions a specifically American romance and thereby inaugurates what amounts to a series of contributions to the lengthy novel-romance controversy in which Andersen's novels serve as catalysts and whose tendency depends on the relative Romantic or realist predilections of the contributors. The severity within the realist camp, which in the case of the *Christian Union*, the *Independent*, and the *Nation* rose (or sank) to the level of flippancy and even sarcasm, derived from an unwillingness to let a romance be a romance rather than a novel. This reluctance, in turn, may well have stemmed from the fact that around 1870—and then, if Howells is to be given credence, for decades to come—the realists had something to prove and thus had a chip on their shoulder. For despite anachronistic individuals and others of variously blended casts of mind and feeling, fundamental elements of Romanticism long constituted the cultural air that most Americans breathed.

This notwithstanding, Andersen's romances, or romance-novels, received their greatest critical exposure in the United States at an unpropitious moment in the country's literary history. Simms's not uncritical approval as well as the straightforwardly positive early notices of *The Improvisatore* suggest that the other works would have fared even better than they ultimately did if they had attracted a larger number of reviewers at a time when the romance was more self-evidently rooted in the American literary landscape.

NOTES

1. See, for example, Paul Binding, *Hans Christian Andersen: European Witness* (New Haven, CT: Yale University Press, 2014), 138.

2. See note 1 in the introduction to this volume. Also see in particular, for example, Troy Wellington Smith, "From Autonomy to Dependency: The Aesthetics of Andersen's First Novelistic Trilogy," *Anderseniana*, 2017, 33–57; Bjarne Thorup Thomsen, "Contesting the Novel: Andersen and the Challenges of Criticism, with Particular Reference to 'De to Baronesser,'" *Scandinavica* 46 (2007): 175–94; Sophie Wennerscheid, "Haben oder Nichthaben: Zur Zirkulation der Werte in H. C. Andersens 'At være eller ikke være,'" *Wechselkurse des Vertrauens: Zur Konzeptualisierung von Ökonomie und Vertrauen im nordischen Idealismus*, ed. Klaus Müller-Wille and Joachim Schiedermair (Tübingen and Basel: A. Francke Verlag, 2013), 69–87.

3. See note 6 in the introduction, and Hans Christian Andersen, *The Improvisatore: A Novel of Italy*, trans. Frank Hugus (Minneapolis: University of Minnesota Press, 2018).

4. See Elias Bredsdorff, *H. C. Andersen og England* (Copenhagen: Rosenkilde og Baggers Forlag, 1954), 43. According to the product information in an ad for the American edition on Amazon.com, the volume was published on December 31, 1844, but that seems unlikely and, to my knowledge, cannot be substantiated in any event; see "Life in Italy: the Improvisatore Hardcover—December 31, 1844 by Hans Christian [Mary Howitt, Translator] Anderson [*sic*] (Author)," accessed April 20, 2015, http://www.amazon.com/Italy-Christian-Howitt-Translator-Anderson/dp/B009OZM2QW. The earliest sign of the edition found in a reliable source is another

ad, placed by Harper & Brothers, in which it is listed among books currently in press; *Commercial Advertiser*, February 22, 1845, 3. The *Advertiser* announces the publication of the novel on April 2, 1845, 2.

5. See, for example, Johan de Mylius, *Myte og Roman: H. C. Andersens romaner mellem romantik og realisme. En traditionshistorisk undersøgelse* (Copenhagen: Gyldendal, 1981), 246; Frank Hugus, introduction to *The Improvisatore: A Novel of Italy*, by Hans Christian Andersen, trans. Frank Hugus (Minneapolis: University of Minnesota Press, 2018), xviii.

6. See Iben Holk, *"Improvisatoren* (1835)," Epoke—Danske Romaner før 1900, last modified August 3, 2004, accessed July 20, 2018, https://www.e-poke.dk/ander sen_imp_1-2.php. Holk uses the terms "snørklet" and "utal."

7. See, for example, Elias Bredsdorff, *Hans Christian Andersen: The Story of His Life and Work 1805–75* (London: Phaidon, 1975), 118; Hugus, introduction to *The Improvisatore*, xviii–xxi; Mogens Brøndsted, "Modtagelse," in *Improvisatoren: Original Roman i to Dele*, by H. C. Andersen, ed. Mogens Brøndsted (Copenhagen: Det Danske Sprog- og Litteraturselskab / Borgen, 1987), 307–10.

8. Unsigned review of *Life in Italy: The Improvisatore,* trans. Mary Howitt, *Broadway Journal*, April 12, 1845, 227. The notice thus appeared only some six weeks after the initial English response in the *Literary Gazette* on March 1; see Bredsdorff, *H. C. Andersen og England*, 428.

9. See Heyward Ehrlich, "Charles Frederick Briggs," *Antebellum Writers in New York*, 2nd ser., ed. Kent P. Ljungquist, vol. 250 of *Dictionary of Literary Biography* (Detroit: Gale Research, 2002), 48–60; and Perry Miller, *The Raven and the Whale: The War of Words and Wits in the Era of Poe and Melville* (1956; repr., Westport, CT: Greenwood, 1973), especially 47–58.

10. See Frank Luther Mott, *A History of American Magazines 1741–1850* (1930; repr., Cambridge, MA: Harvard University Press, 1957), 757–62.

11. *Broadway Journal*, April 12, 1845, 227.

12. To my knowledge, no comprehensive history of American interest in, or views of, Scandinavia in the nineteenth century (or in general) currently exists. However, Benson writes that a series of travelogues, book reviews, and translations related to the North began to appear in the United States as early as 1805 and, by 1845, had grown in number to the point that Poe complained of the country's being flooded with literature from France, Germany, and Sweden; see Adolph B. Benson, "The Beginning of American Interest in Scandinavian Literature," *Scandinavian Studies and Notes* 8 (1925), especially 133–34. Clearly, however, it took some time before acquaintance, not to mention familiarity, with Scandinavian history and culture became more widespread. Surprisingly, Benson fails to mention Andersen, but he does provide a context in which the author's significance can be roughly assessed.

13. Unsigned review of *Life in Italy: The Improvisatore, Ladies' Repository*, May 1845, 439. See Frank Luther Mott, *A History of American Magazines 1850–1865* (1938; repr., Cambridge, MA: Harvard University Press, 1966), 57; and Kathleen L. Endres and Therese L. Lueck, *Women's Periodicals in the United States: Consumer Magazines* (Westport, CT, and London: Greenwood, 1995), 379–89.

14. See Bredsdorff, *H. C. Andersen og England*, 43; and Jens Andersen, *Hans Christian Andersen: A New Life*, trans. Tiina Nunnally (New York, Woodstock, and London: Overlook Duckworth, 2005), 273–75.

15. See, for example, J. Andersen, *Hans Christian Andersen*, 14.

16. Unsigned review of *Life in Italy: The Improvisatore*, *Ladies' National Magazine*, July 1845, 36.

17. See Mott, *A History of American Magazines 1850–1865*, 306–9.

18. See Robert McHenry, ed., *Famous American Women: A Biographical Dictionary from Colonial Times to the Present* (New York: Dover, 1980), 392.

19. *Ladies' National Magazine*, July 1845, 36.

20. Unsigned review of *The Improvisatore; or, Life in Italy*, *Daily National Intelligencer*, May 2, 1845, 1. See Frank Luther Mott, *American Journalism, a History: 1690–1960*, 3rd ed. (New York: Macmillan, 1962), 176–79.

21. *Daily National Intelligencer*, May 2, 1845, 1. Howitt had already had considerable success with her translations of the novels of Fredrika Bremer (1801–1865), a Swedish novelist and feminist activist whose work gained an audience in the United States as well as Europe.

22. William Gilmore Simms, review of *Life in Italy: The Improvisatore*, *Southern and Western Magazine and Review*, September 1845, 215.

23. See Mott, *A History of American Magazines 1741–1850*, 755–56.

24. See *The Oxford Companion to American Literature,* 6th ed., s.v. "Simms, William Gilmore," and Masahiro Nakamura, *Visions of Order in William Gilmore Simms: Southern Conservatism and the Other American Romance* (Columbia: University of South Carolina Press, 2009), 4.

25. David S. Shields, foreword to *William Gilmore Simms's Unfinished Civil War: Consequences for a Southern Man of Letters*, ed. David Moltke-Hansen (Columbia: University of South Carolina Press, 2013), ix. Also see Mary Ann Wimsatt, *The Major Fiction of William Gilmore Simms: Cultural Traditions and Literary Form* (Baton Rouge and London: Louisiana State University Press, 1989), 1. Though long neglected and his status still controversial, Simms has reemerged over the last few decades in scholarship that looks beyond the "Flowering of New England," particularly in studies dealing with the Young America movement and the relationship between the romance and the novel, as we shall see below.

26. See Mott, *A History of American Magazines 1741–1850*, 756; David Tomlinson, "Simms's Monthly Magazine: *The Southern and Western Monthly Magazine and Review*," *Southern Literary Journal* 8 (1975): 99, 124.

27. Mott, *A History of American Magazines 1741–1850*, 383.

28. See Yonatan Eyal, *The Young America Movement and the Transformation of the Democratic Party 1828–1861* (Cambridge: Cambridge University Press, 2007).

29. See Miller, *The Raven and the Whale*, especially 71–117; Edward L. Widmer, *Young America: The Flowering of Democracy in New York City* (New York and Oxford: Oxford University Press, 1999), 107.

30. See Tomlinson, "Simms's Monthly Magazine," especially 99–102. Widmer writes that Simms "offered perhaps the most urgent expression of Young America's

nationalistic aims with his essay 'Americanism in Literature'"; Widmer, *Young America*, 107.

31. Tomlinson, "Simms's Monthly Magazine," 98. Also see Edd Winfield Parks, *William Gilmore Simms as Literary Critic* (Athens: University of Georgia Press, 1961), especially 111.

32. In the issue for November 1845, Simms confided to his readers that he wrote little or nothing for the September, October, and November editions of the magazine "beyond the few pages at the close of each, which is assigned to the Editorial Bureau"; quoted according to Tomlinson, "Simms's Monthly Magazine," 123.

33. *Southern and Western Magazine and Review*, September 1845, 215.

34. See chapter 1, note 4, and Eugene Exman, *The House of Harper: One Hundred and Fifty Years of Publishing* (New York: Harper & Row, 1967), 24.

35. Exman, *The House of Harper*, 26.

36. *Southern and Western Magazine and Review*, September 1845, 215.

37. Eugène Sue, *The Mysteries of Paris: A Novel*, trans. Charles H. Town (New York: Harper & Brothers, 1843); Eugène Sue, *The Mysteries of Paris: A Romance of the Rich and Poor*, trans. Henry C. Deming (New York: J. Winchester, 1844). According to Isabelle Lehuu, Harper & Brothers published the novel serially, apparently before issuing it as a book; *Carnival on the Page: Popular Print Media in Antebellum America* (Chapel Hill: University of North Carolina Press, 2000), 73. Poet, journalist, and newspaper editor and founder Park Benjamin also apparently published the Deming translation in his weekly *New World* prior to its appearance as a book; see, for example, "*The Mysteries of Paris*, by Eugène Sue" (*New World*, October 14, 1843, 446), which reads in part, "On Tuesday morning [October 17] there will be published at the New World office the first number of the most distinguished romance of modern times." However, the serialized version of the work must have appeared in special numbers of the paper, for the regular issues, as reproduced in the American Periodical Series online, show no trace of it. It is difficult to determine whether the Open Library version of the book available online, the only one to which I have had access, was drawn from the *New World* or the book itself. See *The Mysteries of Paris*, by Eugène Sue, Openlibrary.org, accessed April 20, 2015, https://archive.org/stream /mysteriesofpari00suee#page/n5/mode/2up.

38. See Mott, *American Journalism*, 215, 241.

39. Mott, *American Journalism*, 243.

40. See, for example, Stephen Knight, *The Mysteries of the Cities: Urban Crime Fiction in the Nineteenth Century* (Jefferson, NC, and London: McFarland, 2012), especially 13–55 ("Master of the Mysteries: Eugène Sue's *Les mystères de Paris*").

41. Knight, *The Mysteries of the Cities*, 131–55 ("The Philadelphia Version: George Lippard's *The Quaker City*"). Also see Shelley Streeby, *American Sensations: Class, Empire, and the Production of Popular Culture* (Berkeley: University of California Press, 2002), 41–42.

42. David Reynolds, *Beneath the American Renaissance: The Subversive Imagination in the Age of Emerson and Melville* (New York: Knopf, 1988), 183–84.

43. Reynolds, *Beneath the American Renaissance*, 171.

44. Anonymous; quoted according to Reynolds, *Beneath the American Renaissance*, 209–10. Michael Denning presents a differentiated overview of the various forms of sensationalist publications, including their origins, publishers, and sales figures, and such, in *Mechanic Accents: Dime Novels and Working-Class Culture in America* (London: Verso, 1987), 1–16.

45. See, for example, Reynolds, *Beneath the American Renaissance*, 188–201 passim. Also see Parks, *William Gilmore Simms as Literary Critic*, 10–40 and 110–13, and especially G. R. Thompson and Eric Carl Link, *Neutral Ground: New Traditionalism and the American Romance Controversy* (Baton Rouge: Louisiana State University Press, 1999), particularly 70–73, 111, and 114–16. Much of Simms's critical-theoretical writing, like the action in much of his fiction, would seem to justify his treatment in studies of sensationalism. As Thompson and Link point out, however, he was seeking to define and demonstrate his notion of an indigenous American romance rather than to shock and disgust in the service of social reform or low(est)brow entertainment. Thompson and Link, *Neutral Ground*, 70–73.

46. See David Reynolds, introduction to *The Quaker City; or, The Monks of Monk Hall*, by George Lippard (Amherst: University of Massachusetts Press, 1995), vii.

47. Reynolds, *Beneath the American Renaissance*, 192.

48. *Southern and Western Magazine and Review*, September 1845, 215.

49. Parks writes, "Like most nineteenth-century critics, he [Simms] had discarded the idea that the universe is a harmonious machine for the concept that it is a growing organism. Likewise the literary work should grow under the hand of the novelist, but it should develop organically into a planned design"; Parks, *William Gilmore Simms as Literary Critic*, 39.

50. See John C. Guilds, *Simms: A Literary Life* (Fayetteville: University of Arkansas Press, 1992).

51. George Stillman Hillard, "Hans Christian Andersen," in *Six Months in Italy*, by George Stillman Hillard (Boston: Ticknor, Reed, and Fields, 1853), 2:440–43.

52. For biographical information on Hillard, I have drawn on *American National Biography,* s.v. "Hillard, George Stillman," and Francis W. Palfrey, "Memoir of the Hon. George Stillman Hillard, LL.D.," *Proceedings of the Massachusetts Historical Society* 19 (1881–1882): 339–48.

53. Paul R. Baker, *The Fortunate Pilgrims: Americans in Italy, 1800–1860* (Cambridge, MA: Harvard University Press, 1964), 29. In a similar statement elsewhere in the volume, Baker omits the word "probably." Baker, *The Fortunate Pilgrims*, 228. Also see Palfrey, "Memoir of the Hon. George Stillman Hillard, LL.D.," 340. Palfrey's memoir concludes with a memorial poem by noted sculptor William Wetmore Story, a friend and early legal associate of Hillard, that is touching in its elegiac mood and redolent of the cultural world of contemporary Boston. Palfrey, "Memoir of the Hon. George Stillman Hillard, LL.D.," 346–48.

54. Hillard, "Hans Christian Andersen," 2:440. The idea that knowledge is acquired through recognition probably derives from Plato's notion of anamnesis, the "discovery" of ideas innate in man through experience.

55. Hillard, "Hans Christian Andersen," 2:441.

56. Longfellow has generally been credited with awakening Americans' interest in Scandinavia, particularly through the publications noted, thereby fostering the image of the region evoked by Hillard. As Benson shows, however, other Americans preceded the poet in writing and/or publishing work related to the North. Henry Wheaton (1785–1848) wrote extensive reviews of related works as well as the internationally acclaimed *History of the Northmen, or Danes and Normans, from the Earliest Times to the Conquest of England by William of Normandy* (1831), and George Perkins Marsh (1801–1882) authored *A Compendious Grammar of Old Northern or Icelandic* (1834–1835/1838), among other works; see Adolph B. Benson, "Henry Wheaton's Writings on Scandinavia," *Journal of English and Germanic Philology* 29 (1930): 546–61, and Adolph B. Benson, "The Beginning of American Interest in Scandinavian Literature," *Scandinavian Studies and Notes* 8 (1925): especially 136–39. These and other American contemporaries may have been attracted to Longfellow's idealized vision of the Scandinavian past. However, their motivations were primarily scholarly in nature and oriented to the present, relating, for example, to the connection between Old Norse and the modern Germanic languages and the influence of medieval Icelandic law on its English (and American) descendants. Longfellow spent summer 1835 in Sweden and Denmark, principally in Stockholm and Copenhagen, but gained only a superficial acquaintance with the literary history of the countries, not to mention their contemporary literatures and social-political conditions, for which the lover of Scott and the heroic past had little interest in any case. According to Hilen, "he was in no sense the equal of his contemporaries Henry Wheaton and George Perkins Marsh as a student of the Old Norse." Andrew Hilen, *Longfellow and Scandinavia: A Study of the Poet's Relationship with the Northern Languages and Literatures* (New Haven, CT: Yale University Press, 1947), 90; also see 106–12. All the same, Longfellow acquired the status of an authority on the subject for a limited but influential number of friends and acquaintances in and around Boston. Hilen writes, "The poet's [Longfellow's] closest associates—Sumner, [Cornelius] Felton, [George] Greene, and Hillard—undoubtedly discussed Scandinavian literature with him in the Craigie House." Hilen, *Longfellow and Scandinavia*, 111. Moreover, Longfellow's great popularity surely guaranteed a wider audience for his views.

57. Hillard, "Hans Christian Andersen," 441, 442.

58. Hillard, "Hans Christian Andersen," 442.

59. Hillard, "Hans Christian Andersen," 442–43.

60. Hillard, "Hans Christian Andersen," 443.

61. George S. Hillard, *The Relation of the Poet to His Age: A Discourse Delivered before the Phi Beta Kappa Society of Harvard University on Thursday, August 24, 1843* (Boston: Charles C. Little and James Brown, 1843), 12–13.

62. Hillard, *The Relation of the Poet to His Age*, 44–63. In his Phi Beta Kappa address, Hillard creates the impression of a Romantic reluctantly, but decidedly engaging a changing world, and not without some self-contradiction. Early on, he writes,

> The office of poetry is to idealize human life; to connect the objects of thought with those associations which embellish, dignify and exalt, and to keep out of sight, those which debase and deform; to extract from the common world, which lies at our feet, the elements

of the romantic, the impassioned and the imaginative; to arrest and condense the delicate spirit of beauty which hovers over the earth, like an atmosphere, and to give shape, color and movement to its airy essence. . . . We are willing to observe from his [the poet's] point of view, and to overlook the plain facts of the case. (Hillard, *The Relation of the Poet to His Age*, 5–6)

Toward the end, however, he states, somewhat incongruently, or searchingly, "The poetry of our times must be, more than ever before, the poetry of real life, or if an expression may be allowed, somewhat savoring of conceit, the poetry of prose." Hillard, *The Relation of the Poet to His Age*, 46.

64. See Elias Bredsdorff, *Danish Literature in English Translation, with a Special Hans Christian Andersen Supplement: A Bibliography* (Copenhagen: Ejnar Munksgaard, 1950), 173–75, 177, 181.

65. Unsigned review of *The Improvisatore*, *American Literary Gazette and Publishers' Circular*, September 1, 1869, 254.

66. See Frank Luther Mott, *A History of American Magazines 1865–1885* (1938; repr., Cambridge, MA: Harvard University Press, 1966), 491–94.

67. See Mott, *A History of American Magazines 1850–1865*, 159, and Mott, *A History of American Magazines 1865–1885*, 492. For further information on Mackenzie, see "Robert Shelton Mackenzie," Virtual American Biographies, accessed April 20, 2015, http://famousamericans.net/robertsheltonmackenzie/, and "Mackenzie, Robert Shelton (1809–1880)," The Vault at Pfaff's: An Archive of Art and Literature by the Bohemians of Antebellum New York, accessed April 20, 2015, http://digital.lib.lehigh.edu/pfaffs/p117/. For additional information on Rode, see "Obituary: Charles Rudolph Rode," *American Literary Gazette and Publishers' Circular*, March 1, 1865, 238.

68. Mott, *A History of American Magazines 1865–1885*, 494. The entry for the paper in *Rowell's* for 1869 (97) offers no circulation figure.

69. *American Literary Gazette and Publishers' Circular*, September 1, 1869, 254–55.

70. Howitt relates her use of the German translation in *Mary Howitt: An Autobiography*, ed. Margaret Howitt (London: Isbister, 1889), 182. The review in the *Ladies' National Magazine*, for example, concludes with the words, "We need not say that the translation of this book is chaste and beautiful. Mrs. Howitt's name is sufficient to assure the reader of this" (*Ladies' National Magazine*, 36).

71. See Viggo Hjørnager Pedersen, *Ugly Ducklings? Studies in the English Translations of Hans Christian Andersen's Tales and Stories* (Odense: University Press of Southern Denmark, 2004), 85–87. Implicit in the author's "Conclusion" is that he is perhaps the kindest of Danish commentators on Howitt's translations.

72. Carl Woodring, *Victorian Samplers: William and Mary Howitt* (Lawrence: University of Kansas Press, 1952), unpaginated preface. Also see 98–106, especially 105, where we read, "Although they were thought of as Quakers and thus had their greatest following in Philadelphia, they maintained a literary status as high throughout the United States as in Great Britain, with the added enhancement of being eminent foreigners." Bredsdorff's quite plausible explanation for the success of Andersen's fairy tales in English-speaking countries may well apply to all his works

in English translation: "Even if the wonderful freshness and charm of the style was lost, even if the language was reduced to the stalest clichés and most inane banalities, something remained which was unparalleled in English literature. . . . Even if buried under earth and slag, the gold shone through"; Bredsdorff, *H. C. Andersen og England*, 520; translation by Hjørnager Pedersen, *Ugly Ducklings?*, 15. The reviewer of *The Improvisatore* for the *American Literary Gazette and Publishers' Circular* would appear to corroborate this possibility; see note 69 above.

73. Review of *The Improvisatore*, *American Literary Gazette and Publishers' Circular*, September 1, 1869, 254.

74. For the date of publication, see *Boston Journal*, August 28, 1869, 3. Also see Scudder to Andersen, August 27, 1869, where the editor relates that the novel is to be released the following day; *The Andersen-Scudder Letters*, ed. Jean Hersholt and Waldemar Westergaard (Berkeley and Los Angeles: University of California Press, 1949), 52.

75. William J. Clark Jr., review of *The Improvisatore*, *Evening Telegraph*, September 11, 1869, 6; "Book Notices," unsigned review of *The Improvisatore*, *Portland Transcript* (Maine), September 11, 1869, 186.

76. See John Thomas Scharf and Thompson Westcott, *A History of Philadelphia 1609–1884*, 3 vols. (Philadelphia: L. H. Everts, 1884), 3:2034. Also see *Rowell's* for 1869, 97.

77. Scharf and Westcott, *A History of Philadelphia 1609–1884*, 3:2034.

78. Scharf and Westcott, *A History of Philadelphia 1609–1884*, 3:2034. Also see "Clark, Jr., William J. (1839–1889)," Philadelphia Sketch Club, accessed April 20, 2015, sketchclub.org/art-collection/archives/. I have drawn most of the information on Clark from this website.

79. *Evening Telegraph*, September 11, 1869, 6.

80. See, for example, Winifred Hughes, *The Maniac in the Cellar: Sensation Novels of the 1860s* (Princeton, NJ: Princeton University Press, 1980); Kimberly Harrison and Richard Fantina, eds., *Victorian Sensations: Essays on a Scandalous Genre* (Columbus: Ohio State University Press, 2006), especially the introduction, ix–xxiii. Denning locates the demise of the "dime novel" in the United States in the 1890s. Denning, *Mechanic Accents*, 12. The review predated publication of the novel in the Author's Edition by about a year and may have been based on a reissue of the American edition that came out in 1861; see Bredsdorff, *Danish Literature in English Translation*, 173.

81. See Mott, *A History of American Magazines 1850–1865*, 36.

82. See *Rowell's* for 1869, 42. Also see C. A. Cook, *United States Newspaper Directory*, rev. ed. (Chicago: C. A. Cook, 1881), 75, which provides substantial information on the distribution of the paper, among other things.

83. See Joseph Griffin, ed., *History of the Press of Maine* (Brunswick, ME: J. Griffin, 1872), 58–59; Samuel T. Pickard, *Life and Letters of John Greenleaf Whittier* (Boston and New York: Houghton, Mifflin and Company, 1895), 2 vols.

84. *Portland Transcript* (Maine), September 11, 1869, 186.

85. Unsigned review of *The Improvisatore, Christian Advocate*, September 30, 1869, 307; "Editor's Book Table," *Harper's New Monthly Magazine*, November 1869, 925; "Reviews of New Books," unsigned review of *The Improvisatore, Albion*, September 25, 1869, 578.

86. See "About the *Christian Advocate* [Volume] (New York [N.Y.]) 1866–1938," Chronicling America: Historic American Newspapers, accessed April 20, 2015, https://chroniclingamerica.loc.gov/lccn/sn97066043/.

87. See *Rowell's* for 1869, 72.

88. See Mott, *A History of American Magazines 1850–1865*, 102, 391, and Exman, *The House of Harper*, 79. See *Rowell's* for 1869, 77, and 1871, 109.

89. See the scant information on the magazine in Mott, *A History of American Magazines 1741–1850*, 131. Also see *Rowell's* for 1870, 699. The publication lists no circulation figure for 1869; 71.

90. *Christian Advocate,* September 30, 1869, 307.

91. *Harper's New Monthly Magazine,* November 1869, 925.

92. *Albion,* September 25, 1869, 578.

93. Unsigned review of *The Improvisatore* and *The Two Baronesses: A Romance, Nation*, December 9, 1869, 514.

94. See Mott, *A History of American Magazines 1865–1885*, 331–44. Much of the information in the following is indebted to Mott.

95. "Literary Notes and News," *Dial*, July 1885, 81.

96. Mott, *A History of American Magazines 1865–1885*, 339. In the edition for 1869 (74), *Rowell's* has the circulation at precisely six thousand.

97. Mott writes, "The list of the early contributors to the *Nation* enrolls most of the famous scholars and writers of the sixties and seventies"; Mott, *A History of American Magazines 1865–1885*, 335; also see 335–38. For an extensive treatment of the magazine, see Gustav Pollak, "The *Nation* and Its Contributors," in *Fifty Years of American Idealism: The New York* Nation *1865–1915: Selections and Comments*, ed. Gustav Pollak (Boston and New York: Houghton Mifflin, 1915), 3–83, particularly 49–52.

98. See Mott, *A History of American Magazines 1865–1885*, 335–36; Rowland, *More Than Meets the Eye*, 37–39, 41–42, 49–51, 71–73. Howells had worked for the *Nation* in 1865 and 1866, writing reviews and a minor topics column, before moving to the assistant editorship of the *Atlantic Monthly* in 1866, where he was promised time for his own writing; see, for example, Susan Goodman and Carl Dawson, *William Dean Howells: A Writer's Life* (Berkeley, Los Angeles, and London: University of California Press, 2005), xxii–xxiii, 105–8. Another possibility is Fitzedward Hall (1825–1901), who, though specializing in Sanskrit, Hindi, and English philology, was apparently widely read in the European literatures and is known to have reviewed for the *Nation*; see Caskie Harrison, "Obituary. Fitzedward Hall, C.E., M.A., D.C.L., L.L.D.," *Modern Language Notes* 16 (1901): 184–91, and, for example, Fitzedward Hall, "Recent Biographies of Lessing," *Nation*, December 4, 1879, 390–91.

99. *Nation*, December 9, 1869, 514.

100. See, for example, Margarete Kohlenbach, "*Lucinde* 1799. Novel by Friedrich Schlegel," in *Encyclopedia of the Romantic Era, 1760–1850*, ed. Christopher John Murray, 2 vols. (London: Routledge, 2004), 2:699.

101. J. Henry Harper, *The House of Harper: A Century of Publishing in Franklin Square* (New York and London: Harper Brothers, 1912), 322–23.

102. William Dean Howells, *Selected Literary Criticism, 1898–1920*, ed. Ulrich Halfmann, Donald Pizer, and Ronald Gottesman, 3 vols. (Bloomington: Indiana University Press, 1993), 3:218.

103. Unsigned review of "Hans Christian Andersen's Works" (Author's Edition), *Eclectic*, January 1870, 118–19.

104. See Mott, *A History of American Magazines 1741–1850*, 306–9; *Rowell's* for 1870, 706.

105. The reviewer writes, for example, "We have said that it is chiefly as a writer for the young that Hans Christian Andersen is known to American, and, for the matter of that, to English readers"; *Eclectic*, January 1870, 118.

106. *Eclectic*, January 1870, 118.

107. *Eclectic*, January 1870, 118.

108. *Eclectic*, January 1870, 118.

109. Thompson and Link, *Neutral Ground*, especially 188–94.

110. *Eclectic*, January 1870, 118–19.

111. See Mott, *A History of American Magazines 1865–1885*, 328–29.

112. See David J. O'Brien, *Isaac Hecker: An American Catholic* (New York and Mahwah, NJ: Paulist Press, 1992), 200–202.

113. *Nation*, March 26, 1868, 225; quoted according to Mott, *A History of American Magazines 1865–1885*, 329.

114. See *Rowell's* for 1870, 705.

115. See O'Brien, *Isaac Hecker*, 200.

116. Unsigned review of *The Improvisatore*, *Catholic World*, January 1870, 575.

117. *Catholic World,* June 1873, 289; quoted according to Mott, *A History of American Magazines 1865–1885*, 330.

118. *Catholic World,* January 1870, 575.

119. Unsigned review of *The Improvisatore*, *Advance*, October 14, 1869, 6.

120. See Mott, *A History of American Magazines 1865–1885*, 76–77.

121. *Rowell's* for 1869 (20) has the number at 16,500.

122. *Advance*, October 14, 1869, 6.

123. Unsigned review of *The Improvisatore*, *Universe*, October 30, 1869, 145. See Mott, *A History of American Magazines 1865–1885*, 52–53; *Rowell's* for 1869, 20.

124. *Universe*, October 30, 1869, 145.

125. "New Publications," unsigned review of *The Improvisatore*, *Boston Herald*, June 23, 1891, 9. According to *Rowell's* for 1891 (318), the *Herald* had a circulation in excess of one hundred thousand at the time the review was published.

126. For discussions of these two closely related genres, see Gero von Wilpert, *Sachwörterbuch der Literatur*, 8th ed. (Stuttgart: Kröner Verlag, 2001), 215 and 91–92. The terms are often used interchangeably, but the bildungsroman is properly understood as a type of novel of development. The undifferentiated usage of these

terms likely reflects an absence of consensus over what constitutes their referents. This, in turn, may well have led to the prevalent lack of unanimity regarding the genre assignment of Andersen's novels. For Hugus, all of Andersen's novels belong to the bildungsroman (Hugus, introduction to *The Improvisatore*, xviii), whereas de Mylius excludes *O. T.*, *Only a Fiddler*, and, in part, *Lykke Peer* from the category; *Andersen og verden: Indlæg fra den Første Internationale H. C. Andersen-Konference 25–31. August 1991*, ed. Johan de Mylius, Aage Jørgensen, and Viggo Hjørnager Pedersen (Odense: Odense Universitetsforlag, 1993), 57. Binding and Smith share de Mylius's attitude toward *O. T.* and *Only a Fiddler*; Binding, *Hans Christian Andersen*, 155; and Smith, "From Autonomy to Dependency," 33–57.

127. See Bredsdorff, *Hans Christian Andersen*, 128; Mogens Brøndsted, "Modtagelse," in *O.T.: Original Roman i to Dele*, by H. C. Andersen, ed. Mogens Brøndsted (Copenhagen: Det Danske Sprog- og Litteraturselskab / Borgen, 1987), 268.

128. *Brooklyn Eagle*, July 20, 1870, 1.

129. See *Evening Post*, November 12, 1845, 2; *Commercial Advertiser*, November 13, 1845, 2.

130. Samuel Nathan Hart Sr., review of *Only a Fiddler!* and *O. T.*, trans. Mary Howitt, *Southern Patriot*, December 30, 1845, 2.

131. William L. King, *The Newspaper Press of Charleston, S.C.: A Chronological and Biographical History, Embracing a Period of One Hundred and Forty Years* (Charleston, SC: Edward Perry, 1872), 77–87.

132. "The Charleston Book: A Miscellany in Prose and Verse," Simms Initiatives, University of South Carolina, accessed March 29, 2016, http://simms.library.sc.edu/view_item.php?item=132071.

133. *Southern Patriot*, December 30, 1845, 2.

134. See, for example, Iben Holk, "*O. T.: Original Roman i to Deele* (1836)," Epoke—Danske Romaner før 1900, last modified August 30, 2004, accessed March 28, 2016, http://www.e-poke.dk/andersen_ot_1.php. Clifford Albrecht Bernd fails to give Andersen his just due in the present context, principally, it would seem, because the Dane assumed the "wrong" political stance. Clifford Albrecht Bernd, *Poetic Realism in Scandinavia and Central Europe 1820–1895* (Columbia, SC: Camden House, 1995), 54–56 and passim.

135. The *Boston Recorder* gives the date of publication in the issue for June 23, 1870, 200.

136. William J. Clark Jr., "Literature: Review of New Books," unsigned review of *O. T.: A Danish Romance*, *Evening Telegraph*, July 1, 1870, 7. As in the previous year, the paper claimed a circulation of twenty-six thousand; *Rowell's* for 1870, 733.

137. In the Author's Edition, to be sure, both *O. T.* and *Only a Fiddler* (as well as *The Two Baronesses*) bear the word "romance" in their subtitles.

138. Unsigned review of *O. T.: A Danish Romance*, *North American and United States Gazette*, July 7, 1870, 1.

139. See Scharf and Westcott, "The North American and United States Gazette," in Scharf and Westcott, *A History of Philadelphia 1609–1884*, 3:1970–73. See *Rowell's* for 1870, 732–33.

140. See Robert L. Bloom, "Morton McMichael's *North American*," *Pennsylvania Magazine of History and Biography*, April 1953, 166.

141. *North American and United States Gazette*, July 7, 1870, 1.

142. Unsigned review of *O. T.: A Danish Romance*, *Independent*, July 28, 1870, 6 (col. 7).

143. See Mott's sketch of the magazine in Mott, *A History of American Magazines 1850–1865*, 467–79.

144. See *Rowell's* for 1870, 701. Mott states that the periodical was at the high point of its circulation in this year, though he names no figure. He also writes that it sold seventy-five thousand at some point during the Civil War; Mott, *A History of American Magazines 1850–1865*, 375, 372.

145. *Independent*, July 28, 1870, 6 (col. 7).

146. "Book Notices," unsigned review of *O. T.: A Danish Romance*, *Portland Transcript*, July 9, 1870, 114. The paper recorded a circulation of 17,300 in that year; see *Rowell's* for 1870, 660.

147. Unsigned review of *O. T.: A Danish Romance*, *Churchman,* July 23, 1870, 248. See Mott, *A History of American Magazines 1850–1865*, 69.

148. The quotation is drawn from *Rowell's* for 1870, 624.

149. de Mylius, *Myte og Roman*, 103–4.

150. See Binding, *Hans Christian Andersen*, 139; Smith, "From Autonomy to Dependency," 52.

151. See Binding, *Hans Christian Andersen*, 138–39. According to Brøndsted, the novel probably received only one, mixed review in a Danish newspaper. It was the object of sarcastic criticism in an independent publication by Søren Kierkegaard; see Mogens Brøndsted, "Modtagelse," in *Kun en Spillemand: Original Roman i tre Dele*, by H. C. Andersen, ed. by Mogens Brøndsted (Copenhagen: Det Danske Sprog-og Litteraturselskab/Borgen, 1988), 290–92.

152. Binding, *Hans Christian Andersen*, 138–39.

153. *Southern Patriot*, December 30, 1845, 2.

154. "Foreign Literature," unsigned review of *Only a Fiddler*, trans. Mary Howitt, *North American*, October 30, 1845, 1. See Scharf and Westcott, "The North American and United States Gazette," 3:1970–71.

155. See Mott, *A History of American Magazines 1741–1850*, 544–55.

156. See Scharf and Westcott, "The North American and United States Gazette," 3:1970–71.

157. "Foreign Literature," unsigned review of *Only a Fiddler*, trans. Mary Howitt, *North American*, October 30, 1845, 1.

158. The earliest advertisement for the book I have found was placed in the *New-York Tribune*, August 18, 1870, 6.

159. "Literary Notices," unsigned review of *Only a Fiddler*, *North American and United States Gazette*, August 26, 1870, 1.

160. See the unsigned review of *Only a Fiddler*, *Evening Post*, October 11, 1870, 1. The critic for the *Post* writes, "It [the novel] reads in many respects not unlike the home-life tales of Fredrika Bremer." He adds, perceptively, "Andersen is artistically skillful in depicting melancholy scenes and has strikingly displayed his power in the

story of one who was 'only a fiddler.'" Andersen knew Gyllembourg and Bremer as well as their work.

161. *North American and United States Gazette*, August 26, 1870, 1.

162. See Timothy Hilton, *The Pre-Raphaelites* (London: Thames and Hudson, 1970).

163. Unsigned review of *Only a Fiddler: A Danish Romance*, *Christian Union*, September 3, 1870, 34.

164. See Mott, *A History of American Magazines 1865–1885*, 422–35.

165. Mott, *A History of American Magazines 1865–1885*, 425. *Rowell's*, however, states that the periodical claimed a much more modest circulation of fifteen thousand; *Rowell's* for 1870, 700.

166. For information on Gardner, see "Notes for Dorsey GARDNER," Rash's Surname Index, accessed April 21, 2015, www.pennock.ws/surnames/nti/nti142837.html.

167. *Christian Union*, September 3, 1870, 34.

168. See Iben Holk, *"Kun en Spillemand: Original Roman i tre Dele* (1837)," Epoke—Danske Romaner før 1900, last modified January 11, 2005, accessed April 21, 2015, http://www.e-poke.dk/andersen_kun_1.php.

169. Holk, *"Kun en Spillemand: Original Roman i tre Dele* (1837)"; de Mylius, *Myte og Roman*, 125–26.

170. *Christian Union*, September 3, 1870, 34.

171. Unsigned review of *Only a Fiddler*, *Portland Daily Press*, September 21, 1870, 1.

172. An attempt to find the missing portion of the review in later issues of the paper proved futile. According to *Rowell's* for 1870 (660), the *Press* had a circulation of twenty-six hundred.

173. Unsigned review of *Only a Fiddler*, *Daily Evening Bulletin*, September 24, 1870, 1.

174. I am indebted here to Edward C. Kemble, *A History of California Newspapers 1846–1858* (Los Gatos, CA: Talisman, 1962), 121–23. *Rowell's* for 1870 (621) lists the circulation as eleven thousand for the daily edition and thirty-five hundred for the weekly edition, in which the review of Andersen's work appeared.

175. *Daily Evening Bulletin*, September 24, 1870, 1.

176. See Monica Correa Fryckstedt, "Geraldine Jewsbury's *Athenaeum* Reviews: A Mirror of Mid-Victorian Attitudes to Fiction," *Victorian Periodicals Review* 23 (1990): 17–18.

177. In this study, Longfellow serves as a cipher for a largely retrospective, idealized reception of Scandinavia, and, within the American context, with good reason (see note 56 above). It was not by chance that Norwegian American Rasmus B. Anderson, founding head of the program in Scandinavian studies at the University of Wisconsin (the first in the United States), dedicated his hymnic *Norse Mythology* of 1875 to the poet. In fairness, and from an international point of view, however, Longfellow was in excellent company. In his "The Discovery of Norway Abroad, 1760–1905," H. Arnold Barton sketches the genesis of a European view of the country as a region of rugged natural beauty, an exemplary heroic past, and an archetypal simplicity and innocence that originated in the Rousseauist primitivism of the

eighteenth century. Widely applied synecdochally to the rest of Scandinavia, it dominated perceptions of the North in the nineteenth century, actually intensifying interest in the Northern countries themselves in their past and present. H. Arnold Barton, "The Discovery of Norway Abroad, 1760–1905," *Scandinavian Studies* 79 (2007): 25–40. Benson writes, indeed, that Henry Wheaton "arrived in Copenhagen when native interest in Northern antiquity ran high. Never had the time been more propitious for stimulating enthusiasm in the Scandinavian peoples and their culture." Benson, "Henry Wheaton's Writings on Scandinavia," 547.

178. *Daily Evening Bulletin*, September 24, 1870, 1.

179. "Book Notices," unsigned review of *Only a Fiddler*, *Portland Transcript*, October 1, 1870, 210.

180. Unsigned review of *Only a Fiddler*, *Zion's Herald*, October 20, 1870, 497. See Mott, *A History of American Magazines 1741–1850*, 138; "*Zion's Herald*," World Public Library, accessed April 21, 2015, www.netlibrary.net/articles/Zion's_Herald; and *Rowell's* for 1870, 665.

181. Unsigned review of *Only a Fiddler* and *O. T.*, *Gentleman's Magazine*, November 1845, 508.

182. See Emily Lorraine de Montluzin, "The *Gentleman's Magazine*: A Short History," Attributions of Authorship in the *Gentleman's Magazine*, 1731–1868: An Electronic Union List, last modified March 13, 2003, accessed April 21, 2015, bsuva.org/bsuva/gm2/GMintro.html#history.

183. See William Prideaux Courtney, "Mitford, John (1781–1859)," in *Dictionary of National Biography, 1885–1900*, last modified November 12, 2012, accessed April 21, 2015, http://en.wikisource.org/wiki/Mitford,_John_(1781-1859)_(DNB00). I have found no evidence that Mitford wrote reviews for the *Gentleman's Magazine* himself. According to de Montluzin, the magazine had a paid staff for such responsibilities; de Montluzin, "The *Gentleman's Magazine*: A Short History."

184. See Courtney, "Mitford, John (1781–1859)."

185. Twenty-five years separate the English and American reviews, but Gross indicates that the didactic and "uncompromisingly moralistic, political, and religious" character of most early Victorian criticism did not change significantly until the late 1870s. John Gross, *The Rise and Fall of the Man of Letters: English Literary Life since 1800* (Chicago: Ivan R. Dee, 1969), 131. The London *Spectator*, like the *Gentleman's* a general magazine, also refers (briefly) to the moral character of *Only a Fiddler*. Averring the "truth" of Andersen's depiction of Danish life and Christian's death, the reviewer writes, "The laxity of the moral tone is quite as natural, but not quite as well fitted for English readers"; unsigned review of *Only a Fiddler* and *O. T.*, August 30, 1845, 831–32; quoted according to Bredsdorff, *H. C. Andersen og England*, 435–36.

186. Review of *Only a Fiddler*, *Zion's Herald*, October 20, 1870, 497.

187. "Hans Christian Andersen—'Only a Fiddler,'" *Farmers' Home Journal*, September 14, 1876, 568.

188. See *Rowell's* for 1876, 82, and Mott, *A History of American Magazines 1865–1885*, 155–56.

189. See Erik Dal, "Romanens modtagelse," in *De to Baronesser*, by H. C. Andersen, ed. Erik Dal (Copenhagen: Det Danske Sprog-og Litteraturselskab / Borgen, 1997), 248–55.

190. Bredsdorff, *H. C. Andersen og England*, 467.

191. An ad for the novel carries the words "Ready This Day, Oct. 2"; *Boston Daily Advertiser*, October 2, 1869, 2.

192. "Book Notices," unsigned review of *The Two Baronesses: A Romance*, trans. Charles Beckwith Lohmeyer, *Portland Transcript*, October 16, 1869, 226.

193. Unsigned review of *The Two Baronesses: A Romance*, *Presbyterian*, November 27, 1869, 7. See Mott, *A History of American Magazines 1850–1865*, 63; and Mott, *A History of American Magazines 1885–1905* (Cambridge, MA: Harvard University Press, 1957), 293, as well as *Rowell's* for 1870, 734 (the edition for 1869 gives no circulation figure).

194. Beckwith Lohmeyer, however, translated from the original Danish; see Eileen Curran, "Biographies of Some Obscure Contributors to 19th-Century Periodicals: Charles Beckwith(-Lohmeyer)," Victoria Research Web, accessed August 22, 2016, http://victorianresearch.org/Obscure_contributors.html. Beckwith Lohmeyer also signed as "Beckwith" and "Beckwith-Lohmeyer."

195. For the role of politics in Andersen's life and work, see, for example, Johan de Mylius, "H. C. Andersen og politik," in *Myte og Roman: H. C. Andersens romaner mellem romantik og realisme: En traditionshistorisk undersøgelse* (Copenhagen: Gyldendal, 1981), 255–65; Johan de Mylius, "Hans Christian Andersen—on the Wave of Liberalism," in *Hans Christian Andersen, a Poet in Time: Papers from the Second International Hans Christian Andersen Conference 29 July to 2 August 1996*, ed. Johan de Mylius, Aage Jørgensen, and Viggo Hjørnager Pedersen (Odense: Odense University Press, 1999), 109–24.

196. Unsigned review of *The Two Baronesses: A Romance*, *Times*, December 26, 1848, 3.

197. "Literary Notices," unsigned review of *The Two Baronesses: A Romance*, *Connecticut Courant*, October 18, 1869, 1. See "The Oldest US Newspaper in Continuous Publication," ConnecticutHistory.org, accessed April 1, 2016, http://connecticut history.org/the-oldest-newspaper-in-continuous-publication/. The paper is now called the *Hartford Courant.*

198. See Mott, *American Journalism*, 454.

199. Mott, *American Journalism*, 454. Also see "Hawley, Joseph Roswell (1826–1905)," in *Biographical Directory of the United States Congress 1774–Present*, accessed April 1, 2016, http://bioguide.congress.gov/scripts/biodisplay.pl?index =H000377.

200. Mott, *American Journalism*, 454.

201. See *Rowell's* for 1869, 13.

202. *Connecticut Courant*, October 18, 1869, 1.

203. In this connection, it is interesting to note that, as Scandinavian studies arose at American universities beginning in 1858, eastern institutions focused on Old Norse language and literature, whereas their (present-day) Midwestern counterparts emphasized the modern period; see George T. Flom, "A Sketch of Scandinavian

Study in American Universities," *Publications of the Society for the Advancement of Scandinavian Study* 1 (1911): 14–15. The explanation for this state of affairs must lie in important part in the fact that students at the eastern universities were primarily native-born Americans, while those at the Midwestern schools came largely from the extensive Scandinavian American population in the region, for whom the languages and cultures of their parents were still living. Flom, "A Sketch of Scandinavian Study in American Universities," 15. Although the sagas as well as Ibsen and Strindberg were studied in both parts of the country, one is thus perhaps justified in speculating that the Romantic view of the North was stronger and more persistent in the East, where the majority of the review criticism originated. Also see George T. Flom, *A History of Scandinavian Studies in American Universities*, Iowa Studies in Language and Literature 11 (Iowa City: State University of Iowa, 1907), 47–66, on which the author's "Sketch" is based and which includes a useful bibliography.

204. Unsigned review of *The Two Baronesses: A Romance*, *Evangelist*, October 14, 1869, 2. See Mott, *A History of American Magazines 1741–1850*, 373; "About the *New-York Evangelist* [Volume] (New York [N.Y.])," Chronicling America: Historic American Newspapers, accessed April 22, 2015, http://chroniclingamerica.loc.gov /lccn/sn85054545/; *Rowell's* for 1869, 701.

205. *Evangelist*, October 14, 1869, 2.

206. Hans Christian Andersen, *The Two Baronesses: A Romance*, author's ed., ed. Horace E. Scudder (Boston: Hurd and Houghton, 1869), 236–37.

207. *Evangelist*, October 14, 1869, 2.

208. See de Mylius, *Myte og Roman*, 166–68 and 190–95.

209. Unsigned review of *The Two Baronesses: A Romance*, *North American and United States Gazette*, October 28, 1869, 1. *Rowell's* for 1869 (97) offers no circulation figure for the year.

210. *Eclectic*, January 1870, 119.

211. "Literature: Review of New Books," unsigned review of *The Two Baronesses: A Romance*, *Evening Telegraph*, November 26, 1869, 6; unsigned review of *The Two Baronesses: A Romance*, *American Presbyterian Review*, January 1870, 193.

212. See Mott, *A History of American Magazines 1850–1865*, 516–17; *Rowell's* for 1870, 708.

213. *American Presbyterian Review*, January 1870, 193.

214. Unsigned review of *The Two Baronesses: A Romance*, *Detroit Free Press*, November 1, 1869, 3. See Frank Angelo, *On Guard: A History of the* Detroit Free Press (Detroit: Detroit Free Press, 1981), 24, 86–90, and 93–95.

215. See Jennifer L. Weber, *Copperheads: The Rise and Fall of Lincoln's Opponents in the North* (New York: Oxford University Press, 2006); Si Sheppard, *The Partisan Press: A History of Media Bias in the United States* (Jefferson, NC, and London: McFarland, 2008), 152.

216. See Mott, *American Journalism*, 393–94; Richard L. Kaplan, *Politics and the American Press: The Rise of Objectivity, 1865–1920* (Cambridge: Cambridge University Press, 2002), 44–54.

217. See *Rowell's* for 1869, 50.

218. *Detroit Free Press*, November 1, 1869, 3. A search of the newspaper's archive and other electronic sources failed to retrieve the notice of *The Improvisatore* mentioned.

219. "Book Table," *Independent*, October 14, 1869, 6.

220. Unsigned review of *The Two Baronesses: A Romance*, *Providence Evening Press*, October 5, 1869, 1.

221. See Bredsdorff, *H. C. Andersen og England*, 474–75. Extensive extracts of the English reviews are found in Elias Bredsdorff, *H. C. Andersen og Charles Dickens, et venskab og dets opløsning* (Copenhagen: Rosenkilde and Bagger, 1951), 82–83 (= *Lloyd's Weekly London Newspaper*); 88–89 (= *Athenæum*); 90–91 (= *Examiner*); and 96–97 (= *Literary Gazette*).

222. *American Publishers' Circular and Literary Gazette*, February 7, 1857, 84; February 14, 1857, 102; July 4, 1857, 421; July 11, 1857, 439, 441. On June 27 of the same year, the magazine published the news that "Hans Andersen, the Swedish [*sic*] novelist, is now in London, on a visit to Charles Dickens, and will immediately produce a new work of fiction, to be translated into English under his own eye, called 'To Be or Not to Be'" (402). The novel had already been issued in London by this time, but the short article is one more sign that the book did not go entirely unnoticed in the United States, as is another that mentions Andersen's summer visit with the Serre family in Dresden as well as the recent appearance of *To Be, or Not to Be?*; *Rhode Island Schoolmaster*, November 1, 1857, 285.

223. "Literary Intelligence and Gossip," *Putnam's Monthly Magazine*, September 1857, 411–12. Brøndsted writes that the Danish reception of the novel was "extremely mixed" ("*særdeles blandet*"), but the examples he offers suggest that it was largely negative; see Mogens Brøndsted, "Modtagelse," in *"At være eller ikke være": Roman i tre Dele*, by H. C. Andersen (Copenhagen: Det Danske Sprog-og Litteraturselskab / Borgen, 2001), 242–44. According to Holk, indeed, critics annihilated the novel, generally denying it any aesthetic, philosophical, or ethical value; see Iben Holk, "*'At være eller ikke være': Roman i tre Dele* (1857)," Epoke—Danske Romaner før 1900, last modified November 1, 2012, accessed July 30, 2018, https://www.e-poke.dk/andersen_atvaere_1.php.

224. *Putnam's Monthly Magazine*, September 1857, 411; [William Hepworth Dixon], unsigned review of *To Be, or Not to Be? A Novel*, *Athenæum*, June 27, 1857, 815–16; unsigned review of *To Be, or Not to Be? A Novel*, *Examiner*, June 27, 1857, 405.

225. Unsigned review of *To Be, or Not to Be? A Novel*, *Literary Gazette*, June 13, 1857, 561–62.

226. Unsigned review of *To Be, or Not to Be? A Novel*, *Lloyd's Weekly London Newspaper*, June 21, 1857, 8.

227. See the conversations between Niels and Bodil in parts 1 and 2 and those between Niels and Esther in part 3.

228. The reviewer for the *Examiner* writes, for example, "A very good story is this of *To Be, or Not to Be?* wherever (as in the first five chapters, and afterwards in various odd pages) the story runs unweighted by the sermon" (*Examiner*, June 27, 1857, 405). However, he continues, "but, alas! When [Andersen] writes for us a sermon, we

may find in it reason enough to doubt his possession of a soul"—extravagant words that rhetorically verge on subverting the positive element of the comment.

229. See Mott, *A History of American Magazines 1865–1885*, 278, and Mott, *American Journalism*, 244–45. For the *Literary Gazette*, see Denys Thompson, "A Hundred Years of the Higher Journalism," TheFossils.org, accessed April 22, 2015, http://www.thefossils.org/horvat/higher/higher.htm. For *Lloyd's Weekly*, see "Edward Lloyd: Victorian Newspaper Proprietor, Publisher and Entrepreneur," EdwardLloyd.org, accessed April 22, 2015, http://www.edwardlloyd.org.

230. Mott, *A History of American Magazines 1850–1865*, 426, 158.

231. The magazine ran from 1853 to 1857 and then, after a lengthy hiatus, from 1868 to 1910; see Mott, *A History of American Magazines 1850–1865*, 419–31. In the following I have drawn on Miller, *The Raven and the Whale*, especially 47–58; Thomas Bender, *New York Intellect: A History of Intellectual Life in New York City, from 1750 to the Beginnings of Our Own Time* (New York: Knopf, 1987), 156–68; Edward Carey, *George William Curtis* (Boston and New York: Houghton Mifflin, 1894); Gordon Milne, *George William Curtis & the Genteel Tradition* (Bloomington: Indiana University Press, 1956); "Parke Godwin," in *Antebellum Writers in New York*, 2nd ser., ed. Kent P. Ljungquist, vol. 250 of *Dictionary of Literary Biography* (Detroit: Gale Research, 2002), 142–47; and "Parke Godwin," in *American Literary Critics and Scholars, 1850–1880*, ed. John W. Rathburn and Monica M. Grecu, vol. 64 of *Dictionary of Literary Biography* (Detroit: Gale Research, 1988), 82–86.

232. Justification through grace and faith has long been the official belief of the Episcopal Church, as of the Church of England, from which it descended. See, for example, "Justification," The *Episcopal Church*, accessed August 24, 2016, http://www.episcopalchurch.org/library/glossary/justification. However, it may be that the reviewer for *Putnam's* was one of the high-church number who reserved a significant role for good works as well; see Owen C. Thomas, *Theological Questions: Analysis and Argument* (Wilton, CT: Morehouse-Barlow, 1983), 81–82.

233. See chapter 1, note 4. The identity of the translator is unknown, but s/he may have been Anna Raasløff, a daughter of Danish general Valdemar R. Raasløff, or German American sculptor Eduard Kuntze, whom Horace Scudder commissioned to translate some of the fairy tales for his *Riverside Magazine for Young People.* Scudder continued to handle Andersen's works for *Scribner's* after it absorbed the *Riverside* in December 1870; see Erik Dal, "Hans Christian Andersen's Tales and America," *Scandinavian Studies* 40 (1968): 13–14.

234. See *Literary World*, December 1, 1870, 107 (announcement of forthcoming publication in *Scribner's*; currently in translation); *New York Evangelist*, December 15, 1870, 5 (ad for the January 1871 number of *Scribner's*: "The beginning of Hans Andersen's charming story of a Boyish Life, entitled *Lucky Peer*"); *Book Buyer*, January 16, 1871, 17 (announcement of the installment for February in *Scribner's*); *American Publishers' Circular and Literary Gazette*, February 1, 1871, 121 (announcement of the installment for February in *Scribner's*); *Book Buyer*, March 15, 1871, 3 (notice of the last installment of the novel in the April issue of *Scribner's*) and March 15, 1871, 16 (the April issue of *Scribner's* contains "the beautiful closing chapters of Hans Andersen's 'Lucky Peer'"); *Christian Union*, March 22, 1871, 192

(notice of the last installment of the novel in the April issue of *Scribner's*: the novel "is concluded with wonderful power, pathos and genius"); *Reformed Church Messenger*, March 22, 1871, 8 (notice of the last installment of the novel in the April issue of *Scribner's*); *Advance*, March 30, 1871, 6 (notice of the last installment of the novel in the April issue of *Scribner's*); *American Publishers' Circular and Literary Gazette*, April 1, 1871, 231 (content of *Scribner's* for April 1871). The novel received a mixed critical reception in Denmark; see Erik Dal, "Modtagelsen," in *Lykke-Peer*, by H. C. Andersen, ed. Erik Dal (Copenhagen: Det Danske Sprog-og Litteraturselskab / Borgen, 2000), 101–3.

235. See *Rowell's* for 1871, 28 (*Advance*); 65 (*Literary World*); 103 (*Christian Union* and *New York Evangelist*); and 138 (*Reformed Church Messenger*). For the *American Publishers' Circular and Literary Gazette* and the *Book Buyer*, see 108 and 139, respectively. The *Circular* had a circulation of under two thousand in 1869; see *Rowell's* for that year. The *Book Buyer* was at this time an advertising organ for Scribner and Company.

236. See *Rowell's* for 1871, 110–11.

237. E. S. Martin, "New Departures and Old Ways," *Ladies' Repository* (Cincinnati), February 1874, 99–103.

238. Martin, "New Departures and Old Ways," 100.

239. In this connection, one should bear in mind that a certain "petticoat rule" prevailed even in general magazines such as *Harper's* and *Scribner's*; see Mott, *A History of American Magazines 1865–1885*, 90.

240. The term was coined by Karl Morgenstern in 1803 but gained currency only through Wilhelm Dilthey beginning in 1870. Reviewers conversant with German literature may have been familiar with the concept, if not the term, through their reading of *Wilhelm Meister's Apprenticeship* and other German novels or, for that matter, Dickens's *David Copperfield* (1850); see von Wilpert, *Sachwörterbuch der Literatur*, 91.

241. See p. 43 above.

242. See pp. 36 and 61 above.

243. See p. 43 above.

244. See p. 58 above.

245. See p. 63 above.

246. See p. 67 above.

Chapter Three

The Travel Books

Hans Christian Andersen was an inveterate traveler. During the some forty years extending from his first trip to Italy in 1831 to his eighth and final one in 1873, he traveled northward to Sweden and southward to Africa, westward as far as England and eastward as far as Turkey, not to mention the many trips he took within his home country. He spent lengthy periods of time in both Italy and Germany. "To travel is to live," he wrote in his autobiography, but, for him, to travel was also to escape, to escape from the real and perceived literary and personal criticism of his fellow Danes. His attraction to Germany arose not least of all because of the early warm reception he and his work received in the country. Perhaps more important, travel as life and travel as education were inseparable for him. Jens Andersen points out that, more clearly than many another travel writer of the nineteenth century, Hans Christian Andersen repeatedly asserted the enlightening value of his journeys in his diaries and letters home, "which are often peppered with the overwhelming kind of learning to be found in immediate sensory and nature experiences, as well as in a shrewd observation of life."[1]

Between 1831 and 1872, Andersen recorded such experiences and observations and much else in five major travelogues as well as numerous travel sketches. Most were very well received at the time of their publication, by the public if not uniformly by critics, and a few are still generally reckoned among the author's most artistically successful works.[2] No less than the novels, the travel books continue to generate interest among scholars.[3] From the mid-1870s through the mid-1880s three appeared in new English translations, and in 2011, Praesens Verlag of Vienna announced a projected series of five volumes of the works in English, one of which has already been published.[4]

All of the travelogues and some of the travel sketches were translated into English beginning in 1846.[5] Research for the present volume uncovered forty-five American reviews of these writings, all but one of them responses to the books as issued in the Author's Edition. Like their peers in Denmark, American critics generally reacted quite favorably to the works, indeed, more favorably than to the novels, applauding features such as their painterliness and poetic quality that were also highlighted in reviews of the novels. If not uniformly illuminating, the notices disclose an array of personal interest, impression, and opinion almost as varied as the magazines in which they appear. In the present chapter, the works will be discussed in the order of their publication in the Author's Edition.

IN SPAIN AND *A VISIT TO PORTUGAL*

Andersen traveled to the Iberian Peninsula twice during the later years of his life. He visited Spain from July 1862 to March 1863 and sojourned in Portugal for the seven months beginning at the end of January 1866. The products of these stays were *In Spain* and *A Visit to Portugal*, which were originally published in 1863 and 1868, respectively. Of the nineteen chapters that comprise *In Spain*, most reflect Andersen's many diverse experiences in the more than fifteen cities he visited, the remainder describing his impressions along the roads between the cities and in North Africa. Surprisingly, perhaps, the chapter on Granada is the longest of all, even longer than the one on Madrid, largely due to the author's expansive account of Queen Isabella's visit to the city and his description of the Alhambra. Compared to *In Spain*, *A Visit to Portugal* is a slight work, only somewhat over one-quarter the length of its companion piece. In the central chapter (IV), Andersen describes the scenes and events of the month he spent in Setubal, near Lisbon, where he witnessed the Feast of St. Anthony and a bullfight. Otherwise, he appears to have been taken as much with Italian tragedienne Adelaide Ristori's performance as Medea in Bordeaux and sights in Spain on the way to and from Portugal as with Portugal itself.

A British translation of *In Spain* came out in 1864, but *A Visit to Portugal* did not appear in English dress until both works were issued together as volume 4 of the Author's Edition, probably around the first of May 1870.[6] A useful but incomplete introduction to the volume appeared in the *Phrenological Journal*, which ran under varying titles from 1841 to 1914.[7] The contemporary popularity of what in some quarters was still considered a legitimate science is corroborated by the fact that the magazine reported an estimated circulation of around thirty thousand for the year in which the review was printed.[8] Although specializing in phrenological analyses of famous persons accompanied by portraits, the periodical also published a section of miscellany that included book notices.

The review of the present volume is illuminating chiefly for what it says and does not say about Andersen's itineraries: "Reader, would you take a run with a very intelligent guide through an interesting part of the Old World, taking Barcelona, Valencia, Murcia, Carthagena, Malaga, Granada, Gibraltar, Cadiz, Seville, Cordova, Madrid, Toledo, Burgos, and over the Pyrenees to Biarritz? If so, here is the medium and the guide."[9] While presenting an almost complete overview of Andersen's tour through Spain—only his stops in Almansa, Alicante, and North Africa are excluded—the writer omits any mention of the author's stay in Portugal. In this, however, he is like most of his colleagues at the other magazines, who seem not to have noticed that the volume contains a second text.

Andersen's reviewers found various aspects of his work(s) deserving of comment. For the writer at *Zion's Herald*, it was the history of the countries: "IN SPAIN AND PORTUGAL, by Hans Christian Andersen . . . gives pictures of these lands when they sat in the midnight of Papal superstition. Art, worship, beggary, brutality, were their chief traits then."[10] A more expansive notice of similar focus appeared in the *American Quarterly Church Review*, contemporarily the most distinguished organ of the Protestant Episcopal Church in the United States, which listed a circulation of three thousand for 1870:

> Of all the old historic lands, Spain possesses the most thorough romance. Provence with her troubadors—the wandering minstrels of "Old Englande"— the wonderful dwellers of the Hartz Mountains, are but shadows to the deeds of the Cid, and the pranks of Don Quixote. We are apt in the present desolation of Spain to forget its past glory. Our traveler finds somewhat of interest in every spot he visits. He gives one most attractive pictures and amusing scenes among people that are represented to us the very epitomes of squalor and filth. Seville of all Spanish cities seems to have the most charm. Its picture gallery, its Murillos, its luscious fruits and dark-eyed beauties, make it interesting even as compared with any city in sunny Italy. We tread the Alhambra with our friend, and think we see those old Moorish knights and dreaming Sultanas in its marble halls; would fain rest ourselves by those rippling fountains, soothed by the intoxicating perfumes of Oriental flowers, and awake to find ourselves among the ashes of past days.[11]

For this reviewer, Spain is in equal parts Longfellow's land of romance and a particolored landscape where the present is imbued with the past. Indeed, Andersen reflects on many sundry elements of the history of politics, religion, art, and folk tradition in the cities he visits. However, the writer is able to go beyond his preconceived notions of the country, opening himself to the present that Andersen witnessed and depicts: "Washington Irving finds only *ruins*, and can only give his book interest by recalling *old* scenes. Hans Andersen makes Spain most interesting even at the present time. Spite of its poverty and fleas, the travel is comfortable, the food good, the people enjoyable; and one feels as if he would willingly forego the worn-out tour of the continent for a sojourn in this fascinating peninsula." Irving was quite familiar with the Spain of his day, serving as American ambassador to the country from 1842 to 1846. In books such as *The Conquest of Grenada* and *Tales of the Alhambra*, however, he in fact dealt exclusively with the nation's history.

Some reviewers apparently found *In Spain* appealing in important part precisely because of the "present desolation" of the country. The *Presbyterian* writes, for example, "As Spain is now so prominently brought before the whole civilized world, intelligent men are desirous of understanding better its condition and the character of its people. They will find many things, touching land and people, pleasantly told them in this book."[12] The *Eclectic* puts it as follows: "The interest which is now felt in everything connected with Spain makes this book peculiarly opportune, for it is only a few years since Andersen was there, and he gives some suggestive glimpses of the actual condition of the Spanish people."[13] Such contemporary interest in Spain is probably attributable generally to the "Glorious Revolution" of 1868, which ended the reign of Isabella II, sending her into exile in France, and introduced an extended period of instability.[14] For Americans, however, it likely derived more specifically from the fraught relations between Cuba and Spain and their impact on the United States.[15]

Most reviewers disclose awareness that *In Spain* is more a work of the literary imagination than a historical or practical travel guide. For the writer at the *Portland Transcript*, as for many critics of this and the other travel books, Andersen's lively imagination and peculiar way of seeing things stand out:

> This is a charming book of travels in a southern land by a poet from the North, who invests the simplest objects with the wealth of his exuberant fancy. He selects for description the oddest things, and every page abounds in queer conceits. A big hoop skirt sign at Valencia seems to him its principal object of interest. He says "It is so large that it quite obscures everything else in Valencia," and the fun he pokes at it is delicious. He says the Spanish way of striking the castanets is not as we hear them at the North, where they sound like the rattling of wooden cups, but there is an expression in their music, and "the melody they yield is like a poem."[16]

Andersen was indeed fascinated by the play of castanets, which he heard in different cities in Spain, and returned to the subject in several parts of the work, devoting poems to their sensual music in the chapters on Murcia and Cartagena. The reviewer also takes note of the author's even more strongly sensuous, but far less appealing experience of bullfights: "He [Andersen] witnessed the horrors of a specially horrible bull-fight, and one wonders that the gentle poet had the heart to see and describe such things." Andersen in fact saw and described more than one such spectacle and was so appalled by the cruelty to the animals that the wonder is rather that he attended yet another one during his stay in Portugal. He relates that, under "Don Pedro" (King Pedro V?), the "barbarous and bloody" features still typical of bullfights in Spain had been eliminated in the neighboring country. However, it is clear from his description of the event he saw there that it was still barbaric and bloody enough.[17]

Many reviewers also responded to Andersen's imaginative faculty as displayed in the poetry of his prose and, to a lesser extent, the verse interludes and motti that adorn in varying degrees both his travel books and novels as well as his autobiography.[18] Perusal of the volumes of the Author's Edition apparently had a cumulative effect on the writer for the *Sunday-School Times*, an interdenominational journal of Philadelphia that was founded in 1859 in the wake of the revivalist movements of the day and ran until 1966:

> The more we see of the author's writings, the more enamored we become of their rich beauty. His very prose is poetry in ambush. This quality lends its peculiar flavor to these charming sketches of travels in Spain and Portugal. He is a most delightful travelling companion, imparting to the reader some of his own glowing enthusiasm, and by showing everything in the rich colors of his warm, cultivated imagination, gives one more accurate and impressive views of nature, art, and life in the places visited, than could be obtained by volumes of less sympathetic narrations.[19]

Zion's Herald adds, "Snatches of neat verses are scattered through the pages making it [the work?] Spanish in its lively mixture of grave and gay."[20]

By contrast, the reviewer for the *Christian Union* may himself have been one of those who, as he implies, have not read the first three volumes of the Author's Edition and are thus familiar only with Andersen's stories and tales: "This volume, no doubt, will prove to many their first introduction to the great Danish writer in another capacity than that of a teller of children's stories."[21] However, he continues in a similarly complementary way:

> As a traveler, we cannot, it is true, claim for him the entirely unapproached pre-eminence which, as a narrator, is his beyond a question. Yet much that is charming in his writings—his quaint simplicity, dry humor, love of childhood, of purity, of the picturesque—is here, as in his more familiar works; and nothing could be more vivid than his pictures of Spanish manners, nothing more genuine

than the zest with which he writes upon a new life, and which he imparts to his readers. Not seldom, too, he indulges us in the hitherto unwonted luxury of verse.

The reviewer's appreciation proceeds from a restrictive concept of narration and an imperfect knowledge of Andersen's work, but it is appreciation all the same.

The reviewer for the *Eclectic Magazine* cites its earlier extensive notice of *The Improvisatore* and *The Two Baronesses* as justification for now doing nothing more than announcing the successive volumes of the Author's Edition as they come out.[22] However, he in fact says more of substance than most:

> It would be difficult to meet a more agreeable companion in any walk of litera-
> ture than Andersen, but he is particularly pleasant as a traveller. His faculty of
> observation, his culture and sensibility, and his keen eye for the beautiful, give
> a peculiar flavor to the instruction he imparts; and the flowing, rambling style
> has all the ease and *abandon* of oral narrative. Few travellers have so much self-
> restraint as he—that is, few discriminate so nicely between what should be told
> and what can very well be left for the compilers of guide-books.[23]

An unusual capacity for observation, a unique, refined, and discerning personal culture, a poetic sensibility, and a seemingly conversational narrative style—all these features combined form an accurate composite of Andersen the man and the artist. What the reviewer means by "instruction" is uncertain, but since it evidently does not refer to the kind of information found in travel guides, it may well allude to that experiential knowledge imparted by authors who possess the peculiar attributes he ascribes to Andersen.

One finds similar sentiments in *Hours at Home* and the *Christian Standard*.[24] The former was a literary monthly and the first venture into magazine publishing by Charles Scribner and Company. It ran from 1865 until 1870, when, with a circulation of ten thousand, it was discontinued to make way for *Scribner's Monthly*.[25] The editor from 1869 to 1870 was Richard Watson Gilder (1844–1909), in his time a popular poet who formed a "triumvirate" of poet-editors with Thomas Bailey Aldrich (*New York Illustrated News*, *Every Saturday*, *Atlantic Monthly*) and James Russell Lowell (*Pioneer*, *Atlantic Monthly*, *North American Review*). As longtime editor of *Scribner's* and its successor, the *Century*, Gilder became a leading figure in the cultural and civic life of New York City.[26] The magazine published writers on the order of Josiah Gilbert Holland, Henry Theodore Tuckerman, and William Gilmore Simms as well as a considerable amount of review criticism. By the time the notice of *In Spain* appeared, the magazine had lost much of its original religious character but, as the review demonstrates, not all of it:

The fresh, unpretending, sympathetic, tenderly humorous style of Andersen's narrative makes this one of the most winsome books of travel we have seen in many a day. "One must stick to the truth if one wishes to be original as a writer of travels," says the author naively, and throughout it is evident that the pictures presented are faithful to the life, whether he portrays some grand old Spanish cathedral, or the geese that float in the basins in its shadow. But Andersen is essentially a poet, and it is the poetry of his descriptions that constitutes their chief and most enduring charm—while these as well as his other writings are characterized by a spirit of piety, as unobtrusive as it is utterly without affectation.[27]

Though sensing an ambient piety in the work, the reviewer places greater emphasis on the poetic nature of Andersen's prose. Like many others, he also expresses appreciation for the humor that frequently brightens Andersen's accounts of his travels.

Published in Cincinnati, the *Christian Standard* was between 1870 and 1900 one of the two most prominent publications of the Disciples of Christ during the (American) Restoration movement. Emerging from the Second Great Awakening of 1790 to 1840, the movement represented an attempt to unify all Christians in one body modeled after the church as perceived in the New Testament.[28] Still in publication today, the *Standard*'s contemporary influence is suggested by the fact that its circulation of eighty-four hundred in 1870 was one of the largest of all denominational papers.[29] Beyond its briefly stated opinion of *In Spain*, the review is noteworthy chiefly as one more instance of American critics' reading Andersen's "new" works with eyes conditioned by the increasingly consensual, if false, understanding of the stories and tales: "It is only necessary to see the name of Hans Christian Andersen, to secure interest in a book, especially on the part of *youthful* readers. This is a charming volume of travels by one who has eyes to see. And who knows how to describe what he sees as few are able to do. All our *young* readers will want to get hold of it; and if they do, let nothing be expected of them until the book is finished [emphasis added]."[30]

Although most of the responses to *In Spain* were quite positive, the work did not emerge from critical scrutiny entirely unscathed. Two of the magazines took umbrage at different technical aspects of the volume rather than Andersen's creation per se. The reviewer for the *Christian Union* writes, "But we have a complaint against this otherwise admirable edition—that it contains no preface or note from which one may judge the occasion of those leaves of travel, or even their date; nor is there an index or even a table of contents beyond a mere list of chapter-headings."[31] The edition offers no index, it is true, but *A Visit to Portugal* in actuality contains both a preface, outlining the background of the trip, and a rather detailed table of contents, which follows that of *In Spain* at the beginning of the book—another indication that the work somehow escaped the attention of most reviewers.

Another complaint was lodged in the *Southern Review*.[32] Founded two years after the Civil War, the magazine was edited or coedited for most of its twelve-year run by Albert Taylor Bledsoe (1809–1877), who, according to a recent biography, was one of the main originators of the "Lost Cause" mythology in the South.[33] Consequently, as Mott opines, the *Southern* is an almost incomparable source for an understanding of the post-bellum mind of the region.[34] Intended in part as an apologia of the Old South, the magazine was also envisaged as a representative of the current literary culture and scholarship of the region, publishing the work of historian William Hand Browne and poet and critic Paul Hamilton Hayne, among others, as well as a regular section of book notices. Mott writes that the magazine was "uncommonly good in its literary phases," although its excellence was not rewarded with more than fifteen hundred subscribers in 1870.[35]

The reviewer is somewhat disenchanted that the work(s) under consideration fail(s) to conform to his expectations of Andersen: "Those who take up this volume expecting to find in it the inimitable charm of the *Fairy Tales* by the same author will be disappointed; but those who are content to take it simply as a book of travels, will find it pleasant reading for a leisure hour."[36] However, the main object of his displeasure is the translator's work, of which he writes,

> The translation is disfigured by numerous inaccuracies of language; for example: "No one knew each other;" "It really seemed witchcraft to many an old Señora, who made the sign of the cross before placing their feet on the steps;" "But then we should have had to have given up Murcia;" "a couple of years;" "a couple of weeks;" "a couple of days;" etc., etc., etc. Whether the author or the translator is responsible for the following, we cannot say: "Now we were driving through wide, stagnant pools of water with unseen deep ruts; now, over stony slopes that protruded themselves into the road. We expected every moment to be upset, but that certainly did not happen; *we went so fast that it was only the centrifugal power that kept us right*."[37]

In most instances, one cannot quarrel with the reviewer, and he could have cited many another example as well. We have already seen evidence that, in his correspondence with Andersen, Horace Scudder lamented the difficulty he had in securing good, reliable translators for the Author's Edition. However, one can only wonder that such howlers apparently escaped the eye of the usually scrupulously conscientious editor, whose imperfect command of Danish could not have prevented him from recognizing and correcting bad English. The realist (?) writer is not enamored of the traveler's "every now and then breaking forth into song," much less of the English garb of the song.[38] Still, he can conclude with the words, "Spite of the translator, our feeling towards Andersen is that of the daughter of the Danish Consul at Malaga, 'a little girl not quite five years old:'—'Papa! A me mi gusta mucho Andersen, yo lo quiero mucho!'—Muchissimo [*sic*], nosotros."[39]

The only negative notice of *In Spain* itself appeared in the *Congregational Review*, which began its decade-long existence as the *Boston Review* in 1861.[40] The magazine did not prosper as a spirited and well-edited conservative organ of the church and fared no better when attempts to improve its fortunes, which included the name change and a move to Chicago, allegedly made it less brilliant as well as less controversialist—in 1870 it claimed a circulation of only one thousand.[41] The somber reviewer writes,

> We apprehend that many will be disappointed in this book, as we have been, the name and fame of the author raising expectations which are not realized. It is a very common-place account of the author's journey to the principal cities of the peninsula, quite lacking in the charms of incident and style which characterize other productions of his pen. Some valuable information is given, but little more than a good guide-book would furnish. Its descriptions no doubt are accurate, and to such as enjoy the small gossip about the company in a diligence and petty annoyance at hotels, it will afford some entertainment.

This writer's thwarted expectations led to a decidedly dimmer view of the work than that of the commentator for the *Southern.* Andersen would have been pleased that it was a distinct exception to the rule and, on a bad day, might have been glad that the magazine went out of business little over a year later.

The rule is demonstrated by a review published in the *Pittsburgh Weekly Gazette* that implicitly addresses a point of criticism made in the *Congregational Review.*[42] The *Gazette* was established in 1786 under the sponsorship of writer, jurist, and justice of the Pennsylvania Supreme Court Hugh Henry Brackenridge and printed, as one of its first major acts, the recently adopted Constitution of the United States.[43] Retaining its original Whig orientation until the 1850s, it contributed to the founding of a local chapter of the newly organized Republican Party and supported Lincoln in his bids for the presidency. In 1870, the year the notice of Andersen's book appeared, the paper registered a circulation of twelve thousand.[44] Following a number of mergers, it lives on today as the *Pittsburgh Post-Gazette.*

The reviewer focuses on the relationship of Andersen's travelogue to the typical vade mecum: "The contrast between the guide-book account of travel in Europe, and Mr. Andersen's racy sketches of men and things, in Spain and a visit to Portugal, never appeared so diverse to us before, and any one who will take the trouble to compare this work with one of the former, will be surprised at the difference."[45] Why the surprise? The writer offers familiar reasons in explanation: "The reading of this book charms and almost dazzles the mind with the wealth of description, and of the delightful episodes of travel. The peculiarities of the people, its grand old cities, and ancient structures, its wonderful history in bygone years, are all presented in the glowing imagery and prose-poetic style of this gifted writer." The sights themselves and their past seem to pique this individual's fancy, but in contrast to the critic for the *Congregational Review* and like several other commentators, he writes as if almost overwhelmed by the "racy" manner in which Andersen brings them to life.

A POET'S BAZAAR

A Poet's Bazaar was the fruit of a nine-month trip Andersen took through central and southern Europe and as far eastward as Constantinople (Istanbul) from October 1840 to July 1841. Originally published in 1842, the book is divided into sections according to the countries he visited along his route, from Germany to Italy, Greece, and Turkey and then via Austria back to Denmark. In the section on Germany, he dedicates chapters to his first experience of Franz Liszt in concert and his first train ride, among many other things. He dwells at great length and with obvious fondness on his time in Italy, recording Christmas Eve and Carnival in Rome as well as scenes in Naples, Sicily, and Malta. The Acropolis, Easter in Athens, the dervishes' dances and the celebration of Muhammad's birthday in Constantinople, and the *Burgtheater* in Vienna number among the many varied and often colorful sights and experiences he describes or relates, not to forget the original fairy tales he includes.

A *Poet's Bazaar* first appeared in English in Charles Beckwith Lohmeyer's translation of 1846. Apparently the only American review of the edition came out the same year in the *Spirit of the Times* (1831–1902), a New York weekly which, despite its misleading title, was reputedly the first and, for years, the leading sporting magazine in the country.[46] Aimed at an upper-class readership of sportsmen—its subtitle read *A Gazette of the Literary, Fashionable and Sporting World*—the paper had a nationwide reach and even maintained a sales agent in London for some time; it was said to have a circulation of forty thousand in 1856.[47] In addition to its principal subject matter, it included a considerable amount of humor and covered the theater and literature as well.

The writer emphasizes features of the work that are cited over and again in later review criticism:

Mr. [*sic*] Howitt has already made us familiar with the principal writings of this author, and with his romantic history. These volumes present us with sketches of his travels through Italy, Greece, Turkey, and Germany. It was probably from this book that Mr. Dickens took his idea of "Pictures in [*sic*] Italy."[48] Andersen describes as though he were selecting materials for pictures. Whatever he sees from his window, or in his walks through the streets, or from the deck of a vessel, or from a mountain top, that he notes down with accuracy, yet, with the taste of a true artist, for combination and contrast. He is one of the most poetical of tourists. His mind, when in a glow, receives impressions, like sealed wax, that remain firmly fixed there when the traveller's heat has passed away. Some of his chapters will remind the reader of Sterne. The most trifling incidents of travel take a sentimental or romantic turn from his manner of telling them. His active fancy is aided by his quick observation, and his pages are almost as full of human portraiture, as of nature's beauties.[49]

The reviewer focuses his (and his reader's) attention on Andersen's pronounced power of rapid yet accurate observation of people and nature as well as his ability to combine and contrast, i.e., to compose his observations in a unique, poetically picturesque manner. He reveals his own Romantic proclivities most clearly in his characterization of Andersen's creative procedure as the reception of impressions in something like warm sealing wax that grows firm upon cooling, which is strongly reminiscent of Wordsworth's notion of poetic creation. Andersen's reflections on these impressions "in tranquility," partly on the basis of notes taken during his journey, is certainly "sentimental," or Sternesque, at least in their apparently random sequence, united, as they are, principally by temporal progression. Following extensive excerpts from the text—the review covers nearly two compactly printed columns—the reviewer writes,

We have quoted enough to give an idea of these [three] volumes, and it is only by quotations that their character can be made known. In all his descriptions and reflections the poetic faculty of the author predominates. He is the Byron of prose, but, with the exception, that, with the utmost passionate ardour of feeling, with thoughts that rush upon him too thick and fast for expression, his views are always elevated and pious. He has much of Byron's poetic genius, but none of his misanthropy.[50]

According to the reviewer, the poetic nature of Andersen's prose reveals itself not least of all in the impossibility of capturing its essence in discursive language. Altering and foreshortening his earlier portrayal of Andersen's poetics, he expresses a preference for the author's lofty piety and love of man over the English poet's skepticism, though these features in fact occupy the background, rather than the foreground of the *Bazaar*.

The work appeared as volume 9 of the Author's Edition in 1871 and, this time around, met with numerous reviews, the first of which came out in the *New-York Tribune*.[51] Established in 1841, the *Tribune* had since ascended to a prominent position among American newspapers. It was noted for its opposition to slavery, its conciliatory position on Reconstruction, and, soon, for its support of founder and longtime editor Horace Greeley's candidacy for the presidency in his campaign against Ulysses S. Grant in the elections of 1872. At the same time, it had gained great respect for its book reviewing, at different times boasting critics such as Margaret Fuller, George Ripley, and Bayard Taylor.[52]

In this instance, the review is relatively brief but pointed, following a thumbnail description of the volume's contents with the words,

> [the book] forms a delightful mélange of egotism, frankness, garrulity, keen observation, and overflowing kindliness of heart characteristic of the author. His experiences in Italy, especially in Rome, are related with charming simplicity, and surpass in interest most of the tourists' records in that land of artistic and antiquarian enticements. The lapse of years has not impaired the freshness of his descriptions, which afford a better introduction to the curiosities of European travel than most of the subsequent guide-books.[53]

The notice suggests that the writer had a good memory and the book a certain continuity—nothing in the edition indicates that it is a reissue—also that the work continues to offer the reader an immediacy of experience that flows only from the pen of a traveler who is also a poet.

Other reviews of *A Poet's Bazaar* more clearly demonstrate that the poetic quality of the work was not lost, or wasted, on critics during an emerging period of "no-nonsense" criticism. One of these was published in New York's *Evening Post*, which Alexander Hamilton founded in 1801 to espouse the Federalist cause and which currently claims the distinction of being the nation's longest continuously running daily newspaper.[54] Over the course of the nineteenth century, while shifting allegiance from the Federalist and Democratic parties to the latter's Free-Soil and Republican rivals, the *Post* pursued a liberal agenda of support for unions and abolition that earned the respect of English philosopher and political economist John Stuart Mill.[55] Under the general editorship of poet William Cullen Bryant since 1829, the paper also enjoyed a reputation for literary taste and overall refinement. With poet and former editor of the *Southern Literary Messenger* John Reuben Thompson as literary editor, the *Post* entered the 1870s with its stature as one of the most distinguished newspapers in the United States firmly intact, though it had an unremarkable daily circulation of roughly eighty-five hundred.[56]

Andersen's reviewer, if not a poet himself, was apparently someone conversant with the vocabulary and at least one notion of the nature of poetry:

> There is not one page of verse in this pretty volume, though the title gives promise of an olio of song, and its author is apt to poetic measures. "A Poet's Bazaar" is an idealized and sublimated guide-book to Austria, Italy, Greece and the Grecian Archipelago; a guide-book full of unrhymed poetry, pleasant egotism, engaging simplicity, childish fancies, minute observation and delightful good-humor—in a word, a book of European travel by Hans Christian Andersen. There is no need to say more of it.[57]

An "idealized and sublimated guide-book"—with these words and those that immediately follow, the reviewer betrays a Romantic temperament, for in his view the journey on which Andersen takes the reader goes beyond the objectively given into the realm of essential reality, a reality made experiential through its artistic expression. In his closing words, he picks up a thread spun at the very beginning: "Every reader of the Danish novelist will anticipate how charmingly he writes of the classic Mediterranean, and with what stories and legends he diversifies the journey through Greece and the sail down the Bosphorus." This reviewer, perhaps more so than others, appears to have taken the title of *A Poet's Bazaar* at what one might call its "face metaphorical value," evincing admiration for both the poetic character of the work and the great wealth of its diverse contents.

The reviewer for the *Christian Union*, quite mindful of the poetry of the *Bazaar*, seeks to characterize it by comparing and contrasting it with already well-known writings:

> These pictures have little in common with that work of the German humorist which bears the same name, save in the pensive interest which they inspire. Hans Andersen is the embodiment of sweetness and light, and these sketches of wanderings through Germany, Italy, Greece and the Orient are rather poems than narrative. All is dreamy, and far off, and strange. It is like the excursion of a lotos-eater. You catch the color of the sky, the perfume of ever new fields, the glow of sunlight on street and tower. All human life is joyous, the most ordinary existence takes an unaccustomed gladness, and one seems to float on and on in an endless reverie. This delicious glamour gives to the volume an irresistible attraction. We know of no book recently published that is more admirably adapted for Summer-day reading at sea-side or on mountain slope.[58]

The "German humorist" cited by this Romantic was Heinrich Heine, to whose unique style we had occasion to refer in chapter 2. The comparison to the "excursion of a lotos-eater" alludes to Tennyson's poem "The Lotos-Eaters," of 1832, and/or, of course, to the related incident in Homer's *Odyssey*.

One suspects that the reviewer for the *Portland Transcript* read the work as an art lover: "The reader is taken first to Germany, where he is introduced to the best works of art in Munich and Nuremberg, and the finest scenery of the Tyrol; thence to Italy, over the Appenines [*sic*] to Rome, where the poetic enthusiasm of the author finds vent over its art-wonders and beauties."[59] Like the writer for the *Spirit of the Times*, however, the reviewer also has a fine sense for Andersen's characteristic way of seeing, selecting, and presenting the individuals and sights that availed themselves to him along his journey: "[A]nd his quiet humor sets before us pictures Rome never dreamed of, of the most varied and comical character. His facility and fondness for noting the phases of strange people and places, lend a peculiar charm to his descriptions, which abound in quaint and original touches of wit and fancy."

Reviews of a similar tenor appeared in a number of other newspapers. The writer for the *Bangor Daily Whig & Courier* (1834–1900), for example, recognizes "our old friend of the nursery in a new character, that of a tourist, and yet every page, every line has the unmistakable stamp of Hans Christian Andersen upon it, in the simple, unaffected, yet always poetical descriptions of what nobody else thinks it worth their while to write about, but which his magical pen invests with a strange and beautiful fascination."[60] Much in the manner of the *Spirit of the Times* twenty-five years earlier, the San Francisco *Daily Evening Bulletin* writes that the work

> consists of a series of word-pictures of travel in Germany, Italy, Greece, and the Orient, and has the usual characteristics of its author. A bit of graphic description, a rapid sketch of a scene in character, a little touch of sentiment, a spice of quiet satire—such are the leading features of these papers, as of all the writings of the great Danish story-teller. When he traveled he looked about him with the eye of an artist, and noted everything that would be effective in a sketch, or useful as a study. Few writers have so industriously utilized their observations and reflections. The result in the volume before us is a literary mosaic of travel.[61]

The critic for Montpelier's *Vermont Watchman & State Journal* (1836–1883) read the book in a similar fashion: "'A Poet's Bazaar' is full of those odd fancies and curious sketches of people, manners, and customs, which make Andersen's books such racy reading. There is nothing of the pedantic traveller or tiresome copyist in Andersen. He is a chatty, shrewd, gossiping writer, who has an unfailing interest in every scrap of humanity. The genius that can make a shirt collar talk, finds unending material in his travels."[62]

One of the longest and most interesting reviews of the *Bazaar* appeared in the *Overland Monthly*, a magazine based in San Francisco and edited for the first two years of its existence by Bret Harte.[63] Best known for his short fiction about the California Gold Rush, Harte published some of his own work in the magazine as well as pieces by Mark Twain and numerous lesser, but then well-known writers, making it something of a western *Atlantic Monthly* or *Lippincott's*. For this, according to Mott, he was rewarded with a circulation that quickly rose to ten thousand.[64]

The reviewer detects a confessional quality in the *Bazaar*:

> We do not at present recall a writer who confides in the public to so great an extent as Andersen. *The Story of His Life* [*sic*] is a heart-confession that keeps no secret from the world. *A Poet's Bazaar* is a supplement to that confession, as though the poet had not been explicit enough in the story, and hastened, therefore, to elaborate detail. We confess the charm of this ingenuous trust in humanity. The sincerity of the author is stamped upon every page, and few men are so keenly observant and so sympathetic.[65]

Later in the review, the writer returns to Andersen's autobiography, revealing a literal reading of the book in his defense of the Dane from his critics, who "are not satisfied with ill-using his books, but seem to take malicious pleasure in ridiculing every act and misinterpreting every motive of the man who has done more for the glory of Denmark, than any other of the score of Danes whose fame has spread beyond the border of their little kingdom."[66]

In the meantime, the reviewer foregrounds the "highly colored, and exquisitely finished" depictions of Andersen's journey, which are both "extremely poetical" and "musical."[67] As examples, he cites passages describing two very different kinds of concerts, the first set in a Viennese *Volksgarten* where Johann Strauss appears as the "heart" of the orchestra, providing entertainment for the ladies and gentlemen strolling about and conversing there. Immediately thereupon, he quotes lines in which Andersen "discourses of another sort of concert, in which he took an active part": "'A real Danish toothache is not to be compared to an Italian one. Pain played on the keys of my teeth as if it were a Liszt or a Thalberg. Sometimes it rumbled in the foreground, and then anon in the background—as when two martial bands answer each other—whilst a large front-tooth sang the *prima-donna's* part, with all the trills, *roulades*, and cadences of torture.'"[68] Drawn from different parts of the book, these "musical events," if loosely related in content, are totally divergent in tone and intent. By closely juxtaposing them, the reviewer is able to underscore the great variety of the work while at the same time exploiting reader interest in contemporary cultural eminences and delivering (yet another) personal confession of a singular but all too meaningful kind. He concludes by citing passages in which Andersen expresses mixed dread and joy on returning to the land of both his critics and his loved ones.

A number of reviewers candidly confess their inability to name Andersen's equal or to articulate the uniqueness of his work. One of these is the critic for Philadelphia's *Sunday-School Times*, who writes, "The counterpart of this celebrated Dane can scarcely be found among living writers. There may be some who approach him as poet, traveller, and descriptive writer,—and perhaps Bayard Taylor's genius is nearest like his,—but in any mention there must be a wide distance before we reach that child-like simplicity, we had almost said artlessness, which is the pre-eminent characterizing charm of Andersen's style."[69] The writer's admittedly imprecise comparison of Andersen and Bayard Taylor is not fortuitous. The American is now remembered principally for what was once considered the finest translation of Goethe's *Faust* in English. In his time, however, he was a popular author of novels, plays, and criticism who wrote of his own journey abroad in *Northern Travel: Summer and Winter Pictures; Sweden, Denmark, and Lapland*, in which he relates a conversation he had with Andersen in Copenhagen.[70] If unable to think of a contemporary writer truly comparable to Andersen, apparently the Andersen of the fairy tales, the reviewer finds words for the *Bazaar* that bring the blossoms and fruit of the lotus to mind: "The present sketches are well named 'pictures.' They are warm in coloring, and soft and melting as Italian skies. Imagination and fact in them are wedded with wonderfully pleasing effects."[71]

The notice in *Harper's New Monthly Magazine* initially raises expectations of a favorable opinion: "We find Hans Christian Andersen's *Poet's Bazaar* a charming series of 'pictures of travel in Germany, Italy, Greece, and the Orient.' But the charm is indescribable."[72] However, the writer views the *je ne sais quoi* he senses in Andersen's work with a certain ambivalence that might have caused the hypersensitive Dane's eyes to narrow, had he had the misfortune of reading the review:

> [A]nd we are not particularly surprised to find some very appreciative readers pronounce it [the work] dull.[73] In truth, one either likes Hans Christian Andersen's writings without knowing why, or he finds it difficult to understand why any one should like them. It is as impossible to interpret to another the charm of his pen as it is to explain the listless enjoyment of resting on the bosom of a quiet river in the still twilight of a summer's eve.

A plea of ineffability is also found in a review that appeared in *Wood's Household Magazine*.[74] Located first in Newburgh, New York, and then in New York City, *Wood's* ran from 1867 to 1881 and competed successfully for several years with other "home" magazines like *Harper's Bazaar*, attaining a circulation of 115,000 in 1872.[75] The reviewer writes, for example, "We cannot describe the book—there is nothing to which we can compare it; it stands by itself, a collection of beautiful pictures of beautiful things, with not a common thought or conception in a single line."[76] However, these words appear at the end of the notice and are belied by those that precede them:

The book is well named, for though it contains no engravings or illustrations, yet it is full of "Pictures," beautiful, touching, quaint, humorous pictures, such as only Anderson's [*sic*] wonderful imagination can paint. It is delightful to read—pick it up at any time, open it where you will, and entertainment is always found. Its ideas are so original, so poetical, so pleasing, one grows enthusiastic as he reads, and yet the very prettiness of the book is in its simplicity, its artless manner of narrating. And then Anderson [*sic*] has a way of seeing things differently from any one else. It is natural to him, and requires no effort; his sense of the ludicrous is keen, and he excels in description, and though his portrayals may not be always accurate, yet they are most vivid, and his style most refreshing; and you bless him rather than fault-find, for allowing his imagination to run away with him, inasmuch as it accomplishes such happy results.

The varied characterization of the pictures, the attributes of imaginativeness, originality, poeticality, artlessness, uniqueness of perspective, a keen sense of the ludicrous, and excellence of description—all these features in reality say a great deal about the *Bazaar* and, indeed, summarize much of what other reviewers have to say about the book.

PICTURES OF TRAVEL

Pictures of Travel was the tenth and final volume of the Author's Edition, appearing in summer 1871. The book contains four different texts, which were originally published in three different decades. *Rambles in the Hartz Mountains*, Andersen's first travelogue, issued from a tour of more than five weeks' duration in May and June 1831, coming out later in the same year to a reasonably friendly welcome.[77] His trip to Sweden from mid-May to mid-August 1849 led to the publication of *In Sweden* two years later, which, by contrast, registered disappointing sales.[78] Given the great favor that Charles Dickens enjoyed in the United States, it is small wonder that Horace Scudder included *A Visit at Charles Dickens's House* in the volume. The result of a five-week-long stay with the English author and his family in 1857, the sketch first came out in a series of articles published in a Danish newspaper in early 1860 and only later in book form.[79] Trips through Germany and Switzerland in 1858 and 1860, respectively, inspired the three sketches that comprise *In Switzerland*, which were originally brought out separately in 1858, 1860, and 1861.[80]

The twenty notices of *Pictures of Travel* issued in American periodicals are, in aggregate, the shortest and least illuminating of all those written in response to the travel books. Even the *Portland Transcript*, which typically offered sensible to insightful comments on Andersen's works, printed a rather generic notice.[81] One wonders whether, after greeting the nine earlier volumes of the Author's Edition in the short space of around two years, critics experienced a certain "Andersen-fatigue."

In any event, it is a shame that they did not better familiarize their readers with these writings, especially the *Rambles* and *In Sweden*. The author's record of his journey through northern and central Germany to what is now part of the Czech Republic is the spirited revelation of an intelligent and thoughtful, sensitive, and observant young man as he experiences a foreign but respected natural and cultural landscape for the first time, through eyes preconditioned by reading but open to living reality. Replete with people, places, nature, poetry, dreams, sagas, whimsy, and reflections on life, death, religion, and much else, the book mirrors Andersen's present and suggests much that was still to come. Written some twenty years later, *In Sweden* is, by contrast, a more sober work by a mature, widely celebrated author in his middle years. Andersen himself called it perhaps the most carefully written of all his works.[82] Not unlike its predecessor in content, numerous cities, landscapes, and events pass in review. However, its narrator is less self-consciously omnipresent, and it unfolds less linearly, creating space for entire fairy tales and "Poetry's California" ("Poesiens Californien"), the final chapter, in which Andersen expresses his notion of the coming union of poesy and science.[83]

One of the most informative reviews of *Pictures of Travel* appeared in the *College Courant*, a weekly that was published at Yale from 1867 to 1874 and was merged, together with several other periodicals, in the *New England Journal of Education* in 1875.[84] The reason for its participation in the merger is perhaps suggested by the editor's statement to *Rowell's* in 1871 that he objected to giving its circulation.[85] The writer first gives an overview of the contents of the book, proceeding from its position in the Author's Edition:

> The last of these [writings], the work before us, is published for the first time in America, and is a fit companion of the other volumes. The contents are "Rambles in the Hartz Mountains," "Pictures of Sweden" [*sic*], "In Switzerland," and "A Visit at Charles Dickens' [*sic*] House.["] The first three of these parts are respectively descriptive of his [Andersen's] own personal observations in the romantic mountains of Germany, and in the countries of Vasa and Tell, in the latter of which, ten years ago, he witnessed the Passion-play, about which so much has been written of late, at Oberammergau.[86] The last part is a narrative of a visit he made to Charles Dickens at his country seat [*sic*], Gadshill, just at the time of the death of the celebrated playwright and humorist, Douglas Jerold. In this sketch the dramatic performances given by Dickens, Wilkie Collins, the editor of "Punch," Mark Lemon, and others, for the benefit of Jerold's widow, are described.[87]

The reviewer was correct in his assertion that the volume, or, more to the point, the works in it, had been published for the first time in the United States (never mind his geographical placement of Oberammergau). However, he appears to have been unaware that English editions of the first two works had come out in the 1840s and 1850s and that *In Sweden* had indeed been reviewed in this country, which attests yet again to the often observed lack of continuity between the first and third phases of Andersen's American reception. The reviewer then offers his assessment of the book:

> In this department of literature, the author has shown himself as much at home as in those which have made him famous, which is bestowing high praise. His talents appear to be adapted to every kind of work, and his versatility equal to every emergency. In this volume there is a freshness and vivacity which are seldom found now-a-days in books of travel. The sketches are lively, the observations shrewd, the descriptions picturesque, and the entire contents captivating. There is an abundance of humor, a great variety of historical reminiscences, anecdotes of eminent men, and incidents of almost every character. The book is full of fine illustrations of the peculiar genius of Andersen.

The notice could have been written with equal accuracy about any of the other travel books, but despite its lack of tailoring to the volume under examination it is one with which Andersen could have been well satisfied.

Some of the more insightful comments on *Pictures of Travel* appeared in nominally religious magazines, though the remarks were not all of a religious nature. The *Churchman*, whose circulation had swollen to nine thousand since the previous year, published a most appreciative response:

> We do not remember ever having read a more charming book of travels than this. Andersen is a true poet, and sees, as common men do not, the life and meaning of the great world. It is a rare treat to know what he thinks of the objects long since worn threadbare by the descriptions of ordinary tourists; for, whatever picture he deigns to draw for us, is sure to be fresh and full of genius. In going through this volume, we were particularly struck with the vein of Christian earnestness which pervades it. The description of the Passion play at Oberammergau, evinces a calmness of judgment and a nicety of discrimination, which no one would be likely to have, who had not thought much of the meaning of the life of our Lord. Not every one, "it is often said," is fitted to appreciate the benefit to be derived from travel. But it is just as true that only very few are competent to write a book of travels worth reading, and among those few, Andersen stands first of those living.[88]

Andersen begins "The Celebration at Oberammergau" as follows: "Never shall I forget the Passion-play at Oberammergau, so completely did it surpass all my expectation. I could not think of it beforehand without being scandalized at the idea of seeing Jesus acted on the stage; but as it here took place, in religious faith, full of fervor, and with a beauty quite unimagined, all offense was taken away, and one found himself taken possession of,—he came into sympathy with it and was quite borne along."[89] Andersen's relationship to Christianity remains a subject of debate, but his deep respect for Christ and his influence is beyond doubt.[90]

The *Christian Union* sensed a different tone in the texts than its sister publications: "The volume's 'Pictures,' unlike those of its predecessors [in the Author's Edition] are in northerly or midland countries, in Tyrol, Switzerland, the Harz Mountains, Sweden and England. The main characteristics of the author cling to the sketches but the tone is somewhat subdued, the humor less sparkling, and frequent; and the interlinking of story with narration comes seldom, though always sweetly when the author is in the mood for it."[91] However, the *Union*, too, highlights Andersen's experience of the Passion play and, more so than the *College Courant* and the *Churchman*, relates it to the present: "In Tyrol, Andersen saw the famous Oberammergau passion play, that has so greatly interested tourists the present year, and his testimony of its serious and earnest conduct is of weight as showing that the current newspaper eulogy of the performance is not without critical justification."

The reviewer for the *Providence Evening Press* would appear to detect a broadly moral, if not religious spirit in the *Pictures*: "In this volume we are wafted along easily from point to point, seeing with Andersen's eyes and feeling with his soul, and at the close of the volume the reader feels better than when he commenced it. *Wild speculations, startling incidents and surprises are not in the vein of the author*, but in simplicity of heart, free from all guile, he tells the charming story of his travels. He is an author to be reread for there is a mine of wealth in his writing" [emphasis added].[92] One is probably safe in suspecting that Andersen's writing serves here as a foil for sensationalist literature.

The *North American and United States Gazette* touches on some of the same points as the publications previously discussed but gives them greater detail and vividness:

There is the same touching of salient features, the same play of fancy and warmth of feeling in these lighter studies that gave life, warmth and color to the Improvisatore and Bazaar. They are charming; not only in that they introduce the details of life and manners and homely incidents that too many writers ignore, nor not only that little dramas are continually enacted in them and sparkling stories found without promise. There are those reliefs and lures. And there is also a genial and kindly spirit beaming from the descriptions; a lambent humor lighting what is dull, and a poetic fancy irradiating what is dark, so that the reader seems to see through into the core of the matter, and to have a perfect and sympathetic response. Andersen has his fame and a deserved one as a writer for children. The qualities needed for that excellence are an armory for the work discharged in this; and we very much doubt whether so much pleasure will be drawn from the more pretentious compositions, as from this that, without any pretence or apparent labor, distils a perpetual bouquet of fragrance. It is captivating; and we are glad that Andersen has now been naturalized.[93]

Like many or most reviewers of this and other collections of Andersen's works, the writer casts a broad net in order to capture the most striking, yet typical features of the texts under scrutiny—an understandable, perhaps necessary procedure in view of the plethora and diversity of incident in the works and the comparatively meager space allotted book notices in many American periodicals of the nineteenth century. Catch them he does, however, from the seemingly minor but telling particular, to the stories that appear unexpectedly midstream in the narrative, to the gentle humor and poetic imagination that allow the reader to penetrate to the heart of things with a commensurate, implicitly emotional, response. Perhaps he has the apparently desultory, episodic nature of the travelogues in mind when he deems the stories and tales a workshop for them and compares them favorably to the novels.

Like several of his cohorts, the reviewer for the *Trenton State Gazette* of Trenton, New Jersey, sought to come at Andersen by way of comparison:

Hans Christian Andersen has a world wide reputation as one of the most charming and interesting of writers, and in the work before us he surpasses himself. It consists of a truly delightful series of sketches of travel in Sweden; among the Hartz mountains, famous for their [weird] and mysterious associations, and in that land of historic interest and natural magnificen[ce], Switzerland. They resemble, in their genial beauty of description and gossipy humor, the famous sketches of Washington Irving, and are, in many respects, fully the equal of the fascinating pen penciling of "Geoffrey Crayon."[94]

Considering Irving's popularity among his countrymen and the pride they took in his international acclaim, especially in usually supercilious England, the reviewer's favorable comparison of *Pictures of Travel* to *The Sketch Book* is praise indeed.

The reviewer would seem to have had a particular interest in the "weirdness" and mystery associated with the Harz and other parts of Germany:

The usually rather monotonous routine of descriptions of travel, are constantly varied by pleasant stories, and legends, and traditions of the places he visited. Many strange and beautiful stories connected with the superstitions that for centuries have been connected with the wild and lonely Hartz mountains [*sic*], and of the caves, islands, ancient ruins, and other interesting characteristics of the home of the Goths, are related in these charming pages. The work concludes with a deeply interesting account of a visit to the house of Charles Dickens.

One wonders what dusky images of the Harz and its homeland circled in the mind of the critic, predisposing him to an appreciation of Andersen's account. Perhaps they alighted from the famous Walpurgis Night scenes in the first part of Goethe's *Faust*, perhaps from the variously "Gothic" fiction of writers from Horace Walpole and E. T. A. Hoffmann to Mary Shelley and Poe.

A brief review in the *Capital* offers evidence of why *Pictures of Travel* might have been of particular interest to Americans in 1871.[95] The scant information about the weekly reveals that it ran from March 12 of that year to, in all likelihood, sometime in 1888, when the Capital Publishing Company shuttered its doors.[96] Published in Washington, DC, the paper was edited by Donn Piatt, who, according to a biography subtitled *Gadfly of the Gilded Age*, was a polymath, active at different times as a diplomat, historian, journalist, lawyer, judge, lobbyist, and politician as well as a novelist, playwright, and poet.[97] As editor of the *Capital*, Piatt gained nationwide fame for his wit and sharp criticism of President Grant and Congress, claiming to have eight thousand subscribers in 1871.[98] His interest in literature is reflected by the fact that on page 1 of the issue in which the notice of Andersen's *Pictures* appeared, more than five of the eight columns are devoted to poetry, fiction, and reviews.

The objective yet friendly tenor of the critique may lead one to believe that it was written by someone other than the frequently caustic Piatt:

> Mssrs. Hurd & Houghton, who are the recognized American publishers of the works of the charming old story-teller of Denmark, and have heretofore produced in "The Improvisatore," "A Poet's Bazaar," etc., in the same style as the present beautiful volume, which contains the record of his travels in Sweden, among the Hartz Mountains and in Switzerland, together with a sketch of his visit at the house of Charles Dickens—the latter first translated and published, we believe, since the English novelist's death. This visit to Dickens is one of the pleasantest chapters indeed in the volume, and, while it exhibits the popular English writer in some of his most attractive and lovable aspects, it shows at the same time the charming characteristics—not forgetting that of a delightful egotism—of the author. The main part of the volume, devoted to "Rambles among the Hartz Mountains," "Pictures of Sweden," and a brief chapter "In Switzerland," are full of sad interest of incident, persons, legends, stories, &c., as related with the old romancer's vivacity and poetry of expression, make very enjoyable reading.[99]

The review would have benefited from more careful proofreading—it is reproduced exactly as printed, incomplete sentence, faulty grammar, and all.

And it is anyone's guess what features of the texts inspired their characterization as "sad interest of incident," whatever that phrase may have meant to the reviewer. In any event, there is no mistaking his admiration for Andersen or overweening interest in Dickens, which comes as little surprise in view of the fact that the most popular author of the age had died only a year and a half prior to publication of the notice.

Relative commonplaces in Andersen criticism and a conjecture of some significance are found in a review of *Pictures of Travel* that appeared in *Scribner's Monthly* in 1872.[100] The magazine was a quality publication that absorbed three others—*Hours at Home, Putnam's,* and Horace Scudder's *Riverside Magazine for Young People*—on or soon after its founding in 1870.[101] It was edited by Josiah Gilbert Holland, himself a popular poet and novelist who printed some of his own work in the magazine. However, *Scribner's* also published many writers of equal or greater stature, including Hjalmar Hjorth Boyesen, Joel Chandler Harris, Bret Harte, Helen Hunt Jackson, Henry James, and—Hans Christian Andersen, three of whose stories and tales as well as *Lucky Peer* appeared between its covers. In only its second year of existence, the publication claimed a circulation of fifty-five thousand.[102]

Of the volume under consideration, the reviewer writes, "It is marked by all the pleasing characteristics of this popular author, his childish simplicity, his quick and minute observation, his amusing—never offensive—egotism, and his ready recognition of the poetic element in life wherever he may wander."[103] Here, we find yet another of the matter-of-fact, even favorable references to Andersen's vanity made in the reviews of his travelogues, a feature which, as we shall see, is cited repeatedly and judged variously in notices of the autobiography, which had come out in spring 1871. At this point, the reviewer observes more generally, "Andersen's acceptance is very wide, in northern Europe his name is a household word, and in England he is welcome in all circles; but it may be doubted whether, after all, he has not a larger number of admirers in America than in any other land, much of which is due to the intelligent zeal of his American publishers." There is no way to verify the writer's surmise of Andersen's relative popularity in the United States and other countries, but there is certainly reason to believe that it was more than an expression of cultural patriotism, though it was surely that.

As early as 1833, the United States published around three times as many newspapers as England or France and, by 1870, was home to more than one-third of all the papers in the world.[104] In 1871, an English writer for the *British Quarterly Review* informed his countrymen that "America is the classic soil of newspapers; everybody is reading; literature is permeating everywhere; publicity is sought for every interest and every order; no political party, no religious sect, no theological school, no literary or benevolent association, is without its particular organ; there is a universality of print."[105] Tebbel offers perhaps the most decisive reason for this circumstance: "America's drive toward universal literacy . . . produced in the 1840s the largest reading audience anyone had ever seen."[106] A recent study of the history of world literacy shows that the United States ranked second only to the Netherlands in 1880.[107] Moreover, the total population of the United States surpassed that of England during the 1830s and that of the entire United Kingdom (England, Wales, Scotland, and present-day Northern Ireland) during the 1850s, whereafter the gap only continued to widen.[108]

British magazines long dominated their American counterparts, in influence if, over the course of the nineteenth century, not necessarily in number.[109] Mott writes, "It is not easy to realize now how large an American public the great English periodicals had before the Civil War. The *Edinburgh Review* was much more widely read in the United States than the *North American*," and the leading British magazines continued to be reprinted in New York for at least two decades after the end of the conflict.[110] Nonetheless, as early as the 1830s the pirating, or unremunerated reprinting of material, initially the province of American magazine editors, had become mutual, and English participation in the practice only increased.[111] Over the following decades, some American periodicals introduced English editions, and in 1873, *Scribner's* began what has been called an invasion of the mother country by the American illustrated magazine.[112]

In an attempt to explain the predominantly general character of the American book publishing industry, Hellmut Lehmann-Haupt writes, "It can be said that in a country where the periodical press dominated the scene in chronological and functional priority, the publication of books was already in itself a form of specialization."[113] Despite the dominance of periodicals, however, the number of book publishers in the United States grew exponentially over the first half of the nineteenth century, totaling more than four hundred in 1859.[114] A contemporary wrote in 1855 that the country had already far surpassed England in book sales.[115] If true, this could happen in important part because the American book market was large and heterogeneous while its British counterpart was small and homogeneous.[116]

We have already seen abundant evidence that American periodicals and books played a prominent role in the dissemination of Andersen's works and Andersen criticism in the United States and will see much more of the same in the following chapters. Separate studies will also show that the American press regularly reported on Andersen's life and activities, devoted extensive attention to his death, and covered his influence on American artists and artisans as well as certain civic projects. In view of these facts, and especially given the size of a reading public that for much of the nineteenth century still read British as well as American publications, one may well be willing to accord the *Scribner* reviewer's speculation concerning the relative popularity of Andersen at home and abroad a high degree of probability.

In contrast to the novels (as well as the autobiography and the fairy tales), the earliest editions of Andersen's travel books elicited next to no reviews in the United States. However, the number that met the works as published in the Author's Edition more than compensated for the earlier neglect, at least numerically. They appeared in some of the same prominent periodicals as those of the novels, including the *Christian Union* and *Harper's New Monthly Magazine.* However, they also found a place in similarly distinguished ones such as the New York *Evening Post*, the *New-York Tribune*, the *Overland Monthly*, *Scribner's Monthly*, and the *Southern Review*. None of the reviews was signed, and available information leaves a shroud of mystery over critics' identities. However, editors and possible reviewers include figures of contemporary repute such as Albert Taylor Bledsoe, Richard Watson Gilder, Josiah Gilbert Holland, Donn Piatt, and John Reuben Thompson.

Critics tended to consider the travel books on their own merits rather than to compare them with each other, as was the case with the novels. A few rendered mixed verdicts, but *In Spain* was the only work to receive a largely negative commentary. On the whole, the travelogues experienced greater approval than did the novels. It was in a notice of *Pictures of Travel* that the reviewer expressed delight that Andersen "has now been naturalized."[117] All the same, it is evident from several of these reviews that Andersen's naturalization was not uniformly sponsored by *Pictures* and its counterparts. One critic denies him the "entirely unapproached pre-eminence" as a "traveler" that he enjoys as a writer of fairy tales, though he finds much of what is charming in these in the books of travel as well, an opinion that several other reviewers share.[118]

Andersen's excursions into the history of the countries he visited formed a major source of interest for commentators in a history-challenged nation whose citizens had just begun to travel abroad in comparatively significant numbers. Spain, for example, attracted particular attention for the Romantic colorfulness of its past and the ways in which that past imbued its equally colorful present. Germany, with its Harz Mountains, on the other hand, sparked interest through the equally Romantic but darkly mysterious "weirdness" of legendary times gone by. All the same, several reviewers commented on the humor displayed in the travel books, which at times betrays a satiric tinge.[119]

Morality and religion do not figure prominently in the notices of the travel books, but they are certainly present in some of them. In one, we read of opinions "elevated and pious" and in another more explicitly of "Christian earnestness."[120] Indeed, some reviewers make a point to mention Andersen's attendance at, and description of the Passion Play in Oberammergau.[121] That one of them points to the absence of "wild speculations, startling incidents and surprises" in *Pictures of Travel* bespeaks an appreciation that should likely be understood as an oblique criticism of sensationalism.[122]

What appealed to reviewers above all else, however, was the same aspect of Andersen's art that essentially stood above criticism in notices of the novels: his genial ability to describe, often, little noticed but characteristic features of nature, people, and events in a manner that was at once visually acute and highly poetic, an ability that became a veritable leitmotif in reviews of the travel books. Little less appreciated were the opulent richness of the works, captured in the title of *A Poet's Bazaar*, and the liveliness, or "raciness," of Andersen's style. Several writers attempt to come by Andersen as an artist by drawing parallels between him and allegedly similar writers such as Washington Irving and Bayard Taylor, Byron and Wordsworth, Heine and Tennyson. However, one must rely heavily on quotations from the text, and others have to take recourse to pleas of ineffability.[123]

NOTES

1. Jens Andersen, *Hans Christian Andersen: A New Life*, trans. Tiina Nunnally (New York, Woodstock, and London: Overlook Duckworth, 2005), 482.

2. See, for example, Bo Grønbech, *H. C. Andersen: Levnedsløb-Digtning-Personlighed* (Copenhagen: Nyt Nordisk Forlag Arnold Busck, 1971), 171, 180, and Paul Binding, *Hans Christian Andersen: European Witness* (New Haven, CT: Yale University Press, 2014), 193. For more detailed commentary see Henrik Schovsbo, "Modtagelsen," in *I Spanien*, by H. C. Andersen, ed. Erik Dal and Henrik Schovsbo (Copenhagen: Det Danske Sprog- og Litteraturselskab / Borgen, 2004), 241–42, and Lars Handesten, "Modtagelsen," in *En Digters Bazar*, by H. C. Andersen, ed. Finn Gredal Jensen, Lars Handesten, Gunilla Hermansson, and Klaus P. Mortensen (Copenhagen: Det Danske Sprog- og Litteraturselskab / Borgen, 2006), 387–93.

3. See introduction, note 1. Also see, for example, Regina Hartmann, "Selbst- und Fremdbild von Deutschland: Heinrich Heines 'Harzreise' (1826) und Hans Christian Andersens 'Schattenbilder von einer Reise in den Harz [. . .]," *Wirkendes Wort* 51 (2001): 183–94; Bjarne Thorup Thomsen, "Connecting Cultures: Hans Christian Andersen as a Travel Writer," *Northern Studies* 39 (2005): 51–69; and Marie-Louise Svane, "Experimente mit dem orientalischen Blickwinkel in H. C. Andersens 'Eines Dichters Basar,'" in *Romantik im Norden*, ed. Annegret Heitmann and Hanne Roswall Laursen (Würzburg: Königshausen & Neumann, 2010), 175–89.

4. See chapter 7, note 158, and "Hans Christian Andersen: Shadow Pictures," Praesens, accessed August 1, 2018, http://www.praesens.at/praesens2013/?p=2031.

5. See Elias Bredsdorff, *Danish Literature in English Translation, with a Special Hans Christian Andersen Supplement: A Bibliography* (Copenhagen: Ejnar Munksgaard, 1950), 177–78.

6. Bredsdorff, *Danish Literature in English Translation*, 177–78. On April 23, Horace Scudder wrote Andersen that the volume would be published "[n]ext week," and reviews began to appear around mid-May; Scudder to Andersen, April 23, 1870, in *The Andersen-Scudder Letters*, ed. Jean Hersholt and Waldemar Westergaard (Berkeley and Los Angeles: University of California Press, 1949), 75. An outlier was a notice that came out on March 14 of the same year in the *Portland Transcript* (see note 16 below), which may owe its early appearance to an advance review copy. According to John Tebbel, the practice of distributing such copies predates the Civil War; see John Tebbel, *The Expansion of an Industry 1865–1919*, vol. 2 of *A History of Book Publishing in the United States* (New York and London: R. R. Bowker, 1975), 150–70, especially 151–52.

7. Unsigned review of *"In Spain" and "A Visit to Portugal,"* trans. Mrs. Bushby (?), *Phrenological Journal*, June 1870, 437. See Frank Luther Mott, *A History of American Magazines 1741–1850* (1930; repr., Cambridge, MA: Harvard University Press, 1957), 447–48.

8. See *Rowell's* for 1870, 707.

9. *Phrenological Journal*, June 1870, 437.

10. Unsigned review of *"In Spain" and "A Visit to Portugal,"* *Zion's Herald*, May 26, 1870, 245.

11. Unsigned review of *"In Spain" and "A Visit to Portugal,"* *American Quarterly Church Review*, July 1870, 319. See Frank Luther Mott, *A History of American Magazines 1850–1865* (1938; repr., Cambridge, MA: Harvard University Press, 1966), 364–66, and *Rowell's* for 1870, 708.

12. Unsigned review of *"In Spain" and "A Visit to Portugal,"* *Presbyterian*, May 14, 1870, 7.

13. Unsigned review of *"In Spain" and "A Visit to Portugal,"* *Eclectic*, June 1870, 764.

14. Andersen experienced Isabella's entrance into Granada on October 10, 1862, and describes it in some detail in his chapter on the city, adding a footnote on the queen's troubled reign.

15. See, for example, French Ensor Chadwick, *The Relations of the United States and Spain: Diplomacy* (New York: Scribner, 1909), 306–22.

16. "Book Notices," unsigned review of *"In Spain" and "A Visit to Portugal,"* *Portland Transcript*, March 14, 1870, 50.

17. Hans Christian Andersen, *A Visit to Portugal*, author's ed., ed. Horace E. Scudder (New York: Hurd and Houghton; Cambridge: Riverside Press, 1870), 264.

18. The poetry in the original of *A Visit to Portugal* is not included in the translation used in the Author's Edition, possibly for the same reason that editor Horace Scudder ultimately decided against including a selection of Andersen's verse in the edition—he could find no suitable translator; see chapter 4, p. 141.

19. Unsigned review of *"In Spain" and "A Visit to Portugal,"* *Sunday-School Times*, May 21, 1870, 333. See Mott, *A History of American Magazines 1850–1865*,

75, and "About the *Sunday-School Times* [Volume] (Philadelphia) 1859–1966," Chronicling America: Historic American Newspapers, accessed April 23, 2015, http://chroniclingamerica.loc.gov/lccn/sn97067021/. *Rowell's* for 1870 (139) lists no circulation figure for the year.

20. *Zion's Herald*, May 26, 1870, 245.

21. Unsigned review of *"In Spain"* and *"A Visit to Portugal,"* *Christian Union*, May 28, 1870, 343.

22. Unsigned review of *"In Spain"* and *"A Visit to Portugal,"* *Eclectic*, June 1870, 763–64. See *Eclectic*, January 1870, 118–19.

23. *Eclectic* June 1870, 764.

24. "Literature of the Day," unsigned review of *"In Spain"* and *"A Visit to Portugal,"* *Hours at Home*, July 1870, 289; unsigned review of *"In Spain"* and *"In Portugal,"* *Christian Standard*, May 21, 1870, 365.

25. See Frank Luther Mott, *A History of American Magazines 1865–1885* (1938; repr., Cambridge, MA: Harvard University Press, 1966), 32–33; *Rowell's* for 1870, 827.

26. See "The Cyclopædia of American Biography/Gilder, Richard Watson," Wikisource, last modified November 18, 2011, accessed April 23, 2015, http://en.wikisource.org/w/index.php?title=The_Cyclop%C3%A6dia_of_American_Biography/Gilder,_Richard_Watson&oldid=3519470.

27. "Literature of the Day," unsigned review of *"In Spain"* and *"A Visit to Portugal,"* *Hours at Home*, July 1870, 289.

28. For a history of the movement and the role of the *Christian Standard* in it, see Henry E. Webb, *In Search of Christian Unity: A History of the Restoration Movement* (Cincinnati: Standard, 1990), especially 240–42.

29. See Frank Luther Mott, *A History of American Magazines 1885–1905* (Cambridge, MA: Harvard University Press, 1957), 295, and *Rowell's* for 1870, 717.

30. Unsigned review of *"In Spain"* and *"In Portugal,"* *Christian Standard*, May 21, 1870, 365.

31. *Christian Union*, May 28, 1870, 343.

32. Unsigned review of *"In Spain"* and *"In Portugal,"* *Southern Review*, July 1870, 229–30.

33. See Terry A. Barnhart, *Albert Taylor Bledsoe: Defender of the Old South and Architect of the Lost Cause* (Baton Rouge: Louisiana State University Press, 2011).

34. Mott, *A History of American Magazines 1865–1885*, 383.

35. Mott, *A History of American Magazines 1865–1885*, 384; *Rowell's* for 1870, 662.

36. *Southern Review*, July 1870, 229.

37. *Southern Review*, July 1870, 230.

38. *Southern Review*, July 1870, 230.

39. *Southern Review*, July 1870, 230.

40. Unsigned review of *"In Spain"* and *"In Portugal,"* *Congregational Review*, September 1870, 496. See Mott, *A History of American Magazines 1850–1865*, 518–19.

41. See *Rowell's* for 1870, 634.

42. Unsigned review of *"In Spain"* and *"A Visit to Portugal,"* *Pittsburgh Weekly Gazette*, May 13, 1870, 2.

43. See J. Cutler Andrews, *Pittsburgh's* Post-Gazette: *"The First Newspaper West of the Alleghenies"* (Boston: Chapman & Grimes, 1936), 38–39.

44. See *Rowell's* for 1870, 737.

45. *Pittsburgh Weekly Gazette*, May 13, 1870, 2.

46. Unsigned review of *A Poet's Bazaar*, trans. Charles Beckwith, *Spirit of the Times*, November 7, 1846, 441. See Mott, *A History of American Magazines 1741–1850*, 480–81.

47. See, for example, Norris W. Yates, *William T. Porter and the* Spirit of the Times: *A Study of the BIG BEAR School of Humor* (Baton Rouge: Louisiana State University Press, 1957), 28–31.

48. I have found no evidence to corroborate or refute this assertion.

49. *Spirit of the Times*, November 7, 1846, 441.

50. *Spirit of the Times*, November 7, 1846, 442.

51. Unsigned review of *A Poet's Bazaar*, *New-York Tribune*, June 2, 1871, 7.

52. See Harry W. Baehr Jr., *The* New York Tribune *since the Civil War* (New York: Dodd, Mead, 1936), 10, 137. Baehr lists the circulation in 1865 as almost three hundred thousand, but that figure must include all of the paper's editions—daily, weekly, semiweekly, and international. According to *Rowell's* for 1871 (102), the daily edition, in an issue of which the review of the *Bazaar* appeared, sold forty-five thousand copies, still a comparatively large number.

53. *New-York Tribune*, June 2, 1871, 7.

54. Unsigned review of *A Poet's Bazaar*, *Evening Post*, June 9, 1871, 1. See Antonia Felix et al., *The Post's New York: Celebrating 200 Years of New York City through the Pages and Pictures of the* New York Post (New York: HarperResource, 2001), 254. The *Hartford Courant* was originally a semiweekly and did not begin daily publication until 1836. The *New Hampshire Gazette*, which also lays claim to being the country's oldest newspaper, was established in 1756 as a weekly and has remained such to the present day.

55. See Frank Luther Mott, *American Journalism, a History: 1690–1960*, 3rd ed. (New York: Macmillan, 1962), 257–58, 344–45; for an in-depth look at the paper's first hundred years, see Allan Nevins, *The* Evening Post: *A Century of Journalism* (New York: Boni and Liveright, 1922).

56. See Mott, *American Journalism*, 425–28, and *Rowell's* for 1871, 101.

57. *Evening Post*, June 9, 1871, 1.

58. Unsigned review of *A Poet's Bazaar*, *Christian Union*, June 28, 1871, 407. The subtitle of the translation reads, *"Pictures of Travel* in Germany, Italy, Greece, and the Orient" [emphasis added]. The publication claimed a circulation of thirty-five thousand in 1871; see *Rowell's* for the year, 103.

59. "Book Notices," unsigned review of *A Poet's Bazaar*, *Portland Transcript*, July 1, 1871, 106. The paper listed a circulation of 17,280 for the year in question; see *Rowell's* for 1871, 59.

60. Unsigned review of *A Poet's Bazaar*, *Bangor Daily Whig & Courier*, June 8, 1871, 3. See "About *Bangor Daily Whig & Courier* [Volume] (Bangor, Me.)

1834–1900," Chronicling America: Historic American Newspapers, accessed July 11, 2015, http://chroniclingamerica.loc.gov/lccn/sn82015185/. In 1871, the paper had a daily circulation of 1,600; see *Rowell's* for 1871, 58.

61. Untitled review of *A Poet's Bazaar*, *Daily Evening Bulletin*, June 17, 1871, 1. In 1871, the paper registered a circulation of eleven thousand for its daily edition but only fifty-five hundred for the weekly edition, in which the review of Andersen's work was printed; see *Rowell's* for 1871, 16.

62. Untitled review of *A Poet's Bazaar*, *Vermont Watchman & State Journal*, July 5, 1871, 1. The paper was normally a weekly but was published daily when the state legislature was in session. Currently, it had a circulation of twenty-six hundred; see *Rowell's* for 1871, 154. Also see "About *Vermont Watchman and State Journal* [Volume] (Montpelier, Vt.) 1836–1883," Chronicling America: Historic American Newspapers, accessed July 11, 2015, http://chroniclingamerica.loc.gov/lccn/sn84023200/.

63. Untitled review of *A Poet's Bazaar*, *Overland Monthly*, January 1872, 102–3. See Mott, *A History of American Magazines 1865–1885*, 402–9.

64. Mott, *A History of American Magazines 1865–1885*, 405. In the edition for 1872 (18), however, *Rowell's* lists the number as an asserted five thousand.

65. *Overland Monthly*, January 1872, 102.

66. *Overland Monthly*, January 1872, 103.

67. *Overland Monthly*, January 1872, 102.

68. *Overland Monthly*, January 1872, 103.

69. Untitled review of *A Poet's Bazaar*, *Sunday-School Times*, July 15, 1871, 445. See Mott, *A History of American Magazines 1850–1865*, 75, and "About the Sunday-School Times [Volume] (Philadelphia) 1859–1966," Chronicling America: Historic American Newspapers, accessed April 23, 2015, http://chroniclingamerica.loc.gov /lccn/sn97067021/. The paper had roughly forty-five hundred subscribers in 1871; see *Rowell's* for that year, 139.

70. See Herbert Rowland, *More Than Meets the Eye: Hans Christian Andersen and Nineteenth-Century American Criticism* (Madison, and Teaneck, NJ: Fairleigh Dickinson University Press, 2006), 115–16.

71. *Sunday-School Times*, July 15, 1871, 445.

72. "Editor's Literary Record," untitled review of *A Poet's Bazaar*, *Harper's New Monthly Magazine*, September 1871, 623.

73. Which readers the reviewer has in mind and where they made their pronouncements, he does not say. In any case, no trace of them appears to remain today.

74. Untitled review of *A Poet's Bazaar*, *Wood's Household Magazine*, February 1872, 92.

75. See Mott, *A History of American Magazines 1865–1885*, 98–99; *Rowell's* for 1872, 117.

76. *Wood's Household Magazine*, February 1872, 92.

77. See Elias Bredsdorff, *Hans Christian Andersen: The Story of His Life and Work 1805–75* (London: Phaidon, 1975), 81.

78. See (for the year 1851) "The Timetable Year by Year," H. C. Andersen Centret/ Hans Christian Andersen Center, last modified October 8, 2013, accessed April 23, 2015, http://www.andersen.sdu.dk/liv/tidstavle/vis_e.html.

79. See "Hans Christian Andersen: Et Besøg hos Charles Dickens i Sommeren 1857," H. C. Andersen Centret / Hans Christian Andersen Center, last modified April 16, 2015, accessed April 23, 2015, http://www.andersen.sdu.dk/vaerk/register/info_e .html?vid=716&oph=1.

80. For the titles of the sketches, see chapter 1, table 1.1, note *b*.

81. "Book Notices," unsigned review of *Pictures of Travel*, trans. Charles Beckwith (?), *Portland Transcript*, October 7, 1871, 218. The only noteworthy, because unexpected remark reads as follows: "These sketches will be found to contain good illustrations of the humor and geniality of the *poet-novelist* who has ever been a popular writer with Americans *both in prose and verse*" [emphasis added].

82. Hans Christian Andersen, *The Story of My Life*, author's ed., ed. Horace E. Scudder (New York: Hurd and Houghton; Cambridge: Riverside Press, 1871), 365.

83. See Bredsdorff, *Hans Christian Andersen*, 226–27.

84. Unsigned review of *Pictures of Travel*, *College Courant*, September 16, 1871, 115. See Mott, *History of American Magazines 1865–1885*, 168, note 23.

85. See *Rowell's* for 1871, 20.

86. The play, which is performed decennially in years ending in a zero, had been presented the previous year. For a contemporary response, see "The Passion Play in Oberammergau in 1870," *Harper's New Monthly Magazine*, January 1871, 174–86.

87. *College Courant*, September 16, 1871, 115.

88. Unsigned review of *Pictures of Travel*, *Churchman*, October 28, 1871, 348; see *Rowell's* for 1871, 19. The quotation marks in the penultimate sentence are apparently intended to signal conscious use of a hackneyed phrase.

89. Hans Christian Andersen, "The Celebration at Oberammergau," in *Pictures of Travel in Sweden, among the Hartz Mountains, and in Switzerland, with a Visit at Charles Dickens's House*, author's ed., ed. Horace E. Scudder (New York: Hurd and Houghton; Cambridge: Riverside Press, 1871), 260.

90. See, for example, Johan de Mylius, "Religious Views in Hans Christian Andersen's Works—and Their Literary Implications," *Orbis Litterarum* 62 (2007): 23–38.

91. Unsigned review of *Pictures of Travel*, *Christian Union*, September 20, 1871, 183. The publication claimed a subscription list of thirty-five thousand in 1871; see *Rowell's* for that year, 103.

92. Unsigned review of *Pictures of Travel*, *Providence Evening Press*, September 26, 1871, 1.

93. Unsigned review of *Pictures of Travel*, *North American and United States Gazette*, October 3, 1871, 1. The editor objected to furnishing the paper's circulation for the year; see *Rowell's* for 1871, 137.

94. Unsigned review of *Pictures of Travel*, *Trenton State Gazette*, October 9, 1871, 2. The *Gazette* currently had a daily circulation of 1,488; see *Rowell's* for 1871, 92.

95. Unsigned review of *Pictures of Travel*, *Capital*, December 23, 1871, 1.

96. "About the *Capital* [Volume] (Washington City, D.C.) 1871–18??," Chronicling America: Historic American Newspapers, accessed April 5, 2016, http://chroni clingamerica.loc.gov/lccn/sn82015845/.

97. Peter Bridges, *Donn Piatt: Gadfly of the Gilded Age* (Kent, OH: Kent State University Press, 2012).

98. See *Rowell's* for 1871, 22.

99. *Capital*, December 23, 1871, 1.

100. Unsigned review of *Pictures of Travel*, *Scribner's Monthly*, January 1872, 8.

101. See Mott, *A History of American Magazines 1865–1885*, 457–68.

102. See *Rowell's* for 1872, 128.

103. *Scribner's Monthly*, January 1872, 8.

104. See Mott, *American Journalism*, 216, 404–5. In the following paragraphs, I have relied largely on scholarship that was published before the advent of modern electronic technology, together with its potential for discovering and searching periodical literature. Understandably, synthetic studies have been unable to keep pace with the rapid and ongoing proliferation of sources. It is therefore likely that future analyses of this material will at least in part supplant the pioneering work of Mott and others. In the meantime, and probably for years to come, however, that work will remain indispensable. In a recent study of American magazines, for example, Heather A. Haveman describes at some length that her research uncovered more sources than Mott estimated to have existed during the period under investigation. However, she uses his *History of American Magazines* self-evidently as a major point of reference, referring to it matter-of-factly as "still a standard reference work." Heather A. Haveman, *Magazines and the Making of America: Modernization, Community, and Print Culture, 1741–1860* (Princeton, NJ, and Oxford: Princeton University Press, 2015), 284–85, 9. I would replace "a" with "the."

105. Quoted according to Mott, *American Journalism*, 405.

106. John Tebbel, *The Creation of an Industry 1630 to 1865*, vol. 1 of *A History of Book Publishing in the United States* (New York and London: R. R. Bowker, 1972), 207.

107. See "Literacy," Our World in Data, accessed May 2, 2015, http://ourworldin data.org/data/education-knowledge/literacy/#note-1.

108. See "History (1870 Fast Facts)," United States Census Bureau, accessed May 4, 2015, https://www.census.gov/history/www/through_the_decades/fast _facts/1870_fast_facts.html; Robert Woods, "The Population of Britain in the Nineteenth Century," in *British Population History: From the Black Death to the Present Day*, ed. Michael Anderson (Cambridge: Cambridge University Press, 1996), 298.

109. The discovery of previously "lost" magazines proceeds on both sides of the Atlantic.

110. Mott, *A History of American Magazines 1850–1865*, 129; Mott, *A History of American Magazines 1865–1885*, 278.

111. Mott, *A History of American Magazines 1741–1850*, 392–93. Tebbel reports that between 1841 and 1846 British publishers reprinted 382 American books, most of them without permission or royalty payments. Tebbel, *The Creation of an Industry*, 209.

112. Mott, *A History of American Magazines 1850–1865*, 130; Mott, *A History of American Magazines 1865–1885*, 278.

113. Hellmut Lehmann-Haupt, et al., *The Book in America: A History of the Making and Selling of Books in the United States*, 2nd ed. (New York: R. R. Bowker, 1952), 213.

114. Tebbel, *The Creation of an Industry*, 206.
115. Tebbel, *The Creation of an Industry*, 222.
116. Tebbel, *The Creation of an Industry*, 210.
117. See p. 121 above.
118. See p. 105 above.
119. See, for example, p. 114 above.
120. See pp. 111 and 119 above.
121. See pp. 118–19 above.
122. See p. 120 above.
123. See for example, p. 116 above.

Chapter Four

The Poetry and the Plays

POETRY

Over the course of his life, in addition to all his other work, Andersen wrote more than a thousand poems.[1] His verse falls into traditional genres as varied as the ballad and the song, the epigram and the elegy, the occasional piece and the lyric, and is particularly rich in the latter two kinds. Contemporaries gave his poetry a mixed reception, and subsequent commentators have been more consistently critical or even harsh in their judgments; Andersen himself once confessed that he was not really a lyric poet.[2] However, Grønbech's words of 1980 still ring true: "Even though most of Andersen's poems have faded now, it is still possible to collect from the very many a minor nosegay of still fresh flowers," and scholars have not at all forgotten his work in the form.[3] One of the pieces Grønbech mentions is "Denmark, My Fatherland" ("Danmark, mit Fædreland"), which is often considered the unofficial national anthem of the country.[4] Interestingly, a few of the others he names are among those that found their way into American publications.

Although near total ignorance of Andersen as a lyric poet currently prevails in the English-speaking world, he in fact appeared as such in periodicals and books issued in the United States during the nineteenth century. Granted, eighty-two printings of fourteen poems is not impressive, especially when one considers that they were published over a span of fifty-three years. On the other hand, they *were* published, and it is quite probable that the vast majority of present-day Americans, even those well versed in literature, would be surprised to learn even this much. Moreover, some of the poems came out in relatively close proximity to each other, seventeen printings occurring between 1847 and 1848 and twenty-seven from 1845 to 1854. Unlike the reviews and general articles, the poetry experienced no decline in publication after 1876. On the contrary, the number of printings published from then until 1899 exceeded that of the otherwise "halcyon" years of 1869 to 1871 fourfold, and more than 29 percent of the total eighty-two appeared between 1878 and the end of the century.

Some of the poems were published in newspapers with local distribution, such as the *New Hampshire Statesman* (Concord; "The Dying Child"); the *Fremont* (Ohio) *Weekly Journal* ("Lines," or "Dusk"; "Aftendæmring"); the *Bolivar Bulletin* of Bolivar, Tennessee ("The Miracle"; "Miraklet"); and San Francisco's *Daily Evening Bulletin* ("Christmas Carol"; "Barn Jesus i en Krybbe laae," from *The Twelve Months of the Year* [*Aarets tolv Maaneder*]).[5] Others, however, found their way into various types of magazines of high quality and/or extensive reach. Horace Scudder published "Spring Song" ("End ligger Jorden i Sneens Svøb") in his *Riverside Magazine for Young People*, which Mott characterizes as "brilliant but unsuccessful," just as he did several of the fairy tales and stories and, following the magazine's absorption by *Scribner's Monthly*, the novel *Lucky Peer*, in which the poem also appeared.[6] "The Poet's Last Song" ("Løft mig kun bort, Du stærke Død") was included in an issue of *St. Nicholas*, one of the best and most successful children's magazines of the era, which for years following its inception in 1873 enjoyed a circulation of seventy thousand.[7] "The Dying Child" gained a place in *Graham's Magazine*, a general periodical which, according to Mott, published "some important work by the best American writers of the time," including Bryant, Cooper, Longfellow, and Poe, and had sales of eighty thousand around the time of the poem's publication.[8] This piece as well as "Lines" came out in *Peterson's Magazine*, which was soon to become the most widely circulating women's publication in the country, reaching 140,000 subscribers in 1869, while "The Miracle" appeared in *Arthur's Illustrated Home Magazine*, *Peterson's* main, if far less successful, rival.[9] William Dean Howells chose "'Yes, yellow and red are the colors of Spain'" ("'Ja Guult og Rødt er *Spaniens* Farver'") as the only example of Andersen's verse style in his mixed review of *In Spain and A Visit to Portugal* for the top-flight *Atlantic Monthly*.[10]

Andersen's poetry appeared in a number of religious periodicals. "Christmas Carol" and "Little Viggo" ("Lille Viggo") came out in the *Christian Register* and *Christian Inquirer*, respectively, both leading Unitarian weeklies.[11] "'Dance, Dance, Dolly Mine'" ("'Dandse, dandse Dukke min!'") and "Ask Amagerma!" ("Spør Amagermo'er!"), which, though generally reckoned among the fairy tales, consist in good part or entirely of verse, were published in the *Independent*.[12] As we saw in chapter 2, this weekly earned acclaim for its antislavery stance and support of women's suffrage as well as for the visibility of its literary contributors.[13] Probably owing to their publication in such magazines, some of Andersen's poems found a home in spiritually oriented volumes like Methodist clergyman James Henry Potts's *The Golden Dawn* ("The Dying Child") and theosophist J. M. Peebles's *Immortality and Our Employments in the Hereafter* ("The Miracle").[14]

Interestingly, two of the poems were deemed worthy of inclusion in several American Protestant hymnals, eleven in all. "The Dying Child" appeared in the Southern Baptist *Gospel Voices.*[15] The Congregational, Lutheran, and Presbyterian churches as well as the American Unitarian Association incorporated "Christmas Carol" in their hymnody, as did the compilers of a number of hymnbooks that apparently had no denominational affiliation.[16] Neither the only extensive history of the American hymnal currently in existence nor any other source provides specific information about, for example, the distribution and duration of usage of the relevant collections, information that would give a clearer indication of the exposure the hymns had among American churchgoers.[17] However, Caryl Florio suggests the great contemporary familiarity of "Christmas Carol" when in the introductory note to his *Children's Hymns, with Tunes* he writes that his object was to "make a collection which may to a certain extent become a STANDARD one. In pursuance of this end, no Hymn or Tune . . . has been admitted which has not, by long practical use, proved to be at once pleasing and interesting in character and of sufficiently sterling quality to wear well."[18] The editors of three other hymnals make similar prefatory statements.[19] Moreover, a newspaper advertisement for one of them, *The Evangelical Hymnal*, includes, among several passages drawn from reviews, one that reads, "It has only been a few years published, but is already widely adopted."[20] And the editor of *Joyful Songs* writes that "hundreds of thousands" of copies of the hymnal had been sold and that the demand for it "is still very great."[21] Significantly, the hymnals were issued by some of the major denominational and nondenominational publishing firms in the country. Based on such evidence one may surely conclude with some confidence that they were ready to hand in the racks on the backs of pews and in the bookcases of Sunday School classrooms in untold numbers of churches and even in many homes for substantial lengths of time. Children's writer Caroline Snowden Guild's *Hymns for Mothers and Children*, which also contains "Christmas Carol," is more a collection of poetry for use in the family circle than a true hymnal, but its contents are also generally spiritual in nature.[22]

Andersen's poetry also appeared in a variety of secular volumes. These include sometime Columbia professor of elocution and drama critic John William Stanhope Hows's *The Ladies' Reader* ("The Dying Child") and *The Rainbow Calendar* by Kate Sanborn ("The Poet's Last Song"), who was variously active as a professor of English at Smith College, a teacher of elocution at the Packer Institute in Brooklyn, and a New York newspaper correspondent.[23] Widely published educator J. Madison Watson's *Independent Fifth Reader* ("The Dying Child") took Andersen into the classroom.[24]

Andersen's fourteen poems are almost evenly divided between his early and late periods, clustered in the years 1825 to 1833 and 1863 to 1875. In view of the sentimentalism then prevalent in the United States and the country's strong religious tradition, it is not surprising that American editors, and probably their readers, responded most sympathetically to the emotionalist and spiritual strains in the poetry. "Christmas Carol" and "The Dying Child," which recount the promise of the manger and offer solace on the death of a beloved child, respectively, alone account for more than a third of the poems' occurrences. "Little Viggo" also treats of motherly love. Death, together with the Christian covenant, figures importantly in different ways in the poems accessible to Americans ("Lines," "The Miracle," "The Moment of Death" ["Dödsöieblikket"], "The Poet's Last Song," "Spring Song"). "What I Love" ("Hvad jeg elsker") juxtaposes the beauty of nature and human virtues with human vices, while "Consolation" ("Fortrøstning") evokes military heroes of the Danish past in the face of the renewed threat of war between Denmark and Prussian and Austrian forces over Schleswig and Holstein. The subtle irony and humor found in "Ask Amagerma!," which good naturedly spoofs May–December relationships, represents a fundamental aspect of Andersen's lifework, but this example of it remains isolated among the poems published in the United States.

The low profile of Andersen's poetry in the United States is largely due to the neglect of English translators.[25] To be sure, Anne S. Bushby published renderings of some twenty of the poems in British periodicals, primarily the *New Monthly Magazine* and *Bentley's Miscellany*, where they likely found readers in the United States as well as in Great Britain.[26] She apparently intended to publish these and others in book form, and forty were indeed included in a posthumous volume of her original poetry.[27] To all appearances, however, the book received no reviews or other discussion, either in England or the United States, and the selections comprise a small fraction of Andersen's body of poetry in any case.[28] No independent collection of Andersen's poetry was ever published in English during the nineteenth century, which means, among other things, that American critics had no opportunity to inform or remind their readers of its existence and nature.[29] Nevertheless, the poems that were in fact printed in the United States bespeak a degree of awareness, however modest, of the Dane as a poet in the contemporary American public, especially among the many churchgoers.[30] If he was not a great poet, within the Danish context or otherwise, the extent, nature, and caliber of his verse make him a figure of consequence, one who was certainly worth knowing in his own time and some of whose poems repay reading yet today.

PLAYS

The same holds true for Andersen's writing for the theater, and English-speakers' ignorance of it is perhaps even more unfortunate than their lack of familiarity with his poetry, above all with respect to his personal literary program. The young author coveted success on the stage above all else, and his love for Thalia and Melpomene, the muses of comedy and tragedy, respectively, never faded. Between 1829 and 1865, he wrote some forty plays, ranging from one-acters to full five-act dramas, from fairy-tale operettas to traditional comedies and tragedies, many of them in verse or mixtures of verse and prose, constituting, among others, vaudevilles, singspiels, and opera libretti.[31] These were written in collaboration with leading Danish composers such as J. P. E. (Johan Peter Emilius) Hartmann and H. (Henrik) Rung. In her study of Andersen and music, Celenza perforce discusses the Dane's writing for the musical theater and his decades-long prominence in the theatrical life of Copenhagen.[32] Andersen surely owed his stature principally to his plays, but he also gained notoriety for the critical observations on Danish attitudes and practices related to the theater that inform his novels and dramas as well as a number of journal articles.[33] Moreover, and more practically, he became the unofficial house dramatist and served as consultant and member of the board of directors for the Casino Theater, a sort of folk theater and the first private stage in Copenhagen.[34]

Despite such undeniable facts, there exists a long-standing perception, even in Denmark, that Andersen was a failure as a dramatist, with the theater-going public and critics as well as in aesthetic terms.[35] In point of fact, however, he experienced success as well as disappointment, and much more of the former than of the latter, in both the classical Royal Theater and the Casino Theater.[36] Tove Barfoed Møller writes that a third of Andersen's plays were "solid successes," while only three were "fiascos," the remainder ranging somewhere in between.[37] During his lifetime, for example, Andersen's fairy-tale comedies *Ole Lukoie* (*Ole Lukøie*) and *More Than Pearls and Gold* (*Meer end Perler og Guld*) enjoyed 117 and 162 performances, respectively, and several others were presented between forty-six and sixty-eight times; with 310 showings, his *Little Kirsten* (*Liden Kirsten*) was by 1971 the most often produced of all Danish operas.[38] If such numbers pale in comparison to the thousands of performances of some successful Broadway plays, the most obvious, if totally inappropriate point of reference for most Americans, they were quite respectable for the time and place.[39]

Perhaps most contemporary criticism centered on Andersen's supposed inability to construct a drama "properly." However, as early as 1864 critic Erik Bøgh could write,

> The public has realized that although [Andersen] has never succeeded in form-
> ing a work for the stage according to the accepted rules of the art, he is a far
> greater poet than someone possessing the most complete talent for dramatic
> construction, and when he leaves his limitless realm in the world of the fairy-tale
> to visit the narrow stage with the slanting floor, upon which each step must be
> measured, he should be considered as a guest who brings rich gifts from another
> land, where art makes other demands.[40]

One hundred fifty years hence, one may both agree with Bøgh's basic sentiment and yet regret its (gently) concessive nature. One may prefer to think
that Andersen's often eccentric dramatic structures, which are found in his
most and least successful plays, represent interesting experiments or innovations in a rather staid and stagnant field.

Andersen may not have been a great playwright, but his writing for the
theater deserves much better than the neglect into which it has long since
fallen, even in Denmark.[41] Affirming this state of affairs, Frank Hugus asserts
that "if one examines Andersen's works for the stage according to the same
criteria applied to the dramas written by his contemporaries (both Danish and
European), his plays hold up well. And an objective analysis of the plays'
literary value shows that they are not inferior to his other work."[42] Hugus's
study as well as others cited in these pages demonstrate that Andersen's plays
still attract the attention of scholars.

In some of his dramatic writings, Andersen takes up centuries-old traditions but gives them his own personal stamp. *The Bird in the Pear Tree*
(*Fuglen i Pæretræet*; 1842), for example, evinces the age-old comic plot of
young love overcoming the resistance of the beloved's father, here a government official. However, Andersen adds the lover's father, a merchant marine
captain, as a major player to the mix, so that the lovers' victory is at the same
time a victory of the socially "inferior" over the socially "superior," whereby
the work becomes a piece of entertaining social-political commentary. *The
Mulatto* (1840) is a serious, full-scale drama in which Andersen takes up
weighty issues such as slavery and racial prejudice in a story set in exotic
Martinique. His plays are characterized generally, among other things, by
unique, or at least uncommon plot structures, often witty or otherwise imposing dialogue, and skillfully crafted verse. They also reveal a broad knowledge

of literary and political history as well a high susceptibility to emotions such as a melancholy sense of transience in the midst of everyday life.

There is no evidence that any of the plays was ever translated into English, even though *The Mulatto* and several others were available in German, which was far more familiar to Americans than Danish and, as we recall, became the conduit for some of the early English translations of Andersen's works.[43] Whatever conditions may have prevailed in England, a propitious opportunity arose and then passed unrealized in the United States when Horace Scudder and Andersen collaborated on the Author's Edition. Scudder originally intended to include a volume of selected plays and poetry, proposing to translate the works himself.[44] He even completed at least a portion of the "bright little play" *He Is Not [Nobly] Born* (*Han er ikke født*) as an exercise while learning Danish.[45] However, he eventually felt compelled to confide to Andersen that he had little confidence in himself as a translator of Danish verse—*He Is Not [Nobly] Born* is one of the few plays written entirely in prose.[46] A few months later he notified Andersen that he had given up his plan to publish the selection of poems due to the difficulty of finding good translators of Danish poetry, which would have impacted his intention to publish selected plays as well.[47] And he must not have trusted himself even to translate the plays in prose. In any case, within a few weeks, and probably at Scudder's prompting, the Boston *Congregationalist* announced the decision in a literary note that reads in part, "He [Andersen] proposed at first to add some of his dramas and poems to the series, but the best qualities of his poems are untranslatable"—which was true, in both literary and practical senses—"and this plan was finally abandoned."[48] The fact that music was an integral part of most of the plays may have been an additional obstacle.

Only two of Andersen's plays received commentary or other mention in the United States during the nineteenth century. The sole critical remarks relate to *The Elder Tree Mother* (*Hyldemoer*) and appeared in the *International Magazine*, which was established in 1850 by editor Rufus Wilmot Griswold, now best known for his contentious relationship with Poe.[49] The magazine competed with *Harper's New Monthly*, though it turned from reliance on English serials to original American writing sooner than its rival, probably to its financial detriment. Despite a respectable list of contributors and strong literary criticism, it was merged with *Harper's* in less than two years. The magazine's review critic was humorist and folklorist Charles Godfrey Leland (1824–1903), a Philadelphian who, in addition to his editorial work for a number of publications, wrote a sketchbook and German-American dialect poems modeled after Washington Irving and Heinrich Heine, respectively.[50]

In a paragraph under "Authors and Books," Leland notes the rise of literary Scandinavia in the awareness of Americans:

We heard little of Scandinavian literature until the translations of Tegner [*sic*], Frederica [*sic*] Bremer, Oelenschlager [*sic*], and Hans Christian Andersen, called our attention to the rich treasures of intellectual activity produced under that cold northern sky. Of course constant additions are being made to this literature. Among its recent productions is a comedy by ANDERSEN, based on a fairy story, called *Hyldemöer*, which has lately been performed upon the Danish stage with not very brilliant success. It is admitted to be inferior to his stories, as have been his former attempts at dramatic composition.[51]

In reality, *Hyldemoer*, the play, has little in common with "Hyldemoer," the fairy tale, other than the theme of love and the figure of the elder tree mother.[52] It was performed sixty times in the Casino Theater beginning in December 1851 and, thus, like many of Andersen's other theatrical works, especially his fairy-tale plays, qualifies as a success.

Hyldemoer is a *Phantasy Play in One Act* (*Phantasiespil i een Act*), as the subtitle reads, in which conventions of the fairy tale are stood on their head. Fairy-tale characters—a mole, a butterfly, a will-o'-the-wisp, and a merman representing the four classical elements—set out on a quest for love in which human beings are the "true" fairy-tale characters. All four seek the favor of fair Maria, but when the mole resorts to treachery by spiriting her into his lair and forgetfulness, the other three join with Elder Tree Mother, the guardian spirit of the elder tree and fond memory, to rescue her and reunite her with young Peter, just as he had protected the elder tree earlier.[53] Imaginative, sentimental but not cloying, light but not weightless—if brought to life by a sympathetic composer and director, the work could conceivably be as appealing today as it was in its own time.[54] Had it been performed in the United States in 1852, however, the readers of Leland's article in the *International* would probably have stayed at home.

Three contemporary references to Andersen's dramatic writing relate to one and the same play, *Ahasuerus* (*Ahasverus*; 1847). The first appeared in an announcement of Longfellow's "The Divine Tragedy" that was published in the *Pittsburgh Weekly Gazette* in 1871 and reads in part, "In its character and even in its style we think it [the work] bears more resemblance to Hans Christian Andersen's 'Ahasverus,' perhaps, than to any other poem, but yet it is very different from that, too."[55] Longfellow's lengthy dramatic poem of 1871, which presents an account of the life of Christ, indeed manifests certain parallels to Andersen's work, but the article does not go beyond an assertion of similarity.

A more substantial reference occurred in the *Methodist Quarterly Review*, which was inaugurated in 1818 and, according to Mott, reached the height of its influence as one of the best church magazines in the country from 1856 to 1884, during which period the reference was made.[56] The editor of the

Quarterly at that time was Daniel D. Whedon (1808–1885), a minister and professor who played a pivotal role in the struggle between Calvinism and Arminianism that was currently roiling Protestant denominations, particularly with respect to the question of free will.[57] During his editorship, the journal reflected his wide-ranging interests, which included, in addition to theology and matters relating to the church, public affairs, above all abolition, education, science, and general literature.

The allusion to *Ahasuerus* turns up in an article titled "The Wandering Jew and His Congenitors," which is in essence an extensive review of two publications that deal with the legendary Jewish shoemaker who taunted Christ as he walked to his crucifixion and was then condemned to wander the earth until the Second Coming: *The Wandering Jew* (1881), by American Moncure Daniel Conway (1832–1907), and *Curious Myths of the Middle Ages* (1869), by the English Anglican priest S[abine] Baring-Gould (1834–1924).[58] In a section titled "The Wandering Jew in Literature," part of his mixed response to Conway's book, the anonymous reviewer devotes more attention to Andersen than to most of the other writers on the figure whom Conway discusses: "Andersen's Ahasuerus is the angel of Doubt—the incarnation of reverential skepticism. Each step in human progress seems to him to be retrogressive: Constantine, the Crusaders, Columbus, Gutenberg, the Reformers, all appear to be deluded fools; and very slowly does the truth reveal itself to his mind that God is working through all forces for the elevation of humanity."[59]

The reviewer was justified in highlighting Andersen's *Ahasuerus*, for Conway did so as well. Conway's spiritual life was a long and arduous journey that took him from the Methodist pulpit to Emersonian Transcendentalism and then to the Unitarian clergy, whence it led him to free thought in the form of a nontheistic spiritual humanism.[60] It is therefore small wonder that in the longest chapter of his book he committed more space to Andersen's exploration of the medieval myth than to that of any of the other writers, giving an extensive summary of the plot. In it, he must have recognized a parallel to his own experience, both in the spirit of doubt that governs the lengthy work until close to the end and, then, in its open conclusion. Here, while upholding a benevolent divine role in human affairs, Andersen does not specify its manner of manifestation or men's response to it, but rather projects the perfection of humanity into a distant future, when "A better skald will, in a better song,/ Tell us of the journey—that follows."[61]

It should be noted that *Ahasuerus* is not a drama in any traditional sense of the word. While normally grouped together with the plays in editions of Andersen's collected writings, terms such as "closet drama" and even "epic poem" and "epic" have also been applied to it.[62] During the planning stages of the work, Andersen used customary dramatic vocabulary when referring to its structural parts. However, he eventually divided it into what he called a "foreground" ("Forgrund") and four "divisions" ("Afdelinger"), which he subdivided into sections superscribed mainly with place-names and historical times, all of which correspond roughly to a prologue, acts, and scenes. Covering more than a hundred pages in the *Samlede Værker*, and thus longer than any of the true plays and much longer than most, the work's vast yet periodically focused historical scope precludes anything resembling a typical plot.[63] Given its structure, its mixture of various spoken and sung verse kinds and occasional prose passages, and its myriads of "personae," which include historical personages, biblical figures, and purely fictional characters as well as animals, spirits, and forces of nature—in view of such diverse richness the work more closely resembles the second part of Goethe's *Faust* than any conventional drama.[64] A formal experiment of this sort might have been considered innovative in conception, despite the flaws in its implementation, both real and perceived. However, the work was—one is tempted to say, "of course"—roundly criticized on grounds of both form and content.[65]

In his definitive study of the Wandering Jew, all the same, George K. Anderson speaks of Andersen's treatment of the figure as "one of the more important" of its time, as the "first example of the theory of evolution which we have as yet met with in the Legend" and "a conscientious and capable attempt to state the abstract idea of evolution, as many others were doing in the 1840s, nearly a score of years before *The Origin of the Species*."[66] Moreover, as Kofoed points out, there is a direct line of coherent ideas leading from *Ahasuerus* to the novel *To Be, or Not to Be?* that reflect Andersen's mature thinking on history, religion, and philosophy.[67]

Andersen's lifework encompasses more than a thousand poems, enough to fill more than two volumes of the most recent edition of his collected writings. His poetry represents various genres but displays a particular abundance of lyric and occasional verse, the latter owing above all to his exceptionally large circle of friends and acquaintances as well as his social stature in Denmark and other countries. Although he was not a major poet, at least a portion of his production commanded, and commands respect. For unknown reasons, his poetry attracted only a few English translators, but some fourscore printings of fourteen poems nevertheless appeared in a wide range of American periodicals and books, including, quite notably, several hymnals. Most prominent among these works are lyrical expressions of religious faith, especially in the face of death, though Andersen's pronounced satiric-humorous vein comes to the fore in one.

Andersen's lifelong desire to excel as a dramatist led him to write some forty plays. Although misapprehensions still persist, he experienced much greater popular and critical success in the theater than commonly thought. On the whole, his work for the stage is of higher quality than his poetry and still exerts an appeal for scholars and, at times, for the Danish public; five of his works were performed a total of ten times in Denmark between 1995 and 1997.[68] Not surprisingly, perhaps, Andersen's fairy-tale plays found the greatest resonance, but he mined several other dramatic genres as well, often with success. Although none of his plays was translated into English, two received modest mention in the American press. One critic detected a parallel between *Ahasuerus* and a work by Longfellow, while another followed an anonymous colleague in his dismissal of *The Elder Tree Mother.* Two others passed informed favorable judgments on *Ahasuerus.*

NOTES

1. The website of the Hans Christian Andersen Center lists 1,024 titles but reports that others can be found elsewhere; "H. C. ANDERSEN: DIGTE - 1024 TITLER," H. C. Andersen Centret / Hans Christian Andersen Center, last modified August 11, 2015, accessed August 5, 2018, http://andersen.sdu.dk/rundtom/borge/danmark.html.

2. See Bo Grønbech, *Hans Christian Andersen* (Boston: Twayne, 1980), 80.

3. Grønbech, *Hans Christian Andersen.* See, for example, Heinrich Detering, "Hans Christian Andersen, poète inconnu," in *(Re)lire Andersen: Modernité de l'œuvre*, ed. Marc Auchet (Paris: Klincksieck, 2007), 257–77; Lise Bostrup, "H. C. Andersens bouts rimés—sjove digte i en glemt genre," *Anderseniana*, 2015, 5–32. Detering affirms that for a time Andersen was equally well known to Germans as a poet and a teller of tales. He writes that the originality of Andersen's poetry lies in "la répétition de structures et de *constellations de base* déjà connues—et donc la sélection et l'agencement de thèmes stereotypes" (262). Bostrup deals with Andersen's handling of what was essentially a parlor game that required improvisational skill.

4. The Hans Christian Andersen Center affirms the current role of "Denmark, My Fatherland" in present-day Denmark; see "Oversigt digte—poems," H. C. Andersen Centret/Hans Christian Andersen Center, accessed August 5, 2018, http://www.hcandersen-homepage.dk/?page_id=4978.

5. *New Hampshire Statesman*, November 5, 1847, 4; *Fremont Weekly Journal*, October 18, 1872, 4; *Bolivar Bulletin*, June 11, 1875, 1; *Daily Evening Bulletin*, December 24, 1887, 6.

6. *Riverside Magazine for Young People*, June 1870, 264. See Frank Luther Mott, *A History of American Magazines 1865–1885* (1938; repr., Cambridge, MA: Harvard University Press, 1966), 176.

7. *St. Nicholas*, December 1875, 133. See Mott, *A History of American Magazines 1865–1885*, 501.

8. *Graham's Magazine*, March 1851, 278. See Frank Luther Mott, *A History of American Magazines 1741–1850* (1930; repr., Cambridge, MA: Harvard University Press, 1957), 555, 553.

9. *Peterson's Magazine*, November 1854, 284, and February 1853, 118; *Arthur's Illustrated Home Magazine*, June 1875, 394. See Frank Luther Mott, *A History of American Magazines 1850–1865* (1938; repr., Cambridge, MA: Harvard University Press, 1966), 309, 417.

10. *Atlantic Monthly*, September 1870, 378. Immediately following his quotation of the poem, Howells begins, "Our poet (for such he is when he writes prose)," thereby giving a broad hint as to his opinion of Andersen's verse. See Mott's sketch of the *Atlantic* in Mott, *A History of American Magazines 1850–1865*, 493–515.

11. *Christian Register*, December 22, 1898, 1452; *Christian Inquirer*, September 9, 1848, 189. See Mott, *A History of American Magazines 1741–1850*, 138; Mott, *A History of American Magazines 1850–1865*, 72.

12. *Independent*, June 12, 1873, 749; July 10, 1873, 877.

13. See chapter 2, p. 53. Over the three years since its review of *O. T.*, the paper had lost twenty-five thousand subscribers due to the Beecher-Tilton adultery scandal, estimating a circulation of forty-three thousand in the year Andersen's two works appeared; see *Rowell's* for 1873, 151, and Mott, *A History of American Magazines 1850–1865*, 375–76.

14. J[ames] H[enry] Potts, *The Golden Dawn; or, Light on the Great Future: In This Life, through the Dark Valley, and in the Life Eternal, as Seen in the Best Thoughts of Over Three Hundred Leading Authors and Scholars* (Philadelphia: P. W. Ziegler, 1883), 247; J[ames] M[artin] Peebles, *Immortality and Our Employments in the Hereafter* (Boston: Colby and Rich, 1880), 13.

15. *Gospel Voices: For Sunday-Schools, Church Services, Gospel and Evangelistic Meetings, Young People's Societies, Special Occasions, etc.*, ed. D. E. Dortch (Nashville, TN: South-Western Publishing House, 1895), no. 71. Dortch's publisher was Southern Baptist in origin and orientation, but he writes in his preface that "[a]ll songs of special doctrinal differences have been rejected, so that all denominations can use these books, adopting them as theirs" (unpaginated; quoted from the edition of 1900, which introduced a series of three volumes titled *Gospel Voices*); see "The Southwestern Company," in *The Tennessee Encyclopedia of History and Culture,* last modified January 1, 2010, accessed December 13, 2016, http://tennesseeencyclopedia .net/entry.php?rec=1237. "The Dying Child" was published in the original Danish in *Sangeren: En Samling af ældre og nyere kristelige Sange* by the Danish Lutheran Publishing House Forlag of Blair, Nebraska, in 1895 (2nd ed., 1898, 380). However, the firm did not begin to issue hymnals in English until 1915, and I have been unable to locate any other Danish-American hymnals that were published in English during the nineteenth century; "The Danish Lutheran Publishing House of Blair, Nebraska," Danish American Archive and Library: Center for Research and Education, accessed August 5, 2018, http://danishamericanarchive.com/danish-lutheran -publishing-house-blair-nebraska/.

16. *Pilgrim Songs for the Sunday School*, ed. John W. Tufts (Boston and Chicago: Congregational Sunday School and Publishing Society, 1886), no. 157; *The Plymouth Hymnal: For the Church[,] the Social Meeting[,] and the Home*, ed. Lyman Abbott (New York: Outlook, 1893), no. 176 (Congregational); *School and Parish Hymnal: With Tunes*, compiled and ed. J. F. Ohl (Philadelphia: G. W. Frederick, 1892), no. 69

(Lutheran); *The Evangelical Hymnal with Tunes*, ed. Charles Cuthbert Hall and Sigismond Lasar (New York: A. S. Barnes, 1880), no. 586 (Presbyterian); *Hymn, Tune, and Service Book for Sunday Schools*, ed. American Unitarian Association (Boston: American Unitarian Association, 1869), no. 245; *The Chapel Hymnal with Tunes*, ed. S(igismond) Lasar (New York and Chicago: Biglow & Main, 1882), no. 213 (nondenominational); *Children's Hymns, with Tunes: A Book for Use in the Sunday School*, ed. Caryl Florio (New York and Chicago: Biglow & Main, 1885), no. 38 (nondenominational); *The Choral Hymnal*, ed. S(igismond) Lasar (New York: Biglow & Main, 1888), no. 94 (nondenominational); *Choral Song: For the Church School, and the Mid-Week Meeting*, ed. Melancthon Woolsey Stryker (New York and Chicago: Biglow & Main, 1891), 72 (nondenominational); *Joyful Songs: A Choice Collection of New Sunday School Music*, ed. James R. Murray (Cleveland: S. Brainard's Sons, 1875), 116–17 (nondenominational?). Like Dortch, editors of additional denominational hymnals state that they sought to avoid theological narrowness in their selection of hymns, but other assertions and/or the orientation of the publishers justify the attributions made here. Note that four of the songbooks were designed specifically for use in Sunday Schools (i.e., for the young), and two others were compiled with both Sunday Schools and church services in mind. Bigelow & Main has been called "one of the most important and prestigious 19th century publishers of sacred music in America," and a recent dissertation makes clear that the firm's hymnals were nondenominational in character; see George H. Shorney Jr., "The History of Hope Publishing Company and Its Divisions and Affiliates," in *Dictionary-Handbook to Hymns for the Living Church*, ed. Donald P. Hustad (Carol Stream, IL: Hope Publishing, 1978), 1. Hope acquired Bigelow & Main in 1922. See Shorney, "The History of Hope Publishing," 6; John Booth, "A Comparative Study of Four Major Non-denominational, Evangelical, American Hymnals in Current Use" (PhD diss., New Orleans Baptist Theological Seminary, 1986), 9–17. Three different translations of "Christmas Carol" were used, but none of the translators is clearly identified. The melody found in almost all of the hymnals was composed by Niels Gade, who has been called the foremost Danish musician of his time. He also set several other of Andersen's poems as well as his verse drama *Agnete and the Merman* (*Agnete og Havmanden*; Andersen called it a "dramatic poem") to music. Dortch and Ohl composed their own tunes; see notes 15 and 16 (*School and Parish Hymnal*) above, respectively.

17. See Christopher N. Phillips, *The Hymnal: A Reading History* (Baltimore: Johns Hopkins University Press, 2018).

18. Florio, "Introductory Note," 2.

19. Lyman Abbott writes in the preface to the *Plymouth Hymnal* that, in choosing the hymns, he "laid stress on intrinsic excellence alone" (iii), while J. F. Ohl states in his prefatory remarks to the *School and Parish Hymnal* that he "aimed to gather together . . . only such hymns and tunes as have real merit" (3); the *Evangelical Hymnal* represents itself as a sort of reform hymnal, retaining, in the words of editors Hall and Lasar, "the best of the old and the best of the new" (iv). Abbott also references "the Danish of Hans Christian Andersen" as an example of the breadth of his sources (iii).

20. "The Evangelical Hymnal," *Missionary Herald*, January 1885, 46. The excerpt continues, "It [the hymnal] is much used in colleges and other institutions of learning."

21. James R. Murray, "Publishers Preface," in *Heavenward: A Choice Selection of Sacred Songs, Adapted to the Wants of Sunday Schools, Praise Meetings, and the Home Circle*, ed. James R. Murray (Cleveland: Brainard, 1877), unpaginated.

22. Caroline Snowden Guild, *Hymns for Mothers and Children*, 2nd ser. (Boston: Walker and Fuller, 1866), 154.

23. John William Stanhope Hows, *The Ladies' Reader: Designed for the Use of Ladies' Schools and Family* (Philadelphia: E. H. Butler, 1860), 181–82; Kate Sanborn, *The Rainbow Calendar* (Boston and New York: Houghton Mifflin, 1889), November 22.

24. J. Madison Watson, *Independent Fifth Reader* (New York, Chicago, and New Orleans: A. S. Barnes, 1876), 191.

25. Mary Howitt and Anne S. Bushby alone accounted for the translations of more than half of the poems found in American periodicals: "Consolation," "The Dying Child," "Lines," "Little Viggo," "The Moment of Death," "The Poet's Last Song," and "What I Love"; see Elias Bredsdorff, *Danish Literature in English Translation, with a Special Hans Christian Andersen Supplement: A Bibliography* (Copenhagen: Ejnar Munksgaard, 1950), 175–77. Howitt included "The Miller's Journeyman" ("Møllerens Datter") in the biographical sketch with which she introduced her translation of *The Improvisatore*; given the popularity of the novel, the piece may have been the best known of all of Andersen's poems in the United States. "Yes, yellow and red are the colors of Spain" is part of Bushby's rendering of *In Spain.* "The Poet's Last Song" was translated by one Annie Wood, probably British social activist, writer, and translator Annie Wood Besant (1847–1933). "The Miracle" is ascribed to Adamine Sindberg, a Danish painter and teacher who spent time in Boston and/or New York during the 1870s as a teacher or governess; Michele McNabb, Librarian/Manager, Danish Immigrant Museum, e-mail message to author, September 26, 2012. The translation of "Dance, Dance, Dolly Mine!" was the work of a Carl Larsen, about whom I have been able to determine nothing other than that, judging by his name, he was probably of Danish or Norwegian birth or descent. Given its appearance in the same place under the same rubric of the same periodical around a month earlier, the unattributed "Ask Amagerma!" may well have also come from Larsen's pen. The translators of "Christmas Carol" and "Spring Song" resist identification.

26. See Bredsdorff, *Danish Literature in English Translation*, 175–77.

27. See Viggo Hjørnager Pedersen, "Anne Bushby, Translator of Hans Christian Andersen," *Nordic Journal of English Studies* 3 (2004): 160–61; Anne Bushby, *Poems by the Late Anne S. Bushby* (London: Richard Bentley & Son, 1876).

28. I have been unable to locate any reviews or other mention of the collection in either American or British periodicals. The poetry is found principally in volumes 7–8 of the *Samlede Værker*; additional texts appear in volume 9. Hans Christian Andersen, *Andersen: H. C. Andersens Samlede Værker*, ed. Klaus P. Mortensen et al., 18 vols. (Copenhagen: Danske Sprog- og Litteraturselskab / Gyldendal, 2003–2007).

29. The only collections of poems ever published in English are R. P. Keigwin, trans., *Seven Poems by Hans Christian Andersen, Syv Digte af H. C. Andersen*, 2nd ed. (Odense: Hans Christian Andersen's House, 1970), and Paula Hostrup Jessen's

Brothers, Very Far Away, and Other Poems, ed. Sven H. Rossel (Seattle: Mermaid Press, 1991), which contains only six texts.

30. One does find scattered references to the poetry (e.g., in the review of *The Improvisatore* mentioned in chapter 2, p. 38). And in a "tease" designed to attract readers to the literary offerings of an issue of the *Independent*, the editors listed Andersen among the poets Swinburne, Whittier, et al., as opposed to prose writers like Charles Kingsley and Harriet Prescott Spofford (*Independent*, June 12, 1873, 754). While one should not attach too much significance to such things, they do indicate that in some quarters and to a certain limited extent Andersen was thought of precisely as a poet.

31. Here, "vaudeville" refers to a type of light comedy popular in Denmark beginning in the second quarter of the nineteenth century. Works of this kind generally consist of a mixture of dialogue and music drawn from easily recognizable popular songs, operatic arias, and such.

32. Anna Harwell Celenza, *Hans Christian Andersen and Music: The Nightingale Revealed* (Aldershot and Burlington, VT: Ashgate, 2005).

33. Celenza, *Hans Christian Andersen and Music*, 52 and 59.

34. Celenza, *Hans Christian Andersen and Music*, 166–67. Also see Frederick P. Marker, *Hans Christian Andersen and the Romantic Theatre: A Study of Stage Practices in the Prenaturalistic Scandinavian Theatre* (Toronto: University of Toronto Press, 1971), 54; Tove Barfoed Møller, "H. C. Andersen og teatret," *Anderseniana*, 1998, 7–20.

35. That this notion was present, perhaps even widespread, in the contemporary United States is demonstrated by a newspaper article that reads in part, "As a dramatist Andersen was never very successful, though he wrote a great many plays, most of which made a fiasco on the stage or were never performed at all." "Andersen, the Novelist," *Ripley Bee*, November 11, 1868, 1. The fact that the article appeared in a village paper in Ohio suggests that it originated in an (as yet unidentified) metropolitan periodical and, like many a comparable article, was reprinted in numerous similar papers.

36. See, for example, Marker, *Hans Christian Andersen and the Romantic Theatre*, 30–64, and Møller, "H. C. Andersen og teatret," 7–20.

37. Møller, "H. C. Andersen og teatret," 20.

38. The Hans Christian Andersen Center at the University of Southern Denmark maintains a list of the original productions staged during Andersen's lifetime on its website; see "Hans Christian Andersen—FAQ: Stage Performances," H. C. Andersen Centret / Hans Christian Andersen Center, last modified August 24, 2010, accessed April 23, 2015, http://www.andersen.sdu.dk/rundtom/faq/index_e.html?emne=scene. Møller offers figures for the period from 1900 through 1997. Møller, "H. C. Andersen og teatret," 9–10. Marker provides the figure for *Little Kirsten*. Marker, *H. C. Andersen and the Romantic Theatre*, 47. In *Little Kirsten*, Andersen created at once a lasting presence on the Danish stage and the genre of Danish Romantic opera; see Dan Shore, "The Emergence of Danish National Opera, 1779–1846" (PhD diss., City University of New York, 2008), 159–90, especially 159–68.

39. A running list of the fifty most successful Broadway shows, which reflects traditional as well as musical theater, reveals a range of from 1,567 to 11,782 perfor-

mances. "Longest-Running Broadway Shows," Broadway League, accessed March 14, 2017, https://www.broadwayleague.com/research/statistics-broadway-nyc/. By 1943, Johann Ludvig Heiberg's comedy *Elves' Hill* (*Elverhøj*; 1828), which is considered Denmark's national play, had had something over 700 performances, which was more than any other work ever produced at the Royal Theater; see Niels Friis, *Det Kongelige Theater: Vor Nationale Scene i Fortid og Nutid* (Copenhagen: H. Hagerup, 1943), 77. Over the next three decades, that number climbed to more than 1,000; Niels Birger Wamberg, *H. C. Andersen og Heiberg:* Åndsfrænder *og* Åndsfjender (Copenhagen: Politiken, 1971), 275.

40. Quoted according to Marker, *Hans Christian Andersen and the Romantic Theatre*, 62.

41. Møller shows that roughly one-third of the plays were performed during the twentieth century, though a couple were clear favorites, in other words, often repeated (in addition to *Little Kirsten, Ole Lukoie* and *A Night in Roskilde* [*En Nat i Roeskilde*]), and gaps of a decade and more lie between some of the productions. Møller, "H. C. Andersen og teatret," 9–10. According to de Mylius, writing in 1996, the plays had not been reprinted in recent years. Johan de Mylius, "Et stykke, der gav hus," *Anderseniana*, 1996, 60. De Mylius also states that related research had been "terribly modest" ("*uhyre beskedent*"; 61), and a survey of recent bibliographies and issues of *Anderseniana*, a major outlet for Andersen-scholarship, reveals that little has changed in the meantime. The plays do appear in the extensive edition of the collected works published after the turn of the present century (Andersen, *Samlede Værker*, vols. 10–13).

42. Frank Hugus, "En genvurdering af to dramaer af H. C. Andersen," *Anderseniana*, 2000, 53 (my translation). Marker attributes "considerable wit and dramaturgical finesse" to Andersen's vaudevilles and writes that, though Andersen was not the best Danish dramatist of the period, none of his contemporaries "embraces as much of the rich variety and scope of the romantic theatre as he." Marker, *Hans Christian Andersen and the Romantic Theatre*, 40 and xvi, respectively. Also see Tove Barfoed Møller, *Teaterdigteren H. C. Andersen og "Meer end Perler og Guld": En dramaturgisk-musikalsk undersøgelse* (Odense: Odense Universitetsforlag, 1995), especially 13–28.

43. Marker affirms the absence of English translations of the plays. Marker, *Hans Christian Andersen and the Romantic Theater*, xvii. For the German translations, see Ivy York Möller-Christensen, *Den gyldne trekant: H. C. Andersens gennembrud i Tyskland 1831–1850* (Odense: Odense Universitetsforlag, 1992), 166–67, 226–30, 240–41.

44. See Scudder to Andersen, February 5, 1870, in *The Andersen-Scudder Letters*, ed. Jean Hersholt and Waldemar Westergaard (Berkeley and Los Angeles: University of California Press, 1949), 67.

45. Scudder to Andersen, February 5, 1870, in Hersholt and Westergaard, *The Andersen-Scudder Letters*, 67.

46. Scudder to Andersen, June 8, 1871, in Hersholt and Westergaard, *The Andersen-Scudder Letters*, 99.

47. Scudder to Andersen, September 7, 1871, in Hersholt and Westergaard, *The Andersen-Scudder Letters*, 100.

48. "Literary and Art Items," *Congregationalist*, September 28, 1871, 6.

49. "Authors and Books," *International Magazine*, April 1852, 553. See Mott, *A History of American Magazines 1850–1865*, 406–8.

50. See Elizabeth Robins Pennell, *Charles Godfrey Leland: A Biography*, 2 vols. (Boston: Houghton Mifflin, 1906).

51. *International Magazine*, April 1852, 553. Esaias Tegnér (1782–1846) was a Swedish poet, professor of Greek, and bishop whose *Frithjof's Saga* (1825) made him one of the foremost literary figures in Europe. Adam Oehlenschläger (1779–1850) was a Danish poet and dramatist and the foremost representative of Romanticism in Denmark. He was also an early supporter of Andersen.

52. I assume here that the writer refers to Andersen's fairy tale "The Elder-Tree Mother" rather than to any of the many tales associated with the figure in Nordic and British folklore; see, for example, Johannes Tholle, "Hyldebusken," in *Danske Studier for Universitetsjubilæets Danske Samfund*, ed. Gunnar Knudsen and Ejnar Thomsen (Copenhagen: Gyldendalske Boghandel Nordisk Forlag, 1944), 1–38, especially 15–18, and the more popular article by Mara Freeman, "Tree Lore: Elder," Order of Bards, Ovates & Druids, accessed December 29, 2016, http://www.druidry.org/library/trees/tree-lore-elder.

53. In his novel *To Be, or Not to Be?*, Andersen also names memory as the peculiar power of Elder Tree Mother, making reference to his own play; *Samlede Værker*, 6:230; *To Be, or Not to Be? A Novel*, trans. Mrs. Bushby (London: Richard Bentley, 1857), 317.

54. Jørn Langsted points out several aspects of Andersen's artistry in the play and its production in the new Casino Theater, including an effective use of the gas lights and other technical features. Jørn Langsted, "H. C. Andersens 'Hyldemoer,' 1851: En dramaturgisk analyse," *Anderseniana*, 1968, 234–62.

55. "An Unexpected Pleasure," *Pittsburgh Weekly Gazette*, November 27, 1871, 2. The weekly edition of the paper currently had a circulation of fourteen thousand; see *Rowell's* for 1871, 142.

56. Mott, *A History of American Magazines 1741–1850*, 299–300.

57. See, for example, "Daniel Whedon (1808–1885)," Christian Heritage Fellowship, accessed April 23, 2015, http://christianheritagefellowship.com/daniel-whedon-1808-1885/.

58. "The Wandering Jew and His Congenitors," unsigned review of *The Wandering Jew*, by Moncure Daniel Conway, and *Curious Myths of the Middle Ages,* by S. Baring-Gould, *Methodist Quarterly Review*, July 1882, 489–506. *Rowell's* for 1882 (280) lists the journal's circulation as no more than five thousand.

59. *Methodist Quarterly Review*, July 1882, 497.

60. See, for example, Charles A. Howe, "Moncure Conway," in *Dictionary of Unitarian & Universalist Biography,* last modified August 31, 2004, accessed April 23, 2015, http://uudb.org/articles/moncureconway.html.

61. My prose translation of the final two lines of the work.

62. Erik Dal refers to the work as a "closet drama in verse" ("*læsedrama* [literally, "reading drama"] *på vers*"); "Jødiske elementer in H. C. Andersens skrifter," in *Andersen og verden: Indlæg fra den Første Internationale H. C. Andersen-Konference 25.–31. august 1991*, ed. Johan de Mylius, Aage Jørgensen, and Viggo Hjørnager Pedersen (Odense: Odense Universitetsforlag, 1993), 449. Niels Kofoed writes, "This poem was intended to become an epic dealing with the genius of mankind." Niels Kofoed, "Hans Christian Andersen and the European Literary Tradition," in *Hans Christian Andersen: Danish Writer and Citizen of the World*, ed. Sven Hakon Rossel (Amsterdam and New York: Rodopi, 1996), 240. Erik Rindom also refers to the work as an "epic" ("Epos"). Erik Rindom, "H. C. Andersen og *Ahasverus*: En litterærhistorisk Studie ved Andersen-Jubilæet," *Gads danske magasin* 24 (1930): 175.

63. Andersen, *Ahasverus*, in *Samlede Værker*, 12:243–349.

64. The discussion between Niels and Esther in chapter 4 of part 2 of *To Be, or Not to Be?* shows that Andersen was quite familiar with Goethe's work at least by the time of the novel's composition.

65. See, for example, Rindom, "H. C. Andersen og *Ahasverus*," 185–92. Also see Jens Andersen, *Hans Christian Andersen: A New Life*, trans. Tiina Nunnally(New York, Woodstock, and London: Overlook Duckworth, 2005), 405–6 and 525–41. The latter pages of the biography deal with Andersen's views on religion in general, touching on *Ahasuerus* in the process.

66. George K. Anderson, *The Legend of the Wandering Jew* (Providence, RI: Brown University Press, 1965), 221, 222. Unlike most commentators, Anderson speaks highly of the "artistic design" as well as other features of *Ahasuerus*, but criticizes it as a work of poetry (222).

67. Kofoed, "Hans Christian Andersen and the European Literary Tradition," 240.

68. See Møller, "H. C. Andersen og teatret," 10. These were the only statistics of this kind available to me.

Chapter Five

The Autobiographies

At the age of twenty-seven, long before it occurs to most individuals that their memoirs are worth preserving, Andersen recorded reminiscences of his life in *Levnedsbog*, literally *Book of [My] Life*, which begins with his birth in modest circumstances in Odense in 1805 and ends with his first literary successes in Copenhagen in 1831. He left the manuscript unfinished, intending it to be published only in case of his premature death. It was assumed lost for over ninety years, until Danish literary scholar Hans Brix discovered it in the Royal Library in Copenhagen and published it in 1926. However, many American reviewers of later iterations of the work would very likely have supported Andersen's decision to write and publish it, had he chosen to do so. For they deem the period of time covered in it the most interesting and, in some respects, the most valuable phase of his entire life.

Andersen wrote the next version of his autobiography for a German edition of his collected works that appeared in 1847. It was this rendering that served as the basis for Mary Howitt's English translation, which was issued under the title *The True Story of My Life* (*Mit eget Eventyr uden Digtning*) in the same year. In 1855, Andersen published the (provisionally) definitive version of his autobiography in Danish as *Mit Livs Eventyr* (*The Fairy Tale of My Life*), a revised edition of which came out four years later. Before Horace Scudder broached the idea of an author's edition with him, when only an authorized edition of his stories and tales was under discussion, he proposed to write additional chapters to his autobiography covering the years 1855 to 1867—a clear indication of the importance he attached to a project on which he worked for nearly forty years.[1] Scudder then rendered these chapters into English, while another individual, as the editor writes, "incorporated Miss Howitt's translation when it was available, but added all that was new in the Danish edition."[2] This version of the work, which appeared in 1871 under the title *The Story of My Life*, was the one that critics reviewed during the final phase of Andersen's reception in the United States.[3]

The True Story of My Life enjoyed great success internationally on its publication in 1847, especially in Germany, England, and the United States.[4] Reviewers were generally polite, but we shall see that several Americans were exceptions to the rule.[5] American critics were virtually the only ones to take note of *The Story of My Life* in 1871, and their commentaries were even more mixed.[6] Andersen scholars continue to show a lively interest in many aspects of Andersen's life, personality, and thought and routinely draw on his autobiographies in their work, but studies of the books themselves are not common. A republication of Scudder's edition appeared in 2000.[7]

An American edition of Howitt's translation of the autobiography was published shortly after the English edition in summer 1847. Probably owing to Andersen's already established popularity, it quickly drew the attention of reviewers, eventually eliciting nine notices, substantially more than any of the author's other writings during the first phase of his reception in the United States. When the work came out in the Author's Edition in 1871, it met with twenty reviews, thereby exceeding the numbers accorded the other works by an even greater percentage. While reflecting a high degree of interest in Andersen, however, these reviews disclose extremes of approval and disapproval unapproached in those of the other writings. Perceptions of his personal virtues as well as his egocentricity and vanity, his inability to bear criticism, and his subservience to the upper classes figured prominently in critics' responses. Discussion of these reviews will proceed according to the phases of Andersen's reception in which they appeared.

1847

The first American review of the autobiography appeared in Boston's *Weekly Messenger* on August 11, 1847, around three and a half weeks after the initial British notice.[8] The *Messenger*, which ran under varying titles from 1811 to 1861, was edited at the time by Nathan Hale (1784–1863). The nephew of the Revolutionary War hero of the same name, he was the father of Edward Everett Hale and an editor, journalist, and politician who established the long-lived *Boston Advertiser* and cofounded the highly influential *North American Review* and *Christian Examiner*.[9] The paper began as a political journal in the service of the Federalist Party but switched its allegiance twice over the first half of the nineteenth century, first to the Whig and then to the Republican parties.

Aside from its distinction as the first American commentary on Andersen's autobiography, the notice in the *Messenger* is significant more for its comprehensiveness than for its critical engagement with the work. In his opening remarks, the reviewer expresses an opinion that proved to be a dominant, if not always unqualified theme in subsequent assessments of the book:

> This volume, the publication of which we noticed a few days since, proves to be exceedingly interesting. The struggles of a man of genius, placed in the lowest rank of life, and subjected to all the deprivations of extreme poverty, while he makes his way through difficulties, and succeeds at last in overcoming them all, and reaching a point beyond the dreams of his early ambition, cannot but be watched with interest. This interest is deepened when we have all this in the poet's own words, giving a record of his inmost feelings during the whole course of his life. Andersen's language is so simple and beautiful that it gives the best idea of his character.[10]

The reviewer concludes by expressing the hope "that he [Andersen] may be induced at some future time to resume a narrative which is so interesting and which gives so good an example of patient and hopeful perseverance, crowned with success," a hope that was indeed fulfilled, surely beyond anyone's fondest expectations.

In between these passages, the writer provides perhaps his greatest service to the reading public by reproducing five, in part, lengthy excerpts from the text punctuated by accounts of intervening episodes, which, all together, amount to about two and a half densely printed columns. He follows the course of Andersen's life and work faithfully, though devoting noticeable attention to the renowned friends and acquaintances the author made along the way, for example, Fredrika Bremer, Jenny Lind, and Bertel Thorvaldsen. The interest and even fascination with which this and many other reviewers greeted the autobiography are entirely understandable, for Andersen's ascent from poverty and obscurity to financial well-being and international fame was only a heightened realization of Horatio Alger's notion of the American Dream.

The second of three August reviews of *The True Story of My Life* came out in the *Christian World*, a Unitarian weekly published in Boston from 1843 to 1848.[11] Its publisher was George G. Channing, a brother of famed champion of Unitarianism and public intellectual William Ellery Channing (1780–1842) and himself a Unitarian minister. Very little information about the paper is available, but examination of the issue in which the review appeared suggests that, while religious in spirit, it was not theological. The issue's four pages contain, for example, a few articles and letters to the editor on moral-religious subjects and church matters but also local secular news, poetry, and, of course, book notices. The review of Andersen's autobiography is signed "E," but available sources provide no certainty as to the identity of the individual. At the same time, it is worth observing that Channing's nephew, Transcendentalist poet William Ellery Channing the Younger (1817–1901), commonly used his middle name in print.[12]

"E" introduces the review by citing Mary Howitt's dedication of her translation to Andersen's friend Jenny Lind as well as her rather proud prefatory assertion that the author had a "personal" (i.e., financial) interest in the book—treatment that Andersen rarely enjoyed, given the absence of an international copyright law.[13] He then writes, "Andersen has already moved the American heart by his 'Improvisatore,' 'O. T.,' 'Only a Fiddler,' and perhaps still more by his 'Wonderful Stories for Children.'"[14] The statement is significant insofar as it indicates that Andersen's novels had already had an (emotional) impact on American readers and that even at this early date, only a year after the appearance of the first collection, the stories and tales could be seen as being even more impactful.

Subsequently, "E" implicitly raises a question without providing an immediate answer, implicit or otherwise: "The True Story of his Life will be read with great interest. It is natural to desire personal knowledge of a favorite author. We sorrow if we find that the character of one who has charmed us with his writings is below rather than above the common standard of virtue; while, if we find that his life is as beautiful as his word, we rejoice over him as over a personal friend." An answer begins to emerge when "E" continues, "It is a theory of ours that the truest poetry as well as the most unsophisticated feeling is found in humble life. And true to this theory, the childhood and youth of Andersen, as the struggling peasant-boy, has a charm that does not attach to him as the successful man of letters." Failure to perceive in the literary lion the charm one senses in the floundering youth does not necessarily equate to disapproval, but it does make one perk one's ears.

Consequently, the reader attends all the more intently to "E"'s following words: "The first part of Andersen's 'True Story' is the most bewitching; it reminds us of Lavater, that unrivalled reader of his own heart." Here, "E" likens Andersen to Johann Caspar Lavater (1741–1801), the Swiss religious enthusiast, poet, and physiognomist whose confessional candor influenced a generation of German-speaking youth, not least of all the young Goethe.[15] To support his assertion and comparison, "E" quotes the soon-to-become famous opening sentence of the autobiography—"My life is a lovely story, happy and full of incident"—as well as several passages from the first chapter of the book. Among these is one in which Andersen relates how his pride in the loudly squeaking new boots he wore to his confirmation soon gave way to pangs of conscience when he realized that his thoughts were as much on the boots as on God—an episode that became a favorite among editors, reviewers, and, one assumes, other readers.

"E" begins the following paragraph with what might, logically, have been the conclusion to the preceding one, writing, "These little anecdotes of Andersen's childhood, remind of the vein of naturalness which forms one of the chief charms of his writings."[16] He then turns to what he calls Andersen's "two most distinguishing characteristics," a "morbid sensitiveness to unjust criticism" and a "childlike love of God," focusing more on the former than the latter:

> Andersen has more than his share of the sensitiveness which seems peculiarly to attach to men of genius. His nature "struggled its way out of narrow and depressing circumstances." He had a latent consciousness of power, the most unaffected humility, and that craving desire for approval, that makes, for some, approval almost the breath of their life. This approval he long waited for. . . . During a troubled portion of his life he says, "I possessed a peculiar talent—that of lingering on the gloomy side of life, of extracting the bitter from it, of tasting it; and understood well, when the whole was exhausted, how to torment myself." He well knew how ungenial it is for the heart to have "too quick a sense of constant infelicity," when in prosperity he penned the following words: "Too many flattering circumstances, some people argue, may easily spoil a man, and make him vain. But no; they do not spoil him; they make him, on the contrary, better; they purify his mind, and he must thereby feel an impulse, a wish, to deserve all that he enjoys."

Thus, the notice ends, with no overt comment on Andersen's free admission of his "gift" for self-torment and positive view of the influence of felicitous circumstance on the individual, the words apparently assumed to speak for themselves. Coupled with the previously affirmed lack of charm in the established author, however, the very absence of interpretive remarks may be seen as a reflection of "E"'s ambivalence toward Andersen the man, if not the artist, and a reluctance to condemn the one lest he condemn the other in so doing.

A patently mixed review appeared in another Unitarian weekly on August 21, 1847.[17] The *Christian Inquirer* was published by the Unitarian Association of the State of New York, based in New York City, and became one of the leading periodicals of its kind, running from 1846 to 1866.[18] A strong proponent of its liberal brand of Christianity, which was richly represented in its pages, the *Inquirer* resembled numerous other religious publications in that it also manifested typical features of the general family magazine, including stories, poems, and book notices.

Like many another reviewer, the anonymous writer prefaces his comments on the work at hand with interesting observations about the stories and tales, to which we shall return in the next chapter. He launches into his discussion of the autobiography in much the same fashion as his predecessor of the previous week:

> Andersen is a man of genius, unquestionably; and if any one who has read his works shall still doubt this, the perusal of his Life, with its early difficulties, such as only true genius could have surmounted, will be conclusive. The earlier part of the book is naturally the most interesting, from the picture of distresses and obstacles overleaped by the "faculty divine," from which its fixed attention to heavenly glimpses in the distance, scarcely recognises earthly hindrances.[19]

However, this reader of Wordsworth's "The Wanderer" represents other critics who both chide Andersen for his hypersensitivity to criticism and admonish him for what they consider an even more shameful failing:

> Success, wrung from the cold and careless and jealous world, has dazzled our author and enfeebled his wings a little. We are unpleasantly affected by his sensitiveness to a word of criticism,—to a single hiss amid a tempest of applause; but above all, by his almost abject deference to rank and power. Burns, in similar circumstances, never showed an unmanly gratitude—never forgot his self-respect, or mistook the terms upon which he stood with the great.

The writer explains the disparity between the two authors as follows:

> We imagine the difference to be owing, after all allowance for the smaller caliber of the continental man, to the difference in political and national circumstances. Andersen was born where the impassable wall between the great and the low-born allowed not even a glimpse of hope for the less-favored, unless the jealous gates opened to let in amusement or advantage for the exalted; and when he had a momentary admission on these terms, he was transported with a joy which is inconsistent with self-respect. Burns, who had drawn in a free and independent spirit with the air of his native hills, and who felt always that "a man's a man for a' that," carried with him into the great circles to which his genius introduced him—and would have carried to the foot of any throne in Christendom—such a consciousness of his own claims as gave dignity to his manner, and prevented his ever accepting condescension in lieu of consideration.

However one may judge the disparity drawn between the Scot and the continental European, there is no doubt that the reviewer wrote as a proud Anglo-Saxon, or even Celt, of western climes. Nevertheless, he can write, "Andersen's Life is full of interest, however, and well worth perusal—if we need say so after having said he was a man of genius." At this point, he reproduces rather lengthy extracts from chapters 1 and 7 of the book. The first deals with Andersen's sewing clothes for the dolls in his puppet theater and being chased by other boys for being "different"; in the last, Andersen expresses his love for the king and queen of Denmark and his gratitude to them for arranging a dinner at the palace to celebrate the twenty-fifth anniversary of his arrival in Copenhagen—passages likely chosen to illustrate the main points made earlier in the notice.

The reviewer for the *Young American's Magazine of Self-Improvement* takes a position similar to that of the *Christian Inquirer*.[20] The meager information available about the publication suggests that it was issued every two months and lasted only one year, from 1847 to 1848.[21] The editor was George W. Light (1809–1868), a publisher and bookseller in Boston who was active as such in the abolitionist and free soil movements.[22] Light aimed his magazine principally at urban working-class youth, promoting the kind of knowledge necessary to run machinery.[23] Himself a published poet, however, he saw a role for letters and sociopolitical matters in the education even of boys destined to labor in factories, including writings by Longfellow, Lowell, and Goethe as well as abolitionists Wendell Phillips and Charles Sumner in his magazine.[24]

The reviewer writes, "His [Andersen's] story is marked by fine traits of originality and humor, and rendered still more interesting by sketches and anecdotes of many celebrated men with whom he met"—features that recur over and again in the commentaries on the autobiography.[25] Much like his colleagues at the *Weekly Messenger* and the *Christian Inquirer*, he continues, "His early life presents one of those examples of genius struggling with poverty, which always command sympathy; and the artless manner in which the warm-hearted poet relates it, is charming." At this juncture the writer broaches Andersen's weaknesses:

> Even his imperfections of character, through the unconscious frankness with which he exposes them, make him interesting to us. We can willingly pardon in him the apparent obsequiousness with which he acknowledges the favors of his sovereign, it is done with such a hearty gratitude; however repugnant it might be to a true republican, in whose view the *man* stands far above the trappings with which royalty bedecks him.

Much like his counterpart at the *Christian Inquirer*, this reviewer voices distinct distaste for Andersen's "fawnery," but he is willing to overlook it because it appears to him to be of a piece with the ingenuous candor that characterizes the man in general.

Most of the critics discussed heretofore have reservations about Andersen as a man, but they express them in a generally objective, professional manner commensurate with their admiration for him as an artist. The reviewer for *Holden's Dollar Magazine*, on the other hand, seemingly treats neither the man nor the artist with great respect.[26] The periodical was founded in 1848 by Charles W. Holden (b. 1826), a New England journalist and author who died the following year after contracting typhoid fever while seeking his fortune during the California Gold Rush.[27] A representative of the movement for cheap literature, *Holden's* survived its founder and first editor by only two years before merging with the *North American Miscellany.*

At the outset, the reviewer handles Andersen's home country with even less delicacy than the author himself:

> Were it not for Hamlet the Dane, the little antiquated Kingdom of Denmark would hardly be known to the world of every day men. See what literature has done for a kingdom, to make it known to the world by one fictitious character! Hereafter Denmark will be better known as the birthplace of Hans Christian Andersen, whose father was a poor shoemaker, and whose mother was a simple beggar girl. Which of the Kings of Denmark has done so much for it as this, or which of the great warriors or statesmen of that little kingdom has made it renowned and talked about, as this poor person Hans Christian has done?[28]

One cannot accuse the writer of possessing an acute historical memory or an awareness of current world events. Denmark was certainly no longer the European power it had been in earlier centuries, but it still had to be taken into account by its neighbors until the aftermath of World War I. At the very moment the review was written, indeed, the country was engaged in a war with German Schleswig-Holsteiners and Prussian forces over control of the duchies from which the Danes, profiting from international pressure on Prussia, emerged victorious.

The reviewer continues with words that would probably have brought the easily overwrought Andersen to angry tears:

> He has fought no battles, made no laws, killed nobody, but only written a few little songs, and some simple stories for children, and yet he has made himself famous by these trifles, and his country better known. The thought of it must make Hans very happy. We have given in another part of the Magazine a portrait of this feeble little great man, and now we will give the reader some idea of who he is and what he was, which we shall borrow from his own autobiography.

Thereupon follow more than two columns of extracts comprising the first ten paragraphs of Andersen's life story, from the programmatic words, "'The history of my life will say to the world what it says to me—There is a loving God, who directs all things for the best,'" to the introduction of his beloved paternal grandmother, who kept the garden of an insane asylum that was to play an unfortunate role in the youth's development.[29]

The reviewer's final comments, which introduce the extracts, read as follows: "We have rarely read a book so full of pleasant and profitable reading as this. See how simply and like a Christian, as he is by nature as well as name, Hans writes."[30] Only at this point does the unsuspecting modern reader fully realize that he has been taken in. The apparent discrepancy between the body of the commentary and its conclusion becomes even less discrepant when one learns that the current editor of *Holden's* was Charles F. Briggs, who, as we have already seen, had adopted a similar bantering style a few years earlier as editor of (and reviewer for) the *Broadway Journal.*[31] Nevertheless, one wonders how what was intended as witty urbanity, which in parts at least borders on travestying flippancy, affected readers of the magazine, especially those living outside of *Knickerbocker* New York. That is to say, one wonders whether the tone of the review enticed readers to continue on to the extracts or rather induced them to turn to other reading.[32]

One of the lengthiest of all American reviews of Andersen's works appeared in the *American Literary Magazine* in January 1848.[33] The monthly was established the previous year by Timothy Dwight Sprague (b. 1819), a Yale graduate who moved the magazine from its birthplace in Albany, New York, to Hartford in his home state of Connecticut, where it died young, together with him, in 1849.[34] During its brief lifespan, Sprague's monthly published work by popular authors such as Charles A. Goodrich, Lydia H. Sigourney, and Alfred B. Street as well as Yale professors, displaying particular interest in manners, biography, and art.[35] The review is signed "Geraldine," but the identity of the person who wrote it defies determination. Whoever s/he was—"Geraldine" is both a surname as well as a feminine given name—the notice was certainly not the work of the best-known Victorian review critic named Geraldine, (i.e., Geraldine Endsor Jewsbury), who reportedly wrote some twenty-three hundred notices for the London *Athenaeum* between 1849 and her death in 1880.[36] Both the review and another contribution to Sprague's magazine signed "Geraldine" provide clear evidence that the author was an American.[37]

Geraldine opens the review by extolling the joys and benefits of a book:

What luxury can bring so rare a pleasure as a beautifully written book[?] It is a mine of joy. It not only contains new and beautiful thoughts itself, but suggests many others to us, and thus elevates us in the scale of intelligence by making us conscious of our own capacities. And though these thoughts may never be uttered, they enter into our being and we impress them upon the world by our lives. Who has told as it deserves the praises of a beautiful book?[38]

These musings lead to the question, "Who has lauded as he should the merit of its author?," which, in turn, prompts the explanation, "We hardly dare do it. We are afraid of being called extravagant," which would not do in the current age of propriety and decorum.[39] In a book,

> we may find an oblivion for hunger and cold, for sickness, sorrow, loneliness, neglect, or any of the ills of life. We may laugh, weep, aye pray over it, and in the sincerity and fervency of those prayers receive strength for the days which are to come. It may enter with us into our secret chamber—the watches of the night may find us bending over it—its burning words may be graven upon our very soul, and yet if we met the writer of that book, we would touch his hand with cold civility, we would not dare to embrace him and weep upon his breast our gratitude and praise. And he will die, and never know his influence upon the eternal destiny of another.[40]

The reader has yet another reason for withholding any expression of thankfulness to the author: "Because *sin* is in the world and ere those words of gratitude could pass from our lips to the ear of another, they would be tainted by its breath, and he for whom it was intended, would repel it as fulsome flattery."[41] The reader's suppression of his indebtedness has consequences for the author:

> Thus while love and sympathy are all around him, the author often accuses the world of coldness, and he thinks that he is right. He must look to the future life for the true revealings of the heart of man. And after all the railings which are cast upon it, the world though slow in rendering in its verdict, is just at last. He who panders to the prejudices of a clique, may become its pet, and in that he has his reward, while he who speaks the truth boldly, relying upon God for strength, though he may be persecuted and neglected, and be compelled to walk through the "way which is desert," will eventually have justice, even from the world; and though he may not see it in the flesh, the truths which he utters will shine onward and add a lustre to the crown of glory which he wears above.[42]

Up to this point in the review, the end of the first page, Geraldine has not mentioned Andersen's name a single time. However, the reader familiar with his autobiography and a major criticism of the man depicted in it gradually wakens to the realization that the reviewer is presenting a rather convoluted defense and justification of what many consider the Dane's hypersensitivity to indifference or criticism. This s/he does by placing his critics in a poor light, all the while casting a virtually hagiographic glow about Andersen himself qua "the author."

Subsequently, the reader also slowly becomes aware that Geraldine's apologia extends beyond Andersen's oversensitiveness: "He has such a childlike confidence in the world to which he tells his story, that we should condemn ourselves did we doubt a syllable. There is a moral beauty in the simplicity of a soul like his, upon which it is delightful to dwell. He reveals his lowly origin and the poverty of his childhood with the same ingenuousness with which he records the homage of princes."[43] Others may suppress their lowly origins out of cowardly pride, "yet it is struggles and trials like these which make the greatest men. He who has met and conquered them, need not repine that he was poor. He has a moral wealth which gold can never measure, a patent of nobility greater than was ever issued by an Emperor, for it is sealed by the hand of God."[44] The reviewer then deftly turns Americans' criticism of Andersen's alleged obsequiousness against them, entering upon lengthy variations on the theme that "Here where there are no hereditary titles, there is perhaps as great a veneration for them and hankering after them as in any other land."[45]

After two pages of comments dealing primarily with Andersen's moral character, Geraldine turns to his life story, from the shoemaker's room in Odense to the royal dinner table in the nation's capital and the Dane's near tearful expression of gratitude; from the many cultural and political luminaries he met on his journeys—"As a book of travels alone this [volume] would be invaluable"—to the influence of individuals and circumstances on the formation of his intellectual character, a few examples of which warrant mention here.[46] Andersen relates that his father wept when he showed him his schoolbooks and told him what he had learned at grammar school, which leads Geraldine to write, "This simple incident speaks volumes, and in the name and character of the son, we see a glorious temple, which like that of Solomon, it was in the heart of his father to build."[47] Referring to a passage in chapter 4, where Andersen recounts the criticism he suffered on the publication of his Hoffmannesque *Walking Tour from Holmen's Canal to the Eastern Point of Amager in the Years 1828 and 1829* (1829; *Fodreise fra Holmens Canal til Østpynten af Amager i Aarene 1828 og 1829*), the reviewer continues, "At one period of his life, his writings became satirical. Satire is natural to none. It is the refuge of a proud but wounded heart. It is a dangerous art, and one in which none but those of deep and keen feelings can excel. Morbidly sensitive and really humble[,] he had been scourged as the gifted too often are with the imputation of vanity; 'and when those whom we love smite us, scourges become scorpions.'"[48] However,

A new an[d] immense world opens before him. The poet loves, but the lady loves another. He tells not the name nor the abode of the fair one. With true delicacy he devotes but half a page to this great event of his life. Yet we see its influence upon every other page. This trial swallows up all the lesser ones, and that past[,] the light breaks upon him, and his life grows brighter and brighter until the day of popular and poetic favor is full upon him.[49]

Paternal love, romantic love, and, finally, the love of a friend, Jenny Lind, on whose brow Andersen "places a crown in the fragrance of which those of the world are forgotten"—these are for Geraldine the most important formative forces in Andersen's life.[50]

In the final paragraph of the article—for such it is, as much as a review—Geraldine cites a "greater pleasure" in reading the book than any previously mentioned: "It is like reading a song of praise and thanksgiving, that purest but rarest offering to God."[51] What follows assumes the proportions of a sermon, one presented in a state of exaltation:

> We make *confessions* and *petitions* and our souls are in earnest, but how feeble are the notes of *praise* which we offer, how weak our efforts to glorify Him. And it will be so while the spirit chafes and rebels against earthly trials. When we can welcome adversity as a friend, when we can clasp the cross to our breast "uttering songs in the night" then can we give acceptable songs of praise. Then from the heaven to which we are journeying will stream a light which will gild the dark places of this world with its own bright coloring. Then we can exclaim "how beautiful is earth, how noble is humanity!["] "It is a joy to live and to believe in God and man." The religion of our poet is not merely one of *feeling*, it is one of *action*, it is a *living faith.* The holy spirit given at his baptism seems to have illumined his whole life, shining upon the darkest steps with a brighter radiance.[52]

Geraldine knows that Andersen is still living and thus concludes by paraphrasing the last lines of the book, "From that life the world has yet much to hope. But should we be disappointed, should the star of his brightness cease to shine, we have only to say in his own words, "'still it has shone, we have received our portion; let it set.'"[53]

When taking pen in hand to discuss Andersen's autobiography, Geraldine likely had the variously mixed reviews of most of his or her predecessors in mind. For early and late s/he is at pains to counter the three major criticisms leveled at Andersen by his early American commentators and many of their counterparts in Europe, to which Andersen himself had responded with repeated lamentations and explanations or self-justifications—his oversensitivity to criticism, his obsequiousness, and his vanity. If the Geraldine who wrote the notice was not surnamed "Jewsbury," s/he certainly shared the English reviewer's fundamental concern for moral rectitude in literature.[54] For none of Andersen's American critics views him and his work from a more consistently, indeed insistently moral and specifically religious standpoint, an approach to judging art that could obviously still lay claim to validity, if certainly not exclusivity, in the United States of the time. If that moral-religious insistence and its elevated ductus offend a modern sensibility, one cannot deny that they flow from a very close and quite thoughtful reading of the autobiography. And if Geraldine took Andersen's portrayal of himself at face value, one may be inclined to concede that a distinct ideality attached to both the man and his work, so that both the book and the review, while unquestionably incomplete, were and are nonetheless not without their legitimacy.

A notice of similar tendency but entirely different tonality appeared in the *Christian Register* under the title "A Happy and Beautiful Life" in April 1849.[55] The *Register* was the official journal of the American Unitarian Association and spanned a period of well over a hundred years, from 1821 to 1957; merged with the *Universalist Leader* in 1961, it lives on today as the *UU World.*[56] During the nineteenth century, the magazine published theological contributions by such noted figures in Unitarianism as William Ellery Channing, Andrews Norton, and Henry Ware Jr., as well as articles on religion and religious news. However, it also served as an outlet for local, national, and international news, biography, religious poetry, and book reviews.

The notice of Andersen's autobiography was written "For the Register" by an individual residing in "Keene, N[ew] H[ampshire]," as one reads at the top and the bottom of the notice, respectively. The identity of the correspondent is unclear, but he may well have been Abiel Abbot Livermore (1811–1892), a graduate of Harvard College and Harvard Divinity School who served as pastor of the Unitarian church in Keene from 1836 to 1850 before moving on to other pastorates and activities.[57] In any case, he appears to have been familiar with structural features of the Protestant sermon.

At the beginning of the notice, the reviewer quotes a passage from the penultimate paragraph of the book to illustrate and justify the title of his commentary: "'The story of my life, up to the present hour, lies unrolled before me, so rich and beautiful that I could not have invented it. I feel that I am a child of good fortune; almost every one meets me with love and candor, and seldom has my confidence in human nature been deceived. From the prince to the poorest peasant I have felt the noble human heart beat. It is a joy to live and to believe in God and man.'"[58] The writer then explains the reasons for the characteristic qualities of Andersen's life: "The man's life is beautiful and happy, simply because of his child-like purity and innocence. He has passed the midway of mortal life, but his child-heart has not grown old. It beats as high, as hopefully and as warmly as in the fresh days of his boyhood. The candor and confidence of early youth has never departed from him, and his 'belief in God and man' has never faltered."

The reviewer now goes about making an Everyman of Andersen:

He was a poor boy, who, without the assistance of friends, went into the world to seek a *living*, as thousands have done before him, and are doing now. No very great adversity opposed him, and no very kind fortune ever smiled upon him. Little of that which we are apt to call success in life has ever fallen to his portion. Fame which has been falsely called the highest good of earth, has never waited on him,—except indeed that fame which calls his name blessed among the good, not great ones of the earth. Riches have not showered their luxuries nor their cares upon him. In the field of letters he has not glittered, and no shouting multitudes have praised him. His little stories have made him a welcome guest at the evening fireside among the children, and there he is truly famous. He has scaled no dazzling heights of philosophy or science. He calls himself a poet, but the world will never bind his brow with the poet's garland. Still his life is full of poetry, and the simple wreath that he wears shall be fresh and green forever. He is not a great man; he has done no great thing, and notwithstanding he says that his "life is a lovely story, happy and full of incident," yet it is only little incidents which have made it so lovely and happy.

The reviewer gives Andersen and his achievement to date what is in all probability the most modest positive assessment possible. And much as with Geraldine, though at the opposite rhetorical extreme, an observer applying an objective standard would find it difficult to call him absolutely wrong, at least based on the evidence available to him. However, the writer is not concerned first and foremost, if at all, with Andersen's art, intellect, or success:

The lessons which such a life teach are those which we are all too slow to learn; but those lessons acquired and practiced, procure the great good for which we are all striving—happiness. Love and kindness towards each other; contentment in our daily lot, however humble, and a grateful trust and confidence in God; these are the teachings constantly before us. These let us study and consider well. . . . The life and character of Andersen illustrate this effect. Believing in God and man, he trusted both, and as he received the favors of his Maker with delight and gladness, so he dispensed from his full soul its warmth on all around him. Full of confidence and trust, he met his fellow men with an open heart, a cordial hand, and a love-beaming eye; and it is chiefly because of his own rich offerings of good will to all, that he is enabled to say—"every one meets me with love and candor; seldom has my confidence been deceived." So may *we* likewise speak, if in such generous manner we have met our fellow men.

After expanding on the foregoing thoughts for a space, the reviewer writes in conclusion,

We have chosen for our lesson the example of a living man, but an older example and a lovelier life than his speak to us from another land. God be thanked! . . . The Son of our common Father, our elder brother, who suffered and sorrowed on the earth, still loving us more than his own life, smiles kindly from his happy home above and beckons to each one of us, saying—"Friend, come up *higher.*" Little, nameless, unconsidered acts of daily kindness are steps upon the ladder, and treading them ourselves, let us lend an arm to a weaker brother.

The review in the *Christian Register* is the one notice that at least compares to Geraldine's article in its fundamental concern for the role of religion in Andersen's autobiography, if not in its tone or diction. Unobtrusively and conversationally elegant rather than rhapsodic, it would not have been out of place had it been presented from the pulpit—and it may well have been. For formally, it adheres by and large to the text-application type of sermon long common in Protestant churches.[59] Andersen's account of his life, specifically the important passage from the end of the work and other quotations, corresponds to the scriptural text. This, the reviewer, as pastor-exegete, elucidates as evidence of the Christian virtues of *humilitas*, *fides*, *spes*, and *caritas*, which, in turn, constitute the guarantor of happiness. The reviewer then invites his "congregants" to embrace this model existence, to apply its imperatives in their own lives. Only in the final remarks does he approach the lofty tone of Geraldine, likening Andersen to Christ in the process.

The *Christian Review* devotes all of two sentences to the autobiography, one of them rather commonplace, the other rather puzzling.[60] The quarterly was founded in 1836 by James D. Knowles, a Baptist minister and professor at Newton Theological Institution in Newton Centre, Massachusetts, which was a graduate seminary affiliated with an organization now known as American Baptist Churches USA and part of the Andover Newton Theological School.[61] Its articles, virtually all of which were written by clergymen, covered a wide range of subjects, including literature and education, but were heavily weighted toward theology. It was never profitable and succumbed to poor circulation in 1863. The editor at the time the Andersen review appeared was Samuel F. Smith, best remembered now as the author of the text for "America" ("My Country, 'Tis of Thee"). He reportedly told Evert Duyckinck that he wrote fourteen hundred pages as well as short notices for the *Review* and is thus probably responsible for the critique presently under consideration.[62]

The review reads as follows: "This beautiful earnest sketch of the life of a man of extraordinary simplicity, is adapted to furnish innocent entertainment to an hour of recreation, having the merit of being true and honest, as well as sparkling and poetical. It will be chiefly interesting to the lovers of dramatic literature."[63] Now, by 1848 Americans had been introduced to Andersen as the author of novels, travel books, a certain few poems, and fairy tales. As we have seen, however, not a word of any of his plays had crossed from Danish to English or from Denmark to England or the United States. Why his autobiography should be interesting "chiefly" to lovers of drama is thus a matter of some curiosity, to say the least. Perhaps the reviewer was one of apparently few to whom Andersen was still unfamiliar, perhaps he did not bother to read the book. On the other hand, and more charitably, it may have been precisely his and other Americans' ignorance of Andersen's work for the stage that piqued his interest and elicited the statement. Certainly, Andersen devotes considerable space in the autobiography to his first and most passionate literary love. Whatever the case may have been, readers of the volume, as well as the review, could no longer claim ignorance of the fact that he was a playwright of distinct pretension.

1871

At the beginning of the chapter, we saw evidence of the importance Andersen attached to the publication of an updated version of his autobiography in the United States. In his correspondence with Horace Scudder, he recurred to the subject time and again, from his proposal to write additional chapters in April 1868, to his response to the appearance of the volume in May 1871, to his repeated inquiries about a corrected edition that was never issued due to apparent poor sales of the first.[64] In September 1871, Andersen wrote to Scudder, "I am anxious to hear how *The Story of My Life* is going in the American book trade. To judge from the many letters I receive from many persons over there who are unknown to me, I conclude that it is being widely read."[65] There is no record to support or contradict Andersen's conclusion, though Scudder's periodic apologies for the small royalty payments he was able to send him provide a telling clue to the true state of affairs.[66] However, the book was certainly widely reviewed in the American press. Between mid-March and November 1871, twenty notices (and another ten of lesser import) came out, this in addition to the six discussed in *More Than Meets the Eye*. As with the reviews of Andersen's other works, not all are illuminating. Many repeat each other, if not necessarily intentionally, or make only one or two noteworthy points. Many others, however, not least of all the negative ones, are quite revealing.

Hurd and Houghton prepared the American publishing world well for the forthcoming appearance of the Author's Edition of the autobiography. As early as October 1870, six months prior to its issuance, a pre-publication announcement appeared in the *Trade Circular and Publishers' Bulletin*, and an unsuspecting reader of another published in the same periodical four months later may have assumed that the book had already come out: "*The Story of My Life*, by Hans Christian Andersen, . . . is now first translated into English."[67] A month and a half hence, indeed, Hurd and Houghton's house organ, the *Riverside Bulletin*, proclaimed more accurately that the "autobiography is now for the first time given complete in English," providing a brief overview of the work's genesis and signaling the romance and eminent figures the reader would discover in it.[68] According to a letter from Scudder to Andersen, however, the volume actually appeared, after several delays caused by problems with translators, on April 8, 1871.[69]

Even taking into account the contemporary use of advance review copies, it is a matter of some wonderment that the next notice of the autobiography came out the very same day as the book itself, and across the continent in San Francisco's *Daily Evening Bulletin* at that.[70] The reviewer's comments are uniformly positive and, though hardly undiscriminating, reflect a sunny disposition:

> The reading world is curious to know all about its favorite writers, and no author has more thoroughly unbosomed himself than Andersen. His confidences are as full and fond as those of one intimate friend to another. The picture of his life and struggles, his successes and triumphs, is fascinating by its simplicity and candor. We learn to like even the little vanities and foibles of the man, and can laugh good naturedly at his splenetic strictures upon his critics, concerning some of whom he says: "we feel a desire to flagellate such wet dogs, who come into our rooms and lay themselves down in the best places there." There are many such naive confessions, as we might expect from a sensitive artist and poet who has made his own way in the world and who is able to say: "My life is a lovely story, happy and full of incident."

In contrast to many of his peers, this reviewer responds to Andersen's "little" personal weaknesses with humorous good nature, owing in part to traits commonly associated with artists, but not least of all, one suspects, because of Andersen's frankness and perceived ability to meet adversity with an optimistic smile. Like them, however, he also notes a simplicity in the book that he surely associates with its author and that may well be attributable to the prominence of the fairy tales and stories in critics' minds.

The reviewer offers one uncommon opinion which, were it not for the overall tone of his remarks, could be taken as a criticism of the bulk of Andersen's lifework:

> It happens often that a well told story of a notable man's life is better than any of his works. Max Muller [*sic*] thinks the life and character of Schiller worth as much to mankind as his poems; and we all know how much oftener we look into *Johnson's Life* [*sic*] by Boswell than into anything that Johnson himself wrote. In like manner we are inclined to like Andersen's autobiography better than any of his other stories—although, these are themselves full of the man's kindly, ebullient nature, and often based on true incidents in his experience.[71]

There are indeed many parallels relating to character and incident between the autobiography and both the novels and especially the travel books. However, the writer's formulation of his preference for the autobiography is particularly striking: he likes it "better than any of [Andersen's] *other* stories" [emphasis added]. Whatever one may think of his valuation per se, the reviewer appears to have had at least a vague prescient understanding of the fictitious nature of much of what Andersen offered the public in the work most important to him—that is, a sense of his self-conscious construction of his life *story*.

In addition to a buoyant personality and an original perspective, the critic discloses a distinctly empathetic nature in his response to the passage where Andersen relates his father's unrealized literary aspirations:

> Ah, to how many of us, drudging in lines of toil foreign to our capacities and yearnings, as to our early ambitions perhaps, comes the moment when we look back in an ecstacy of regret and self pity, inwardly weeping over opportunities lost or never known, and exclaiming as we look at the fate of others, "that was the path upon which I ought to have gone!" It is with such unaffected touches all through his writings that Andersen moves our sympathies, making us feel better for reading him, although we may often feel sadder.[72]

Insight into the virtue of sorrow further marks the reviewer as a person of uncommon sensibility.

In conclusion, he applies a more individual touch to a couple of very common responses to Andersen's work:

> Then his autobiography is full of graphic sketches of society, customs, character and scenery that are out of the beaten track of description and literary reference. These show us how much of the early Norse traits remain in Scandinavian lands, chiefly a peculiar vigor and heartiness, mixed with a naive humor and racy individuality. The book is sure of as wide a circle of readers in America[,] where Andersen is very popular, as any of his stories command.

The reviewer's comments reveal an appreciation for Andersen's rare descriptive ability and, at the same time, indicate that even in the 1870s his work still struck some American readers as foreign to their own literary experience, yet interesting for that very reason. If falling victim to Longfellow's myth of the Northland, he at least gives "the other" some definition.

Less than a week after publication of the autobiography and its first notice, reviews appeared in three different periodicals, one of which was the *Harvard Advocate*.[73] The *Advocate* was and remains the undergraduate literary magazine of Harvard University, whose close proximity to Hurd and Houghton in Cambridge may explain the publication's quick response to the book.[74] Founded in 1866 as a fortnightly tabloid, the journal early on enjoyed the support of James Russell Lowell and Oliver Wendell Holmes and has published fledgling writing by a host of American cultural luminaries, including Conrad Aiken, Van Wyck Brooks, E. E. Cummings, and T. S. Eliot.

The anonymous, but presumably undergraduate reviewer was sufficiently competent to sound notes often re-sounded by seasoned critics:

> All those who have been delighted by the gentle genius of Hans Christian Andersen—and their name is legion—will take a peculiar pleasure in reading his autobiography. It is written in the simple, unaffected style which characterizes his stories, and is, as Andersen himself says, the "Wonder Story" of them all.... He says, at the outset, "My life is a lovely story, happy, and full of incident;" and in this initial sentence one may see that his happiness and uniform success are due to the nature of the man himself.[75]

The first sentence of the autobiography is probably the most often quoted passage in the entire work, and the uncritical identification of man, story, and style forms one of the most common features of American critics' appraisal of it. Like many other commentators, the reviewer appreciates becoming acquainted with "many distinguished men and women, who are now either dead or rapidly passing away," but finds that "the main interest of the story centres in the author himself, a man who unites to rare ability a childlike simplicity and purity of character."[76] Andersen's unique *naturel*, significantly, does not make him attractive to children alone: "This child-nature, which he seems never to have outgrown, not only puts him *en rapport* with children themselves, but has evidently won for him an easier access than is usual to the good-will of all whom he has wished to please. His genial, winning disposition seems to have smoothed many of the difficulties which every young author must overcome."[77] The appeal Andersen's "child-nature" held for adults as well as for children was clearly apparent to this reviewer of the autobiography, whose notice may thus serve as a preview of an important finding detailed in chapter 6. At 569 pages, the book understandably strikes him as being long, "but throughout its entire length one's interest cannot flag, nor can he tire of reading the story of a life which deserved to be, and has been, eminently successful."[78]

Another of the earliest reviews of Scudder's edition of the work came out in the *North American and United States Gazette* of Philadelphia.[79] The writer numbers among those who confuse Andersen's native tongue and, perhaps, his nationality as well: "He won fame with his pen and has spread his reputation wherever the English language or the German is read." Much of the review revolves around Andersen's sense of self:

> This is the first complete and connected narrative, and is told in so simple and charming a manner, with such evident appreciation of all his achievements and

such kindly mention of other distinguished persons whose friendship he has had
. . . as will edify all. There is a curious resemblance in Andersen's simplicity
and self-appreciation to Goldsmith's familiar character; and his story is more
interesting through his own self-portraiture than for any of many interesting
descriptions.

"[E]vident appreciation" of all one's achievements, "self-appreciation"—
there is obviously a wide rhetorical gap between such characterizations and
the "vanity" sometimes thrown in Andersen's face. Whether critics assumed a
position at one edge or the other appears to have depended on the weight they
placed on the idiosyncratic geniality that would indeed seem to have linked
Andersen, whom *Peterson's* termed an "erratic genius," and the congenial
and impetuous author of *The Vicar of Wakefield* and *She Stoops to Conquer*.[80]

The review in the *Phrenological Journal* was one of the later ones to appear but greeted the autobiography as if it were one of the first: "Here we
have it. This most popular of all the modern Danish writers gives us the story
of his life—including the pedigree of his progenitors—in that familiar col-
loquial style which interests and holds the reader."[81] In the manner of certain
reviewers of the 1840s, however, the writer is concerned with more than
pleasurable reading: "Nor is this story merely entertaining, it is very instructive. Without being sectarian or dogmatic, it is full of good counsel, given in
acceptable language. Every young man should read it." At the same time, the
critic does not enlarge upon the nature of said good counsel, though it was
plainly of a broadly moral-religious kind.

His counterpart for the *Christian Union* found instruction of a very different sort in the book:

Hans Christian Andersen has afforded too many delightful hours to readers
through many lands, and in many languages, to be refused the indulgence which
we are very sorry to find his Autobiography requires. In a striking degree, he is
one who forces his readers to form an ideal of the man who has inspired them
with so much of personal affection for himself; and the discovery on conclusive
evidence that the reality is other than we have painted to ourselves, is as painful
a dissipation of an illusion as that which befell Tom Pinch on learning that the
Pecksniff evolved from his own inner consciousness, had all along been non-
existent in the actual world. Of the same kind will be the shock to the admirers
of Hans Christian Andersen on finding that his self-portraiture consists of an
array of qualities so pitiful that, had it been presented on other evidence than his
own, it must have been incontinently rejected as incredible.[82]

The comparison of Andersen to the likes of Dickens's Seth Pecksniff, together with the equation of the reader and Tom Pinch, is perhaps the harshest
criticism ever brought to bear on Andersen in the United States. However, the

deception long perpetrated on an unsuspecting American public relates not to hypocrisy, as with Pecksniff, but rather to other failings pilloried in *Martin Chuzzlewit* and other novels by Dickens:

> It is not only that the book—evidently a true reflex herein of the man's life—is instinct with a self-conscious vanity, than which Goldsmith's was not more exaggerated, and with a complacent self-absorption, whereby the world of men and things exist only in their correlation with literary productions obtruded by their author upon every audience with the same egotistical persistency that made Wordsworth a social incubus upon every company; together with this is an unintermittent strain of that most disagreeable species of egotism, which has been immortalized in the 'umbleness of Uriah Heep, mingled with a querulous petulance over a series of sedulously cherished grievances that becomes inordinately tedious. Detailed recitations of the injustices which, in our author's fancy, the Danish literary world primarily exists for the purpose of inflicting upon him constitute the most impressive feature of the book.

The reviewer appears to proceed no more critically than certain others in his stated assumption that the autobiography is a faithful reflection of its author's life. And yet he contradicts himself in what would seem to have been a painful and reluctant concession:

> Under the accumulation of these excrescences which incrust the book, there is, to be sure, an element of matter-of-fact wherefrom many incidents of the author's life may be extracted with the same sort of pains that one exercises in getting kernels out of nuts; similarly, like Virgil's *rari nantes in gurgite vasto* [rare survivors in the immense sea], among the swarm of celebrities unheard of out of Denmark, there, now and then, appear those whose sketches by Andersen's pen have real interest—Jenny Lind, Heine, Victor Hugo, Miss Bremer, Oehlenschläger, Thorwaldsen, Balzac, Au*erbach*, *Ladies Morgan* and *Blessington*, *Dickens*, etc. etc. And it must be added that the hold which Andersen secured upon minds like those goes far to show that the conceptions one forms from his works must be truer than that embodied in his more formal self-portraiture.[83]

Here, however, the reviewer makes another volte-face, continuing, "That very childishness, indeed, which forms one of the charms of [Andersen's] writings, goes a long way toward accounting for the utter lack of dignity and reserve, for the tedium, and weakness, and prattle, that make the book one of the most wearisome we have ever come upon, and leave upon its reader much the kind of exhaustion produced by setting and holding one's mind in accord with that of an exacting child." Proceeding from these comments, the critic's closing could not be more elegantly, and therefore more exquisitely, damning: "The indulgence which we have spoken of as due to the author, may be combined with that which every man has a right to show toward himself, by a refusal to make acquaintance with this unfortunate book, in which we are persuaded its author has done himself injustices greater than any of those of which he so bitterly complains."

The *National Sunday School Teacher* published a briefer but similar and more uniformly condemnatory notice of the autobiography.[84] Founded in Chicago as a nondenominational monthly, the magazine ran from 1866 to 1882, claiming a very respectable circulation of 33,600 in 1871.[85] Much of this success must be attributed to Edward Eggleston (1837–1902), a clergyman, novelist, and historian who edited the journal from 1867 to 1871 before moving to New York City, where, among many other activities, he wrote his best-known novel, *The Hoosier School-Master*.[86]

Whether the reviewer was Eggleston or someone else, he clearly felt that Andersen was not the best person to tell his life story: "Andersen is widely known for the genial nature of his voluminous writings, mainly imaginative. We should be glad to read what some judicious friend would tell us of the man himself, but Andersen is not that judicious friend."[87] For this reviewer, as for others, indeed, Andersen quite injudiciously betrays a pronounced lack of *humilitas*:

> Here is an account of a man whom we find to be badly diseased in two particulars. All along he has been eaten up with self-esteem; saying, for instance, that, in his year at school, "four *great* poets were made students;" to-wit, "Arnesen, Hansen, Nielsen, and *H. C. Andersen!*" And then he has all along been sick with disappointment, to use no stronger term, because the world, and Denmark in particular, did not recognize his ability, as fast as he thought he made it evident. He describes himself as a sort of butterfly, flitting from flower to flower through all the cities of Europe, and all the time declaring that he was not appreciated.

Whether writing from a specifically religious standpoint or not, the reviewer deems Andersen guilty of the capital sin of *superbia.*

The writer for the *Congregational Review* does not go as far as his most displeased colleagues in his criticism of Andersen's self-portrait, but he is not taken with it, either.[88] At the outset, to be sure, he raises no red flags: "It reads just like Herodotus—was the report of one who had preceded us in perusing this singular autobiography,—just such quaint simplicity, and naive, unconscious egotism. Weird and wild too, in incident and costume at times, and altogether strange throughout to American experience and thought. We read for ourselves and found the report of the home critic accurate and just."[89] Indeed, the parallel drawn to the Father of History could be intended as a badge of honor, even if borrowed from an unidentified, perhaps Danish ("home") critic, and the writer appears rather to appreciate than to object to the difference between Andersen's "exotic" ambient and his own. However, he continues in a less complementary way: "To one that has little that is more tasking at hand, the innocent garrulousness of Andersen may be, we can conceive quite charming; to one whose reading must needs lie in more laborious fields, it is a trifle wearisome. It has all his graces, however, of diction and expression."[90] In other words, the book is worth one's time if one has nothing of a serious nature to occupy it, which qualifies the review as decidedly mixed.

Although generally less expansive and incisive in their praise than the three preceding reviewers in their criticism, the large majority of commentators evinced the same quite friendly response to the autobiography as the writer for the *Daily Evening Bulletin.* In the process, they reveal individual bits of opinion presumably shared by other readers. Like his colleague in San Francisco, the reviewer for a Macon, Georgia, newspaper prefers the work to any of those that preceded it, which, of course, include the stories and tales.[91] The *Cleveland Morning Herald* states that it "has for years been a great favorite with the admirers of the Danish story-teller," demonstrating that the early phase of Andersen's reception had not been forgotten by all.[92] For the *Christian Standard*, the (fictional?) interest of the book is such that the reader is seldom aware that he is "conning" a life story.[93] While some accuse Andersen of name-dropping, the reviewer for the *Sunday-School Times* opines that "his visits to, and personal recollections of his contemporaries in the world of literature, art and the drama, make the 'story of his life' a rich repository of facts and impressions in the current history of belle [*sic*] lettres."[94]

In contrast to the critic for the *National Sunday School Teacher*, the reviewer for the *Portland Transcript* feels that only Andersen could have written his autobiography: "*The Story of My Life* . . . is just such an autobiography as none in the world but Hans Christian Andersen could have written, even though his life had been duplicated in theirs. The charming, childlike simplicity with which the good man tells of all that has happened to him, the innocent vanity with which he has treasured the compliments of small and great, is indeed a curious study."[95] The critic for the *Churchman* quite agrees: "It is well that Andersen, whose name has become honored and beloved in so many lands, has written the history of his own life, and not left the task to those who, notwithstanding their knowledge of, and intimacy with, him could not have learned all that Andersen has himself told us."[96] For this reviewer, the book's claim on the attention of the reader is great indeed:

We need not say that this story is like everything he has written—charmingly told. That quiet naturalness and sweet simplicity which have already won the hearts of thousands, are here especially prominent. The life thus sketched and laid open to the world, is one which, for the power of awakening interest and sympathy, has never been surpassed, even in the delineations of fiction. We read it with all the breathless absorption of attention that chains children to his

"Wonder Stories," and yet we feel all the time that we are following the chain of a real life.

Given the overwhelming popularity of fiction, especially novels, at the time, the last two assertions are especially meaningful. The reviewer speaks for many others when he writes,

> And, aside from the value which attaches to this work as being a life-story of a wonderful man, and a story which no one knows or can tell us as well as he, it throws much light upon the other volumes which Andersen has written, telling us who were the originals of the characters drawn there, and now universally known, and what scenes in his previous stories have been drawn from his own experience. Thus this story is in some sort a key to the treasures he has already given to the world.

In short, the autobiography furnishes a guide to understanding much of Andersen's other work.

The reviewer for Montpelier's *Vermont Watchman & State Journal* agrees that Andersen is the right person to tell his life story: "Such a delightful story teller as Hans Christian Andersen ought to tell his story interestingly. And so he has in 'The Story of My Life.'"[97] While finding the "mingling of personal adventures and accounts of [Andersen's] literary performances . . . intensely interesting," however, the writer locates the principal appeal of the book elsewhere: "But the crowning charm is the spirit of faith and hopefulness with which he received every thing, and the evident soul of the genuine poet that makes of his own lot and his own life the best that Providence could have given him. This is its moral, and it is the grandest theme that any biography could have." This reviewer shares the *Daily Evening Bulletin*'s appreciation for Andersen's positivity but highlights its religious dimension, which was quite appropriate, yet nonetheless uncommon for the time and place.

The *Aldine* issued one of the briefer but most pregnant notices of the autobiography.[98] From its modest beginnings as the house organ of a New York printing firm, the monthly developed into a magazine that deserved its ultimate subtitle, *The Art Journal of America.*[99] It distinguished itself through high-quality printing and original woodcuts as well as reproductions of works by both European and American artists, including Gustave Doré and members of the Hudson River School. At the same time, it bore the stamp of a general literary magazine. The issue in which the review of Andersen's autobiography appeared, for example, contains familiar essays, stories, poetry, biography, articles on travel and an art exhibit, and short book notices. The publication ran for only eleven years, from 1868 to 1879, but had a circulation of twenty thousand in 1871 and, according to one source, double that number the following year, including sales at home and abroad.[100]

The *Aldine*'s reviewer describes Andersen's book as a "rambling, gossiping, cheerful story of a rambling, gossiping, cheerful old gentleman, whom every one knows for his 'Improvisatore' and 'Tin Soldier' ("The Steadfast Tin Soldier"; "Den standhaftige Tinsoldat"). For sixty years he goes up and down the world, traveling everywhere, seeing everything, making friends with everybody. It is a pleasant mosaic of the most varied scenes and people, and can be read by snatches, or in course, at the reader's pleasure."[101] In very few words the writer manages to encapsulate many, if certainly not all of the key features of Andersen's autobiography and the man described in it, features that recur in perhaps the majority of reviews written in the United States, and he does so in a style and tone that correspond to the image presented.

In view of the particular importance Andersen placed on his autobiographies, he might well have been pleased that *The [True] Story of My Life* attracted more critical attention in the New World than any of his other writings.[102] Among the publications that issued reviews of the works, the *Christian Union* was the only one that was roughly comparable to periodicals such as the *Atlantic Monthly*, the *Christian Examiner*, and *Harper's New Monthly* in quality and/or circulation. However, a host of less prestigious but eminently respectable magazines entered the discussion, most prominent among them originally religious publications like the *Christian Inquirer*, the *Christian Register*, the *Churchman*, and the *National Sunday School Teacher* that had generally become family-oriented magazines with broader interests. All of the reviewers are either anonymous or unidentifiable, but possibilities such as Briggs, Channing, Eggleston, and Smith suggest the sophistication of their work. Ultimately, the commentaries speak for themselves, whether they are appreciative or disparaging, and there are significant numbers of both kinds.

Indeed, the autobiography elicited the most extreme expressions of approval and disapproval of any of the works. For several reviewers, Andersen's egotism is "naive," "unconscious," and thus forgivable, while for others it is apparently unredeemable.[103] According to the critic for the *Christian Union*, such vanity debases him to the level of Dickens's despicables Seth Pecksniff and Uriah Heep, a level not elevated by his excessive sensitivity to criticism. Another reviewer compares him most unfavorably to the Bard of Ayrshire with respect to sense of self before the powerful.[104] Inspired by his moral-religious character, however, Geraldine launches a spirited, if in part overly subtle defense of him for all these flaws.[105] Similarly, the "pastor" from Keene delivers an apologia of the poet as a model of a Christian life well lived.[106] Some early reviewers, had they been writing twenty-five years later, might have drawn a parallel between Andersen and Horatio Alger's Raggedy Dick and his many cousins, though by that time the comparison appears to have lost much, if certainly not all of its force.

Certain reviewers for whom Andersen's egocentricity was no disqualifying factor disclose an uncritical, often implicit identification of the man, his life story, and its style, noting its simplicity, naturalness, and beauty. Some, indeed, treat the autobiography more like a work of art than as a revelation of character. Closer to the truth than they realized, they find it as interesting as a romance or more appealing than the author's (other) creative writing. Or they see in it something akin to the travel books, "full of graphic sketches of society, customs, character and scenery that are out of the beaten track of description and literary reference."[107] Several writers consider the book a key to understanding Andersen's other works and appreciate the insight he provides into the many notable contemporaries he met during his many travels.

NOTES

1. See Hans Christian Andersen to Horace Scudder, April 21, 1868, in *The Andersen-Scudder Letters*, ed. Jean Hersholt and Waldemar Westergaard (Berkeley and Los Angeles: University of California Press, 1949), 11–12.

2. Horace E. Scudder, "Advertisement," in *The Story of My Life*, author's ed., ed. Horace E. Scudder (New York: Hurd and Houghton, 1871), iii. Also see Scudder to Andersen, April 23, 1870, in Hersholt and Westergaard, *The Andersen-Scudder Letters*, 75.

3. As far as the United States is concerned, the publication history of the autobiography came to an end at this point. However, it continued in Denmark, initially with the separate printing in 1877 of the additional chapters written for the Author's Edition. The Danish manuscript from which the first German and English versions were translated was not published in Denmark until 1942. The truly definitive version (i.e., the revised edition of 1859 together with the Danish original of the additional chapters) appeared in 1951. For a detailed historical overview of the work beginning in 1847, see Helge Topsøe-Jensen, "Inledning," in *Mit Livs Eventyr*, by Hans Christian Andersen, ed. Helge Topsøe-Jensen, 2 vols. (Copenhagen: Gyldendal, 1951), 1:8–23.

4. See Bo Grønbech, *H. C. Andersen: Levnedsløb-Digtning-Personlighed* (Copenhagen: Nyt Nordisk Forlag Arnold Busck, 1971), 56.

5. See Jackie Wullschlager, *Hans Christian Andersen: The Life of a Storyteller* (New York: Knopf, 2001), 287–88.

6. See Grønbech, *H. C. Andersen*, 214. According to Bredsdorff, the autobiography in the Author's Edition found only one reviewer in England; Elias Bredsdorff, *H. C. Andersen og England* (Copenhagen: Rosenkilde og Baggers Forlag, 1954), 481–82.

7. Hans Christian Andersen, *The Fairy Tale of My Life: An Autobiography* (New York: Cooper Square Press, 2000).

8. Unsigned review of *The True Story of My Life*, trans. Mary Howitt, *Boston Weekly Messenger*, August 11, 1847, 2. According to Bredsdorff, the first English review appeared on July 17. Bredsdorff, *H. C. Andersen og England*, 451.

9. See "About the *Weekly Messenger* [Volume] (Boston) 1811–1815," Chronicling America: Historic American Newspapers, accessed April 5, 2016, http://chronic lingamerica.loc.gov/lccn/sn84045041/; "About *Boston Weekly Messenger* [Volume] (Boston [Mass.]) 1833–1861," Chronicling America: Historic American Newspapers, accessed April 5, 2016, http://chroniclingamerica.loc.gov/lccn/sn83021311/; and "Hale, John," in *Appletons' Cyclopædia of American Biography*, ed. John Fiske and James Grant Wilson (New York: D. Appleton, 1888), 3:30–33 (John Hale and his descendants are treated in one article; Nathan Hale the journalist is discussed on p. 31).

10. *Boston Weekly Messenger*, August 11, 1847, 2.

11. E. (William Ellery Channing, the Younger?), review of *The True Story of My Life*, *Christian World*, August 14, 1847, 3. See "About the *Christian World* [Volume] (Boston) 1843–1848," Chronicling America: Historic American Newspapers, accessed May 30, 2015, http://chroniclingamerica.loc.gov/lccn/00221510/.

12. In the only full studies on Channing I have been able to find, no mention is made of any reviewing activity for the *Christian World*. See Frederick T. McGill Jr., *Channing of Concord: A Life of William Ellery Channing II* (New Brunswick, NJ: Rutgers University Press, 1967); Robert N. Hudspeth, *Ellery Channing*, Twayne's United States Authors Series 223 (New York: Twayne, 1973). However, aside from brief periods in New York, where he worked for Horace Greeley's *Tribune*, and sojourning in Rome, Channing lived near Boston in Concord during the period in question. McGill, *Channing of Concord*, 82–89. For Channing's use of his middle name in print, see "William Ellery Channing," PoemHunter.com, accessed October 27, 2016, http://www.poemhunter.com/william-ellery-channing/biography/.

13. According to Erik Dal, however, Andersen received only £368 for *all* the work published in England over the course of his life, an amount surpassed by the sum he got during the late 1860s and early 1870s for the writings that appeared in the *Riverside Magazine*, *Scribner's*, and the Author's Edition. Erik Dal, "Hans Christian Andersen's Tales and America," *Scandinavian Studies* 40 (1968): 10–11.

14. *Christian World*, August 14, 1847, 3.

15. The reviewer's phrase "reader of his own heart" likely alludes to Lavater's *Geheimes Tagebuch: Von einem Beobachter Seiner Selbst* (1771), literally *Secret Diary: By an Observer of Himself.* In chapter 3, we saw that certain critics also detected a confessional quality in *A Poet's Bazaar* and *Pictures of Travel.*

16. *Christian World*, August 14, 1847, 3.

17. Unsigned review of *The True Story of My Life*, *Christian Inquirer*, August 21, 1847, 180.

18. See "*Christian Inquirer*," Worldcat, accessed June 2, 2015, http://www.world cat.org/title/christian-inquirer/oclc/8371032.

19. *Christian Inquirer*, August 21, 1847, 180.

20. Unsigned review of *The True Story of My Life*, *Young American's Magazine of Self-Improvement*, December 1, 1847, 364.

21. See *Young American's Magazine of Self-Improvement*, ed. George W. Light, vol. 1 (Boston: Charles H. Pierce, 1847), accessed June 2, 2015, https://books.google.com/books?id=REFAAAAAYAAJ&pg=PA371&lpg=PA371&dq=%22Young+American's+Magazine+of+Self-Improvement+%22&source=bl&ots=GtS8R3NpcS&sig=hddxDCd4qDh7RO4yUjcQGXu8Nts&hl=en&sa=X&ei=ACpuVe-3J4fvtQX2koKICw&ved=0CCAQ6AEwAA#v=onepage&q=%22Young%20American's%20Magazine%20of%20Self-Improvement%20%22&f=false. Searches for a second volume were unsuccessful.

22. See "Robert G. Valentine Family Papers," Massachusetts Historical Society: Collection Guides, accessed June 2, 2015, http://www.masshist.org/collection-guides/view/fa0383.

23. See Lorinda B. Cohoon, *Serialized Citizenships: Periodicals, Books, and American Boys* (Lanham, MD: Scarecrow Press, 2006), 32.

24. See Light's prospectus and selected reviews of the magazine, note 21, end of the site, pp. 3–4 and 1–4.

25. *Young American's Magazine of Self-Improvement*, December 1, 1847, 364.

26. "Hans Christian Andersen," unsigned review of *The True Story of My Life*, *Holden's Dollar Magazine*, July 1849, 446–48. In view of Andersen's popularity since the appearance of *The Improvisatore* and the first collections of tales, the publication of the notice almost two years after the initial review of the autobiography may incline one to speculate that the book sold well enough that publisher James Munroe issued further editions or impressions, though Bredsdorff lists none in *Danish Literature in English Translation.*

27. See Mott, *A History of American Magazines 1741–1850* (1930; repr., Cambridge, MA: Harvard University Press, 1957), 348; H. Fowler, "A Tribute to the Memory of Charles W. Holden," *Holden's Dollar Magazine*, January 1850, 33–38.

28. *Holden's Dollar Magazine*, July 1849, 446–47.

29. *Holden's Dollar Magazine*, July 1849, 447.

30. *Holden's Dollar Magazine*, July 1849, 447.

31. See Miller, *The Raven and the Whale: The War of Words and Wits in the Era of Poe and Melville* (1956; repr., Westport, CT: Greenwood, 1973), 226–27. Miller supplies evidence that Briggs also reviewed for *Holden's* (294). This, coupled with the style of the review, suggests that Briggs very possibly wrote it himself. Also see chapter 2, pp. 27 and 76, of the present study.

32. Victorian book reviews indeed played a significant part in determining what was read—and bought—through the often lengthy extracts from works they provided; see Monica Correa Fryckstedt, "Geraldine Jewsbury's *Athenaeum* Reviews: A Mirror of Mid-Victorian Attitudes to Fiction," *Victorian Periodicals Review* 23 (1990): 14.

33. Geraldine, review of *The True Story of My Life*, *American Literary Magazine*, January 1848, 56–60.

34. See Oliver Crane, "Timothy Dwight Sprague," in *Record of the Class of 1845 of Yale College* (New York: Jenkins & Thomas, 1881), 182–84.

35. Mott, *A History of American Magazines 1741–1850*, 347–48.

36. See Fryckstedt, "Geraldine Jewsbury's *Athenaeum* Reviews," 13.

37. See below and "Geraldine," "The Cavern of Waneonda," *American Literary Magazine*, February 1848, 106–11.

38. *American Literary Magazine*, January 1848, 56.

39. *American Literary Magazine*, January 1848, 56.

40. *American Literary Magazine*, January 1848, 56.

41. *American Literary Magazine*, January 1848, 56.

42. *American Literary Magazine*, January 1848, 56.

43. *American Literary Magazine*, January 1848, 57.

44. *American Literary Magazine*, January 1848, 57.

45. *American Literary Magazine*, January 1848, 57.

46. *American Literary Magazine*, January 1848, 58.

47. *American Literary Magazine*, January 1848, 59.

48. *American Literary Magazine*, January 1848, 59. The original of the quotation reads, "and when those who smite are those we love, then do the scourges become scorpions." Hans Christian Andersen, *The True Story of My Life: A Sketch*, trans. Mary Howitt (Boston: James Munroe, 1847), 91.

49. *American Literary Magazine*, January 1848, 59.

50. *American Literary Magazine*, January 1848, 59.

51. *American Literary Magazine*, January 1848, 60.

52. *American Literary Magazine*, January 1848, 60. "[U]ttering songs in the night" appears to allude to Job 35:9–10, which reads, in the King James Version, "By reason of the multitude of oppressions they make *the oppressed* to cry: they cry out by reason of the arm of the mighty. / But none saith, Where *is* God my maker, who giveth songs in the night." "It is a joy to live and to believe in God and man" comes from the end of the autobiography (*The True Story of My Life*, 297). I have been unable to locate a source for "how beautiful is earth, how noble is humanity," though each half of the phrase appears separately in various poems. It is possible that Geraldine paraphrased passages from the text such as, "From the prince to the poorest peasant I have felt the noble human heart beat" (297).

53. Andersen, *The True Story of My Life*, 297. The original reads, "But should it set, perhaps whilst I conclude these lines, still it has shone, I have received my rich portion; let it set!" Andersen, *The True Story of My Life,* 298.

54. See Fryckstedt, "Geraldine Jewsbury's *Athenaeum* Reviews," 17.

55. "A Happy and Beautiful Life," unsigned review of *The True Story of My Life*, *Christian Register*, April 28, 1849, 1.

56. "The *Christian Register* (1821–1957)," Unitarian Christian Journals: Yesterday and Today, accessed June 9, 2015, http://www.americanunitarian.org/journals.htm.

57. See "Keene Congregational (Unitarian) Society of Keene, NH," Access Genealogy: A Free Genealogy Resource, accessed June 9, 2015, http://www.accessgene alogy.com/new-hampshire/keene-congregational-unitarian-society-of-keene-nh.htm. Livermore later assumed the editorship of the *Christian Inquirer* (1856–1863) and, ultimately, the presidency of Meadville Theological School in Pennsylvania, now called Meadville Lombard Theological School and located in Chicago.

58. *Christian Register*, April 28, 1849, 1.

59. See "Sermon Structures: Text-Application," Concordia Theology, accessed June 10, 2015, http://concordiatheology.org/sermon-structs/.

60. Unsigned review of *The True Story of My Life*, *Christian Review*, March 1848, 151.

61. See Mott, *A History of American Magazines 1741–1850*, 666–68; Margaret Lamberts Bendroth, *A School of the Church: Andover Newton across Two Centuries* (Grand Rapids, MI, and Cambridge: Eerdmans, 2008).

62. Mott, *A History of American Magazines 1741–1850*, 667.

63. *Christian Review*, March 1848, 151.

64. See Hersholt and Westergaard, *The Andersen-Scudder Letters*, 11–12, 96, 117, 144, 148.

65. Andersen to Scudder, September 17, 1871, in Hersholt and Westergaard, *The Andersen-Scudder Letters*, 103.

66. My request to Houghton Mifflin Harcourt for related information went unanswered. Of course, it is quite possible that such records no longer exist.

67. "Notes on Books and Authors: *The Story of My Life*," *Trade Circular and Publishers' Bulletin*, October 18, 1870, 9; "Literary Bulletin: *The Story of My Life*," *Trade Circular and Publishers' Bulletin*, February 1, 1871, 11.

68. "Just Ready," unsigned review of *The Story of My Life*, trans. Mary Howitt, Horace E. Scudder, and unknown, *Riverside Bulletin*, March 15, 1871, 10.

69. Scudder to Andersen, April 10, 1871, in Hersholt and Westergaard, *The Andersen-Scudder Letters*, 96, also see 64 and 69.

70. "Andersen's Autobiography," unsigned review of *The Story of My Life*, *Daily Evening Bulletin*, April 8, 1871, 1.

71. Max Müller (1823–1900) was a German-born and German-educated philologist and orientalist who spent most of his life in England, the greatest part of it as a professor at Oxford. Schiller's idealism, popular in America during the first half of the nineteenth century, thereafter indeed became a liability that influenced attitudes toward his work, if not his character; see, for example, Henry A. Pochmann, *German Culture in America: Philosophical and Literary Influences 1600–1900* (Madison, WI: University of Wisconsin Press, 1961), 337–38. The reviewer lends support to the long-standing notion of a "double tradition" in the nineteenth century's reception of Johnson, "by which the cult of Johnson's personality dominated popular perceptions, while his actual works became more and more the preserve of the learned," though recent scholarship has placed the notion in question. See Katherine Turner, "Critical Reception to 1900," in *Samuel Johnson in Context*, ed. Jack Lynch (Cambridge: Cambridge University Press, 2012), 49.

72. *Daily Evening Bulletin*, April 8, 1871, 1.

73. Unsigned review of *The Story of My Life*, *Harvard Advocate*, April 14, 1871, 74–75.

74. See *Harvard Advocate*, accessed December 3, 2016, http://theharvardadvocate .com/about. The editor objected to stating the magazine's circulation in 1871; see *Rowell's* for that year, 66.

75. *Harvard Advocate*, 74.

76. *Harvard Advocate*, 74.

77. *Harvard Advocate*, 74.

78. *Harvard Advocate*, 74–75.

79. Unsigned review of *The Story of My Life*, *North American and United States Gazette*, April 14, 1871, 1.

80. Unsigned review of *The Story of My Life*, *Peterson's Magazine*, September 1871, 227.

81. Unsigned review of *The Story of My Life*, *Phrenological Journal and Life Illustrated*, June 1871, 435. The magazine had a circulation of thirty thousand in 1871, as in 1870. See *Rowell's* for 1871, 110.

82. Unsigned review of *The Story of My Life*, *Christian Union*, April 26, 1871, 263.

83. The quote from Virgil comes from *The Aeneid*. Bertel Thorvaldsen (1770–1844) gained an international reputation as a sculptor. Berthold Auerbach (1812–1882) was a German writer who is best known for a series of local color stories called *Schwarzwälder Dorfgeschichten* (*Village Tales from the Black Forest*). Ladies Morgan (Sydney Owenson) and Blessington (Marguerite Gardiner, née Power, Countess of Blessington) were Irish novelists who played significant roles in literary and social circles in London. The italicizations appear to be printer's errors.

84. Unsigned review of *The Story of My Life*, *National Sunday School Teacher*, September 1871, 358.

85. See Frank Luther Mott, *History of American Magazines 1865–1885* (1938; repr., Cambridge, MA: Harvard University Press, 1966), 84; *Rowell's* for 1871, 30.

86. See Arthur W. Shumaker, *A History of Indiana Literature: With Emphasis on the Authors of Imaginative Works Who Commenced Writing Prior to World War II* ([Indianapolis]: Indiana Historical Bureau, 1962), 261–72. Shumaker and others assert that Eggleston moved to New York City in 1870, but the issue of the magazine in which the review of the autobiography appears still lists him as editor. This suggests that, while perhaps having moved, as claimed, he continued to edit the magazine for some time afterward.

87. *National Sunday School Teacher*, September 1871, 358.

88. Unsigned review of *The Story of My Life*, *Congregational Review*, November 1871, 577–78. As in the preceding year, the publication listed a circulation of one thousand; see *Rowell's* for 1871, 30.

89. *Congregational Review*, 577–78.

90. *Congregational Review*, 578.

91. Unsigned review of *The Story of My Life*, *Georgia Weekly Telegraph and Georgia Journal & Messenger*, April 18, 1871, 6.

92. "The Republic of Letters: Notices of New Publications," unsigned review of *The Story of My Life*, *Cleveland Morning Herald*, April 15, 1871, 5.

93. Unsigned review of *The Story of My Life*, *Christian Standard*, May 13, 1871, 149.

94. Unsigned review of *The Story of My Life*, *Sunday-School Times*, April 22, 1871, 253.

95. "Book Notices," unsigned review of *The Story of My Life*, *Portland Transcript*, April 29, 1871, 34.

96. Unsigned review of *The Story of My Life*, *Churchman*, May 13, 1871, 156.

97. Unsigned review of *The Story of My Life*, *Vermont Watchman & State Journal*, May 3, 1871, 1.

98. Unsigned review of *The Story of My Life*, *Aldine*, June 1871, 100.

99. See Mott, *A History of American Magazines 1865–1885*, 410–12; Janice Simon, "Consuming Pictures: The *Aldine: The Art Journal of America* and the Art of Self-Promotion," *American Transcendental Quarterly* 12 (1998): 220–45.

100. See Mott, *A History of American Magazines 1865–1885*, 410–12; Simon, "Consuming Pictures," 220–45.

101. *Aldine*, June 1871, 100.

102. In aggregate, the collections of fairy tales and stories received the most reviews, but they, of course, contained various selections, large and small, from the oeuvre as it existed at the many respective times of publication.

103. See, for example, pp. 159, 169, and 172–73, above.

104. See p. 158 above.

105. See pp. 161–65.

106. See pp. 165–67.

107. See p. 170 above.

Chapter Six

The Fairy Tales and Stories

The seventeenth-century French poet and critic Boileau furnished the motto for one of the earliest American reviews of Andersen's fairy tales and stories: "From grave to gay, from lively to severe."[1] The line certainly captures the spirit of the volume in question, *The Nightingale, and Other Tales*, as of Andersen's fairy tales in general. For in addition to the title story, which itself ranges from grave to gay, the collection includes works as disparate in tone as "The Traveling Companion" ("Reisekammeraten") and "The Emperor's New Clothes," "The Buckwheat" ("Hørren"), and "Ole Lukoie."[2] On a lighter note, however, the reviewer might have done better to include the entire couplet, which reads, "Happy the poet who with ease can steer, / From grave to gay, from lively to severe."[3] For Andersen "steered," or inspired many review critics to discuss the works most closely associated with him, in both approbation and disapproval, and to a far greater extent than was true of any of the other genres he cultivated. As the bibliographies cited in this study show, his fairy tales and stories continue to dominate the international scholarly discussion of Andersen's work to this day.[4]

We saw earlier that Andersen's first three novels appeared in English translation in 1845 and determined the American (and British) public's impression of him for some time, prompting thirteen reviews by the end of the first phase of his reception in 1853. However, research for the present study brought to light eighteen reviews of seven different collections of his fairy tales and stories that came out between 1846 and 1848 alone, twenty-one of eight, if one includes *Picture Book without Pictures*; by 1853, another eight reviews had been published. This surfeit is precisely what one would have predicted for the years in which Andersen's stories and tales were introduced to Americans.[5] What one might not have expected, given the relative dearth of attention paid Andersen's tales, indeed, his entire work, in England after

1848 and especially after 1872, is that in the United States reviews continued to appear over the course of the nineteenth century, reaching high points in the 1860s and 1870s. All told—that is, counting *Picture Book*—eighty-five additional reviews of thirty collections came out in American periodicals during the period.

Like numerous notices of the other works, many of the reviews are brief. During the 1880s and 1890s, by which time "Andersen's fairy tales" had already attained classical status, moreover, they tended to focus on the editions and illustrations rather than the works themselves, and their numbers thinned considerably. Despite no small amount of repetitious banality, which will go unexamined here, the response to the tales that takes shape in these reviews nonetheless discloses considerable insight into the works per se and reflects important aspects of the cultural and sociopolitical world in which they found a new and secure home. For example, many writers inquire after the works' target, or most appropriate audience(s), a question that still occupies scholars today.[6] In a few instances, they position the texts within the framework of current national affairs.

For the most part, the commentaries are treated in sections determined by the chronological groupings into which they fall: 1845–1853, 1860–1867, 1870–1871, and 1872–1899. However, three of the writings are outliers, chronologically and/or in terms of their nature. They are not reviews in the customary sense but, rather, commented translations or "palimpsests" of Andersen texts that deal with specific topical issues within the American context while implying an understanding or evaluation of the texts per se. These three pieces are considered in an excursus placed between the third and fourth sections, where, in view of their dates of publication and/or subject matter, they most properly belong. Although the chapter has a summary at the end, it may be helpful to identify some salient points made by reviewers at the end of each main section.

1846–1853

Between February 1846 and December 1847, no less than eleven collections of Andersen's fairy tales and stories came out in London.[7] The first and best known of them was Mary Howitt's *Wonderful Stories for Children*, which was soon published in an American edition and quickly elicited the prescient comment, "This is a new vein for juvenile books and one that is likely to prove popular."[8] Before April 1846 was out, three short notices of the collection had appeared in American magazines, which, in aggregate, demonstrate the contradictory way in which critics initially reacted to the works. The earliest was issued in the *Spirit of the Times*, while the other two appeared in the *Churchman* and the *Presbyterian*.

The reviewer for the *Spirit of the Times* writes, "This is a collection of ten marvelous tales, bearing a strong resemblance to the fairy legends of our own childhood, written by a highly agreeable author, and translated by one whose ability needs no commendation at our hands to enhance her popularity. They are neatly issued, in a form proper for the juveniles."[9] According to Andersen, only three of the stories in the volume were in fact based on folktales, most of them shooting forth from his own fertile imagination.[10] Part of his genius was indeed an ability to transform the gifts of his fancy into creations that exuded much the same air as the often anonymous stories that he and other readers of the world's many cultures heard or read in their childhood. In addition to sensing this common experience, the writer for the *Spirit of the Times* has kind words for the author and, less propitiously, perhaps sets the stage for all those who shared his literal understanding of the part of the collection's title that reads "for Children."[11] The reviewer for the *Churchman* makes some of the same points as his close predecessor:

> The name of the translator, than whom few have produced more pleasing and healthy tales for young readers, would be alone a strong inducement to many to pay their respects to this attractive looking volume. We feel inclined to add, however, that from personal examination our own prepossessions have been confirmed, and that the contents of the volume are quite equal to what we looked for. The tales are happily conceived, gracefully told, and of the right calibre for children.[12]

The writer does not elaborate on what he considers the "healthiness" of the tales, which he apparently ascribes to Andersen's stories as well as Howitt's, but others do so, and in different senses of the word at that.

The critic for the *Presbyterian* begins the single sentence of his comment on the collection in much the same way as his colleagues at the other publications but ends it with what could be construed as a non sequitur: "Here we have specimens of Swedish [*sic*] story-telling, highly imaginative, often prettily conceived, but not in the style which we should like to see popular in this country."[13] The notice offers little grist for conjecture as to the reason or reasons for such ambivalence. However, another short review that appeared in the *Mothers' Journal and Family Visitant* (1836–1872) provides the likely appropriate frame of reference.[14] As the title suggests, this monthly was a class magazine designed for women and the home, one of many like *Godey's* and the *Ladies' Repository* that flourished during the Victorian era.[15] Its editor at the time the notice appeared was Eliza C. Allen (1803–1848), the wife of a clergyman, who was active in various women's organizations and contributed to sundry religious magazines.[16] Of the *Wonderful Stories* she or a like-minded associate writes, "Two pretty quartos of the German stamp, but not objectionable in moral teaching. The whole class of fairy, marvelous and supernatural tales should be put into the hands of children cautiously, if at all. Of many of them, the moral is good; and when they are rightly explained, and placed on the ground of fables, they may be quite as harmless to the minds of children as many modern juvenile tales."[17]

The "but" between the clauses of the first sentence, not to mention the remainder of the notice, establish the context in which some of the early reviews of Andersen's tales and stories must be evaluated. For these writers, religious and moral instruction was of the utmost importance in literature for the young, superseding entertainment and any other consideration. In an issue of the *Mothers' Journal* published the preceding year, Allen had written, "One very general cause of failure to accomplish religious or moral training, is the neglect to cultivate conscientious motives in children. To secure compliance from them, parents too often appeal to other motives than principle."[18] Fantasy was not considered an appropriate vehicle for cultivating such principle. Indeed, Samuel Griswold Goodrich introduced his highly successful series of Peter Parley stories precisely as a morally edifying alternative to fairy tales such as those of the German Brothers Grimm, which were viewed as lacking moral value or, at best, as morally opaque.[19] Allen's judgment that Andersen's tales are "not objectionable" tacitly applies only if, as with the genre as a whole, they are presented as modern counterparts of Aesopian fables and are "rightly explained," and even then they are no better than "harmless." For many Americans of the antebellum period, the Calvinist sensibility going back to the Puritans suppressed the emergence of highly imaginative entertainment as a positive value in education, let alone German Romantic notions of such amusement as implicitly or inherently moral.[20]

But by no means for all. In the review of *The Nightingale, and Other Tales* cited earlier, morality is an important consideration, but it is not the first noted and was thus likely not uppermost in the reviewer's mind:

Everything produced by Andersen carries the stamp of originality and genius with it; and on the present occasion he has received the advantage of a strictly correct and admirable translation—communicating his own spirit to the English text. It is, then, a charming little volume of Fairy Tales, full of invention and fancy, and yet pointed with excellent morals, as it is adorned with pleasant and characteristic embellishments. We are gratified to exemplify such a performance of modern taste and ingenuity on the same sheet which is informed by the recondite biblical learning of Mr. Osburn."[21]

The review appeared in the *Anglo American,* an eclectic magazine edited by a transplanted Englishman named Alexander D. Paterson, who had been in the United States at least since 1833 and was a former editor of the *Albion.*[22] He or his reviewer emphasizes the originality and imaginativeness as well as the style, or artistry, of the tales, also underscoring their moral character.[23] Following a lengthy excerpt from "The Flying Trunk" ("Den flyvende Kuffert"), the writer describes "The Garden of Paradise" ("Paradisets Have") as a "fine morality"; however, he also enthuses that "The Wild Swans" ("De vilde Svaner") is a "genuine excursion upon fairy land" and concludes with excerpts from "Ole Lukoie," which was based on the mythical folk figure of the Sandman and is called here the "giver of dreams."[24]

A certain tension between art and morality can be detected in reviews of other early collections, and Andersen's artistry itself is placed in question by some observers. In its notice of *The Shoes of Fortune, and Other Tales,* the *Presbyterian* maintains its ambivalent posture toward Andersen: "The book itself is one of the highly imaginative and curious productions of the Danish story-teller, Anderson [*sic*], who is an oracle with young folks abroad, and not unknown among them here. His stories are wild, Esopian, fairy-like, very ingenious, sometimes with good moral, and while calculated to amuse, of no great potency to instruct."[25] Anticipating certain later reviews of different import, indeed, the *Christian World* finds that some of the tales go over the heads of youthful readers: "Children will not be sorry for the multiplication of Andersen's stories [the critic had just reviewed a collection containing the same works as the present one], though they may sometimes find it hard to get at his application."[26]

A brief notice that came out in the *Boston Evening Transcript* reflects a similar reading of *A Danish Story Book.*[27] The *Transcript* filled a void in the Boston press world when in 1830 it became the only evening paper in the city.[28] "[M]odest, conservative, nonpartisan, and in good taste," as Mott writes, it early on included literature and the theater among its specialties.[29] On the accession of *Knickerbocker* poet and playwright Epes Sargent to the editorship in 1847, the paper became even stronger in these areas and maintained its leading role in Boston culture until close to the end of its existence in 1941. The comments on *A Danish Story Book* do not reflect this strength, but they make a relevant point: "Andersen is a favorite writer with the young. His style has the charm of vivacity; and the moral tone of his stories is always good. Sometimes he makes a little too free with the patience of his readers and narrowly escapes from tediousness; but in the little volume before us he is more than usually sprightly and companionable."[30] While pleased with the morality of Andersen's tales, the reviewer finds something, left unspecified, that approaches tedium in some of them, something perhaps stemming from the opacity of their "application" mentioned in the *Christian World*. Now, "The Snow Queen" ("Sneedronningen"), one of six works contained in the collection, is among the least thematically transparent—and longest—of the tales, and "sprightly" is not an attribute most readers would attach to "The Fir Tree" ("Grantræet") or "The Bell," which are also included in the book. Nonetheless, those three texts in fact show Andersen at his best, which may explain why the volume found particular favor with the critic.[31]

The *Literary World*, on the other hand, senses anything but opaqueness in the tales: "Andersen's style is by this time well known to our readers, so far at least as they can estimate it through the means of translation; and these are not the least favorable specimens of his manner, even though they give one the idea that the author is laboring for simplicity, and using his utmost efforts to pare down his conceptions to the level of infantine understanding."[32] This reviewer voices what proved to be a distinctly minority opinion, both here and when he continues, "Fairies and other supernatural machinery are, in his hands, objects of patronage, and seem to require a little patting on the head, by way of encouragement to perform their functions; they resemble puppets rather than real existences, and consequently the illusion is not so well sustained as it might be by a different treatment." However, he concludes on a positive note: "Still we are thankful for anything imaginative, anything that can enlist the sympathies, even though imperfectly: and would cheerfully place this neat little volume in the hands of a child as a source of amusement not likely soon to fail." Such privileging of imagination, emotion, and entertainment to the exclusion of explicit moral concern came to dominate criticism of the fairy tales and stories. It is of incidental interest that the reviewer comments on the high degree of visibility the tales had attained in the United States in the space of only two years.

It is of course no fluke that a magazine called the *Literary World* reflected this emerging attitude toward verbal art, whether for children or for adults. In its review of *The Shoes of Fortune, and Other Tales*, artistic considerations take center stage:

> "The Shoes of Fortune" is one of Andersen's best and most characteristic stories. Its imperious turns remind us strongly of two American tales, "Shepherd [*sic*] Lee" and "The En*chanted Moccasins* [*sic*]," in Schoolcraft's Algic Researches. The whimsical feature, however, of carrying a person back as well as forward, suggests some very amusing situations; as in the case of Counsellor Knapp, after praising "the good old times" finding himself suddenly wading through the mud of the unpaved streets of Copenhagen of three centuries ago. Our young readers will find much entertainment, too, in the other stories of this volume.[33]

The comparison to the American works is inexact. Henry Rowe Schoolcraft's "The Enchanted Moccasins" (1839) is an Indian legend involving quests for a wife and vengeance that the ethnologist discovered during his studies of Native American cultures.[34] Meanwhile, Robert Montgomery Bird's *Sheppard Lee: Written By Himself* (1836) is a dark satire posing as an autobiography that takes a jaundiced look at a young nation in which everything can be bought for the right price.[35] Andersen's "The Galoshes of Fortune," while also satiric, does not set its sights quite so high, aiming at individual human foibles such as the assumption that the "good old days" were indeed preferable to the present. However, the device of enabling characters to inhabit different bodies is a direct and valid point of comparison, though the reviewer fails to mention it. And Andersen's allowing Counsellor Knapp to also move backward and forward in time, which the writer does touch on, is similarly ingenious.

It is perhaps not by chance that the *Literary World* sees a resemblance between Andersen's tales and works by American authors or deems his simplicity of style labored and his treatment of his airy creations mechanical. The magazine was born of the desire of Evert Duyckinck to found a review journal that would pursue what proved to be the incongruent dual aims of exercising objective, sophisticated, and scholarly criticism and upholding the cultural patriotism of Young America.[36] The *Literary World* was indeed the first important American weekly of its kind and, over the five years of its run, from 1847 to 1852, succeeded in accompanying literary developments at home and abroad with a generally high level of commentary.[37] The ill-advised manner in which Duyckinck set about implementing the doctrine of a distinctly American literature, however, led to his dismissal after three months of editorship, at which point he was replaced by Charles Fenno Hoffman, who conducted the affairs of the periodical according to a new policy of inoffensive neutrality until September 1848.[38] It is unclear to what extent these circumstances affected reviewers' readings of individual works. The two notices of Andersen's tales appeared during Hoffman's editorship, but it is quite possible that the original aspirational sophistication and "Americanism" of the *World* colored the assessments of the collections to a greater or lesser degree. Certainly, the dream of a peculiarly American literature did not fade with the firing of Duyckinck, or, for that matter, with the demise of the Young America movement.

In its review of Charles Boner's *A Christmas Greeting*, in any event, the *Christian Inquirer* presents a comfortably matter-of-fact and warmly commendatory appraisal of the tales as art:

> What is it that gives such a wonderful power to Andersen's stories? The Old House, the Drop of Water, the Happy Family, the False Collar, the Dream of

Little Tuk, the Darning Needle, the little Match Girl—each and all, indeed, are creations, and their author is a genius—that must be the secret. One must be churlishly disposed to be able to read one of these little stories without a sort of thrill of pleasure, quite different from the slow and measured approbation which it costs us an effort to call up, after we have read something which we feel bound to praise on certain established grounds. Invention, humor, tenderness, vivacity, gentle humanity, sly satire—all these are expended upon these little stories for children, with a carelessness which shows conscious affluence.[39]

The reviewer experiences a certain exhilaration over the originality that distinguishes Andersen's tales from the well-wrought but pedestrian work of others and delights in the artistic and human qualities lavished on them with such a seemingly light hand. Unlike his colleague at the *Literary World*, however, he finds little in American writing to compare to them:

Why is it that these Northern authors—Miss Bremer and Andersen in particular—have such a knack at awakening youthful feelings, and making us remember that we have hearts, though they may be less easily reached than of yore? Has not the simplicity of their habits of life something to do with their power? If they were steeped in imperious conventionalisms, could they break through our crust as they do? Hardly any body among us, but Mrs. Child and Mr. Jacob Abbott, possesses any thing of this power, and we have reason to believe they are both, theoretically and practically, advocates of simplicity of life, naturalness of habit, and a Christian plainness of speech.

Lydia Maria Child (1802–1880) certainly broke with convention in the novels, stories, and other works she wrote in solidarity with oppressed groups in American society such as Indians, slaves, and women.[40] Some of these writings she directed specifically at children, not least of all in *The Juvenile Miscellany*, the first American children's magazine, which she edited from 1826 to 1834. Having spent her adolescence in rural Maine, she indeed never felt entirely at home in the patrician society of Boston in which she later moved. In 1834, Jacob Abbott (1803–1879), himself a Mainer who spent lengthy periods of his life in his home state, published the initial volume of a long series of popular children's books revolving around a boy named Rollo. These books were among the first, and certainly the most influential, American publications of their kind to combine entertainment and instruction.[41] Only in Child and Abbott did the writer for the *Christian Inquirer* sense at least something that reminded him of Andersen's characteristic individuality, simplicity, and ability to reawaken his readers to their youth through movements of the heart.

The *Literary World*, back in the hands of a chastened and regenerate Duyckinck and his brother, George, as of October 1848, published a similarly spirited commentary on *Hans Andersen's Story Book* in which the reviewer touches on central features of Andersen's artistry in the tales:

> A treasure house of wonder and invention for children, coupled with a fine culture of the sensibilities, and a sense of nature and possibility in the wildest passages. We know no writer who is a greater favorite with children (aye, and grown people too), or more deservedly so. A common sense fantasy, distinguished from the usual German moonshine, is the characteristic of Andersen's stories. He puts life in inanimate but tangible objects, always naturally and simply; and oftentimes the moral of his stories is unsurpassed by any world-used fable of Æsop. "The Emperor's New Clothes" is a capital satire, admirably told, with a thousand applications.[42]

Hans Andersen's Story Book contains the largest selection of fairy tales of all the early English-language editions, twenty-one specimens covering a wide range of Andersen's work in the genre. They range from the touching "Story of a Mother" ("Historien om en Moder") and "The Little Match Girl" to the philosophically or psychologically charged "The Bell" and "The Red Shoes" ("De røde Skoe"); from the darkly or opaquely enigmatic "The Shadow" ("Skyggen") and "The Snow Queen" to the variously satiric "The Princess on the Pea" ("Prindsessen paa Ærten") and "The Drop of Water" ("Vanddraaben").[43] It is thus no wonder that the reviewer begins by extolling the richness of Andersen's imagination and creativity and their refining influence on the sensibilities. He expresses an awareness that the tales address adults as well as children, a key insight which, as we shall see, places him among the most discerning of his guild.[44] Whatever he may have understood by a "commonsensical" turn of imagination, stories like "The Old House" ("Det gamle Huus") and "The Fir Tree" evoke a sense of lived reality that anticipates Andersen's later development toward realism and differ in that way from the more fantastic products of the Brothers Grimm, E. T. A. Hoffmann, and their German brethren. Most perceptive is the reviewer's recognition that Andersen invests his shirt collars, garters, scissors, darning needles, etc., with personalities that correspond to their respective "natures" (i.e., their shapes and/or functions). Little less impressive is his knowledge that symbolic action can represent myriads of specific instances.

In its notice of the autobiography, the *Christian Inquirer* makes similarly salient comments on the fairy tales and stories:

> Andersen is the author of some charming stories for children, which have been translated by Mrs. Howitt. They are of that class of children's stories which have abundant interest for grown people. Originality, wit, humor, pathos, and poetry, all abound in them; and there is also a flow of spontaneous humanity—a term which we adopt advisedly, and in contradistinction from that protruded

humanity which has become almost nauseous in a certain class of writings—
quite delightful and inspiring.[45]

The review is noteworthy for its acknowledgment of the adult dimension of
the tales but is perhaps even more remarkable for its contrastive comparison
of their "spontaneous humanity" to the sickeningly "protruded humanity" of
a "certain class" of literature. Other critics also demonstrate that Andersen's
novels were not his only works that were perceived as "healthy" alternatives
to the sensationalist writing of the day.

Andersen's early American reviewers gave their readers a generally brief
but decidedly mixed opinion of *Picture Book without Pictures.* In Denmark,
the work is not normally reckoned among the fairy tales and stories, and for
good reason.[46] Andersen himself distinguished between it and the tales, publishing it in two parts in 1839 and 1844 in close proximity to collections of
stories specifically designated as fairy tales (*eventyr*).[47] The use of the moon
as narrator, recounting experiences it undergoes during its nightly flights, is
reminiscent of techniques employed in certain of the tales, but few, if any, of
the individual "accounts" could be mistaken for such. *Picture Book* consists
of a series of thirty-three prose sketches called "evenings" (*aftener*) that vary
widely in historical, geographic, and cultural setting as well as in tone and
theme, though a melancholy sense of transience, or the presence of death in
the midst of life, looms very large in them. None of these prose poems evinces
the preternatural or supernatural elements—the talking plants, animals, and
inanimate objects—found in many or most of the true fairy tales. Perhaps simply because the volume appeared amid the avalanche of collections of tales
that occurred in the English-speaking world in 1846 and 1847, commentators
made no principal distinction between them, and this has continued to be the
case ever since, which explains the treatment of the work here.

The *New York Evangelist* makes the commonplace but positive observation that the sketches are "charming pictures, full of the very poetry of
feeling and expression, and replete with the gentlest and most excellent sentiments."[48] By contrast, the critic for the *Literary World*, perhaps the same
one who wrote on *A Danish Story Book* a couple of months later, is less
favorably impressed: "The 'pictures' are some of them highly poetical, and
though Andersen's simplicity verges at times upon affectation and mawkish-
ness, there is for the most part great freshness and directness of expression in
these sketches."[49] And in an extensive department of *Holden's Dollar Magazine* called "Topics of the Month," the writer harnesses his short comment
to a British persiflage of the work that pulls even harder in the direction of
the pretentious and maudlin.[50] The English piece is titled "A Page by Hans
Christian Andersen" and first appeared in *The Man in the Moon*, a monthly
humor magazine then edited by Angus B. Reach which competed from

1847 to 1849 with *Punch*, whose staff Reach later joined.[51] In *Holden's*, the "Page" reads in part as follows:

> There was a Daffy-down-dilly once, and it grew in the ground; and when the rain came down the poor daffy-down-dilly was wet. Naughty rain! But when it was moonshine, then the daffy-down-dilly saw the moon and the moon saw the daffy-down-dilly. So the Daffy-down-dilly said, one night, to the moon, "Moon! Moon! What are you doing?" And the moon smiled when she heard the question; and the birds which built in the garden all woke and twittered, and wondered what the moon would say, for they loved the daffy-down-dilly very much indeed. But then there was silence in the air and on the earth—only an impudent blade of chickweed said to a swaggering mangel-wurzel, "Listen to that impudent daffy-down-dilly, who asks the moon what she is doing?" . . . Still the moon answered not; so the daffy-down-dilly raised its tiny voice again and said, "Moon! Moon! What are you doing?" Then, indeed, a change came over the face of the moon, and it replied in low deep tones,—"What's that to you?"—and then sinking behind a cloud it was seen no more, and darkness was upon the garden, and the daffy-down-dilly wept, and the chickweed and the mangel-wurzel quite chuckled to themselves. And this is the story of the Daffy-down-dilly. *** Mrs. Mary Howitt is respectfully informed, that in future she need not trouble herself to translate Mr. Andersen's lucubrations from the Danish, as the MAN IN THE MOON has succeeded in discovering a charity-boy, of tender years, who is competent to undertake the above style at four-pence a chapter.[52]

Holden's commentator agrees wholeheartedly with the English writer's travesty of Andersen's purportedly saccharine style, for he introduces the "Page" with the words, "Mr. Hans Christian Andersen thinks he has the English reading world in his clutches; but people are already beginning to cry, 'Hans off.' Here is a very good burlesque of the style of Andersen."

The reviewer for the *Christian Inquirer* was not one of these people:

> The name of the Author and the name of the Translator combined are enough to commend this little book. The "Picture Book without Pictures" contains 30 stories of various things that the moon had seen, which she came back to tell the writer. "Make a sketch," said she, on her first visit, "of what I tell thee, and thou shalt make a really beautiful picture book." Here the author has a free field in which his gay and ever sportive, yet always chaste and loving fancy, can roam whithersoever it will. Very beautiful are many of his pictures, and sometimes full of meaning, too. Children, unaided, would not always perceive the sentiment through its veil of imagery, but they could hardly fail to be attracted by the beauty of these little fables.[53]

The critic recognizes that the narrative frame formed by the moon and its youthful "ghost writer" offers Andersen the latitude to range matter-of-factly wherever his imagination takes him. Given the dark mood of the "evenings" over Pompeii and Venice (twelve and eighteen), among many others, one may well disagree with his characterization of Andersen's fancy as "gay and ever sportive." And if it is indeed "always chaste," it is only because both Howitt and Taylor expurgated the eleventh "evening," which ends with a new bride putting out the lamp in what is clearly the nuptial bedroom, which the moon nonetheless illuminates, and because both, as well as the reviewer, apparently failed to recognize the implication in the third evening that the blossoming child and bride of yore dies in despair as a prostitute, which might have led to its expurgation as well.[54] However, the reviewer is correct in his contention that the "sentiment" of some (perhaps many) of the sketches would escape the understanding of children—which applies, clearly, to some adults as well.

The *Christian Parlor Book* (1844–1854) also rendered a favorable review of *Picture Book*, but its claim to interest lies less in what it has to say about the work per se than in how it relates to the mission of the periodical.[55] The magazine was, as Mott writes, "part of the movement by which the religious press attempted to compete with the lady's books and popular family magazines of the time."[56] As we read in an earlier issue, indeed, it sought to "'combat the overwhelming flood of impure and corrupting literature, which has come in upon us.'"[57] Thus, the mere presence of the review in the periodical broadly represents the instrumentalization of yet another of Andersen's works in the struggle of the establishment press against sensationalism. The notice itself reads in part as follows:

> We have been much pleased with this story book by Andersen. Though we have heard a great deal of late of this remarkable man, this book is the first of his efforts which has come under our observation; and we find that he has been by no means overrated. His tales, especially when taken in connection with his early poverty, and the difficulties through which he hewed his way to genius and popularity, must be greatly interesting to every class of readers.[58]

The writer attends neither to the artistry of *Picture Book* nor to the artist who created it, as such, but rather highlights the social dimension of its author. As we have seen, Andersen's rise from impoverished obscurity became a prominent feature in the American reception of his work. However, there is some irony, what one might call a socio-moral discrepancy, in the fact that a review of this tendency appeared in a magazine that expressly oppugned a current in contemporary American literature which, at least as represented by George Lippard, sympathized with the plight of people of Andersen's background.[59]

A number of reviews published in the early 1850s seem bathed in the afterglow of Americans' introduction to the fairy tales and stories from 1846 to 1848. The writer who commented on Charles Boner's *The Story Teller* for the *Dollar Magazine*, as *Holden's* was called after its founder's death, was patently not Charles F. Briggs or the Briggsian who reviewed the autobiography two years earlier: "C. S. Francis & Co. have lately published . . . the tales of Hans Christian Andersen, the wonderful Danish story teller. Those stories delight everybody—the young, because of their charming, simple nature, and their flavor of fairy land—and the old, because of their beautiful thoughts and words so full of pathos and living truths hidden under the guise of childish tales."[60]

In its review of Boner's *Wonderful Tales from Denmark*, the *Raleigh Register* of North Carolina expands upon this point and makes others as well: "These are altogether the most charming Fancy Tales we have ever read. While they abound in beautiful thoughts, splendid descriptions, and marvellous adventures which please the childish fancy, there is a rich flow of thought in the strong undercurrent of deeper meaning which teaches the more mature, instructive and useful lessons."[61] In observing the appeal of the tales to young and old, this critic draws a distinction between thought that charms the imagination of children and thought which stimulates the adult mind—an interesting notion that virtually demands elaboration, though any amplification is at best only implicit in his subsequent comments: "The simplicity and quaint drollery of the style is very attractive. All things seem endowed with life; we converse freely with birds and flowers and our hearts warm with kindlier emotions towards every living thing. We love the man who was so full of kindness and love to all God's creatures." The writer recognizes Andersen's humor as well as Ruskin's pathetic fallacy as central features of the tales but does not think the latter fallacious, at least in Andersen. Far from any solipsistic sentimentality, or emotional extravagance, indeed, this element of the tales has for him a humanizing power that is directed at all creation. The notice concludes with the words, "We are tempted to extract one of the tales entire, but not having room, must content ourselves with referring our young and old readers to Mr. Turner's Bookstore, where it may be found." There is something endearing in the reviewer's transition from the warm idealism of his critical comments to the quite practical referral of his readers—young and old, he repeats—to a local gentleman's bookstore.[62]

A notice of similar insight appeared in the *Una*, a monthly that has the distinction of being the first American periodical to be owned, written, edited, and published entirely by women.[63] It was established in Providence, Rhode Island, in 1853 by abolitionist, suffragist, and educator Paulina Wright Davis (1813–1876), one of the founders of the New England Women Suffrage Association (1868–1920), but was moved to Boston in 1855, where financial problems ended its short run the same year.[64] The notice relates to *A Poet's*

Day Dreams, a collection of twenty tales in the translation of Anne S. Bushby that came out in 1853:

> This is a charming little book, fully equalling its predecessors, designed for the young, but should be read by the old, for it tells wholesome truths in a few words and a kindly spirit. His [Andersen's] love of the beautiful leads him to study nature, and in doing so it becomes suggestive and illustrative of the best lessons. He understands the songs of the birds, the voice of spring as she carols through the leafless forests calling out the flowers, and breathing over the meadows, changing their countenance as by magic.[65]

The reviewer falls victim to the most common misapprehension associated with the stories and tales—namely, that they were "designed [only] for the young." However, she makes an imperative of their also being read by adults for the pithily and humanely expressed "wholesome truths" they convey. She attributes the wisdom as well as the varied usage of personification in the tales to Andersen's love of beauty and study of nature, sources of inspiration rarely cited in American criticism of these works. For her, a little girl's sorrow over being unable to pay a button to see a dog that has died ("Heartache"; "Hjertesorg") is sufficient to draw tears from the already grieving, which strikes this reader as a personal confession. Nonetheless, she chooses the humorous "It's Quite True!" ("Det er ganske vist!") to exemplify the contents of the volume.

Over the years from 1845 to 1853, critics expressed both censure and praise of the works. Several early commentators found that the tales had an uneasy or uncertain relationship with morality. Although others soon determined that art and morality could coexist in them or that morality was no issue in the first place, the "moralists" denied them the virtually uniform acceptance they later enjoyed. This, together with the earlier appearance and general popularity of the novels, likely provides an explanation for why the current misconception of Andersen as exclusively a writer of tales for children did not arise for some time. Another reason must lie in the fact that several of the reviewers recognized that the tales in fact address adults as well as children.

1860–1867

The 1850s saw a distinct decrease in the number of reviews of Andersen's fairy tales and stories vis-à-vis the second lustrum of the 1840s, only four appearing in the entire decade, and those in the short space from 1850 to 1853. The decrease cannot be attributed to diminished interest in the works, at least among book buyers, for fourteen collections were published during the period, some of which went through two, three, and as many as five editions.[66] Whatever the reasons for critics' abated attention may have been, the 1860s witnessed another burgeoning of both collections and notices, fifty-three of the former, including the first translated by an American, and twenty-six of the latter.[67] As table 1.2 (p. 12) shows, indeed, more reviews of the tales appeared between 1860 and 1867 than in any other period. The great majority were devoted to only two collections, most of them to one, but those two elicited some of the most perceptive and well written commentaries of all.

By 1860, Andersen's stories and tales had circulated in the United States for only fourteen years, but, as a few of the notices considered below make clear, they had already found a cherished place in the childhood memories of some reviewers. It is unclear how many, if any, of them had read the reviews of the 1840s, but given the ephemeral nature of magazine writing then as now one suspects that their critiques reflect fresh readings. In any case, their comments add nuance and substance as well as occasional novel insights to the opinions of their predecessors.

The year 1860 witnessed the publication of *The Sand-Hills of Jutland*, a collection of eighteen tales translated by Anne S. Bushby.[68] One reviewer observed that the title story ("En Historie fra Klitterne," literally, "A Story from the Sand Dunes") introduced an unwonted sobriety in Andersen's short prose, which was true, at least for readers who had overlooked the more or less transparent seriousness of many an earlier work.[69] Published in Danish only the year before, the piece indeed exemplifies the aforementioned general trend in Andersen's stories toward greater realism. This trend is also discernible in "The Wind Tells about Valdemar Daae and His Daughters" ("Vinden fortæller om Valdemar Daae og hans Døttre"), "The Nightcap of the Pebersvend" ("Pebersvendens Nathue"), and wide stretches of other stories such as "Anne Lisbeth" and "The Child in the Grave" ("Barnet i Graven"), which are also included in the collection. However, the volume contains a broad cross-section of the fairy tales and stories that drew the attention of some seventeen reviewers, making it the second most widely noticed of all the collections discussed in the United States.

Series of descriptive adjectives and noun phrases continue to abound: "Wild, fantastic, droll, lively"; "quaint conceptions . . . subtle drollery . . . genial sympathy . . . exquisite pathos . . . limpid style . . . capital good-sense"; "sweetness and grace . . . simplicity . . . quaintness and humor."[70] The *Eclectic*, on the other hand, stresses the pictorial nature of the tales: "This neat volume of 267 pages contains nineteen [*sic*] Sand-Hills, alias beautiful stories, alias beautiful word-paintings, which attract strongly the mental gaze."[71] The writer then exemplifies Andersen's style by reproducing the first few sentences of the title story: "This is a story from the Jutland Sand-Hills, but it does not begin there; but far away towards the South in Spain. The sea is the highway between the two countries. Fancy yourself there. There blossoms the scarlet pomegranate amidst the dark laurel-trees: from the hills a refreshing breeze is wafted over the orange-groves and the magnificent Moorish halls, with their gilded cupolas and their painted walls."[72] The *Providence Evening Press* writes in a similar vein, "[The stories] are charming prose idylls—full of the fascination of imagination and pathos, and almost stereoscopic in their descriptive power."[73] "Y," of the *Boston Evening Transcript*, adds, "It is a series of fairy tales or rather of allegorical and imaginative stories, with just enough admixture of real observation to give them verisimilitude."[74] Elsewhere in the notice, "Y" makes observations shared by numerous other reviewers: "He [Andersen] loves to watch the scenes of ordinary life and to interpret them by the light of his Northern fantasy; he is very human in his sympathies and quite ideal in his invention." The tales are "often so original, in their conception, as to interest adults"; "they are novel in their scene and scope, suggestive in their moral, and quaintly charming in their spirit and character."

In the years since Andersen's introduction in the United States, reviewers had generally become comfortable with the fairy tale as reading matter for children as well as for adults and had accepted the Horatian notion that literature both instructs and entertains. The *Independent* writes that the opening story of the collection "is full of tenderness and of profitable religious sentiment," while the volume as a whole "has quite a fund of entertainment."[75] For the *Monthly Religious Magazine and Independent Journal*, the tales are not only wild and fantastic, etc., but always have a "good purpose, and [are] always illustrative of some important practical truth."[76] It is of some significance, incidentally, that the notice was written by the influential Unitarian pastor and theologian Edmund Hamilton Sears (1810–1876), now best known perhaps for the text to the Christmas carol "It Came upon the Midnight Clear," who coedited the periodical at the time in question.[77] The reviewer for the *Lady's Home Magazine* opines that Andersen possesses "a power which only those enjoy who can unite grave wisdom and bewitching fancy."[78]

A number of magazines set aside more space to discuss the combination of entertainment and instruction in Andersen's tales. One of these was the monthly *Hunt's Merchant's Magazine and Commercial Review*, a forerunner of the *Wall Street Journal* and *Barron's* that began publication in 1839 and lived on as the weekly *Commercial and Financial Chronicle* until 1987.[79] The reviewer writes approvingly,

> Among the many story books we are receiving, it is long since we have perused one so charmingly interesting as are these fanciful sketches of Mr. Anderson's

[*sic*], whether viewed in their moral light, or in the peculiar winning style in which they are written, [for] which, though purely imaginative, a much higher object seems to have been kept in view than is usual to works of this class. Thus while exciting the fancy to the utmost, each tale is characterized by a well defined and useful moral purpose, which cannot but prove beneficial to those for whom they are intended.[80]

For the *Monthly Journal of the American Unitarian Association* (1853–1869), children's books can be *too* edifying. The writer describes *The Sand-Hills of Jutland* as "[o]ne of the *good* story-books for children,—good, because (1) interesting; (2) with a good moral tone; healthy, not morbid; (3) instructive, but not too instructive. Such are all Andersen's books: so far as we have read them, they are all good for children. They are not *sloppy*; but bright, as children's books ought to be."[81] He goes on to emphasize the importance of fine writing for children, including Andersen's work among the best:

> Many suppose that the rinsings of weak brains are good enough for children; but this is a mistake. Children need the very best books: the first impressions made on young imaginations should be of the best quality. They should read only such books as "Robinson Crusoe," "Gulliver's Travels," "The Vicar of Wakefield," "The Pilgrim's Progress," "Don Quixote," "Uncle Tom's Cabin," Walter Scott, Miss [Maria] Edgeworth. Younger children should read Jacob Abbott, Andersen, and the like. The parents may read silly books; but children should have the best. This work is one which may be added to your child's library.

As the nineteenth century progressed, moral-religious concerns receded into the mid- or background of reviews of most of Andersen's works or disappeared altogether. However, they remained present and, often, prominent in many critiques of the fairy tales and stories, particularly those whose authors consider the works written principally or exclusively for children. Note that the reviewer for the *Monthly Journal* thinks of them as being especially appropriate for younger children, perhaps because they are "healthy, not morbid"—that is to say, not sensationalist.

The writer for the *Portland Transcript* implies that the wisdom and artistry evinced by the stories are of great sophistication: "There is also a deep philosophical insight of life that enables him [Andersen] under the most fanciful forms to convey the most impressive lessons. The first story in this volume strikingly illustrates the uncertainties and vicissitudes of fortune. It has fine descriptive touches of the sand hills of Jutland, and the church sepulchre with which it concludes betrays an imaginative power of a high order."[82] The *Methodist Quarterly Review* finds that the morality of the tales is implicit rather than manifest:

> Another very readable story-book from Herr Andersen, a great writer of stories. . . . The book savors of the old Norse legends, occasionally entering those bewitching regions of the marvelous which lie between fact and fancy, between myth and history; but it does so without disturbing our credence, like Munchausen, or shocking the moral feelings like Paul de Kock. Andersen is a prolix Æsop in his use of the lower forms of life; but puts the moral, not at the end, but in the stories themselves, which breathe throughout a fine spirit of piety, and afford pleasant reading to wonder-loving youth and genial old age.[83]

Unlike Baron Munchausen, who could ride on cannonballs and travel to the moon, or Paul de Kock, whose novels of lower- and middle-class Parisian life were widely considered to be vulgar, Andersen's creations are at once pleasing and credible as well as moral.[84] However, in contrast to the works of Æsop, their morality permeates them, residing integrally in their form and content, so that one must draw their meaning from them, as the Romantic Goethe wrote of all literature, as from life.[85]

The *Ladies' Repository* of Boston provides both an explicit context for the reception of the present volume and further corroboration of the perceived nature of Andersen's achievement in it.[86] The current editor was E[lizabeth] A. Bacon, wife of former editor and Universalist minister Henry Bacon and apparently, herself, a figure of some consequence in Universalist church and literary circles in contemporary Boston.[87] Together with two other women she continued to publish mainly female and clerical writers while maintaining her deceased husband's positive but rather patriarchal view of women. The reviewer writes of *Sand-Hills*,

> Here is a charming book for the home circle. The pleasant mingling of myth and sweet, holy lessons of trust in God and the right, will make the eye of youth and age sparkle alike with wonder and delight. Our good puritan grandmothers need not frown over their spectacles at these legends and stories, for they are very unlike those of our own childhood. And here let us give a tribute to one of those same old books—"German Popular Stories." Ah, how it was hunted down and hidden from our sight, and what exultation did we express when on reading Mrs. [English poet Felicia] Hemans' Memoir, we discovered in one of her letters a pleasant reference to the same book, where she tells us with what zest her little boys sung the fisher's song to the fisherman's ambitious wife. There was many a truth in these rare stories that we shall never forget.[88]

Much the same as the reviewers discussed in the preceding paragraphs, this writer perceives a balance of entertainment and instruction in the collection. However, s/he also endeavors to allay the concerns of those older individuals who still harbor reservations toward the fairy tale as children's reading material. Indeed, s/he goes so far as to disclose the relish with which she and her generation read a respected author's fond recollection of a circumstance involving the "taboo" tales of the Brothers Grimm. It is thus all the more telling when s/he continues, "and so we dare recommend a book that is far above comparison with that, even though myths and legends are woven into its lovely and beautiful teachings, and to those who would have a volume worthy to lay beside Ruskin's 'King of the Golden River,' we say purchase 'The Sand-hills of Jutland.'" The writer holds Andersen's tales in far greater esteem than the highly popular, but in some quarters still suspect gleanings of the German folklorists, most likely because of the union of pleasure and profit in them.

It is worth noting in passing that Ruskin might well have been offended by the reviewer's comparison of Andersen's stories to his own already classic fairy tale, "The King of the Golden River" (1851). In his introduction to an edition of *German Popular Stories* published in 1868, Ruskin decries the attempt to "substitute the pervasive influence of moral precept, intruded in the guise of amusement, for the strength of moral habit compelled by righteous authority"; he adds that the "effect of the endeavor to make stories moral upon the literary merit of the work itself, is as harmful as the motive of the effort is false."[89] He would have the story's representation of a fictional reality appeal immediately to the imagination, exercising the child's fundamental "power of grasping realities," and cautions against the danger of enfeebling this power through rich illustration and, by extension, richly imaginative narrative.[90] If history is any indication, however, Ruskin credited children for being more perceptive than they in fact were and are, for they—as well as many or most adults—have proven quite capable of reading Andersen's stories for their imaginative appeal, altogether untroubled by any transcendent value.[91]

Most American reviewers of *The Sand-Hills of Jutland* would have rejected Ruskin's caveat against making fairy tales as attractive to adults as to children,[92] for they consider his success in doing so one of his major achievements, as recently quoted passages from the *Portland Transcript*, the *Methodist Quarterly Review*, and the *Ladies' Repository* suggest. Indeed, the "fund of entertainment" of which the *Independent* speaks, is also "for old and young," and Edmund Sears writes in the *Monthly Religious Magazine and Independent Journal* that while the collection "is a book mightily to take the fancy of young readers," it is "calculated to make any readers better and more hopeful for the perusal."[93] The *Lady's Home Magazine* states the case in fond retrospection:

If the publishers of this book had any misgivings as to its merits, they would certainly have put upon the title page, "By the author of 'The Ugly Duckling;'" for there is no one of the present generation of critics, however hard or severe he may be to others, but has a soft place in his heart for the writer of that inimitable child-story, which he laughed and cried over when tottling about in petticoats

2

and crinoline, or strutting in the dignity of first jacket and trousers. But Hans Andersen needs not to borrow a charm from childish associations. He has the rare power of pleasing alike the infant and the mature man.[94]

This, the reviewer adds, coupling the phenomenon to a related one already mentioned, is "a power which only those enjoy who can unite grave wisdom and bewitching fancy." Indeed, *Peterson's Magazine* seems to be writing mainly with adults in mind: "This is a collection of tales, most of them for children, and printed from early sheets for the author's benefit. The writings of Andersen are singularly original. They have a peculiar charm which is almost indescribable. 'Waldemar Daae and his Daughters,' 'Something,' and 'The Sand Hills of Jutland,' are, in different ways, three of the best of the stories. With *persons of culture*, this will be the favorite book of the summer" [emphasis added].[95]

The critic for the *Daily Ohio State Journal* of Columbus, which ran from 1848 to 1865, however, leaves no doubt that he deems both children and adults beneficiaries of Andersen's stories:

There is the sweetness in our memory of a Christmas story of Andersen's, which we think can never wholly pass from it. How fresh, out of the childhood days, rise the thoughts that it suggested[.] How tenderly glow all the beautiful pictures that it touched in divine colors, as we run over the pages of this charming book, with an envy harmless, we hope, of all the happiness it shall bring to the little people, and to the large people, too, for the matter of that. For does not such a child's book as this find everybody a child? He is a very dull fellow and less than a child, whom it will not please and interest.[96]

This reviewer also has kind, imaginative words for Andersen's imagination and its power over the finer emotions of the reader: "With our admiration for the quaint and peculiar beauty of Hans Christian Andersen's stories, there is mingled that love for the writer, which men always feel for one who has deeply moved their better sentiments. It is the good wizard only who can tell where the hidden springs are running. The divining-rod, moved by the pulses from his own heart, turns toward them[.] He strikes there, and the tears come. But in the hands of the ungenuine, the mere sorcerer, the fine wand is only a common stick." The title story "has a rare breath of Northland sea-life in it—picturesque and grand, yet very tender and affecting." The remaining stories are "all beautiful and fantastic. The vivid imagination of the author, plays about the commonest theme, and it springs out of the common place, with a new and charming life[.]" Indeed, "[t]his Scandinavian poet almost out Germans [Jean Paul] Richter in the profusion and quaintness of his fancies in these Northern stories." The reviewer is particularly impressed by the breadth of Andersen's imaginative faculty. Proceeding from the previous sentence, he writes, "though when we read his 'Improvisatore,' it seemed as if the book were steeped in the wine, and sun and sadness of Italian life. Christian's [i.e., Andersen's] nature is opulent—he is a mine of such riches as never were digged from the ivory mines of the Arctic ice."

Perhaps the most interesting and revealing American review of *Sand-Hills* was written by possibly the most compelling little-known figure of American literature during the first half of the nineteenth century, John Neal.[97] Born in 1793 in Falmouth, Maine, now part of the greater Portland area, Neal spent his most productive years as a writer, from 1817 to 1835, in Baltimore, London, and then again in Portland, where he remained until his death in 1876, still engaged in literary activity.[98] In certain important respects, he bears comparison with William Gilmore Simms, his junior by thirteen years. Both shared a central interest in promoting and helping to create a specifically American literature. Though Neal approached the project as a decided Yankee, Simms as an unmistakable Southerner, both employed the native materials they knew best in their writing, including regional dialect. The two tried their hand at various literary genres but achieved their greatest success in the novel, or romance. Both were unusually, perhaps inordinately, prolific—Neal wrote his six novels in the space of eight years and estimated that his lifework would fill more than eighty substantial volumes. Unfortunately, they both wrote hastily and, to make matters worse, had a broken relationship with the virtue of revision; Neal indulged in the practice of well-nigh automatic writing, which was consistent with his poetics, as outlined below, but detrimental to his ultimate artistic achievement. According to Donald A. Sears, he was nonetheless the equal of most authors of his generation, overshadowed only by Cooper and Bryant, and influenced Poe, Hawthorne, and Whitman, much as Simms influenced Melville. Neal and Simms alike, finally, were magazinists who edited and contributed to periodicals for much of their lives, publishing theoretical work and critical opinion that have stood the test of time.

Neal took Byron as his model in both his belletristic writing and his personal life. It was thus not by chance that Hawthorne referred to him as "that wild fellow," for he created a superhuman image of himself, full of individualistic and, often, mercurial vitality that impressed itself on his work.[99] As suggested earlier, his writing also bore the stamp of his Romantic reliance on the *coup génial* in contrast to the rationalized neoclassical aesthetic of the preceding century. His literary-theoretical thought was definitively shaped by August Wilhelm Schlegel's concept of the unity of effect on the reader, which Neal understood as the impact of passion, from which, for him, poetry issues forth.[100] In general, he sought to adapt British and German Romanticism to American conditions. And it may have been the Romantic's prizing of nature and everything associated with origins, not to mention his own fatherhood, that led him to write extensively about and for children, including fairy tales. By intellectual and psychological predilection and personal experience, Neal was thus by no means the least prepared American critic to render an opinion on Andersen's collection of stories and tales.

By 1860, Neal had been out of the public eye for many years. However, the introduction to a reprint of his review of *The Sand-Hills of Jutland* published only a few weeks after the notice itself provides a sense of the esteem in which he was still held and what the reader of the reprint may expect:

> Those who remember John Neal, editor, in the days of the "Boston Galaxy"— some twenty-two or three years gone by—have some spicy things treasured up. The ink in which he dipped his pen seemed to be always bubbling with wit, fun, satire, and poetry. The inside form of the "Galaxy," when he and [H. Hastings] Weld covered it with their sage and saucy paragraphs, was one of the best anti- dotes for the blues to be found in those days. After he left the Galaxy, we believe Neal retired from editorial life; but, recently, in the Portland Transcript, his pen has been at work again as a reviewer of books, and we see the old quaintness and originality coming out again as fresh, peculiar, dashing, and independent as ever. John Neal's idea of a book is always worth reading, and it is sometimes a curious comparison to lay it alongside of your own. We take from a recent number of the Transcript a couple of paragraphs on Hans Christian Andersen, written on the text of his new book, "The Sand Hills of Jutland." Don't pass it by, reader.[101]

Neal's review follows here in its entirety:

> Not a child's story book—but fairy tales for "children of a larger growth." Some of the teachings here might be called lay sermons, written upon the meadows and blue sea, with flowers and rippling sunshine; "The child in the grave" [*sic*], for example. That Hans Christian Anderson [*sic*] is a poet—a real flesh and blood poet: one whose flesh is not *doughy*, and whose blood you may almost hear ratling [*sic*] through his arteries, every body knows—who knows anything about him; but how few are they that understand him. Of conventional poetry, we are sick, heartily sick, "tired to death," as the young ladies of the high school say. But of such poetry as we have here, the wine of life, the true blood of the grape—the melted ruby—the subterranean sunshine, which people are digging for, under the name of gold, in all parts of the world—how little there is, and how little it is felt or understood. Our very newspapers, and some of the dullest and least promising, often turn off better poetry and truer poetry, than goodly portions of the British classics—but how little of it, after all, has the ferver [*sic*] and flash, the glow and sparkle we meet with in such norther[n] lights as we have imprisoned here, just for the fun of the thing, like fire-flies in a transpar- ent globe. There is a heartiness—a downright rough and tumble way of doing his work, which always characterizes this strange man—this living Aurora

Borealis. And this, after all, is the kind of northern literature we most need; that which healthy people, whether young or old, must hanker for and hunger and thirst after—something new and startling. Not that it should be in verse—for the grandest poetry in the world may be but prose in shape—not that we need fairy tales and hobgoblin extravagancies to keep us alive and stirring, but we do need something which is not altogether what we have always been acquainted with—in one shape or another; something to stir the blood—to wake us up—and to keep us awake. And so three cheers for Hans Christian Anderson! [C]ome in what shape he may! J. N.[102]

The large majority of Andersen's most insightful American critics recognize with greater or lesser clarity the maturity necessary to fully comprehend the stories and tales, but John Neal is the only one to assert unequivocally that they address themselves to adults *rather* than to children. He speaks of the "teachings" of some tales as of "lay sermons," aware of their moral-religious depth, but his metaphoric diction—the stories are "written upon the meadows and blue sea," for example—leaves little doubt that he finds their thematic substance woven into their imaginative fabric. A systematic comparison of *Sand-Hills* with other collections in terms of sophistication makes little sense in the context of the present study, if at all, but it is undeniable that the "message" of a significant number of the tales contained in it goes well beyond a child's apprehension. How many children have the perspicacity or life experience to appreciate, for example, the variform folly of human endeavor measured against eternity or the grand sense of transience expressed in the title story, the tale of Valdemar Daae and his daughters, and "The Bell Deep" ("Klokkedybet"); how many possess the cultural awareness necessary to discern Andersen's satire of literary critics in "Something" ("'Noget'")? "The Child in the Grave" is one of the few stories that are more immediately accessible to the young.

The remainder of Neal's review, which is to say the largest part of it, deals less with the collection under scrutiny than with Andersen and his tales as a whole in the context of contemporary American literature. In the romantically effusive, metaphoric diction of the notice, to be sure, the poet whom Neal so appreciates in Andersen impresses one as being more like Neal, himself, than the Dane, whether in his work or his personality. However, it is patent that Neal recognizes in Andersen, this aurora borealis or northern light, something unique, vibrant, and truly poetic, be it in his verse or in his prose, something missing in American letters. Periodical literature published in the United States is superior to much of its British counterpart, he writes, unable to resist delivering another lash of the whip to what for him and many other Americans was still a living horse. But he acknowledges that it could profit from the vitality and naturalness of Northern literature, as exemplified by the stories in *Sand-Hills*, and, nota bene, as interpreted by Longfellow. For many in the United States, indeed, the literature of the North served as a lodestar for the rejuvenation of an American literature freed from its British origins. Again revealing his innermost proclivities, Neal states that Americans, young and old alike, need a literature that is at once novel and perennially enlivening. They do not need fairy tales per se any more than they need verse. Genre is far less important for him than "healthy," living content realized integrally in living form, a requirement he shares with many other American reviewers of Andersen's tales. In sum, Neal uses the review as an opportunity to lend the weight of Andersen's example to his own Romantic poetics, and in a most romantically poetic manner at that. At the same time, he gives heightened expression to the "magic" that certain other reviewers sense in Andersen.

The *Crayon* also writes, with much less pretension, from within the context of American letters: "Indeed, so delicate are [Andersen's] touches, and so naturally painted his pictures of humble life, to say nothing of his power of enlisting the reader's sympathies for his characters, that he at times reminds us of Irving."[103] However, the reviewer appears to have read only the title story: "The volume before us is made up of a series of stories relating events that occurred on the coast of Jutland." While most of the notices underscore, or even confine themselves to the initial tale, New York's *Evening Post*, reflecting the general American predilection, highlights a more fanciful work. For this paper, the book "is a collection of a number of pleasant and unpretending stories and legends, the principal and largest of which is the 'Mud King's Daughter,' a fairy tale with the scene laid alternately in Scandinavia and Egypt. Through the story, wild and curious as it is, there runs a vein of quiet humor that is by no means its least charm."[104] For unstated reasons, the reviewer judges the other pieces to be "of varied merit" and condemns some of them, including "The Bottle Neck" ("Flaskehalsen"), as "too insignificant to find a permanent place in a book like this."

A handful of reviews of other collections appeared between 1860 and 1867, and a few of them warrant some comment. Not surprisingly, Fanny Fuller's *The Ice-Maiden, and Other Tales*, the first collection by an American translator, received considerable scrutiny precisely as a translation. The *Independent* contents itself with the laconic pronouncement that, while "[t]here is always something graceful and good in Andersen's stories, [t]hese are not very well translated."[105] *Peterson's*, on the other hand, terms Fuller's work a "very creditable performance," declaring the following year that "[t]he popularity of the [title] story has secured for [the collection] a second edition."[106] The *American Literary Gazette and Publishers' Circular* claims that the volume is "so admirable that, without losing any of the author's literal truth, it reads like an original English book," and the *Press*, also of Philadelphia, agrees: "His latest work, consisting of four tales, has just been so well translated into English, by Miss Fanny Fuller, a young lady of this city, that it reads as if it had originally been written in our language."[107] A recent commentator stands somewhere between the extremes, calling Fuller's rendering "fairly accurate, but undistinguished," and concluding that it is a "relatively modest one, both with regard to quality and quantity. But it is yet another example of the fact that quite decent English translations can be prepared on the basis of a German one."[108]

The *Press* had other things to say about Fuller's collection:

> A new work by Hans Christian Andersen, well translated, must be acceptable to persons of all ages. His stories are among the household treasures of the world. . . . His first story ["The Ice Maiden"], which is the longest, has its scene in Switzerland, and is imaginative and fanciful, with a sorrowful conclusion. The "Butter-fly" is a charming sketch of only a few pages. "The Psyche," located in Rome, is the story of a sculptor's fancy, and "The Snail and the Rose-Tree," in Andersen's own natural, best style, is a delightful little apologue. Altogether, the book has its author's leading characteristics—invention, grace, and sustained interest.[109]

If saying little of substance, the reviewer differs from the majority of Andersen's critics by saying at least something about individual tales, which the large number of stories contained in many collections need not have entirely precluded.

A notice similar in content but quite different in locution appeared a couple of months later in the New York *World*.[110] The daily began its some seven-decade-long existence in 1860 as a moral-religious weapon in the fight against sensationalism, only, after 1883, to drink and then spout the yellow poison itself under Joseph Pulitzer.[111] Soon acknowledging the spiritual and financial failure of its original mission, the *World* became a general newspaper that, in Mott's words, "was as well edited, in both news and editorial departments, as any paper in the country" and was solvent as well.[112] It was during this period that the review of Fuller's collection came out.

The critic avails himself of the vocabulary of the garden to express his undiluted praise of Andersen:

> What Shakespeare is in poetry and the drama Hans Christian Andersen is in children's stories—the "myriad-minded" master of Fairy Land. No other writer of the kind compares with him for a moment, or is worthy to unloose the latchet of his shoes, sparkling as they are with the eternal dews of childhood. Story after story grows like a flower beneath his genial pen, the true magician's wand, every once in a while to be gathered and bound up with some of its fellows in a nosegay of perennial bloom. The latest growth of his prolific mind is a little

knot of divers-colored blossoms—four in all, "The Ice Maiden," "The Butter-fly," "The Psyche," and "The Snail and the Rose Tree." The first-named is the longest—a pretty historiette, brim full of the daintiest poetry; the other three are short fantastic anecdotes, as it were, of art and nature—but short as they are they are radiant with the genius of Andersen.[113]

Little analytical force as such metaphorical language may possess, it certainly has the power to evoke the imaginative magic that this reader, like many others, experienced on reading Andersen's tales and to suggest its perceived source in nature, its fecundity and multiformity, and its ultimate imperishability. In a more matter-of-fact vein, "dainty" is not a word most readers would attach to "The Ice Maiden." For its "poetry," which must refer to its descriptions of the Swiss mountainscape, is better described as magnificent rather than delicate. And its conclusion, which relates the main character's death through the thoughtlessness of individuals and the action of a demonic natural force, is indeed "sorrowful," as the *Press* states, but perhaps awe and fear inspiring as well.

Philadelphia was the site of some additional brief but relevant observations made during the decade of the 1860s. In its mid-month issue for December 1864, the *American Literary Gazette and Publishers' Circular* printed a short notice of several children's books issued by James Miller of New York, including a reprint of *A Danish Story Book* of 1846 and 1848 and two new American collections of Andersen's tales rendered by English translators, *Little Rudy* ["The Ice Maiden"]*, and Other Stories* and *The Mud-King's Daughter* ["Dynd-Kongens Datter"]*, and Other Stories.*[114] The reviewer writes,

> The volumes written by Mary Howitt will, of course, meet with favor. But the best feature in the list [of eight] is the copious reproduction of the delightful Stories of Andersen. These present a striking contrast in every respect to our own child-literature. The scenes and events are new, and a wild and weird-like mystery invests them such as could only be born out of the wondrous mythology of the North. Andersen's stories are in their way works of literary art. . . . They will doubtless attract the attention of grown up as well as of juvenile readers.

Almost twenty years after their appearance in the United States, Andersen's stories and tales still strike the writer as being as unwonted, fresh, and unique as ever, even now differing from the fare served at home. In light of the reserve and even disdain which children's literature, especially fairy tales, still encountered in certain sectors of the reading public, it is of no little significance that the writer views Andersen's stories as works of art, even if "in their way." He belongs to the growing number of critics who recognize their appeal to adults as well as the young.

Less than a week later, the author of a review article published in the *North American and United States Gazette* wrote the following: "Hans Christian Andersen . . . has made himself a great reputation as a writer of tales for children. It is his specialty, and in it he is unapproachable. From a cold, chill field he weaves the richest tissues of fancy to amuse the young, and informs every tale with a kindly, human spirit."[115] The reviewer apparently finds Andersen's success all the more admirable for having been achieved in an inhospitable realm of endeavor. After a space, he enlarges on his implied criticism of juvenile authors as a class: "If all writers for children would remember that they are neither providing fools nor philosophers, and work as Andersen does, upon childhood's level, with childhood's material, there would be fewer failures and greater profit."[116] Although the critic clearly intended his statement as high praise, from a historical perspective he essentially helped escort Andersen politely into the nursery.

The *Round Table* did much the same thing a few years later in a review of *The Will-o'-the-Wisps Are in Town, and Other New Stories.*[117] Founded in New York in 1863, the magazine was a journal of opinion that pursued literary criticism as one of its main interests according to the principle expressed in the programmatic statement, "'We have had too much of the mutual admiration style of reviewing. Let us have mutual detestation rather than that.'"[118] It thus anticipated the stance of the *Nation*, which came into being two years later. Following an editorial change predating the Andersen review, the periodical assumed a more conciliatory critical posture that proved unpopular, costing it many of its three to five thousand subscribers and leading to its merger with another publication in 1869. Andersen's reviewer, however, retains a humorously sharp tongue, though he does not direct it at the Dane himself:

> Of *Will-o'-the-Wisps* it is superfluous to say more than that it contains half-a-dozen new stories by Hans Christian Andersen, who stands *facile princeps* among the benefactors of children—the authors of *Robinson Crusoe* and the *Arabian Nights* not excepted—insomuch that, as we may have said before, we regard it as among the gravest of all possible parental derelictions to withhold his writings from the little ones. Indeed, it may not be too much to say that the good Andersen's charming tales have as much capacity for exquisite juvenile delight as the [Presbyterian] *Westminster Catechism* for exquisite unhappiness.[119]

In his review of *The Improvisatore* for the *Daily Telegraph*, however, Philadelphian William J. Clark Jr. releases Andersen from the nursery, or rather grants him admittance to the study and sitting room as well:

Andersen is principally known here as the fascinating writer of brief stories and sketches, professedly designed for children, but about which older readers find a strange and indefinable charm that always makes them attractive. Many a boy has read the story of the "Ugly Little Duck," and wondered what there was about such a common-place theme that should please him so, and it was only on reperusing it with even greater pleasure in after years that he was able to perceive how much that was charming lay in the quaintly humorous style and the graceful poetry that embellished trivialities and made them great.[120]

One should note that Clark, like John Neal and the reviewer for the *American Literary Gazette and Publishers' Circular*, makes no mention of the "moral" of "The Ugly Duckling" ("Den grimme Ælling"), choosing instead to highlight its deceptively sophisticated artistry.

Before proceeding to the eventful 1870s and subsequent decades, it will be instructive to examine a writing that departs in various ways from those considered heretofore but nonetheless casts a bright light on different aspects of the tales and their place in the United States of its time. It appeared in the *Boston Evening Transcript* in 1865 under the title "Hans Christian Andersen" and over the signature "K. E."[121] It is more a general article than a review per se, but since it deals exclusively with the stories and tales, discussion of it in the present chapter seems appropriate. Despite its relative length, the piece makes few observations of an analytical nature, but those it does make it makes in unwonted ways and is illuminating for other reasons as well.

"Among the many new and attractive books which have been published for children during the last few months," K. E. begins, "we find several new editions of the wondrous tales of the prince of story-tellers, whose name is familiar to all children who like imaginative literature, and there are few who do not."[122] He refers here to the at least seven new or reprint editions of Andersen's tales that came out in 1865.[123] He then makes statements that are of potential significance for the history of the author's presence in the United States: "For thirty years, Andersen's tales have been familiar to children in America as well as in Denmark and Germany. It may be very late, now, to speak of an author who has written for a whole generation, but, on seeing the many new editions of his works, we cannot refrain from expressing something of our own feeling toward him." We have seen that the first editions of Andersen's stories and tales appeared in England and the United States in 1846. K. E. thus misses the mark by eleven years when he traces their arrival in the United States back to 1835, and what was in reality a period of nineteen years does not qualify as a generation. All the same, the first young American readers of the works, born, like Horace Scudder, in or around 1838, were by 1865 in their mid-to-late twenties. Given current life expectancies and Americans' telescopic view of history, the older and more reflective of them may have indeed been capable of looking back on their childhood with the elegiac sense that a generation had passed since then. In any event, K. E. creates the impression that during his lifetime Andersen had become firmly ensconced in the American mind, so self-evident a part of it, in fact, that even lettered admirers could lose track of the beginnings of his presence there, lending him a certain timelessness.

Or perhaps K. E.'s recollection was more accurate than would initially appear to be the case. He continues by recounting his first experience of Andersen:

> We well remember the impression produced upon us, years ago, by reading two or three of his tales, in a book compiled from various sources. Several years passed by before we knew who was the author of "Little Ida's Flowers" and "Ole Lückoie," and our delight was unbounded when we had a whole volume written by the same "Wizard of the North," who perhaps deserves the title as well as the one upon whom it was originally bestowed. Since that time we have eagerly greeted every new work from his pen, and have read the old tales many times over.[124]

"A book compiled from various sources" that preceded "a whole volume" written by Andersen by "several years"—unless K. E. read those first tales in another language, which is nowhere indicated, this means that at least a few of Andersen's stories predated Boner's and Howitt's collections by as many as some four years: "Little Ida's Flowers" ("Lille Idas Blomster") appeared in Danish in 1835, "Ole Lukoie" in late 1841.[125] Locating that book, however, may require the gifts of a John Henry Anderson, the Scottish magician and original "Great Wizard of the North," who inspired Harry Houdini.[126] For searches in the catalogs of the Library of Congress and the British Museum as well as WorldCat, among others, have failed to lift the shroud of mystery that surrounds it. Although it apparently failed to attract any reviewers, either in England or in the United States, the book patently roused the interest of K. E. and, conceivably, numerous others, thus paving the way for the grand entrance of Andersen's tales into the United States in 1846.

K. E. laments the fact that many of the works have been translated from German sources rather than the original Danish. For though German is related to Danish and "we have the general outline of each story, we must necessarily lose many of the delicate shades of meaning, which can never be quite successfully translated," a circumstance, however, that also applies to English translations from the Danish originals, as many Danish scholars affirm.[127] Despite this disadvantage, K. E. finds that "the little stories remain fresh and beautiful, even in a foreign dress." They can do this, he suggests, because of the kinship of Danish, German, and English as Germanic languages. A

French translation "can hardly convey an idea of [the tales'] spirit, however faithful to the letter it may be," since French, "in its construction and idioms, belongs to a different group."

K. E. has glowing words for Andersen's faculty of observation and supports them with a quote from a contemporary who was even more famous for his visual gifts:

> One of Andersen's most prominent characteristics is his power of observation, as shown in his minute descriptions of things which seem to us too common to be noticed. He finds in the most homely and familiar objects a beauty and significance which make them, in his mind, worthy of notice, and he straightway makes them the chief characters in a little romance. When we reflect upon the truth of Ruskin's observation, "A hundred people can talk for one who can think, but a thousand can think for one who can see," we appreciate the power which is so rare, but, when it exists, produces such wonderful results.

If Ruskin's pronouncement is even approximately correct, then Andersen's ability to "see," which also impressed other commentators discussed in these pages, was singular indeed.

For K. E., Andersen's "visual acuity" was not limited to the phenomenal world:

> Only the Northern nations have the power of imagining the 'Mährchen,' as we must call it for want of an English word which exactly expresses its meaning. The fairy tales of the north and south of Europe are as different as their ancient religious beliefs—one vague, dreamy yet pervaded by a certain grandeur and heroism, and with deep truths lying below much that is hardly intelligible—the other, after its earliest period, polished, elaborate, yet sensual and false to its first ideal.

Though his notion of the role of climate in cultural development derives in part from Montesquieu and Comte, K. E. is obviously a Germanophile in the broadest sense of the term: "Both religions [those of Germanic and classical antiquity] have vanished, but the races which followed them remain, and we find the descendants of the Scandinavian Vikings in our own New England, and in Old England, too, while we must look for the remains of the ancient Greeks and other nations which had the same belief, modified, perhaps, but essentially the same in the Greek, Italian, and Spaniard of today. The contrast needs no comment." German(ic) profundity and French/Romance superficiality—such is K. E.'s tacit distinction, which survived him in some quarters of the United States (and elsewhere) into the second half of the twentieth century and still lingers, even less likely to be uttered, in the hypercautious, politically correct twenty-first.

K. E. continues, "Perhaps some of the old dreams of the northern deities, of the 'Twilight of the Gods,' and many another strange scene, have had their influence over the northern nations, whose imaginative works take so prominent a place in modern literature. The Germans, of course, are included in this category. Under a veil of poetic fiction, they have often hidden the deepest truths." One can only speculate which Nordic "dreams" and German authors K. E. had in mind on writing these words. However, he would seem to have been at least generally acquainted with the German and Scandinavian Romantics' discovery of the Germanic medieval past and its influence on writers such as Ludwig Tieck (e.g., *The Wanderings of Franz Sternbald* [*Franz Sternbalds Wanderungen*] and *Fair Eckbert* [*Der blonde Eckbert*]); Adam Oehlenschläger ("The Golden Horns" ["Guldhornene"] and *Hakon Jarl*); and, for that matter, Hans Christian Andersen, some of whose plays (*Little Kirsten*) and tales ("Holger the Dane" ["Holger Danske"]) show distinct traces of this influence.[128] Years before K. E. wrote his article, German Romantics such as Tieck, Goethe, and Jean Paul had made inroads into the United States, particularly through the writing of the Transcendentalists.[129] Although Longfellow's view of the North remained a force after the Civil War, significant scholarship in Scandinavian history and philology had been conducted decades earlier, as we saw in chapter 2. Furthermore, a professorate in Scandinavian studies was established in 1858 at what is now the City University of New York, while a department of Scandinavian languages and literatures was soon to be introduced at the University of Wisconsin; Norwegian was already the language of instruction at Luther College in Decorah, Iowa, which was founded in 1861.[130] Additionally, modern writers such as Andersen and Swedish novelists Fredrike Bremer, Emelie Flygare-Carlén, and Marie Sophie Schwartz had reached wide audiences in the country, and numerous others had been introduced.[131] Though not all of Andersen's reviewers were aware of the fact, in short, the cultural landscape in the United States was more favorable than ever before for an accurate and realistic assessment of the Scandinavia of past and present.

Pursuing the theme of poetic profundity, K. E. writes, "Andersen's tales are beautiful, even without a thought of their higher meaning, which, however, gives them new interest to the attentive reader."[132] As instances, he mentions "The Little Mermaid" ("Den lille Havfrue"), "The Marsh King's Daughter," and "The Garden of Paradise" ("Paradisets Have"). One is left to wonder what aspects of the stories and tales he was thinking of when choosing these as examples. However, the religious element central to all three looms large—the immortality of the soul in the first two and the expiation of sin in the last. And few passages in the tales rival the description of the underwater palace in "The Little Mermaid" or of Eden in "The Garden of Paradise" in luminous, varicolored beauty. K. E. concludes, rather sentimentally, by suggesting that Andersen "has surely drunk of the Fountain of Youth, for he has kept his child-heart, in spite of his three-score years. He will always keep it, we know, and will attract children of all ages while he lives to tell his charming stories"—a prescient if, as time has shown, very shortsighted statement.

In their responses to *The Sand-Hills of Jutland* of 1860, American reviewers displayed a keen eye for the realistic turn in Andersen's handling of his short prose, his "stories" in contrast to his "fairy tales." Andersen never abandoned the genre that established his worldwide fame, as certain of the texts included in Fanny Hill's collections of 1863 and 1864 show. However, his later fiction, both long and short, generally reveals more attention to descriptive detail and topical theme than his earlier work. Critics also exhibited greater sophistication than their predecessors in their articulation of the union of (moral) guidance and art (entertainment) they perceived in the tales, some of them stressing the obliqueness of their edificatory nature. Many of them thus found, virtually of necessity, that the works have as much to say to adults as to children, or even more.

1870–1871

As we have seen, the period from 1846 to 1848 and the year 1860 were times of great exposure for Andersen's fairy tales and stories in the United States—that is, times when they were very much in the eye of American review critics and thus in the eye of their readers as well. However, the works received their most intense critical and, arguably, public scrutiny in the twenty months between January 1870 and August 1871, during which reviewers responded to them as issued in two volumes of the Author's Edition. The notices discussed below are significant, first of all, because of their sheer number: *Wonder Stories Told for Children* and *Stories and Tales* received ten reviews each. If one considers the books as a single two-volume anthology, as we shall do here, furthermore, these twenty notices make it the most widely reviewed compilation of all those published in the United States. Indeed, the flurry of reviews elicited by these volumes probably represents the most concentrated critical activity devoted to the tales after 1850 in any country, certainly in the English-speaking world, chiefly because English reviewers all but totally ignored the Author's Edition.[133] On top of this, the collection assembled 139 fairy tales and stories, the largest number heretofore subjected to critical examination in the United States, and perhaps elsewhere as well. Finally, several relevant comments were made in notices of other works by Andersen published during the same brief space of time. Viewed as a whole, these notices confirm and expand upon the insights expressed in earlier commentaries.

A considerable number of reviewers continue to write as if the fairy tales and stories were addressed primarily or exclusively to children. Some wax so enthusiastic in their praise of them, however, that they betray a quite mature appreciation of them. The critic for the *Advance*, for example, writes, "The first [of the two volumes of tales] is before us and is running over with the odd fancies and fairy creations of this prince of juvenile story tellers. Any one who finds it difficult to get material to answer the ever-present child demands for a 'story,' should take a course of lessons with Andersen. He will thereafter find in bug, bottle, pebble, weather-vane, wind, poker, snuff-box, rose-bush, and river, inexhaustible material for romance."[134] He then copies "The Sweethearts" ("Kjærestefolkene"), that sadly ironic, wilted petal from Andersen's first—and not last—unrequited love, as an illustration. "Romance" is not a word commonly applied to the fairy tales, but, as used here, it probably alludes to the prominence of imagination vis-à-vis realism in the works contained in *Wonder Stories*, in accordance with Horace Scudder's differentiation between the contents of the two volumes in the Author's Edition.[135]

The reviewer for the *Sunday-School Times* is even more lavish in his commendation of the tales:

> In this handsome volume the publishers have collected some sixty of the most beautiful marvels of the fancy that have ever been written in any language. This renowned Danish writer seems to have imbibed more of the spirit of the child's weird-world, and to have interpreted its far-reaching fancies more truly than any writer living. The marvelous creativeness of his imagination, by which, as with a magic wand, indeed, he turns things animate and inanimate into shapes that sing and smile and soar, and the poetic beauty and grace of diction with which he clothes his fancies, continually extort one's admiration and delight. Without question, Andersen's are among the best conceived and executed fairy tales written.[136]

If the preceding review enumerates some of the creatures and objects that Andersen found suitable for use in "romance," the present one complements it by illustrating a few of the varieties of life with which Andersen invests them. *Moore's Rural New-Yorker* channels its approval of the stories in a different direction: "ANDERSEN never has failed, that we know of, to meet the expectations of his readers. This beautiful volume of miscellaneous tales will enliven many a fireside, and make happy and contented at home, many a boy and girl who otherwise might 'love to roam' from the house-nest" (i.e., who might otherwise get into trouble).[137]

Despite the impression perhaps created by these notices, some 60 percent of reviewers held the opinion that Andersen's tales offer something for both young and old. The *Providence Evening Press*, for example, opines: "Written professedly for children, [the tales] gladden the spare hours of children of larger growth, even old children who find their heads tinged with the grey of life's autumn."[138] Like certain other critics, the writer for the *Portland Transcript* cites an appeal to the still young in spirit: "All [the stories] bear the impress of [Andersen's] magical touch, which metamorphoses the commonest incidents into fairy like marvels, the delight, not of children only, but of all who have been so fortunate as to keep young hearts under heads that have grown, or are growing, old."[139] The *Independent* writes of *Stories and Tales*, similarly, "The present volume is a companion to the well-known 'Wonder Stories for Children' . . . and is quite as likely to be welcome to the young folks, and to all older people who have not lost the happy faculty of seeing at times with young folks' eyes."[140]

Implicit in these statements is the commentators' sense of being transported imaginatively back to the magic of their own childhood. The reviewer for the *Ladies' Repository* of Cincinnati (1849–1876) avers as much in no uncertain terms.[141] A Western pendant to its namesake in Boston, the journal was founded by Methodist Samuel Williams to counter the "worldliness" of *Godey's* and similar publications and was edited by a succession of Methodist ministers in this spirit, though they eventually grew more tolerant of fiction.[142] Publishing the work of then popular New Englanders as well as Midwesterners, the magazine had 40,000 subscribers at the high point of its run and still claimed 33,500 in 1871.[143] Of Andersen's *Stories and Tales* the reviewer writes,

> A very excellent test of a story-writer for children is how his stories are appreciated by adults. A first-class story for a child is of equal interest to a pure-minded, generous-hearted man or woman. We have all been children. A good child's story carries us back to our childhood. We love to be reminded of it, to be re-introduced to it, to live it over again, to enter into its simplicity, its imagination, its wonderment. Hans Christian Andersen has stood this test, and it is the secret of his popularity as a story-writer. We doubt if many of his books enter into a reading family without being read as well by the older as the younger members of the family.[144]

Lest one hastily dismiss the reviewer's approbation of such retrospective reverie as shallow, one should consider that no less a figure than Dickens shared the same conviction. In an article criticizing George Cruikshank's moralizing retelling of fairy tales, he writes that the fairy literature of his generation's youth "has helped to keep us, in some sense, ever young, by preserving through our worldly ways one slender track not overgrown with weeds, where we may walk with children, sharing their delights."[145]

At the same time, other review critics recognize features of the tales that beguile the adult as such. The writer for the *North American and United States Gazette* reflects, inexactly but relevantly, "Andersen is the very Blitz of letters. Take him all in all, there has never been such a magician for childhood. And it is a rare peculiarity of his writings that, while more than a moiety are designed and expressly prepared for children, they retain so much of a grander human interest, that they appeal to all ages and educations in a hardly less degree than the fables of Æsop and La Fontaine."[146] The *Christian Union* observes, with comparable generality,

> It is idle at this day to dwell upon the charms of the greatest child-poet in all literature, unless it can be done on a scale beyond our reach. We need only say that, from the first glimmer of poetic fancy in childhood—and who can say how early that appears?—until the last spark of childlike freshness and sympathy is extinguished, there is no age which may not derive delight from the exquisite purity and sympathy that overlie great depths of meaning in these quaint stories.[147]

The *Bangor Daily Whig and Courier* provides specific examples of such meaning, writing that *Wonder Stories Told for Children* is a "collection of tales of that veteran story teller who has delighted all hearts, old and young, for so many years. In many of these simple stories is hidden beneath a gay, whimsical exterior some deeper lesson of human hope and trust, like that of the 'Ugly Duckling,' for instance, who, beaten and abused in his callow state, grew to be a beautiful white swan, at the last."[148] The *Phrenological Journal* adds to the list:

> Always refined, chaste, just, and exceedingly entertaining and instructive, this author teaches valuable lessons in kindness, good nature, affection, and in nearly all the interests of life. It is such a work as will please every member of the family, from the youngest to the oldest. What a fund of thought, experience, and suggestion is here! Indeed, parents, teachers, and others need never want for conversational topics, or the means of entertainment with this book within reach.[149]

The *Christian Union* extends the list even further:

> The tales are mainly sketches in outline, and only a few are elaborated with great detail and fullness. But the spirit of Andersen is in them all, and that exquisite charm and grand simplicity, which characterizes whatever the fable-spinner of Copenhagen writes, appears to special advantage in the lighter pieces which make up the bulk of the book. To the children it will prove a rare delight, while the airy delicacy of the style and the piquancy of the morals

underlying almost every one of the stories, will make it captivating to all the seniors of the household.[150]

Human hope and trust, kindness, good nature, affection, and nearly all the interests of life, airy delicacy of style, and piquancy of morals—the meaning the reviewers discern in the tales largely relates to the finer elements of spirit that constitute high character. These writers thus find in Andersen's tales that ennobling influence which Romantics attributed to all art and which we, chastened by events of the intervening century and a half, still believe, or would like to believe, that it can, and sometimes does have.

At the end of its review of *Stories and Tales*, the *College Courant* allows candidly that, "Andersen's stories have an interest for the older people, as well as for children, and many a reader has felt himself more moved than he perchance would care to own, by some simple trait of nature beautifully presented in a touching little story."[151] The writer's comment bespeaks a possible reluctance on the part of no few readers—mostly men, one suspects—to acknowledge their emotional response to the tales as writing ostensibly addressed to children. One wonders whether in the later decades of the nineteenth century a misguided notion of manliness—or, more broadly, adulthood—indeed consorted with inattentiveness, imperceptiveness, and other factors to consign Andersen's tales and stories well-nigh exclusively to the child's library. Experience teaches that young adults such as college students are entirely capable of apprehending the relevance of the tales to mature concerns like morality, religion, art, society, science, and any number of aspects of personal experience, once they are presented with the opportunity to do so, and even if they initially react with (usually pleasant) surprise. Many of Andersen's American reviewers of the early 1870s obviously shared this capacity. The question then arises: Precisely what happened? Danny Kaye's often cited and indicted portrayal of the author in the film *Hans Christian Andersen* of 1952 still lay the better part of a century in the future, and it is questionable how many Americans of the last two generations have ever heard of the movie, or even of its star.

Critics who recognize the sophistication of Andersen's tales often find it difficult to put their finger on its source or nature. The *Congregationalist and Boston Recorder*, a major organ of the Congregational Church that spanned most of the nineteenth century (1816–1901), states the case succinctly: "*Hidden away* in these quaint little narratives is great store of good feeling, and good wisdom" [emphasis added].[152] The *Press*, a short-lived Chicago quarterly that registered two thousand subscribers for 1871, offers a more extensive illustration:

Andersen is the Magician of the North in current literature, and to all little folks, and many not so little, all over the world. We might write a page of critical praise, without being able to say anything more convincing than is conveyed to a myriad of readers by the mere name of Andersen—incomparable Hans Andersen—who is as familiar and as dear to bright eyes and bright hearts wherever books are known as are violets and robins, or whatever best represents the smiles and songs with which Nature greets the pattering feet of childhood and the reverent feet of her older worshipers.[153]

In order to convey an impression of the volume, the reviewer relies not on ratiocination but, rather, on telling images, feelings, and ideas evoked in the reader's mind by Andersen's name alone, confident of their presence and impact. The writer for *Golden Hours* states much the same principle more explicitly:

Now, nearly all of Andersen's tales have a moral, though, perhaps, it is not so apparent as in the one we have mentioned ["The Ugly Duckling"]. Writers of fiction often err in making the lesson to be taught more prominent than the story. The moral should be kept in the background; *it should be inferred rather than expressed*, and while not, therefore, obscure, should have an inferior place in the narrative, but be so impressed that if the incidents are forgotten the principles taught may be remembered [emphasis added].[154]

The critic for the *New York Evangelist*, the most Romantic of all these Romantics, also uses near Goethean locution in his tentative analysis of the matter:

Just wherein the charm and power of these stories lies, it is not easy to say. The meaning of them makes itself felt, even as the meaning of nature does to one who loves her; but it cannot be formulated in a "moral," or defined in words. It pervades the story and steals into the soul of the reader, whether he be child or man, as the subtle flavor of some delicate fruit surrenders itself to the taste, or as the perfume of some sweet flower steals in upon the sense, and lingers half unnoticed.[155]

As we saw earlier, some reviewers find that the flavor of Andersen's tales is *too* subtle to steal into the soul of a child, and the writer for the *Portland Transcript* is another such: "We find that there are many youthful readers who do not enter into the author's peculiar humor, and who find it difficult to tell what he is driving at when in his fanciful vein."[156] All the same, the critic's reservation is a roundabout testimony to the stories' thematic depth.

The most expansive discussion of meaning in children's literature involving Andersen focused precisely on the relative merit of overt didacticism,

addressed principally to the intellect, and inductive learning through the refinement of sensibility. It appeared in the *Eclectic Magazine* as a rebuttal to
an article titled "The Worship of Children" that was published anonymously
in the *Spectator* of London in 1869.[157] The reviewer relates the following:

> A very clever writer, in a recent number of the *London Spectator*, makes a
> forcible protest against "The Worship of Children," which he believes to be pe-
> culiarly the characteristic of our times, and which is constantly becoming more
> exaggerated in its display. More particularly, he maintains, is this tendency
> observable in the literature designed for children. The sound and respectable
> old legends of Jack the Giant Killer, and the like, which wore so good after
> their kind, together with the ineffable but at least intelligible stories in which
> George the Saint and Tom the Sinner figured so largely, are now relegated to
> the limbo of bygone barbarisms, and children's literature has taken upon itself
> all the refinement, subtlety, and elaboration which characterize modern life.
> He complains . . . that Mrs. Alfred Gatty has for years been solely occupied
> in producing a child's magazine which is equal, if not superior, to any of its
> contemporaries designed for adults; and calls upon parents to go back to the
> good old times of simplicity in toys and genuine downrightness . . . in literature,
> and leave off the psychological refinements which are now supposed to supply
> children with mental food.[158]

Indeed, the writer for the *Spectator* asserts that "[t]he best thing benevolent
uncles and aunts can do, if they have been so injudicious as to buy much of
the admirable children's literature of the present day for their nephews and
nieces, is to keep it themselves and try to enjoy it. If they can do so, they
may be sure that, in the fitness of things, it is more suitable for them than for
the little ones. If they can't, it is a sign their minds need refreshing, and they
should keep it till they can."[159] Although approving of modern, sophisticated
children's literature as reading for adults, the author adheres to a now fading
notion of writing for the young: "If you tell them a fairy story, tell them one
genuinely marvelous, capricious in its details, and wholly devoid of allegory.
If you tell them a moral tale, put the moral in the nakedest possible form before them;—make your good boy very good, your naughty boy very naughty;
your reward very plain, your punishment very clear,—and above all, avoid
the finesse and complexity of real life. They will come to all that in time."[160]
Citing a recent play he characterizes as a "poetic adaptation of the theology
of St. Paul," he continues, "If it did not bewilder children, it would only be
because they would miss its meaning as completely as if it had had no meaning to miss."[161] He is convinced, finally, "that children learned more by the
old, plain didacticism, both when they sympathized with it and when they
could not refrain from ridiculing it, than they do by the higher art of modern
times."[162] It is only his suspicion that such art confuses children as well as

his fear, expressed elsewhere, that it stunts the development of the child's imagination (cf. Ruskin earlier) that renders his disregard for the dual appeal of fairy tales on the order of Andersen's understandable, if hardly compelling. In any case, the reviewer for the *Eclectic* pursues his argument as follows:

> Our critic might have added the names of many other writers of the very highest abilities to those he has mentioned as furnishing the children's literature of our day, such as Jean Ingelow, Miss [Charlotte Mary] Yonge, Miss [Dinah Maria] Mulock, Miss Alcott, and, greater than all, of him whose name stands at the head of this notice—Hans Christian Andersen. And we venture to say that, not withstanding his quaint astuteness, and the cleverness with which he has made some of his points, our critic would heartily agree with us that the final reclamation by these and other great writers of a field of such infinite importance, which had hitherto in great part been given over to dunces, is the most beneficent, if not the most splendid, of recent achievements in literature. Who that has read the fairy and other stories of Andersen alone (for it is as a writer for children that he is principally known to American readers), does not cherish a sense of personal gratitude—does not feel that they alone furnish a *raison d'*être for this branch of literature?[163]

It is not at all clear that the author of the article in the *Spectator* would have agreed with the reviewer's opinion of Andersen, at least with respect to his role in the "reclamation" of children's literature for children. Though mentioning foreign (i.e., German and French) writing only in passing—perhaps merely a consequence of English insularity—it is more probable that he considered Andersen part of the "problem."[164] At any rate, the reviewer for the *Eclectic* represents the majority opinion among his American colleagues. However, he also perpetuates the perplexing and vexing verity that, despite the express opinion of many other commentators to the contrary, Andersen was increasingly known in the United States mainly as a writer for children.

The Author's Edition as such and the tales published in it experienced a modicum of criticism. We saw earlier in passing that the *Christian Union* faulted both the translation and the illustrations of the *Wonder Stories* and an alleged "sketchiness" of the *Stories and Tales*.[165] However, the *North American and United States Gazette* surely spoke for many when it wrote, "The art is so great that it is not seen, and none of the native *raconteurs* could have made the problematic more highly probable and more effective."[166] And the *New York Evangelist* leaves no doubt that in the 1870s, as in the 1840s, Andersen's tales as well as his novels furnished welcome respite from a certain class of writing: "It is a blessed thing to get away from the sensational romances that come flying from the press now-a-days, and to refresh one's soul with anything so pure and restful as these wonder stories. It is like getting a whiff of sweet country air, blown over hay fields and through green leaves, where all one's soul has become weary with the dust and heat and wickedness of the malodorous city."[167] The *Indianapolis News*, with its thirty-six hundred subscribers, writes, similarly,

> There is an entire absence of the sensational in all his [Andersen's] stories, particularly in those for children. The latter are always pervaded with a sort of pleasing quietness throughout, which attracts and holds the child in breathless attention from beginning to the end, and at the close he can retire to his slumber and be undisturbed by the nightmare dreams that, too often[,] follow the read-ing of many of the blood-curdling narratives of the day, the Macbeths of the nursery.[168]

The *Hartford Daily Courant* (Connecticut), after predicting that the *Stories and Tales* will not lie idle in a home where children are present, adds that they will offer relief from reading of another sort: "And how much better is it that [children] should read a book like this than the ordinary slop of the Sunday school library."[169]

If there was any doubt by the end of 1869 where Andersen stood in the esti-mation of American critics, it was removed by the reviews of the two-volume collection of tales in the Author's Edition that appeared within less than two years. The books received virtually no criticism, and several reviewers stated unambiguously that Andersen was the world's leading figure in the field of children's literature, by which they meant in the writing of fairy tales. Some still believed that the works were the purview of children alone, but a signifi-cant majority opined that they were also relevant for adults, as a source either of nostalgia for childhood or of something akin to nourishment for the adult soul. Indeed, they wrote more expansively than their predecessors of 1860 on the recipients and modality of the tales, and a number underscored the sophis-tication of the meaning often residing integrally in the works. Twenty-five years after the publication of Andersen's first novels and critics' comments on them, a couple of reviewers can still extol the tales as a wellspring of relief from sensationalism.

EXCURSUS

This section deals with the chronological and/or thematic outliers mentioned in the introduction to the chapter. As indicated there, they are not reviews in the true sense of the term. However, they bear a varyingly close relationship to texts discussed by Andersen's reviewers, sometimes at length, and reflect an ultimately critical attitude toward them. In their respective unique ways, they may be best described as creative instrumentalizations of those texts.

The earliest of these is a translation of "The Emperor's New Clothes" preceded by a telling introduction. Published in New York's *Evening Post* in 1852, the translation was apparently executed by the anonymous "B. R." who signed it, together with its parenthetical introduction, for it differs from all those contained in collections registered by Bredsdorff through that year.[170] The translator's work itself, which, though often inexact, clearly proceeds from Andersen's story, is of interest here only insofar as it predates Fanny Fuller's collection of tales by more than ten years. Of far greater relevance is the introduction:

> [If the following story should be found to have an allegorical significance, and should appear to reflect upon any of those patriots who have been most active in saving the Union, when it was in no danger, the responsibility lies with the distinguished Swe e (Swede; *sic*) from whom we translate. We had not been aware, until the manuscript was placed in our hands, that he had watched the political history of this country with so much interest as this brief but pithy sketch seems to indicate. Will any one tell us who are meant by the two weavers?][171]

Clues to the empirical correlates of the "allegory" are spare, but the reference to the so-called patriots busying about to save the unendangered union offers a useful one. The contention between North and South over the slavery issue had recently led to the Compromise of 1850, which was intended to provide a way out of related difficulties that arose from the acquisition of Mexican territory during the Mexican-American War of 1846–1848.[172] According to its provisions, for example, California was admitted to the Union as a free state, while the Fugitive Slave Law was made more stringent. Pursuing their Free-Soil Democratic convictions, however, the editors of the *Post* opposed the Compromise, not least of all because they supported the Wilmot Proviso, a victim of the agreement that would have prohibited the introduction of slavery in all the newly acquired lands.[173] For them, the status quo, tense as it was, was apparently preferable to the Compromise with its concessions to slavery. They reserved special criticism for senators Henry Clay of Kentucky and Daniel Webster of Massachusetts for their intimate involvement in the conception and passage of the series of bills. It may be that B. R. had these individuals in mind when asking the ultimately rhetorical question of who was meant by the two weavers in Andersen's tale. Accordingly, the fraudulent "garment" and/or the fraud who wore it represent, in the *Post*'s eyes, the illegitimate Compromise. Whatever the referents of the story may have been, it is undeniable that B. R. made Andersen, with his tale, an ironic witness to a key period in the drama that led to the Civil War.[174]

In the second of the three texts, the author utilizes *Picture Book without Pictures* as a point of departure for an original narrative in which he comments on the Civil War itself. Drawing its title from a recent translation of Andersen's work, he published "What the Moon Saw" in *The Land We Love*, subtitled *A Monthly Magazine Devoted to Literature, Military History, and Agriculture*, in 1868.[175] The publication has been called in many respects one of the best to emerge in the South after the Civil War.[176] It originated in Charlotte, North Carolina, the year the war came to an end, and ran until 1869, when it was consolidated with the *New Eclectic* in Baltimore and some of its printers joined to found the *Charlotte Observer*, currently the largest circulating newspaper in the state. It claimed a subscription list of twelve thousand in 1867 but, at the same time, complained of subscribers' failure to settle their accounts, "'owing probably to the extreme poverty of the South.'"[177]

The magazine was established and edited by ex-Confederate general Daniel H. Hill (1821–1889), an academic who before the war taught mathematics at Washington College, now Washington and Lee University, and Davidson College; after war's end, he served as the fourth president of the University of Arkansas, where he also taught "mental and moral philosophy and political economy."[178] Hill saw *The Land We Love* as a vehicle for advocating replacement of the classics with science and engineering as the basis of higher education, as a repository for Southern memory, especially memory of the Civil War, and as a means of encouraging the development of Southern literature.[179] Atchison provides long lists of known contributors to the magazine, which include Southern poets Paul Hamilton Hayne, Margaret J. Preston, and John R. Thompson as well as a wide variety of former Confederate generals and governors.[180]

According to the index of the pertinent volume of the periodical, the author of "What the Moon Saw" was "F. H. Farrar, of La." The name most likely refers to Frederick Howard Farrar, about whom scant information is available. He took his family to Pointe Coupee Parish, Louisiana, in 1849 and wrote a letter from Bayou Sara in adjacent West Feliciana Parish in 1894, which suggests that he indeed lived for many years in the Pelican State.[181] Farrar was a judge and thus a person of some consequence in his community. Most relevant for our purposes is the fact that he was the father of Frederick Hillsman Farrar, who as a lieutenant colonel in a Louisiana infantry regiment was killed at age twenty-five in the battle of Murfreesboro in 1863.[182]

The counterpart to Andersen's introduction in *Picture Book without Pictures* provides readers with the appropriate literary frame of reference:

> Far away north, in Denmark, there lived a man named Hans Christian Andersen, to whom the moon was wont to narrate many of the curious things which she saw in her nightly journeys over the world. These he wrote down and published

in a little book, which has been translated into every civilized tongue. Now, the moon speaks English as well as Danish, and perhaps seeing how sad I was when I looked on the condition of my native Southern land, and its oppressed people, and wishing to amuse me, she told me too, of many sights she had seen—some pleasant and some sad,—bright and dark intermingled, like the web of human life. Some of these, I will now relate as she told them to me.[183]

Whether the moon's wish to "amuse" the narrator is intended as irony, indeed sarcastic black humor, is uncertain, but the sights she shows him are unquestionably more sad and dark than pleasant and bright. The first of two "evenings," simply called Nos. 1 and 2, is set on a battlefield somewhere in the South:

> Dark groups were scattered over the plain. Some lay silent and still in death— their heart's blood soaked into the earth around them.—In some it was still welling forth freely, but their laborious respiration was growing hurried and short, and the cold death dews were standing on their foreheads. The most of them were youths, born in wealth, carefully taught, gently nurtured, and trained to a patriotic love of their Southern native land, in defence of which they had fallen—fallen in doing [w]hat they religiously thought a duty.[184]

In depicting the scene of carnage, death, and dying, Farrar portrays the majority of the fallen as young gentlemen and thus, implicitly, as sons of the planter aristocracy, perhaps thereby reflecting his sympathies, if not necessarily his background, and giving a broad suggestion of the ethos of his work.

The author then turns to individual soldiers. A surgeon and his assistants move among those who are still alive, seeking to aid and collect messages from the dying to send to their distant families. One young officer asks them to take his sword and deliver it to his father in Virginia: "'It was borne by his grandfather in the first war with the English. We fought for a like cause, the right of self-government, and it has not been disgraced in the hands of his descendant.'"[185] Another, older officer asks that his sword be sent to his widow in Texas, "'and tell her to hang it up, till our eldest boy can wield it, and then—.'"[186] At this point, another dying officer interjects, "'Peace, my darling brother . . . let not our last moments be filled with ideas of vengeance, but with supplications to the Throne of Mercy.'"[187] The first officer admits his error and beseeches the second, a clergyman, to pray, as befits his sacred office. Hereupon, the pastor

> raised his weakening voice and prayed for their hard pressed native land, for their own souls soon to appear before their Maker, for the helpless ones at home, soon to be left orphans and widows, and then prayed for their enemies— that He would forgive them for having made cruel war on their former brethren,

because they wished, in accordance with the political doctrines of their common ancestors, to be allowed to govern themselves in peace, and lastly, if it should be His will that the Southern people should be conquered, that the hearts of their conquerors might be filled with a generous pity for those who could no longer resist.[188]

Distant loved ones in distress, a family tradition of honorable service to the nation, a strong sense of betrayal of a common political ideal by the former countrymen, a desire for revenge suppressed in deference to divine mercy, and a hope for compassion on the part of the conquerors—these ideas and emotions appear to issue from the mind of a conciliatory, if unregenerate Southerner surveying the past and peering into an uncertain future.

However, the pastor's words to his comrade ring hollow in light of what follows. The surgeon and his men go to another part of the field, where lies, among other wounded, a "handsome, delicate lad from Arkansas, his young life's blood welling from a ghastly wound in his breast, and his lips parched with thirst."[189] The youth requests that a lock of his hair be sent to his mother back home: "Tell her it is her Willie's hair, sent with his dying blessing, and that he has not disgraced his father's name. If our country is successful it will not let her, who has lost husband and son in its battles, suffer, and if it is not, a brave and generous foe will protect her helplessness."[190] However, the boy's conviction regarding the enemy's magnanimity, identical in import to the pastor's prayer, proves illusory, for the omniscient narrator then continues,

Poor boy, he did not know that even while he spake, in his distant home in Arkansas, some of those generous foes—soldiers wearing the blue uniform, were at that moment holding burning coals to the naked feet of that shrieking mother, to make her tell of hidden plate, which they had been disappointed in not finding. She had told them, and told them truly, that it had been sold to buy bread for the little ones, but they would not believe her. Poor Willie's death was enviable compared with hers.[191]

The ruthless cruelty of the Union soldiers forms a stark contrast to the essential nobility of their Southern counterparts. Interestingly, Daniel H. Hill made friendliness toward the North an express part of his editorial policy.[192] Like much of the writing in his magazine, however, "What the Moon Saw" betrays an unmistakable ambivalence toward the region tending greatly in favor of the South.

While differing from "No. 1" in tonality, indeed, (Evening) "No. 2" discloses the same evaluative dichotomy as its predecessor. Here, the moon looks down on two old men, "one in a New England town, the other in the mountains of Virginia. Each had been a General in the late war. One is scorned and execrated by millions, and only lauded by a few thousands, because he is the enemy of those they hate, with a fiendish and insane hatred. The other is honored, loved, and lauded by the whole civilized world. One is rich in the plunder of prisoners, widows, and orphans. The other is poor, working daily for his daily living."[193] The roles the ex-generals played in the war now affect their state of mind:

> I looked in at the windows of each, as they were about retiring to rest. The thought that will now and then strike the aged, of their near approach to that eternal resting place, the grave, struck both. The one called hoarsely for an opiate, to drown thought and procure sleep. His sleep was restless and disturbed. The other kneeled down meekly, and prayed, with humility and faith, while my rays rested lovingly on his white hair and beard. He then lay down, and slept like a peaceful and innocent child.[194]

It is perhaps not going too far to see in the ex-Confederate general a representation of Robert E. Lee, though the meager depiction of the figure does not correspond to the historical personage in every respect. In 1868, Lee indeed lived in his home state of Virginia, but in the small town of Lexington in the Shenandoah Valley, *between* the Blue Ridge and Allegheny Mountains, rather than *in* one or the other of the ranges.[195] He had lost his home in Arlington during the war, but as president of Washington College from 1865 until his death in 1870 he, unlike many formerly wealthy Southerners, cannot be considered to have been poor. On the other hand, Lee's long gray hair and beard already stand out in the iconic photographs taken by Julian Vannerson and Matthew Brady in 1863 and 1865, respectively. And he was revered in the South and respected even in the North after the war, particularly for his moral-religious character and opposition to continuing Southern resistance to federal authority and violence against blacks.

If, when sketching his Union general, Farrar had a specific individual in mind, it may well have been William Tecumseh Sherman. In 1868, "Cump," or "Uncle Billy," as Sherman was variously known, resided in St. Louis rather than in New England, to be sure.[196] Furthermore, he was only forty-eight years of age and still an army officer, too young and too deeply engaged in life to be contemplating eternity; indeed, he was soon to relieve newly elected President Ulysses S. Grant as commanding general of the army. From a Southern point of view, however, no enemy commander was richer "in the plunder of prisoners, widows, and orphans" or could better typify a "fiendish and insane hatred" of the South than the architect of the sacking of Atlanta and the March to the Sea and through the Carolinas. And none was more hated in return by Southerners, though he was celebrated in the North. Hill, for example, wrote in his magazine, "The atrocious declaration of Sherman that rebels had no rights of person and property gave sanction to theft, robbery, rape, arson and murder.—The 'march to the sea' was as infamous as any of the desolating raids of Attila the Hun."[197] Sherman was convinced that his scorched-earth policy was the best means to end the war quickly and to reunify the country. However, he wrote a personal letter shortly after the Confederate surrender that Farrar could reasonably have construed as an explanation for insomnia.[198]

In any case, Farrar was more interested in creating representative figures in an account designed to vindicate the South and portray its suffering than in limning particular actors in the great national tragedy. He would appear to have written the tale at least partly in response to circumstances surrounding the Reconstruction Acts of 1867 and 1868, which placed the Southern states under military administration and enfranchised male freedmen, causing outrage and consternation in the region.[199] For present purposes, it is more germane that in responding to recent events he establishes an intimate allusive and formal relationship with Andersen's *Picture Book.* The sobriety that dominates "What the Moon Saw" stands in an effective ironic contrast to the "magical" associations attaching to the name "Hans Christian Andersen" and the alternative title the piece shares with the Dane's work.[200] Moreover, the narrative's general homogeneity of form, content, and tone diverges ironically from the variety of these elements in *Picture Book.* In an intertextual sense, "What the Moon Saw" is thus a quite favorable "review" of, or commentary on, Andersen's work. For through a kind of travesty, or, better, pastiche of it in which he is able to achieve his own essentially unrelated ends, Farrar pays Andersen the ultimate compliment of imitation, implicitly acknowledging the artistic success and renown of the piece—and exacting a measure of vengeance for the death of his son.

In 1872, as the dust was settling around the publication and critical reception of the Author's Edition, a piece titled "The Invisible Web" appeared in the weekly *Ægis and Gazette* of Worcester, Massachusetts, a piece that warrants attention for several reasons.[201] Established in 1801, the *National Ægis*, as it was called at the time, supported Thomas Jefferson and the Republican Party.[202] Its political allegiance over the next few decades is uncertain, but during the presidential election of 1848 it took the side of General Zachary Taylor and the so-called "Hunker," or "Cotton" Whigs, who benefited from the cotton trade with the Southern states and therefore campaigned against former president Martin Van Buren and the Whig-Democrat splinter movement called the Free Soil Party.[203] At some point during the following years, however, the paper changed its stance toward the South and the question of abolition. The issue had preoccupied many in Worcester, leading in 1838 to the formation of the Worcester County South Division Anti-Slavery Society, and reached a climax in 1854 in a near riot that broke out when a deputy

U. S. marshal arrested a black man in pursuance of the Fugitive Slave Law.[204] The *Ægis and Gazette* was definitely in the Republican camp by 1866: "Republican in politics, but . . . independent of dictation from any quarter."[205] From its inception, the paper devoted a page of each issue to literary essays, and its continuing interest in literature is reflected by, among other things, its publication of two of Andersen's tales.[206] Even less a true review than "What the Moon Saw," "The Invisible Web" nonetheless represents an implicit comment on one of the Dane's best-known works and, by extension, numerous others as well. It also relates even more unequivocally than its predecessor to the dominant historical events of the 1860s and 1870s in the United States, if from the diametrically opposed social-political standpoint.

The authorship of "The Invisible Web" is uncertain. Following the tale stand the words "*From the German of Hans Andersen*," but this attribution is erroneous. The resemblance of the story to "The Emperor's New Clothes" is obvious, but it derives from another source, a truly German one, to be sure, but not a translation of Andersen's tale, as one might reasonably assume given the early English renderings of his stories from German translations. In fact, both Andersen and the writer of "The Invisible Web" were indebted to a tale titled "So ist der Lauf der Welt" ("Such Is the Way of the World"), which is contained in *Das Novellenbuch, oder hundert Novellen* (*The Book of Novellas, or A Hundred Novellas*), a four-volume anthology edited by Eduard von Bülow and published between 1834 and 1836, the year before Andersen's work appeared.[207] This story, in turn, is a translation of "Of That Which Happened to a King and Three Impostors," a piece contained in *El conde Lucanor* (*Count Lucanor*), which was written in 1335 by Spaniard Juan Manuel, Prince of Villena (1282–1348), and first published in 1575.[208] Quite apart from the true genesis of the Danish and American tales, however, it seems clear that the "author" of "The Invisible Web," as we will call him in the broad sense of "originator," thought he had used Andersen as his model, or, perhaps better, wished his readers to think so or to call Andersen's story to mind. In any case, the intertextual relationships between these two adaptations vis-à-vis von Bülow's translation are revealing in various ways. For particularly in their major departures from their German source and each other they uncover certain assumptions about the social-political environments and literary forms in which they were written.[209]

A central difference in the three texts lies in the specific power of the garment professedly made by the visiting charlatans. In von Bülow's translation of the story, the cloth is alleged to be visible only to men who are legitimate sons of their fathers, while remaining invisible to those who are not—a question of paramount importance in places where royal succession was (or is) of critical importance.[210] Andersen's scoundrels claim that their new "web" will be invisible both to officials who are unfit for their duties and the incorrigibly stupid, while in the American's story the swindlers seek to ensnare liars and cowards in their scheme. The two stories thereby retain the political-satirical character of the original. However, Andersen focuses, more humorously than aggressively, on what are essentially limited endowments of nature, whatever their broader implications, whereas the American aims at serious matters of personal integrity or character (i.e., matters ultimately subject to the will).

Andersen and the American writer also differ significantly in the kind of figure they choose to reveal the truth to their respective ruler and community. In Andersen's tale we read, "'But he hasn't got anything on,' a little child said. 'Did you ever hear such innocent prattle?' [literally, "Hear the innocent's voice"] said its father. And one person whispered to another what the child had said. 'He hasn't anything on. A child says he hasn't anything on.'"[211] The biblical allusion is implicit but unmistakable. In Matthew 21, Christ angers the chief priests and scribes by expelling the dealers from the Temple; in so doing and by healing some of the blind and lame, he earns hosannas from the young. Verse 16 contains the following, in part proverbial words, "[The priests and scribes] said to [Christ], 'Do you hear what they are saying?' Jesus answered, 'Yea; have ye never read, Out of the mouth of babes and sucklings thou hast perfected praise?'"[212] That it is a child who speaks the truth, and that it speaks the truth oblivious of the circumstances and to no one in particular, makes the "revelation" both conciliatory and, with the allusion in mind, highly ironic, for the Emperor is anything but praiseworthy.

In contrast to Andersen, the American author adheres to von Bülow's translation on this head, choosing to retain as truth-teller a "negro, a hostler of the king's stable who had nothing to lose."[213] The black man says to the king, "My Lord, it makes but little difference to me, whether you hold me for a liar or a coward or both together; therefore, I tell you plainly and I surely know, that you sit on your horse with no different dress from the one you wear at night in your bed." The king then strikes the black in anger, calling him a "wicked, dishonorable man." The truth once out, however, others follow the black man's lead, and all eventually acknowledge the deception that has been practiced upon them, whereupon they set out after the three rogues, who in the meantime have escaped with their booty.

I have called the author of "The Invisible Web" an American. That is not demonstrably true, but, taking into account the time and place of its publication, the story's relationship to its co-texts offers strong evidence that it was indeed written by someone from the United States. It differs in important points from Andersen's tale, not only in the peculiar power of its "magical" garment and the nature of its truth-teller but also in the directness and aggressiveness of its truth-telling. In the latter two respects, it remains close to von Bülow's text but exceeds it in forthrightness and especially forcefulness. Whereas von Bülow translates, for example, "The king commenced mistreating the poor man" ("Der König hub an, den armen Mann zu mishandeln"),[214] the American writes, "The king struck angrily upon the respectable black," thus emphasizing the violence of the king and the dignity of the black man.[215] He underscores this dignity ex negativo by having the discredited king call the black man "wicked" and "dishonorable" rather than illegitimate, another matter of nature rather than of will, as one would expect of a story remaining faithful to its source, or rather than a liar and a coward, for the man is clearly none of these things.

It seems evident that "The Invisible Web" was written within the broad historico-political context of slavery, abolition, and Reconstruction in the United States. The details of the story suggest that the author aimed his barbed satire at "liars and cowards" who dismissed or minimized the evils of slavery or its immediate aftermath, thereby denying the innate dignity of blacks, as of all men. Such individuals were to be found in the North, especially before the Civil War, as well as in the South. However, the king's blatant mistreatment of his servant, who cannot make things worse for himself than they already are, all but confirms that the targets of the tale were Southern whites, either slaveholders or those who resisted Reconstruction, often perpetrating acts of violence on blacks, which led Congress to pass the Enforcement Acts of 1870 and 1871 the year before the work was published.[216] Considering the time of publication and the *Ægis and Gazette*'s allegiance to the Republican Party, at least after the Civil War, one may prefer to view the tale in connection with Reconstruction. Its author was probably a resident of a Northern state, most likely Massachusetts, and all available evidence indicates that it appeared for the first time in the *Ægis and Gazette.*

"The Invisible Web" differs from Andersen's tale in additional particulars. In it, as with von Bülow, the king and his people see the error of their ways: "[P]utting aside their fear of confessing the truth, [they] saw the deception which the three villains had played upon them."[217] After the child and townspeople cry out the truth in Andersen's story, by contrast, the Emperor shivers, "for he suspected they were right. But he thought, 'This procession has got to go on.' So he walked more proudly than ever, as his noblemen held high the train that wasn't there at all."[218] The author of the American tale seems to be confident, at all events more hopeful of the regenerative capacity of his Southern countrymen than Andersen apropos the centuries-long firmly ensconced Danish or European aristocracy.[219]

However, the American apparently had less faith than either the Dane or von Bülow and his source in the power of fabular fiction to express truth immediately, or in the ability of readers to perceive it, so expressed. For, while

Andersen and the German allow their stories to speak for themselves, the American appends a moral to his, in the manner of the overtly didactic fable: "If anyone offers you unusual advantage, but makes the condition silence or some secret proceedings, you have every cause to be on your guard."[220] In addition to its national-historical motivation, the tale with its cautionary lesson must have been inspired by some specific, perhaps local affair now long since forgotten. Its message would appear to bear at least as much on the real-world correlates of the courtiers as on those of the king himself. Regardless, it is good advice for anyone, for those who ignore it, as Danes might say, "riskerer at lægge sig blot"—that is, run the risk of compromising themselves.

However, the king in the American tale compromises himself *only* in the metaphorical sense of the word. The remaining difference between "The Invisible Web" and the other two stories lies in the fact that Andersen's Emperor and von Bülow's king are indeed "exposed," while the American's ruler is not. The "villains" in the American tale work an imaginary weave decorated with beautiful colorful flowers, fruits, trees, and such, to adorn His Highness's nightshirt, which he wears in the critical moments of the story—unseemly attire for one of his rank to sport in public, to be sure, but not the breach of all decency committed by the Emperor and the other king! Mid-century Worcester was active not only in the antislavery effort but also in the struggle against demon rum and its spirituous kith as well as the general advancement of morality. A contemporary local historian writes the following of a noted temperance orator: "The consecration to a life of sobriety and moral effort made by John B. Gough [1817–1886], when, at the Worcester Town Hall on October 31, 1842, he took the pledge of total abstinence, had doubtless a more beneficent effect upon the whole land in the grand efforts for the reclamation of those addicted to the excessive use of liquor and in the elevation of the moral sentiment of the country, than any other agency."[221] The author of "The Invisible Web" clearly shares at least one aspect of the nation's "moral sentiment," intertextually faulting "Such Is the Way of the World," "The Emperor's New Clothes," and, by extension, similar tales for offending Victorian sensibilities respecting human corporeality. In the same manner, he also exhibits some dissatisfaction with his "co-creators'" artistic management of their material, censuring their "equivocal" use of the fable. On the other hand, his tale reflects an overwhelmingly positive assessment of both co-texts as literary creations, for, recognizing their potential usefulness, he adopts their basic form and content and self-consciously modifies them to achieve his own ends.

1872 AND BEYOND

The some 130 new and reprint editions of the tales published between 1872 and the end of the century attest to the continuing popularity of the works and their author.[222] However, the floodtide of their presence in American review criticism had receded, yielding to a relative stillness disturbed only occasionally by someone who evidently believed that not everything worth saying about them had been said. Over these nearly three decades, numerous advertisements and announcements accompanied the appearance of the editions, but, to all appearances, only twelve notices registered opinions of their contents. At the same time, they appear in some of the most respectable periodicals in the country during the period in question, including the *Critic*, *Lippincott's Monthly*, the *Nation*, and the *New-York Tribune.* Some of them focused on the work of the translators, editors, and illustrators rather than on the author's creations. However, even a couple of these warrant attention for varying reasons, and others complement or extend earlier critical commentary.

One of the former appeared in 1873 in the *Boston Daily Advertiser*, a business newspaper founded in 1813 that enjoyed a run of well over a century.[223] The reviewer writes,

> The critic has now and then the pleasant task of calling attention to books which have a half-private character; yet, while lacking the appointments of a regularly published book, are eagerly taken up by any who are fortunate enough to discover them. There are certain genuine qualities about "Hans Andersen's Good Wishes for the Children, interpreted by A. A. B. & S. G. P.," which will commend it to all lovers of good books, who will never hear it praised in any publisher's advertisement.

The origin of the book and the identity of the "interpreters" form a backstory that first came to light in 2010 in a post to the blog of the American Antiquarian Society.[224] The initials refer to Avis A. Bigelow (?–?), the translator, and Sarah Gould Putnam (1851–1912), the illustrator, respectively, both of whom were socialites in contemporary Boston and amateur, rather than professional artists, though Putnam later gained some notoriety as a portrait painter. They collaborated on the slender volume as a means of supporting the Children's Hospital of Boston—hence *Good Wishes for the Children*—and relied on the good offices of Horace Scudder to have it published by the Riverside Press in Cambridge.

The reviewer writes that the illustrations

are so abundant that though there are but forty-one pages of text there are thirty-nine illustrations on stone, almost all full-page. These are characterized by free handling and a good deal of very nice humor, especially in the treatment of those humorous creatures, chickens, which have been the inspiration of so much drollery; the figure-work is not always equally good, but there are some touches in the treatment of the designs which are effective by little effort, especially the suggestion of a cross in the window-sash, at which the little match-girl is looking.[225]

Perusal of the illustrations indicates that the reviewer's judgment is accurate. The individuality of the cook's fingers in "The Darning Needle," to give another example, is humorously captured by their depiction "in character," separate from each other and the hand to which they would normally be attached.

The reviewer has uniformly kind words for Bigelow's rendering of the tales: "The translation is unusually well done, crisp and unconventional as befit Andersen's naïve style. There is a happy success in the straightforward use of homely words which gives a charm in the Danish, often lost in our English renderings, and the abrupt transitions which mark the genuine child-narrative are here well preserved."[226] The writer concludes with the words, "As amateur work, for such [the collection] shows itself to be, it has special interest to the friends of the 'interpreters,' as they modestly call themselves, but it has good right to take its place along with books regularly published." It would be interesting to know whether or to what extent Hjørnager Pedersen or someone similarly conversant with English translations of the tales would agree with the reviewer's assessment. Whatever the case might be, Bigelow apparently has the distinction of being the second American translator of a collection of Andersen's fairy tales and stories.[227]

The *Nation*'s review of *The Little Mermaid, and Other Stories* of 1893 deals principally with the translation, but in so doing it approaches a truth about the language of the tales per se that is still worthy of heed.[228] Having noted the seemingly endless succession of renderings, the critic writes,

The multiplicity of translations, however, is possibly at bottom to no small extent owing to an inherent characteristic of the tales themselves, rather than to an inordinate demand for new renditions. They belong, in short, to that class of literature apparently so simple that, if it is in the vernacular, it is a matter of wonder that one has not written it one's self, or, if in a foreign language, that one should not sit down immediately and translate it off-hand[.] There is scarcely a schoolboy or a schoolgirl who has read Andersen in the smooth German versions, as many do, who has not felt this almost uncontrollable desire to put the easy sentences into fluent English. Where, in later life, there is the reasonable hope of a publisher at the end of one's labors, the desire becomes irresistible, and another translation is added to the already long list. The very simplicity, however, of the tales is their principal difficulty.

Whatever one may think of the reviewer's explanation of the relationship between the plethora of editions and the demand for them, he is correct with regard to the problematic simplicity of Andersen's language. For it conceals a wealth of topical and literary allusion and wordplay that escapes the insufficiently initiated translator, and reader. It is not clear that the critic has this in mind when he then notes translator R. Nisbet Bain's prefatory reference to "the transparency of meaning and the unaffectedness and straightforwardness of Andersen's language." And he wanders from the point when he opines, "If it be true, as is asserted, that nobody but a poet can translate a poet, it may be equally maintained that nobody who is not at heart a child can translate Andersen[.]" Though agreeing with the translator that Mary Howitt's rendering best catches the spirit of the tales, in any case, the reviewer does show appreciation for Bain's own handling of Andersen's language, which "is . . . to be commended. If it is not better than the best of its predecessors, it very far surpasses most of them, and well deserves a place in the front rank of English versions of the tales"—an opinion shared by Hjørnager Pedersen, who calls it "one of the best."[229]

Not all critics were content to allow the disproportionate attention presently paid illustrations in new collections of the tales to pass unchallenged. One of them published a short representative comment in Chicago's *Dial* (1880–1929), a monthly that distinguished itself for much of its existence for intelligent, if rather heavy and conservative literary criticism.[230] The writer begins, "A new edition of 'Tales from Hans Andersen' (Lippincott) is illustrated by Mr. [*sic*] E. A. Lemann, who has endeavored to embellish the tales more fitly than has been done before," alluding to a statement to that effect made in the preface. However, he then puts the accent where it belongs: "This is, however, rather like painting the lily; since the chief interest remains in the tales themselves," though he does not elaborate on his assertion, likely assuming that its truth is self-evident.

Some of the reviews disclose what may have been a trend in American readers' predilections with respect to Andersen's tales during the later nineteenth century. One such appeared in New York's *Critic*, a weekly which, while publishing original work by Whitman, Joel Chandler Harris, and numerous other then-prominent writers, saw its principal function as book reviewing, in which it was, according to Mott, "usually bright, incisive, and impartial, with a tendency to be conservative in judgments and not very profound."[231] The magazine ran from 1881 to 1906 but never saw its circulation rise much above five thousand.[232] It was edited by pioneer female journalist

Jeannette L. Gilder (1849–1916), sister of poet Richard Watson Gilder, and, for twenty years, by their brother, Joseph.

The two siblings did much of the reviewing themselves, and one may well detect a feminine touch in the notice of Carl Sievers's *Fairy-Tales and Stories*: "How lovingly, how longingly remembered are the twilight aisles of this rich and strange Gothic structure, reared by the wonder-builder, Hans Andersen! Here we wandered long ago; we know by heart these tender traceries of flower and vine, these sculptures of sleeping children, these surprises of merry grotesque; we know the dark and terrifying demons on these towers, in whose curved claws and gaping jaws the swallows nest."[233] Much of the review is devoted to the volume's illustrations, but the critic's comments on them reflect her or his view of the tales as well:

> The present translation . . . of the dear Dane, to whom we are liegemen all, boasts, as its special attraction more than two hundred illustrations by Scandinavian artists, from whom a sympathetic embodiment of the author's ideas would naturally be expected. We are surprised to find that the experiment has not been altogether successful. The rudeness of the drawings is certainly quite forgivable for the sake of their sincerity; but whatsoever of harshness, of horror, inheres in Andersen's work, is here brought into the foreground. Vampire and bearded witch and the bony mediæval Death are insisted upon; the northern spirit is intensified just where, for our less hardy imaginations, it required to be somewhat softened.

The introductory metaphorical retrospective and, ex negativo, the characterization and examples of the illustrations both clearly display the reviewer's preference for the stories that do not test the "less hardy imaginations" of American readers (i.e., those that are brighter in tone and more positive in outlook).

Lippincott's Monthly Magazine of Philadelphia demonstrates a similar inclination.[234] The magazine competed more or less successfully with *Harper's* and the *Atlantic* for the near half-century extending from 1868 to 1916, reaching a circulation of as many as seventy-five thousand copies in 1893.[235] It published an array of authors from across the country that included major figures such as Henry James and Sidney Lanier as well as a host of now lesser lights. The *Nation*, not known for puffery, frequently wrote of the magazine's distinctiveness, part of which resided in its literary criticism and book reviewing, which compared well with the offerings of the much acclaimed *Atlantic*, and the *Nation*, itself.

The reviewer's comments pertain to Englishwoman Madame [Clara] de Chatelain's collection of tales (re)published by the magazine's parent company, J. B. Lippincott & Co., under the title *Tales from Hans Andersen*:

The present generation of young ladies and young gentlemen of tender years is so much engrossed with the reforms of the school-room and the discipline of parents that it is feared it does not take enough unstudied fun in the fairy-books of other days. Any boy or girl who ignores Hans Christian Andersen has a doubtful future before him or her, for it is a test of sweet temper and manly and womanly traits to love these perennial tales when one is under one's teens; and not to like fairy-lore is a very bad omen indeed.[236]

In other words, pupils wending their way through the modernization of education and the family programs of the early Progressive Era should be exposed, not to the many grays, sables, and opaques of Andersen's tales but, rather, to those lighter and brighter shades that promote "unstudied fun" and a "sweet temper."[237] Though thus undervaluing some of Andersen's best works, the reviewer does suggest how far American critics had come over the course of the nineteenth century in their attitude toward the fairy tale as reading material for children.

A review published in the *New-York Tribune* reflects the same bias but offers an entirely different reason for it. With R. Nisbet Bain's collection before him, the critic writes,

The republication, in a new and excellent translation, of a number of Hans Christian Andersen's fairy tales is an occurrence of more consequence than might be hastily inferred in view of the Danish author's long-established fame. Every one knows the tale of Ib and Little Christina. Every one knows the three marvelous dogs of "The Tinder Box." Why exclaim over them at this late day? It is for the unfamiliar tales that Mr. Lang, Mr. Jacobs, Mr. Hartland and others have sought out that we are apt to be most grateful now; and the older readers who have a taste for myths are not a little pleased by the scientific flavor that is somehow injected into many a fairy book.[238]

The somewhat misleading final sentence would be clearer if it read, "It is because of the unfamiliar tales that [the men named] have sought out that we are apt to be most grateful for them [i.e., Andersen's tales] now; and the older readers who have a taste for myths are not at all pleased by the scientific flavor that is somehow injected into many a fairy book." For, as the subsequent remarks make clear, the writer greatly prefers Andersen's stories to those of Scottish author and collector Andrew Lang (1844–1912); Australian writer, historian, critic, and folklorist Joseph Jacobs (1854–1916); and English folklorist Edwin Sidney Hartland (1848–1927):

There is no denying the attraction of the folk-lore and racial legends which have been made the objects of enthusiasm by several recent editors. It is good to know the source of a fairy tale and the manner of its development from primitive to modern days. But it is just as good, if not better, from the standpoint of pure enjoyment, not to know anything about these archaeological data, and therein is Andersen's power. His erudition is unobtrusive. The volume before us is practically innocent of notes, a fact full of meaning.

Andersen's learning, like his moral and religious convictions, is indeed largely unobtrusive, for, though early tales such as "The Emperor's New Clothes" were based on the work of older authors and folk stories, he was essentially a creative writer of the later Romantic period. Hartland, Jacobs, and Lang, on the other hand, are now remembered primarily for their contributions to folkloristics as an emerging discipline.[239]

The reviewer's bent toward Andersen's lighter fairy tales clearly emerges from his subsequent comments:

> As translated by Mr. R. Nisbet Bain, "The Little Mermaid and Other Stories" . . . is a collection of tales permeated by the naivete and irresponsibility of tone of which there has been a tendency to rob us. His phraseology is unaffected; the movement of his versions is not only smooth, but spirited, whimsical and suggestive of the personality of the author. The book wins sympathy at once, and that in a collection of fairy tales is after all the sole recommendation it needs.

The critic goes on to discuss the illustrations in the volume, concluding that "they are a creditable addition to what ought to be one of the most popular of Christmas publications." Interestingly, he then renders a generally positive but unenthusiastic review of a new collection by Joseph Jacobs.

In 1886, the Gilder siblings published another revealing commentary on Andersen in the *Critic*.[240] The author was James A(lbert) Harrison (1848– 1911), a Mississippian educated in philology at the University of Virginia who was variously a professor of Latin, English, and Romance and Germanic languages at Randolph-Macon College, Washington and Lee University (his alma mater), and Johns Hopkins University.[241] He authored numerous books, including histories of Greece and Spain and a biography of George Washington, and edited or coedited editions of *Beowulf*, Heine, Poe, and Madame de Sévigné, among others. The present piece is not a notice but, rather, a critique of developments in Italy since the Risorgimento, much of it a retrospective of the Rome of Andersen's time and in Andersen's descriptive style that is still worth reading.[242] The first part, however, is a striking, review-like tribute to both *Picture Book without Pictures*, which Harrison read in German translation, and the author's own deep appreciation of the work.

Harrison writes, "In his charming 'Bilderbuch ohne Bilder,' Hans Andersen constructs a series of dissolving views which for beauty and quaintness stand unrivalled in the realm of imaginative fiction. The moon is his one *dramatis persona*; she wanders from land to land, 'takes up the wondrous tale,' and tells in pictures what she has seen evening after evening in many lands."[243] Following a couple of examples drawn from the text, he continues, "Picture succeeds picture in this wonderful Bilderbuch, each artistically wrought out, each dramatized, each endowed with lips to tell its own tale."[244] Harrison's poetic comparison of the sequence of "evenings" to a series of "dissolving views" refers to what Richard D. Altick calls "one of the most widely attended of all forms of Victorian entertainment."[245] By means of progressively refined devices subsumed under the umbrella term "magic lantern," visual images appeared to fade, or dissolve, as others were superimposed upon them, much as in modern film and television. Used for various purposes, including the popularization of scientific and technical information and the illustration of lectures by evangelists and temperance reformers, dissolving views gained their greatest popularity as means of pure entertainment.

Harrison also employs another contemporary form of popular amusement to characterize the "evenings" in *Picture Book*: "At the end of the book one has seen more than pictures; they are *tableaux vivants*, landscapes gifted with souls, poems that speak, voices that sing, which have passed before the mind's eye and left on its sensitized retina an indelible touch, light as a camel's hair, lasting as bronze. The *Improvisatore*'s genius has scored one more triumph, and his talking pictures, his spiritual landscapes, live after the eye is shut, glimmer after the work is done."[246] Especially popular in Europe during the earlier nineteenth century, the *tableau vivant*, or living picture, presented individuals or groups of them posed in various ways in still life, often within a picture frame.[247] Interposed between the acts of plays or staged as self-contained performances, sometimes in sequences, the "pictures" represented famous paintings or scenes from literary works, utilizing classical, biblical, and secular themes. *Tableaux vivants* also served as parlor games in fashionable society, as suggested notably by Goethe's novel *Elective Affinities* (*Die Wahlverwandtschaften*) of 1809. That they could also be put to good effect in literature is demonstrated precisely by Goethe's novel, in which Ottilie's participation in a series of them ironically prefigures her appearance at the end of the novel in a glass coffin, exemplifying an ultimate "still life." In addition to *tableaux vivants* and dissolving views, Harrison utilizes "talking pictures"—years before the advent of "talkies"—and other images as metaphors for Andersen's series of "evenings" and their various, largely visual and emotive comments on life.

One of the last reviews of the tales to appear in the nineteenth century came out in 1897 in the *Kansas City Journal*, a newspaper that ran under different titles from 1858 to 1942, distributing 22,185 copies daily during the year in question.[248] With regard to its central concern, the notice of *Tales from Hans Andersen* would not have been entirely out of place among the more progressive ones of the 1840s:

It would be a work of supererogation to praise the fairy stories of Hans Christian Andersen. For half a century his name has been a household word all over the world. The story of "The Ugly Duckling," "The Constant Tin Soldier," "Little Tuk" and dozens of others, have been the daily food of millions of happy children. They are rightly held up as models, not only of simple style and beauty, but also of wholesome moral instruction. If they depict selfishness and cruelty, they show them up as they are in life and make them detestable; if they paint the virtuous suffering injustice, they make it evident that courage and virtue are their own reward, even if they do not always seem to triumph in the end. The present collection . . . may be recommended to the attention of parents and others who desire to find unexceptionable literature for the young. These tales offer the right stimulus to the imagination and are a treasure for any household.

The notice discloses important features of Americans' view of the works at the end of the century, first of all their self-evident status as classics of world literature, read children's literature. The many voices of the early 1860s and 1870s that appreciatively recognized the fascination the tales held for readers of all ages appear to have found little echo.[249] The examples of tales portrayed as the daily sustenance of myriads of happy children further confirm the aforementioned preference for Andersen's lighter, affirmative pieces. The reviewer is certainly mindful of their artistry, their "simple style and beauty," as well as their salutary influence on the imagination. By force of emphasis, however, he nonetheless intimates that their greatest value lies in their (apparently implicit) transmission of moral principle. In this, he seems to be out of step with the times.

More typical is a notice of Arthurian scholar H. Oskar Sommer's collection of Andersen's tales that appeared in the *New-York Tribune* in 1895: "Nowhere can one find stories for children so simple and so unaffected as in the books of Hans Christian Andersen. Nobody else can point so many morals and not impress every child as an insufferable prig."[250] This reviewer, perhaps the same one who commented on R. Nisbet Bain's collection for the *Tribune*, evidently approves of the moral content of Andersen's tales, but his rather humorous choice of words indicates particular gratitude for the subtlety of its expression. His subsequent remarks show that he, like Andersen, has retained his "child-heart," a heart surely formed by some of the same cultural forces that shaped Andersen's: "But he [Andersen] is one with [children] in faith in everything that is not seen, in the wisdom which makes dreams real, in fellowship and understanding of every creature and blade of grass with which they play. His 'Stories and Fairy Tales' ought to have a first place in every collection of children's books." The heart revealed in these lines was probably also a young old one, one largely untouched by the dominant cultural currents of the times.

Hearts of similar constitution reveal themselves in two reviews published in newspapers of the Midwest. One of them appeared in the *Inter Ocean*, which began as the partisan *Chicago Republican* in 1865 and, briefly edited by Charles A. Dana, became an "upper-class arbiter of cultural taste" before going into decline as the political tool of mass-transit "boss" Charles T. Yerkes and succumbing in 1914.[251] The notice reads in part, "No writer excels Andersen in fairy tales. He knows and measures the child mind, and plays upon its strings as a master artist. His art is well nigh magical, and sleep vanishes from the tired eyes of childhood when Andersen waves his fairy wand. Happy childhood, and happy the artist who caters to its enjoyment. Let them dream; the realities of life will soon enough awaken them." The writer for the *Detroit Free Press* avers, "Andersen's stories appeal directly to the childish fancy: they accommodate themselves absolutely to the child's point of view, to the faculty of childhood which magnifies and personifies everything in nature. That this is the right way to tell a fairy tale, there can be no doubt."[252]

Perhaps the ultimate child-heart beat in the breast of the individual who wrote a general interest article on fairies for the *Daily Picayune* of New Orleans in 1878.[253] The *Picayune*, named after a Spanish coin worth 6.25¢, the price of a single copy, came into being in 1837 and continues in publication today as the *Times-Picayune*.[254] During the nineteenth century, the paper was noted particularly for its coverage of the Mexican War, serving as a major source of related information for newspapers across the country, and for its humorous sketches.[255] As late as the 1880s, it was the most successful newspaper in New Orleans, but its circulation did not exceed twenty thousand until after 1890 and was listed at only six thousand for the year in question.[256] The article, in which Andersen and his tales occupy a key position, bears the title "Something Lost." It is signed "Charlotte Goodwyn," about whom the piece itself discloses all that is essential here, and may serve as a coda to the present chapter.

Goodwyn concedes that the nineteenth century is "heir to the knowledge and experience of the past"; it "folds about itself all the glory of the present, and can even pierce the future with the glance of keenest prophecy."[257] All the same, the century "has lost something—something very beautiful while it stayed, but which has vanished as completely as the colors from an evening sky." She then invites the reader to accompany her in thought from the hustle and bustle of city life to the wooded countryside: "You must imagine it is summer, for the flowers must be throwing out their sweetness, the trees waving their leaves in the pleasant breeze, the streams moving on in music, and the grass soft and fresh enough to make a lovely carpet for our feet." After continuing in this vein for a space, Goodwyn reflects, "We can talk with freedom, and perhaps with confidence, of the works of nature around us. There is no mystery in her presence now, for science has unveiled her to us, and laid her secrets bare."

The author next asks the reader to wish away the influence of the past two centuries and then to look around to see what change has taken place:

From bosom of flower and heart of tree—sliding down the slanting moonbeams and dancing on spires of grass, come multitudes of fairy creatures not bigger than your thumb! Some brighter than the breast of the Southern hummingbird; some in clothing spun of shining cobwebs; some with tiny faces as exquisite as the face of the one you love when she looks close into your eyes and sees herself mirrored therein; others with faces full of elfin mischief and little ugliness. The music of their mingled laughter is not louder than the brook's. They float on wings more delicate than those of the dragon fly. The rustle of the leaves is but the echo of their chatter, and the hue of the glorious flowers the reflection of their varied beauty.

After pausing for a moment in assumed ignorance of modern scientific law and watching "in superstitious fear and pleasure the monuments of the wondrous little creatures," Goodwyn returns to the present to lament the absence of fairies amid the "wonderful discoveries" and "grand inventions" of the age; even children have put them aside, skeptical of their existence. Drawing on fairy lore and perhaps creating a fairy legend of her own, she subsequently casts blame on a giant called Reality for banishing the fairies into a mountain, "where in darkness and bondage they live and weep." However, she is confident that they will be delivered, and that a child will be their deliverer,

one who has not yet learned that water is composed of gases . . . who still believes that the stars are jewels on God's hand almost low enough to reach—who does not know that the moon goes on its way with the prophet's silver veil about it, hiding desolation and death—who still watches morning and evening for ships to come from Spain . . . a child that "Shall lean her ear / In many a secret place, / And beauty born of murmuring sounds / Shall pass into her face." A child to whose childhood no novels are known and whose poet and prophet is Hans Anders[e]n.

Goodwyn goes on to tell how such a child will break the magic spell and return the fairies to their native haunts, who will repay her with "[w]hatever is most beautiful and desirable . . . but the child must first be found."

The modern reader may chafe, detect symptoms of hyperglycemia, or even smile with quaint pleasure over the questionable content and florid language of Goodwyn's article. Certainly, her quintessentially Victorian notion of fairies in no way corresponds to the wide range of historical folk tales that gave rise to the contemporary "traditional" fairy tale or even to the breadth of Andersen's stories, which she views as embodying the true spirit of fairydom. However, she does capture a sense of the enchantment attendant upon a certain variety of the genre that includes works such as Andersen's "Little Ida's Flowers" and "Thumbelina" ("Tommelise"). And she points to a real problem of the time, addressed to one extent or another by certain other writers treated in this chapter. Referring to the giant and fairies, she writes, "Justly is he called Reality, for he has entered into the holiest plans of the ideal world to scatter their beauties to the wind." For her, fairies hypostasize the old Romantic ideals of the Good, the True, and the Beautiful as realized and experienced through imagination, ideals which, only three years past the third quarter of the century, she can portray as not merely endangered but already extinct, surely with monitory and/or hortatory intent. Nevertheless, she has hope for their return, which is discernible not only in the meaning of her closing words but also in the effusively literary nature of her style: in her allusion to Thomas Moore's "The Veiled Prophet of Khorassan" (1817); her inclusion of the stanza from the fourth of Wordsworth's "Lucy" poems (1798); the biblical resonance of the figure of the child-deliverer; and, certainly not least of all, her choice of Andersen as the child's poet and prophet. What Goodwyn says about progress in the sciences confirms that she was no Luddite. Her ultimate ideal was probably a balance between the left and right sides of the brain. Indeed, she would exclude novels from the list of approved reading in a regenerate reality, likely adverting to the sensationalist fiction against which other writers also employed Andersen.

Given the subject and diction of Goodwyn's article, it is remarkable that she nowhere uses the word "charming" in her reflections. The reviews discussed in the present chapter alone contain some thirty occurrences of the term or related words, and a search of the other chapters of the book discloses many, many more. In fact, "charming" is attached to Andersen's works so often that it can appear almost meaningless and thus tedious. If one understands it in the original sense of "entrancing," as if by an act of magic, which would certainly have justified its use in Goodwyn's piece, however, one can be content with its frequent incidence. For if most applicable to a (significant) subset of the stories and tales, the word aptly describes much of Andersen's other work as well, and the quality to which it refers is perhaps the primary source of his appeal, past and present.

The reviews of Andersen's tales that appeared between 1872 and the end of the century were sparse and, in aggregate, focused more on the translations and illustrations than on the tales themselves. Appearing in some of the best periodicals in the country, however, they were not bereft of individual insights into the works and reveal a couple of important trends in the American perception of Andersen. One critic speaks of the deceptive simplicity of the tales, while another comments on their unobtrusive erudition. Yet another employs sophisticated means of social entertainment such as dissolving pictures and *tableaux vivants* as metaphors to characterize them. Several reviewers disclose an apparently widespread preference for the lighter works over those of a more complex nature that seem to elicit greater interest among scholars today. Most regrettably, the great majority of commentators proceed from the assumption that the tales are the exclusive bailiwick of those who have not yet crossed the threshold of adolescence.

Research for the present volume uncovered considerably more notices of Andersen's fairy tales and stories than of any of his other works, which underscores their widespread familiarity and popularity. Interestingly, one writer provides unconfirmed evidence that a few of the tales were published in English translation up to four years before the earliest recorded collections. If this is true, however, they apparently escaped the ken of American (or any other) review critics. Most of the many reviewers were anonymous, but the ebullient and insightful, if eccentric John Neal heads a list of (possible) critics that includes Charles F. Briggs, Jeanette Gilder, James A. Harrison, and Epes Sargent, all of whom were significant figures in their time. The notices came out in an impressively broad array of largely respectable to high-quality magazines and newspapers such as the *Boston Evening Transcript*, the *Christian Union*, the *Critic*, the *Dial*, the *Independent*, *Lippincott's Monthly*, and the *New-York Tribune*.

Some early reviewers seem not to have known quite what to make of the tales, sniffing about them cautiously or relying on Mary Howitt's credibility to form or support their own opinions. Over the entire fifty-four years covered in this chapter, however, only one notice was entirely of a dismissive nature, and that was *Holden's* rather flippant "Hans off," uttered in approval of an English persiflage of Andersen's style.[258] Of mixed reviews there was a goodly number, though they were limited almost exclusively to the years 1846 to 1848. For some commentators, Andersen's simplicity was labored or affected, or his tales were sketchy or evoked an ill-defined sense of tedium; for others, their "application" went beyond the comprehension of children and, in some instances, even adults.

However, the overwhelming majority of reviewers were unanimous in their appreciation of the tales, many of them voicing their opinion that Andersen was unique or the best in his field. Some were unable to find words to adequately express the nature or impact of the works, resorting to evocations of Andersen's mere name, some unspecified emotion, or an indescribable charm, or "magic"; others compared him, with admitted futility, to familiar

American and English authors.[259] Those who were able to go beyond assertions of ineffability cited features also adduced in reviews of the novels and travel books that are in part even more applicable to the tales, for example, imaginativeness, originality, descriptive accuracy, and poetic beauty. John Neal's effervescent metaphoricity and James A. Harrison's technological comparisons are particularly effective in communicating these elements of Andersen's narrative art. Some writers touch on the emotional depth of the tales and their influence on the sensibilities. Others recognize the humor found in many of them, as in the long fiction and travelogues; still others possess an organ for its satiric usage, though Geraldine deems satire foreign to Andersen's nature. A number speak of a humane spirit that pervades the stories, while several detect an unsuspected profundity of meaning related to the finer qualities of character beneath the often fanciful surface of the works. A few of the most discriminating acknowledge the life that Andersen breathes into inanimate objects commensurate with their shapes and functions.

Such insights led to a conclusion that represents perhaps the signal achievement of American Andersen criticism in the nineteenth century, certainly with respect to the stories and tales. Throughout the period, there were those who took Mary Howitt's title *Wonderful Stories* for Children and Horace Scudder's variation of it at face value or assumed that the fairy tale as a genre was the exclusive purview of "innocence" [emphasis added]. In the later years of the century, these became the dominant voices, voices that evidenced what one might consider a logically consistent preference for the lighter *fairy* tales as opposed to the more realistic *stories.* Their perspective continues to preponderate in the United States (and elsewhere) today and is not at all unknown even in Denmark. All along, however, a far greater number of writers claimed Andersen for "experience" as well, citing, among many other things, the subtleties of style, the inventiveness, and the currents of thought discernible only to the adult eye. Indeed, some felt that the tales overtax a child's powers of apprehension, at least without the guidance of an adult, and John Neal went so far as to assert that they were intended only for the mature.

None of Andersen's reviewers would appear to have shared the ideal of an autotelic art propounded by Poe, members of the aesthetic movement in England, and the French symbolists. To one degree or another, all reflect the conviction that art has, or should have a raison d'être outside itself, certainly beyond its "mere" entertainment value. Early reviewers in particular would have agreed with their colleague who saw the purpose, or at least a major feature of "The Sand-Hills of Jutland" in the transmission of a "profitable religious sentiment."[260] As the century progressed, however, more and more critics spoke of the—implicitly Christian-moral—"wisdom" of the tales. And in what was paradoxically both a historical regression and progression, several approached the Romantic wellsprings of *l'art pour l'art* by suggesting, often in quite poetic locutions, that the moral, or wisdom of a work should be "unobtrusive," "inferred rather than expressed," and by affirming that Andersen's tales fulfill this ideal.[261] Such thinking reflects a growing sophistication among reviewers that in some instances includes awareness of the realism of the later works.

Reviewers identified several other "uses" of Andersen's tales. Possibly related to their religious or moral convictions, some spoke of the "healthiness" of the works, the absence of morbidity or "protruded humanity" in them, their capacity, amid the "sensational romances that come flying from the press," to "refresh one's soul."[262] Such refreshment also derived from their origin in northern Europe, where certain writers still found traces of the grandeur of medieval Scandinavia, which K. E. contrasts so starkly with the "polished falseness" of Greek antiquity and its cultural descendants, as well as a source for the renewal of American letters. Most noteworthy, perhaps, are the actualizations of "The Emperor's New Clothes" and *Picture Book without Pictures* (*What the Moon Saw*) within the context of slavery, abolition, Civil War, and Reconstruction in the United States. Though most observers would surely consider them wholly unanticipated, they each in their own way represent effective superimpositions of Andersen's most characteristic art form onto American sociopolitical life.

NOTES

1. Unsigned review of *The Nightingale, and Other Tales*, trans. Charles Boner, *Anglo American*, October 17, 1846, 605–6.

2. Hans Christian Andersen, *The Nightingale, and Other Tales*, trans. Charles Boner (London: Joseph Cundall, 1846).

3. The first line of the couplet is an inexact rendering from Boileau's *L'art poétique* (*The Art of Poetry*); I have been unable to determine the translator. The second line is drawn from Alexander Pope's *Essay on Man*, which, in turn, was based on Boileau's work. In the Soames-Dryden translation of *The Art of Poetry* the couplet reads, "Happy, who in his Verse can gently steer, / From Grave, to Light; from Pleasant, to Severe"; *The Art of Poetry Written in French by the Sieur de Boileau; Made English*, Early English Books Online: Text Creation Partnership, accessed July 23, 2015, http://quod.lib.umich.edu/cgi/t/text/text-idx?c=eebo;idno=A28571.

4. See introduction, note 1. These bibliographies reflect the vigor as well as the broad scope and thematic richness of current Andersen scholarship. However, they also show that studies of the stories and tales far exceed those of any of the other genres numerically, whether the works are the central focus of attention or part of more comprehensive investigations.

5. The situation described in *More Than Meets the Eye* looked considerably different. Herbert Rowland, *More Than Meets the Eye: Hans Christian Andersen and Nineteenth-Century American Criticism* (Madison, WI, and Teaneck, NJ: Fairleigh Dickinson University Press, 2006), 18–19.

6. See, for example, Anette Øster, "Hans Christian Andersen's Fairy Tales—Children's Literature?"; Tom Lundskær-Nielsen, "Language for Children? An Examination of the Language and Intended Readership of the Fairy Tales"; and Yoichi Nagashima, "For Adults Only," in *Hans Christian Andersen: Between Children's Literature and Adult Literature*, ed. Johan de Mylius, Aage Jørgensen, and Viggo Hjørnager Pedersen (Odense: Hans Christian Andersen Center, University of Southern Denmark, 2005), 398–408, 466–77, and 369–73, respectively.

7. Elias Bredsdorff, *H. C. Andersen og England* (Copenhagen: Rosenkilde og Baggers Forlag, 1954), 438–39. Two of the eleven were pirated editions of collections that had appeared earlier.

8. Hans Christian Andersen, *Wonderful Stories for Children*, trans. Mary Howitt (London: Chapman & Hall, 1846); "Notices of Books," *Commercial Advertiser*, April 4, 1846, 1. By 1848, most of the other collections had also appeared in American editions; see Elias Bredsdorff, *Danish Literature in English Translation, with a Special Hans Christian Andersen Supplement: A Bibliography* (Copenhagen: Ejnar Munksgaard, 1950), 121–22.

9. Unsigned review of *Wonderful Stories for Children*, *Spirit of the Times*, April 4, 1846, 72.

10. See Andersen's notes on the tales and stories, "Bemærkninger til *Eventyr og Historier*," in *Andersen: Samlede Værker*, edited by Klaus P. Mortensen et al. (Copenhagen: Danske Sprog- og Litteraturselskab / Gyldendal, 2003–2007), 3:394–401. An earlier version appeared in a previous collected edition of the works as well as in Scudder's "Advertisement" in the second volume of the fairy tales and stories issued in the Author's Edition; see Horace E. Scudder, "Advertisement," in *Stories and Tales*, by Hans Christian Andersen, author's ed., ed. Horace E. Scudder (Boston and New York: Hurd and Houghton, 1871), vii–xix.

11. Andersen dropped "for Children" from the title of his collections of tales after 1841. However, the influence of Howitt's first compilation and the prevalent understanding of the genre likely contributed greatly to Americans' early perception of the stories.

12. Unsigned review of *Wonderful Stories for Children*, *Churchman*, April 26, 1846, 27.

13. Unsigned review of *Wonderful Stories for Children*, *Presbyterian*, April 11, 1846, 60.

14. Unsigned review of *Wonder Stories for Children*, *Mothers' Journal and Family Visitant*, February 1847, 61.

15. See Frank Luther Mott, *A History of American Magazines 1850–1865* (1938; repr., Cambridge, MA: Harvard University Press, 1966), 57n48.

16. "Eliza C. Allen (1803–1848)," in *Portraits of American Women in Religion That Appeared in Print before 1861*, LibraryCompany.org, accessed July 25, 2015, http://www.librarycompany.org/women/portraits_religion/allen.htm.

17. *Mothers' Journal and Family Visitant*, February 1847, 61.

18. *Mothers' Journal and Family Visitant*, January 1846, 5.

19. See Selma G. Lanes, *Down the Rabbit Hole: Adventures and Misadventures in the Realm of Children's Literature* (New York: Atheneum, 1972), 92–93. Goodrich's first Peter Parley book appeared in 1827.

20. See Anne Scott MacLeod, "Children's Literature in America from the Puritan Beginnings to 1870," in *Children's Literature: An Illustrated History,* ed. Peter Hunt (Oxford: Oxford University Press, 1995), 102–6.

21. *Anglo American*, October 17, 1846, 605.

22. See Frank Luther Mott, *A History of American Magazines 1741–1850* (1930; repr., Cambridge, MA: Harvard University Press, 1957), 618–19; Vera Brodsky Lawrence, *Strong on Music: The New York Music Scene in the Days of George Templeton Strong*, 3 vols. (Chicago: University of Chicago Press, 1988), 1:196.

23. The issue of the paper in which the review appeared contains no article of biblical scholarship, by a Mr. Osburn or anyone else, but the comfortable relationship between art and morality established in the review remains noteworthy nevertheless.

24. *Anglo American*, October 17, 1846, 606.

25. Unsigned review of *The Shoes of Fortune, and Other Tales*, trans. Charles Boner, *Presbyterian*, May 13, 1848, 80.

26. Unsigned review of *A Christmas Greeting*, trans. Charles Boner, *Christian World,* March 4, 1848, 3.

27. "Literary," unsigned review of *A Danish Story Book*, trans. Charles Boner, *Boston Evening Transcript*, June 12, 1848, 1.

28. See Frank Luther Mott, *American Journalism, a History: 1690–1960*, 3rd ed. (New York: Macmillan, 1962), 217.

29. Mott, *American Journalism*, 217.

30. *Boston Evening Transcript*, June 12, 1848, 1.

31. The other stories are (the lengthy) "Shoes [Galoshes] of Fortune" ("Lykkens Kalosker"), "The Leap Frog" ("The Racers"; "Hurtigløberne"), and "The Elder Bush" ("The Elder Tree Mother"), all of which might be considered "sprightly and companionable" and also rank among Andersen's better or best tales.

32. Unsigned review of *A Danish Story Book*, *Literary World*, July 1, 1848, 432.

33. Unsigned review of *The Shoes of Fortune, and Other Tales*, *Literary World*, May 6, 1848, 268.

34. Henry Rowe Schoolcraft, "The Enchanted Moccasins: A Maskego Tale," in *Algic Researches, Comprising Inquiries Respecting the Mental Characteristics of the North American Indians*, by Henry Rowe Schoolcraft, 2 vols. (New York: Harper & Brothers, 1839), 1:226–32.

35. *Sheppard Lee: Written By Himself*, 2 vols. (New York: Harper & Brothers, 1836).

36. See Perry Miller, *The Raven and the Whale: The War of Words and Wits in the Era of Poe and Melville* (1956; repr., Westport, CT: Greenwood, 1973), 183–201, 238–40.

37. "The *Literary World*," OCLC WorldCat, accessed July 28, 2015, http://www.worldcat.org/title/literary-world/oclc/17880978.

38. See Miller, *The Raven and the Whale*, 188–89, 204.

39. Unsigned review of *A Christmas Greeting*, *Christian Inquirer*, March 25, 1848, 93.

40. See Carolyn L. Karcher, *The First Woman in the Republic: A Cultural Biography of Lydia Maria Child* (Durham, NC: Duke University Press, 1994), for example, 80–125, 151–248, and 57–79.

41. See John Boles, "Jacob Abbott and the Rollo Books: New England Culture for Children," *Journal of Popular Culture* 6 (1973): 507–28, especially 509 and 514.

42. Unsigned review of *Hans Andersen's Story Book*, trans. Mary Howitt, *Literary World*, December 2, 1848, 873. Hoffman had displayed erratic behavior and was therefore relieved of his duties in October 1848. He entered an institution for the mentally ill in January of the following year and was declared permanently insane in March; see Miller, *The Raven and the Whale*, 238–40.

43. The volume also includes *Picture Book without Pictures* as well as excerpts from *A Poet's Bazaar*.

44. In a letter to his friend, novelist and poet Bernhard Severin Ingemann, Andersen once wrote, "I seize an idea for the grown-ups . . . and then tell the story to the little ones while always remembering that Father and Mother often listen, and you must also give them something for their minds." Cited according to Jackie Wullschlager, *Hans Christian Andersen: The Life of a Storyteller* (New York: Knopf, 2001), 156. With Andersen, in other words, consideration for adults actually took precedence over that for children, as far as content is concerned. According to Andersen biographer Jens Andersen, this was also true with regard to the form of the tales. Andersen's public readings were divided between those for adults, which perhaps only a couple of children were permitted to attend, and those for children, where typically only two or three little ones would be present. The former were formal occasions, where "art poetry" prevailed, the latter informal events in which Andersen usually improvised, creating "natural poetry." Jens Andersen, *Hans Christian Andersen*, 218.

45. Unsigned review of *The True Story of My Life*, *Christian Inquirer*, August 21, 1847, 180.

46. See Viggo Hjørnager Pedersen, *Ugly Ducklings? Studies in the English Translations of Hans Christian Andersen's Tales and Stories* (Odense: University Press of Southern Denmark, 2004), 116. An exception to the rule is the inclusion of the work in the list of collections of tales maintained on the website of the Hans Christian Andersen Center at the University of Southern Denmark: "H. C. ANDERSEN: EVENTYRSAMLINGER - 38 TITLER," H. C. Andersen Centret / Hans Christian Andersen Center, last modified December 29, 2011, accessed August 3, 2015, http://www.andersen.sdu.dk/vaerk/register/esamling.html. However, those responsible for compiling the list are at pains to explain their decision, which attests to the problem of classification the work presents. While mindful of the differences between it and the fairy tales and stories, the present reader agrees that it is better placed among them than together with the novels or travel books, which has also occurred. The editors of the *Samlede Værker* included the work in a volume of miscellaneous texts (9).

47. See Klaus Mortensen, "The Poetry of Chance: On Hans Christian Andersen's 'Picture Book without Pictures,'" *Fabula* 46 (2005): 58. The first collection contained

twenty "evenings," the second, eleven. The final two came out in an almanac in 1848, and not until 1854 did all thirty-three appear together, in a volume of Andersen's collected works. Here, as elsewhere, I have used the dates provided on the website of the Hans Christian Andersen Center. All of the American reviews of *Picture Book* relate to the 1848 American edition of Mary Howitt's translation of 1846, which contains only thirty of the "evenings" (Meta Taylor's translation of 1847 also excludes three of the sketches).

48. Unsigned review of *A Picture Book without Pictures, and Other Stories*, trans. Mary Howitt, *New York Evangelist*, June 15, 1848, 96.

49. Unsigned review of *A Picture Book without Pictures, and Other Stories*, *Literary World*, May 6, 1848, 269.

50. "Topics of the Month," *Holden's Dollar Magazine*, June 1848, 384.

51. "A Page by Hans Christian Andersen," *The Man in the Moon* 3, no. 15 (May [?] 1848?): 143. See "Angus Reach," *Spartacus Educational*, accessed December 1, 2016, http://spartacus-educational.com/Jreach.htm. In principle, the piece could be considered a satire of all Andersen's short prose, but the prominent role of the moon in it suggests its inclusion here.

52. *Holden's Dollar Magazine*, June 1848, 384.

53. Unsigned review of *A Picture Book without Pictures, and Other Stories*, *Christian Inquirer*, May 6, 1848, 120.

54. See Hjørnager Pedersen, *Ugly Ducklings?*, 116–18. The thirty-second and thirty-third "evenings" appeared in the *Dansk Folkekalender* for 1848, after both early English translations of *Picture Book*; see Mortensen, "The Poetry of Chance," 58.

55. Unsigned review of *A Picture Book without Pictures, and Other Stories*, *Christian Parlor Book*, January 1849, 63.

56. Mott, *A History of American Magazines 1741–1850*, 745.

57. *Christian Parlor Book*, May 1844; quoted according to Mott, *A History of American Magazines 1741–1850*, 745.

58. *Christian Parlor Book*, January 1849, 63.

59. See David Reynolds, introduction to *The Quaker City, or The Monks of Monk Hall*, by George Lippard (Amherst: University of Massachusetts Press, 1995), especially xiv, xxxii, xxxvi. Reynolds emphasizes the social-critical motivation behind Lippard's work.

60. "Holden's Review," unsigned review of *The Story Teller*, trans. Charles Boner, *Dollar Magazine,* June 1851, 40.

61. Unsigned review of *Wonderful Tales from Denmark*, *Raleigh Register*, April 23, 1851, 2.

62. Other reviewers inform their readers where they can purchase the books noticed, but in my reading, none work the information into their text so naturally.

63. Unsigned review of *A Poet's Day Dreams*, trans. Mrs. Bushby, *Una*, July 1853, 84. See Mott, *A History of American Magazines 1850–1865*, 52; "The *Una*: American Periodicals," in *Encyclopædia Britannica*, accessed August 9, 2015, http://www.britannica.com/topic/The-Una.

64. See "Davis, Paulina Kellogg Wright," *American National Biography Online*, accessed December 4, 2016, http://www.anb.org/articles/15/15-00166.html.

65. *Una*, July 1853, 84.

66. See Bredsdorff, *Danish Literature in English Translation*, 122–24.

67. Bredsdorff, *Danish Literature in English Translation*, 124–27.

68. *The Sand-Hills of Jutland*, trans. Mrs. Bushby (London: Richard Bentley, 1860).

69. See unsigned review of *The Sand-Hills of Jutland*, *Lady's Home Magazine*, September 1860, 176 (from the *Home Journal*).

70. See unsigned review of *The Sand-Hills of Jutland*, *Monthly Religious Magazine and Independent Journal*, August 1860, 143; *Independent*, August 16, 1860, 8; *Portland Transcript*, July 14, 1860, 115.

71. Unsigned review of *The Sand-Hills of Jutland*, *Eclectic*, August 1860, 571.

72. Unsigned review of *The Sand-Hills of Jutland*, *Eclectic*, August 1860, 572.

73. "Literary Intelligence: Poems in Prose," unsigned review of *The Sand-Hills of Jutland*, *Providence Evening Press*, July 6, 1860, 2.

74. "Literary," unsigned review of *The Sand-Hills of Jutland*, *Boston Evening Transcript*, July 26, 1860, 1.

75. Unsigned review of *The Sand-Hills of Jutland*, *Independent*, August 16, 1860, 8.

76. S. [Edmund Hamilton Sears], review of *The Sand-Hills of Jutland*, *Monthly Religious Magazine and Independent Journal*, August 1860, 143.

77. See Mott, *A History of American Magazines 1850–1865*, 72n113; "Edmund Hamilton Sears," in *Dictionary of Unitarian and Universalist Biography*, accessed December 2, 2016, http://uudb.org/articles/edmundhamiltonsears.html. Since the review is signed "S." and others in the same issue bear the signature "E.," which probably stands for Sears's coeditor, Rufus Ellis, it is reasonable to conclude that Sears wrote the review.

78. *Lady's Home Magazine*, September 1860, 176–78.

79. See Mott, *A History of American Magazines 1741–1850*, 696–98.

80. Unsigned review of *The Sand-Hills of Jutland*, *Hunt's Merchant's Magazine and Commercial Review*, August 1860, 272.

81. Unsigned review of *The Sand-Hills of Jutland*, *Monthly Journal of the American Unitarian Association*, October 1860, 487. See Mott, *A History of American Magazines 1850–1865*, 72.

82. Unsigned review of *The Sand-Hills of Jutland*, *Portland Transcript*, July 14, 1860, 3.

83. Unsigned review of *The Sand-Hills of Jutland*, *Methodist Quarterly Review*, October 1860, 695.

84. See David Blamirez, "The Adventures of Baron Munchhausen," in *Telling Tales: The Impact of Germany on English Children's Books 1780–1918* (Cambridge and London: Open Book Publishers, 2009), 9–22; *New International Encyclopedia*, 2nd ed., s.v. "Kock . . . Charles Paul de."

85. The relevant passage reads as follows: "All poetry should be instructive, but unobtrusively so. It should draw our attention to something worth learning; but it should be left to us to draw the lesson from it, just as we learn from life"; see Johann Wolfgang von Goethe, "Didactic Poetry: 1827," in *Essays on Art and Literature*,

ed. John Geary, trans. Ellen and Ernst von Nardroff (New York: Suhrkamp, 1983), 194–95.

86. Unsigned review of *The Sand-Hills of Jutland*, *Ladies' Repository* (Boston), August 1860, 104.

87. See Kathleen L. Endres and Therese L. Lueck, *Women's Periodicals in the United States: Consumer Magazines* (Westport, CT, and London: Greenwood, 1995), 386.

88. *Ladies' Repository* (Boston), August 1860, 104. The writers for the *Methodist Quarterly Review* and the *Ladies' Repository* note the "northernness" of the tales with approval, and in this they are not alone.

89. John Ruskin, introduction to *German Popular Stories*, ed. Edgar Taylor (London: John Camden Hotten, 1868), viii, ix.

90. Ruskin, introduction to *German Popular Stories*, x–xi.

91. Ruskin criticized Andersen directly for other perceived flaws, writing in his diary in 1856, "*Wet* all day. Read Andersen's tales. There is a strange mingling of false sentiment, unchildlike, with their delicate fancy and wit: too much of rose-bowers and crystal palaces, prettily heaped together, but without detail of fact and bearing on the story. On the whole I am disappointed in him. The Ugly Duck is perfect. The 'Fat Needle' very good. Nearly all the others, too much of opera nymph in them, and of pure ugliness and painfulness—the princess making the nettle-shirts ["The Wild Swans"], and the grand Klaus, killing his nurse ["Little Claus and Big Claus"; "Lille Claus og store Claus"], and many other such pieces quite spoiling the tone of the book for me." See John Ruskin, "Arrows of the Chace," in *The Works of John Ruskin*, ed. E. T. Cook and Alexander Wedderburn (London: George Allen, 1908), 34:585–86, note 2. However, Ruskin appears to have eventually come to terms with the Dane, in 1886 lamenting the treatment of his tales in English editions as follows: "Then there used to be Andersen! But he has been minced up, and washed up, and squeezed up, and rolled out, till one knows him no more. Nobody names him, of the omnilegent judges: but a pure edition of him gaily illustrated, would be a treasure anywhere—perhaps even to the workers, whom it is hard to please"; Ruskin, "Arrows of the Chace," 34:585–86, note 2.

92. Ruskin, introduction to *German Popular Stories*, vi.

93. See *Independent*, August 16, 1860, 8; *Monthly Religious Magazine and Independent Journal*, August 1860, 143.

94. *Lady's Home Magazine*, September 1860, 176.

95. Unsigned review of *The Sand-Hills of Jutland*, *Peterson's Magazine*, September 1860, 237.

96. Unsigned review of *The Sand-Hills of Jutland*, *Daily Ohio State Journal*, October 26, 1860, 2. See "About *Daily Ohio State Journal* [Volume] (Columbus [Ohio] 1848–1865," Chronicling America: Historic American Newspapers, accessed April 11, 2016, http://chroniclingamerica.loc.gov/lccn/sn84024216/.

97. John Neal, review of *The Sand-Hills of Jutland, Portland Transcript*, July 21, 1860, 123.

98. Much of the factual information in this section is indebted to Donald A. Sears, *John Neal* (Boston: Twayne, 1978). For a discussion of the reasons for Neal's present

obscurity and an attempt to rehabilitate him, see Edward Watts and David J. Carlson, eds., *John Neal and Nineteenth-Century American Literature and Culture* (Lewisburg, PA: Bucknell University Press, 2012), especially xi–xxxiv.

99. Nathaniel Hawthorne originated the epithet in "P.'s Correspondence," one of the *Mosses from an Old Manse*; see "P.'s Correspondence," in *Mosses from an Old Manse*, by Nathaniel Hawthorne (London: Wiley & Putnam, 1846), 2:130.

100. For a reading of Neal's scattered writings on such matters, see Benjamin Lease, *That Wild Fellow John Neal and the American Literary Revolution* (Chicago and London: University of Chicago Press, 1972), 69–80.

101. For Neal's activity on the *Portland Transcript*, see "John Neal," *Lady's Home Magazine*, September 1860, 190.

102. *Portland Transcript*, July 21, 1860, 123.

103. Unsigned review of *The Sand-Hills of Jutland*, *Crayon*, September 1860, 270.

104. Unsigned review of *The Sand-Hills of Jutland*, *Evening Post*, September 20, 1860, 1.

105. "Some Juvenile Books," *Independent*, August 13, 1863, 2.

106. Unsigned review of *The Ice-Maiden, and Other Tales*, trans. Fanny Fuller, *Peterson's Magazine*, April 1863, 321; unsigned review of the second edition of the same collection, February 1864, 159. In the second edition, "The Silver Shilling" ("Sølvskillingen") and "The Old Church Bell" ("Den gamle Kirkeklokke") were added.

107. Unsigned review of *The Ice-Maiden, and Other Tales*, *American Literary Gazette and Publishers' Circular*, May 1, 1863, 20; "Literature," *Press*, February 26, 1863, 2. The *Press* ran from 1857 to 1925; see Mott, *American Journalism*, 347 and 656.

108. Hjørnager Pedersen, *Ugly Ducklings?*, 226, 228.

109. *Press*, February 26, 1863, 2.

110. Unsigned review of *The Ice-Maiden, and Other Tales*, *World*, April 18, 1863, 2.

111. See Mott, *American Journalism*, 350–51; George W. Juergens, *Joseph Pulitzer and the New York World* (Princeton, NJ: Princeton University Press, 1966).

112. Mott, *American Journalism*, 351.

113. *World*, April 18, 1863, 2.

114. Review of "Book Notices: Juvenile" (*A Danish Story Book*; *Little Rudy, and Other Stories*; *The Mud-King's Daughter, and Other Stories*), *American Literary Gazette and Publishers' Circular*, December 15, 1864, 114.

115. "Literary Notices," *North American and United States Gazette*, December 20, 1864, 1.

116. These comments relate to Mary Howitt's *Wonderful Stories for Children*: "His [Andersen's] stories having been collected and prefaced by Mary Howitt . . . are republished here in a volume divided into two parts." However, neither this collection nor any other prefaced by Howitt that has come to the author's attention appeared in the years leading up to 1864. In a couple of lengthy paragraphs further along in the "Notices," the writer comments explicitly on *The Mud-King's Daughter, and Other*

Stories, but his remarks are unrelated to the earlier ones (and are of negligible interest); moreover, the collection is not divided into parts.

117. "Library Table," unsigned review of *The Will-o'-the-Wisps Are in Town, and Other New Stories*, *Round Table*, April 6, 1867, 218. The Danish title of the title story is "Lygtemændene ere i Byen, sagde Mosekonen."

118. See Frank Luther Mott, *A History of American Magazines 1865–1885* (1938; repr., Cambridge, MA: Harvard University Press, 1966), 321.

119. *Round Table*, April 6, 1867, 218.

120. Review of *The Improvisatore*, *Evening Telegraph*, September 11, 1869, 6.

121. "Hans Christian Andersen," *Boston Evening Transcript*, December 29, 1865, 1. Chamberlin's history of the *Transcript* provides no information concerning the identity of K. E. Joseph Edgar Chamberlin, *The* Boston Transcript: *A History of Its First Hundred Years* (Boston and New York: Houghton Mifflin, 1930).

122. *Boston Evening Transcript*, December 29, 1865, 1.

123. See Bredsdorff, *Danish Literature in English Translation*, 122–26.

124. *Boston Evening Transcript*, December 29, 1865, 1.

125. This assumes that K. E.'s recollection of the first tales he read was accurate. See Erling Nielsen and Flemming Hovmann, eds., *Kommentar*, vol. 7 of *H. C. Andersens Eventyr*, ed. Erik Dal et al. (Copenhagen: C. A. Reitzels Forlag, 1990), 26, 56. "Little Ida's Flowers" first appeared in German translation in 1839, "Ole Lukoie" only in 1845; see Ivy York Möller-Christensen, *Den gyldne trekant: H. C. Andersens gennembrud i Tyskland 1831–1850* (Odense: Odense Universitetsforlag, 1992), 317–18, 334–35.

126. For information on Anderson, see, for example, Simon During, *Modern Enchantments: The Cultural Power of Secular Magic* (Cambridge, MA: Harvard University Press, 2002), 114–18.

127. *Boston Evening Transcript*, December 29, 1865, 1.

128. The unfinished *Wanderings of Franz Sternbald* is in some respects a prototypical German Romantic novel, *Fair Eckbert* a similarly characteristic novella. "The Golden Horns" is a dramatic ballad that stands at the beginning of Scandinavian Romantic retro- and introspection, while *Hakon Jarl* is a historical tragedy. *Little Kirsten* was discussed in chapter 4; "Holger the Dane" is a story. Though the earliest sketches of Wagner's *Götterdämmerung* (*The Twilight of the Gods*) go back to the 1840s, incidentally, the opera was not completed until 1874; see J. K. Holman, *Wagner's Ring: A Listener's Companion & Concordance* (Pompton Plains, NJ: Amadeus, 1996), 27.

129. See, for example, Stanley M. Vogel, *German Literary Influences on the American Transcendentalists* (New Haven, CT: Yale University Press, 1955), and Sigrid Bauschinger, *The Trumpet of Reform: German Literature in Nineteenth-Century New England*, trans. Thomas Hansen (Columbia, SC: Camden House, 1999).

130. See chapter 2, notes 56 and 177; George T. Flom, *A History of Scandinavian Studies in American Universities*, Iowa Studies in Language and Literature 11 (Iowa City: State University of Iowa, 1907), 4–8; Albert E. Egge, "Scandinavian Studies in the United States," *Modern Language Notes* 3 (1888): 66–68.

131. See Adolph B. Benson, "The Beginning of American Interest in Scandinavian Literature," *Scandinavian Studies and Notes* 8 (1925): 141 and passim, and the bibliography in Flom, *A History of Scandinavian Studies in American Universities*, 47–48.

132. *Boston Evening Transcript*, December 29, 1865, 1.

133. See chapter 5, note 6.

134. Unsigned review of *Wonder Stories Told for Children*, *Advance*, March 10, 1870, 6. The periodical currently had a circulation of 20,500; see *Rowell's* for 1870, 28.

135. In the "Advertisement," or preface, of the book, Scudder writes, "Thus the present volume contains those compositions in which the element of wonder is especially prominent, the basis of very many of them being in the supernatural and superhuman. The other volume will contain those stories in which the basis is more matter-of-fact"; Horace E. Scudder, "Advertisement," in *Wonder Stories Told for Children*, by Hans Christian Andersen, author's ed., ed. Horace E. Scudder (New York: Hurd and Houghton, 1870), unpaginated [iii]. Also see chapter 1, note 9.

136. Unsigned review of *Wonder Stories Told for Children*, *Sunday-School Times*, May 7, 1870, 301.

137. Unsigned review of *Stories and Tales*, *Moore's Rural New-Yorker*, April 15, 1871, 240. The publication claimed a subscription list of eighty thousand in 1871; see *Rowell's* for that year, 105.

138. Unsigned review of *Wonder Stories Told for Children*, *Providence Evening Press*, February 28, 1870, 1. The paper recorded a circulation of four thousand in 1870; see *Rowell's* for 1870, 741.

139. "Book Notices," unsigned review of *Wonder Stories Told for Children*, *Portland Transcript*, March 5, 1870, 386.

140. "Hurd & Houghton Publishes under the Title *Stories and Tales*," unsigned review of *Stories and Tales*, *Independent,* March 16, 1871, 6. The *Independent* claimed sixty-five thousand subscribers in 1871; see *Rowell's* for that year, 104.

141. Unsigned review of *Stories and Tales* and *From Fourteen to Fourscore*, *Ladies' Repository* (Cincinnati), August 1871, 153.

142. See Mott, *A History of American Magazines 1850–1865*, 301–5.

143. Mott, *A History of American Magazines 1850–1865*, 303. Also see *Rowell's* for 1871, 121.

144. *Ladies' Repository* (Cincinnati), August 1871, 153.

145. "Frauds on the Fairies," *Household Words*, October 1853, 97. According to Kotzin, Dickens became an admirer of Andersen's tales soon after they began to appear in English translation in 1846. Although Kotzin deems it "highly unlikely" that the Dane influenced Dickens's own writing, it is entirely possible that he had an impact on the English author's understanding of the genre in its modern manifestations, however that understanding may have differed from Andersen's; see Michael C. Kotzin, *Dickens and the Fairy Tale* (Bowling Green, OH: Bowling Green University Popular Press, 1972), 36–37, 54.

146. Unsigned review of *Wonder Stories Told for Children*, *North American and United States Gazette*, March 7, 1870, 1.

147. Unsigned review of *Wonder Stories Told for Children*, *Christian Union*, March 12, 1870, 167. Though praising the tales as such, the reviewer finds certain "blemishes" in the translation and deems the illustrations "of uneven merit."

148. Unsigned review of *Wonder Stories Told for Children*, *Bangor Daily Whig and Courier*, March 15, 1870, 2. The paper had a circulation of sixteen hundred for the year in question; see *Rowell's* for 1870, 659.

149. Unsigned review of *Stories and Tales*, *Phrenological Journal*, April 1871, 291.

150. Unsigned review of *Stories and Tales*, *Christian Union*, March 1, 1871, 135.

151. Unsigned review of *Stories and Tales*, *College Courant*, April 1, 1871, 151.

152. Unsigned review of *Wonder Stories Told for Children*, *Congregationalist and Boston Recorder,* March 3, 1870, 6. See "About the *Congregationalist* [Microform Reel] (Boston) 1870–1901," Chronicling America: Historic American Newspapers, accessed February 10, 2017, http://chroniclingamerica.loc.gov/lccn/sf89091700/. The website has substantial information about the paper's contents. According to *Rowell's* for 1870 (664), the periodical claimed a circulation of twenty-seven thousand. The *Boston Recorder* was founded in 1816 and merged with the *Congregationalist* in 1867; see Mott, *A History of American Magazines 1741–1850*, 138.

153. Unsigned review of *Stories and Tales*, *Press,* April 1871, 8. See *Rowell's* for 1872, 32. The review appeared in vol. 1, no. 3, of the journal, which suggests that it initiated publication in February 1871. However, *Rowell's* has no entry for it for that year, nor for 1873–1875, which suggests a run of only a couple of years.

154. Unsigned review of *O. T.: A Danish Romance*, *Golden Hours,* November 1870, 574.

155. Unsigned review of *Wonder Stories Told for Children*, *New York Evangelist*, March 31, 1870, 8. The publication's circulation had increased by one thousand to seventeen thousand by 1870; *Rowell's* for 1870, 701.

156. "Book Notices," unsigned review of *Stories and Tales*, *Portland Transcript*, March 18, 1871, 402.

157. Unsigned review of "Hans Christian Andersen's Works," *Eclectic*, January 1870, 118–19. The review deals primarily with *The Improvisatore* and *The Two Baronesses* and was treated in those contexts in chapter 2, pp. 44–46 and 72. However, what amounts to a lengthy introduction focuses on the tales.

158. *Eclectic*, January 1870, 118.

159. "The Worship of Children," *Spectator*, November 6, 1869, 11.

160. *Spectator*, November 6, 1869, 11.

161. *Spectator*, November 6, 1869, 11.

162. *Spectator*, November 6, 1869, 12.

163. *Eclectic*, January 1870, 118.

164. In this respect, the writer for the *Eclectic* need not have looked any farther than crosstown New York for someone to criticize. In a notice of Horace Scudder's collection *Stories from My Attic* the reviewer opines,

But it is by the so-called fairy tale of modern times that our little ones are in especial wronged and confounded. The flood of heavy morality conveyed under these bewildering parables is enough to swamp for life the intellect of any ordinary child. Hans Christian Andersen is responsible for much of this. His most exquisite stories were meant, not for children, but child-like adults. The man, single-hearted as himself, reads the beautiful parable through the joy or mischance of his own life and finds in it an inexpressible tenderness and pathos. (Unsigned review of Horace E. Scudder, *Stories from My Attic*, *New-York Tribune*, November 30, 1869, 6).

165. See notes 147 and 150.

166. (William J. Clark Jr.?), unsigned review of *Wonder Stories Told for Children*, *North American and United States Gazette*, March 7, 1870, 1.

167. Unsigned review of *Wonder Stories Told for Children*, *New York Evangelist*, March 31, 1870, 8. The *Evangelist* claimed seventeen thousand subscribers in 1870; see *Rowell's* for the year, 701.

168. Unsigned review of *Stories and Tales*, *Indianapolis News*, March 13, 1871, 3. See *Rowell's* for 1871, 40.

169. "Literary Notices," unsigned review of *Stories and Tales*, *Hartford Daily Courant*, March 2, 1871, 1. The paper had a daily circulation of 4,920 in 1871; see *Rowell's* for 1871, 19.

170. B. R., "The Emperor's New Clothes. By Hans Christian Anderson [*sic*]," *Evening Post* (New York), February 7, 1852, 1. See Bredsdorff, *Danish Literature in English Translation*, 121–23.

171. *Evening Post* (New York), February 7, 1852, 1.

172. The standard work on the Compromise is Holman Hamilton, *Prologue to Conflict: The Crisis and Compromise of 1850* (1964; repr., Lexington: University Press of Kentucky, 2005).

173. See Allan Nevins, *The* Evening Post: *A Century of Journalism* (New York: Boni and Liveright, 1922), 244–47.

174. The portrayal of the Union as being in no danger is certainly puzzling, perhaps reflecting an unusually sanguine assessment of current circumstances. It is possible that B. R., unlike many others, believed that those behind the Compromise had taken a reasonably tolerable situation and made it worse, at least morally. Andersen's tale was published in the *Post* some seventeen months after passage of the final bill of the Compromise in September 1850, a seemingly long delay. However, the Compromise was unquestionably the most important related event of national proportions to occur between the aftermath of the war with Mexico in 1848 and the passage of the Kansas-Nebraska Act of 1854, which repealed the Missouri Compromise of 1820, opening the West to the possibility of slavery and escalating tensions between North and South. It would thus appear to be the most likely historical context for B. R.'s handling of Andersen's story. Some years earlier the *Post* published another translation of the work that had recently appeared in *Blackwood's Edinburgh Magazine* (October 1847, 406–7). Unlike B. R.'s introduction, however, the prepended moral is general in nature: "The following story, translated from Hans Christian Anderson [*sic*], shows how easy it is to trick people into seeing with an inward sense what the five senses cannot take hold of"; *Evening Post*, November 30, 1847, 1.

175. "What the Moon Saw," *Land We Love*, April 1868, 493–94. The piece was also published, with minor deviations, in the *Tarboro* (North Carolina) *Southerner*,

May 7, 1868, 1, and the *Fayetteville* (North Carolina) *News*, May 19, 1868, 1. The piece was apparently inspired by *What the Moon Saw, and Other Tales*, trans. H. W. Dulcken (London: George Routledge and Sons, 1866 [1865]).

176. See Ray M. Atchison, "The *Land We Love:* A Southern Post-Bellum Magazine of Agriculture, Literature, and Military History," *North Carolina Historical Review* 37 (1960): 506; Mott, *A History of American Magazines 1865–1885*, 46; Julian Mason, "The *Land We Love*," in *NCpedia*, accessed May 12, 2016, http://ncpedia.org/land-we-love.

177. Mott, *A History of American Magazines 1865–1885*, 46. Also see Atchison, "The *Land We Love*," 506–9.

178. See Atchison, "The *Land We Love*," 506; "Daniel H. Hill," Office of the Chancellor: UA Presidents and Chancellors, accessed May 17, 2016, https://chancellor.uark.edu/presidents-chancellors/daniel-h-hill.php.

179. See Atchison, "The *Land We Love*," 506–7. Mott writes, "Histories of campaigns, tales of heroism, and the humor of the camp vied with agricultural and literary articles, poetry, and travel in [the magazine's] pages." Mott, *A History of American Magazines 1865–1885*, 46.

180. See Atchison, "The *Land We Love*," 511–12.

181. See "F H Farrar Civil War (Confederate): Confederate Army," Fold 3 Ancestry, last modified November 9, 2014, accessed August 15, 2018, https://www.fold3.com/page/636154877-f-h-farrar; and "Geneology," *Virginia Magazine of History and Biography* 9 (1902): 323.

182. See "F H Farrar Civil War (Confederate)."

183. *Land We Love*, April 1868, 493.

184. *Land We Love*, April 1868, 493. The original printing in the *Land We Love* has "that" instead of "what," but the version in the *Fayetteville News* has the (apparently) correct "what," which I have used here. I have been unable to locate the relevant issue of the *Tarboro Southerner.*

185. *Land We Love*, April 1868, 493.

186. *Land We Love*, April 1868, 493.

187. *Land We Love*, April 1868, 493.

188. *Land We Love*, April 1868, 493–94.

189. *Land We Love*, April 1868, 494.

190. *Land We Love*, April 1868, 494.

191. *Land We Love*, April 1868, 494.

192. Hill wrote, for example, "The South, then, so far from feeling the rancor and bitterness of defeat . . . should feel that she stands on high moral vantage-ground and that she can afford to be generous and magnanimous, forget past differences and extend the friendly greeting to good men of every creed and every section"; *Land We Love*, July 1867, 269; quoted according to Atchison, "The *Land We Love*," 510. It bears emphasizing that Hill proceeds from an assumption of Southern moral superiority.

193. *Land We Love*, April 1868, 494.

194. *Land We Love*, April 1868, 494.

195. See, for example, Emory M. Thomas, *Robert E. Lee: A Biography* (New York and London: Norton, 1995), especially 367–417.

196. See, for example, James Lee McDonough, *William Tecumseh Sherman: In the Service of My Country: A Life* (New York and London: Norton, 2016), 648–65.

197. *Land We Love*, December 1868, 175.

198. "I confess, without shame, I am sick and tired of fighting—its glory is all moonshine; even success the most brilliant is over dead and mangled bodies, with the anguish and lamentations of distant families, appealing to me for sons, husbands and fathers . . . and it is only those who have never heard a shot, never heard the shriek and groans of the wounded and lacerated (friend or foe) that cry aloud for more blood, more vengeance, more desolation." Letter to James E. Yeatman, May 21, 1865, in *Sherman and His Campaigns: A Military Biography*, by S. M. Bowman and R. B. Irwin (New York: Charles B. Richardson, 1865), 488. Whether Farrar read the biography containing Sherman's letter to Yeatman is unknown, but it is certain that he had some three years in which to do so.

199. See, for example, Michael Perman, *Emancipation and Reconstruction 1862–1879* (Arlington Heights, IL: Harlan Davidson, 1987), especially 48, 54–59, 61–62, and 112–13.

200. Whether or not the author knew that Andersen was still alive, the first sentence of the piece—"Far away north, in Denmark, there *lived* a man named Hans Christian Andersen" [emphasis added]—immediately lends the narrative a fairy-tale quality. As suggested elsewhere in this chapter, Andersen himself plays with the expectations he creates in his introduction and first couple of evenings, truly intermingling "bright and dark."

201. "The Invisible Web," *Ægis and Gazette*, September 14, 1872, 2. The weekly had a circulation of only twelve hundred in the year in question; see *Rowell's* for 1872, 79. For the little information I have found about the paper, see "Brief Histories of Printing Companies Cited in This Survey," Print Worcester: Documenting Worcester's Printing Industry, accessed April 18, 2016, https://www.wpi.edu/academics /library/collections/printworcester/histories_worcester.html; and *Proceedings of the American Antiquarian Society*, n.s., 25 (1915): 498–501. The piece was reprinted in the *New Hampshire Sentinel* (Keene), October 24, 1872, 1, and the *Indiana Progress* (Pennsylvania), November 21, 1872, 3.

202. "Brief Histories of Printing Companies Cited in This Survey."

203. See Albert B. Southwick, *150 Years of Worcester: 1848–1998* (Worcester, MA: Chandler House, 1998), 32–34.

204. See D. Hamilton Hurd, *History of Worcester County, Massachusetts with Biographical Sketches of Many of Its Pioneers and Prominent Men* (Philadelphia: J. W. Lewis, 1889), 2:1448–51.

205. Hurd, *History of Worcester County, Massachusetts*, 2:1539. Also see "About the Aegis and Gazette [Volume] (Worcester, MA) 1866–1896," Chronicling America: Historic American Newspapers, accessed April 18, 2016, http://chroniclingamerica .loc.gov/lccn/sn83020967/.

206. See "The Buckwheat," *Ægis and Transcript*, June 28, 1862, 1; "Something," *Ægis and Gazette*, January 29, 1876, 4.

207. See Eduard von Bülow, "So ist der Lauf der Welt," in *Das Novellenbuch, oder hundert Novellen: Nach alten italienischen, spanischen, französischen, lateinischen, englischen und deutschen bearbeitet*, ed. Eduard von Bülow (Leipzig: F. A. Brockhaus, 1836), 4:40–44; also see "Keiserens nye Klæder," in Nielsen and Hovmann, *Kommentar*, 40.

208. The translation of the story's title is drawn from Don Juan Manuel, *Count Lucanor; or, The Fifty Pleasant Stories of Patronio*, trans. James York (London: Gibbings, 1868). The Spanish title is "Lo que sucedió a un rey con los burladores que hicieron el paño" and is "cuento" 32 of *Libro de los ejemplos del conde Lucanor y de Patronio*, better known simply as *El conde Lucanor*. In his preface to the volume in which "The Emperor's New Clothes" originally appeared, Andersen himself attributed "the whole comic idea" ("hele den morsomme Idee") of the story to Juan Manuel. However, the editors of the critical edition of his tales name the story in von Bülow's collection as his immediate model; see "Keiserens nye Klæder," in Nielsen and Hovmann, *Kommentar*, 40. Also see Annette Madsen, "*Count Lucanor* by Don Juan Manuel as Inspiration for Hans Christian Andersen and Other European Writers," in *Hans Christian Andersen, a Poet in Time: Papers from the Second International Hans Christian Andersen Conference 29 July to 2 August 1996*, ed. Johan de Mylius, Aage Jørgensen, and Viggo Hjørnager Pedersen (Odense: Odense University Press, 1999), 173–76.

209. There are also some less meaningful differences between the three works. For example, Andersen's tale has three scoundrels, while the American and German texts have two.

210. In an article about his anthology, von Bülow writes that Juan Manuel aimed his satire at a king of the Moors, against whom he long fought. E[duard] v[on] Bülow, "Das Novellenbuch: Fortsetzung" [continuation], *Heidelberger Jahrbücher der Literatur* 43 (1837): 686–87.

211. Hans Christian Andersen, "The Emperor's New Clothes," in *The Complete Andersen: All of the 168 Stories by Hans Christian Andersen*, trans. Jean Hersholt (New York: Heritage Press, 1942–1947), pink pages 83.

212. The passage from the King James Version, used here, probably rings familiar to most English speakers. However, some more recent translations, such as the New International Version and the New Jerusalem Bible as well as the Aramaic Bible in Plain English have "children" in place of "babes." For the latter, see "Matthew 21:16," Bible Hub, accessed April 22, 2016, http://biblehub.com/matthew/21-16.htm.

213. *Ægis and Gazette*, September 14, 1872, 2.

214. von Bülow, "So ist der Lauf der Welt," in von Bülow, *Das Novellenbuch*, 4:44.

215. *Ægis and Gazette*, September 14, 1872, 2.

216. See Perman, *Emancipation and Reconstruction 1862–1879*, 127.

217. *Ægis and Gazette*, September 14, 1872, 2.

218. Andersen, "The Emperor's New Clothes," in *The Complete Andersen*, pink pages 83.

219. One could argue that the American simply remained faithful to von Bülow's translation, but we have seen that in other important respects he had no compunction

to depart from it, so one must assume that the dénouement of the original suited his purposes. Of course, all three intertexts have applications beyond the political sphere, bearing in principle, for instance, on any relationship where pretense and deception are involved. However, the American tale exceeds Andersen's legend-like story and even the German's work in transparent political topicality.

220. *Ægis and Gazette*, September 14, 1872, 2.

221. Hurd, *History of Worcester County, Massachusetts*, 1451. Also see "John B. Gough (1817–1886): The Temperance Orator as Revivalist," TeachUSHistory.org, accessed April 19, 2016, http://www.teachushistory.org/second-great-awakening -age-reform/approaches/john-b-gough-1817-1886-temperance-orator-revivalist. For Worcester's role in the temperance movement as well as the women's rights movement, see Southwick, *150 Years of Worcester*, 28–32, 59.

222. See Bredsdorff, *Danish Literature in English Translation*, 128–38.

223. "Current Literature," unsigned review of *Good Wishes for the Children*, by Hans Christian Andersen, trans. Avis A. Bigelow, *Boston Daily Advertiser*, December 24, 1873, 2. See Mott, *American Journalism*, 187; *Rowell's* for 1873, 99, according to which the paper reported a subscription list of 10,800 for the year.

224. Laura Wasowicz, "A Small Masterpiece and Its Illustrator Are Re-discovered!" *Past Is Present: The American Antiquarian Society Blog*, December 1, 2010, http:// pastispresent.org/2010/curatorscorner/a-small-masterpiece-and-its-illustrator-are-re -discovered/comment-page-1/.

225. *Boston Daily Advertiser*, December 24, 1873, 2. In addition to "The Little Match Girl," the collection contains "It's Quite True" ("Det er ganske vist!"), "The Darning Needle" ("Stoppenaalen"), "The Story of a Mother," "The Angel," and "A Story" ("En Historie"), which Bigelow translated as "Only One Other Story"—thus, mainly sentimental religious tales with an admixture of humorous ones.

226. Bigelow actually translated from German versions of the stories; see Scudder to Andersen, 15 January 1874, in *The Andersen-Scudder Letters*, ed. Jean Hersholt and Waldemar Westergaard (Berkeley and Los Angeles: University of California Press, 1949), 141.

227. Fanny Fuller, of course, was the first. It should be added here, however, that Fuller was not the first American to publish translations of individual tales. That honor apparently goes to "B. R." of the New York *Evening Post* (see note 170 above). He was followed by Luella Clark (1832–1915), a poet, hymn lyricist, and translator who was the "preceptress of mental science and belles lettres" at the North West Female College in Evanston, Illinois, and later "the school's lady principal . . . and teacher of German," after which she taught for many years in New York, Wisconsin, and Ohio, as well as in Illinois, retiring in 1888 to New Hampshire; Frances E. Willard, *Writing Out My Heart: Selections from the Journal of Frances E. Willard, 1855– 1896*, ed. Carolyn De Swarte Gifford (Urbana and Chicago: University of Illinois Press, 1995), 80–81. Beginning in the late 1850s, Clark published original poetry in magazines and newspapers such as the *Atlantic*, the *Chautauquan, Golden Hours*, the *Ladies' Repository* (Cincinnati), the *Little Corporal*, and the *Springfield Republican* (Massachusetts). Her translations from Andersen include "The Buckwheat" (*Salem Register* [Massachusetts], September 19, 1861, 1); "The Fir Tree" ("The Discontented

Fir-Tree"; *Ladies' Repository* [Cincinnati]), February 1862, 90–93; and "The Little Match Girl" ("The Maiden with the Matches"; *Ladies' Repository* [Cincinnati]), June 1863, 335–36. With regard to the collection in the Author's Edition, Hjørnager Pedersen writes, "Scudder simply selected stories from whatever translations already existed and included them without acknowledgement in their original or a slightly edited form." Hjørnager Pedersen, *Ugly Ducklings?*, 207.

228. "Children's Books," unsigned review of *The Little Mermaid, and Other Stories*, trans. R. Nisbet Bain, *Nation*, November 23, 1893, 398. In 1893, the *Nation* had a subscriber list of 10,234; *Rowell's* for 1894, 542. Concerning *Rowell's*, Mott writes, "It should be remembered that circulations are for the year of the date of the directory until 1893." Mott, *A History of American Magazines 1865–1885*, 7n6. Thereafter, it is implied, the figures refer to the year before the date of the directory.

229. Hjørnager Pedersen, *Ugly Ducklings?*, 242.

230. "Books for the Young," unsigned review of *The Little Mermaid, and Other Stories, Dial,* December 1, 1894, 339. See Mott, *A History of American Magazines 1865–1885,* 539–40. The entry in *Rowell's* for 1895 (151) lists the magazine's circulation at between four thousand and seventy-five hundred.

231. Unsigned review of *Fairy-Tales and Stories*, trans. Carl Sievers, *Critic*, November 26, 1887, 272. See Mott, *A History of American Magazines 1865–1885*, 549.

232. *Rowell's* for 1887 (466–67) lists the magazine's circulation at between four thousand and five thousand.

233. *Critic*, November 26, 1887, 272.

234. Unsigned review of *Tales from Hans Andersen*, trans. Madame [Clara] de Chatelain, *Lippincott's Monthly Magazine*, December 1893, 770.

235. See Mott, *A History of American Magazines 1865–1885*, 396–401. In *Rowell's* for 1894 (689) the circulation figure stands at between forty thousand and seventy-five thousand.

236. *Lippincott's Monthly Magazine*, December 1893, 770.

237. For progressivism in education, see, for example, William J. Reese, "The Origins of Progressive Education," *History of Education Quarterly* 41 (2001): 1–24. For a technical but illuminating study of the relation between progressivist and traditionalist notions of the family, see Gwendoline Alphonso, "Hearth and Soul: Economics and Culture in Partisan Conceptions of the Family in the Progressive Era, 1900–1920," *Studies in American Political Development* 24 (2010): 206–32.

238. "Books for Young People: Amusing and Instructive Fiction," unsigned review of *The Little Mermaid, and Other Stories, New-York Tribune*, December 19, 1893, 8. According to *Rowell's* for 1894 (535), the *Tribune* had a circulation of between forty thousand and seventy-five thousand.

239. See, for example, "Folklore," in *Encyclopædia Britannica*, 1966 ed., in which all three men are mentioned.

240. James A(lbert) Harrison, "The Destruction of Rome: An Epilogue to Hans Christian Andersen," *Critic*, December 11, 1886, 287–88. According to *Rowell's* (413), the magazine had a subscriber list of between four thousand and five thousand for the year.

241. See "Harrison, James Albert: 1848–1911," in *Lives of Mississippi Authors, 1817–1967,* ed. James B. Lloyd (Jackson: University Press of Mississippi, 1981), 221–24.

242. The article appears to have been inspired by an essay published by art historian Herman Grimm, son of philologist and fairy tale collector Wilhelm Grimm, titled *The Destruction of Rome* in 1886 (*The Destruction of Rome: A Letter* [Boston: Cupples, Upham, 1886]). For the background of the essay, see "Destruction of Rome, The: Herman Grimm (1886) on the Development of the Rione Ludovisi," Archivio Digitale Boncompagni Ludovisi: Toward a History of the Boncompagni Ludovisi and Their Palace Ludovisi, accessed October 6, 2016, https://villaludovisi.org.

243. *Critic*, December 11, 1886, 287.

244. *Critic*, December 11, 1886, 287.

245. Richard Daniel Altick, *The Shows of London* (Cambridge, MA, and London: Harvard University Press, 1978), 220.

246. *Critic*, December 11, 1886, 287.

247. See Altick, *The Shows of London*, 343–49. The "living nativity," or "living manger," now common during the Christmas season, is a modern instantiation of the phenomenon.

248. Unsigned review of *Tales from Hans Andersen*, trans. Clara [Mme.] de Chatelain (?), *Kansas City Journal*, October 11, 1897, 6. See "About *Kansas City Journal* [Volume] (Kansas City, Mo.) 1897–1928," Chronicling America, Historic American Newspapers, accessed September 18, 2015, http://chroniclingamerica.loc.gov/lccn /sn86063615/. See *Rowell's* for 1898, 515.

249. See, however, "Uncle Sam's Paradise," *Sunday Inter Ocean*, September 6, 1896, 36. Here, the author describes a tour through Yellowstone National Park as a journey through a fairyland in which, recognizing a mistake of his youth, he regains the "fairy-tale" Andersen as an adult friend.

250. "Holiday Books: Adventure, History and Fairy Tales for Young People," unsigned review of *Stories and Fairy Tales*, trans. H. Oscar Sommer, *New-York Tribune*, November 20, 1895, 8. *Rowell's* for 1896 (683) records the paper's circulation at between 20,000 and 40,000. *Ayer and Son's* for 1895, however, indicates that the Wednesday edition, in which the review appeared, had a circulation of 108,000; N. W. Ayer and Son, *N. W. Ayer and Son's American Newspaper Annual* (Philadelphia: N. W. Ayer & Son, 1895), 556.

251. Unsigned review of *Fairy Tales*, trans. Clara [Mme.] de Chatelain, *Inter Ocean*, December 1, 1894, 9. See "Newspapers," in *Encyclopedia of Chicago*, accessed May 19, 2016, http://www.encyclopedia.chicagohistory.org/pages/889.html. Also see Mott, *American Journalism*, 463, 563–64. According to *Rowell's* for 1895 (139), the paper had a circulation of between forty thousand and seventy-five thousand in 1894.

252. "Little Mermaid," unsigned review of *The Little Mermaid, and Other Stories*, *Detroit Free Press*, November 6, 1893, 3. *Rowell's* for 1894 (345) lists the circulation as 31,817. The reviewer goes on to write, with a perhaps surprising sense of history, "[N]evertheless the public had to get used to it [Andersen's narrative style]. It was an

entirely new idea." As we have seen, however, Americans generally grew pleasantly or enthusiastically accustomed to Andersen's style in relatively short order.

253. Charlotte Goodwyn, "Something Lost," *Daily Picayune*, February 3, 1878, 11.

254. See "The Press," Historical New Orleans, accessed December 5, 2016, http://www.storyvilledistrictnola.com/newspapers.html.

255. Mott, *American Journalism*, 248–50.

256. Mott, *American Journalism*, 456n10; *Rowell's* for 1878, 113.

257. *Daily Picayune*, February 3, 1878, 11.

258. See p. 195 above.

259. We have seen that such comparisons also occur in reviews of the novels, the travel books, and even the plays.

260. See p. 200 above.

261. See p. 248 above.

262. See p. 248 above.

Chapter Seven

The Critical General Interest Articles

It is a truism that reviews can play an important part in the success or failure of the books they assess and the authors who write them. They bring both to the attention of a readership that is potentially at least as large as the number of subscribers to the periodicals in which they appear. Depending on their appraisal, they may predispose or disincline readers to spend their money and time on the books in question. However, they are essentially snapshots along the course of a writer's career and can change color, chameleon-like, with every new work ventured, according to the vagaries of time and taste. A favorable notice may appear injudicious if the author's next work is ill received or fails to conform to current expectations. A general interest article, on the other hand, is more like a portrait, for by its very nature it presupposes widespread familiarity and an established appeal among readers. It may need retouching over time but is unlikely to require wholesale reworking. Additionally, it reveals more, and greater detail than a review. Such is certainly the case with most of the articles discussed in the present chapter, which take a comparatively broader and closer look at Andersen and his work, at the same time recapitulating much of what reviewers had to say.

The majority came out in the later stages of Andersen's career or after his death. The authors include some of his most knowledgeable and/or insightful commentators, Hjalmar Hjorth Boyesen and J. Ross Browne, Horace E. Scudder and Bayard Taylor. Several of the articles appeared in highly regarded periodicals such as the *Critic*; *Harper's Weekly*; the *Independent*, or *Outlook*, as the *Independent* was called after 1893; and *St. Nicholas*. Not all deal exclusively with Andersen, but he figures significantly in every one. They are all principally or partly critical in nature and thus complement or supplement the reviews examined in the preceding chapters in different ways. Most are ambivalent toward Andersen as an individual and his work, with the notable exception of the fairy tales and stories. Significantly, they comment on numerous writings that escape the attention of the reviewers.

The years 1857 and 1858 witnessed the appearance of two general articles, the first of which came out anonymously in *Ballou's Pictorial Drawing-Room Companion.*[1] In it, the writer sketches Andersen's life from his childhood to his first literary successes, ignoring his later life and work, a pattern that was to be repeated with slight variations over and again in the subsequent years. His interpretive comments, if unremarkable per se, disclose opinions held by many Americans, especially in the first decade or so of Andersen's presence in the United States: "Sprung from the people, sympathizing with humanity in its struggles and joys, unspoiled by flattery, but earnest and simple as a child, the Danish author makes friends wherever he goes."[2] *The Improvisatore* is "one of the most exquisite works, whether for truthful delineation of character, or pure and noble sentiment, that ever was penned. The work most harmoniously combines the warm coloring and intensity of Italian life with the freshest and strong simplicity of the north." *O. T.* is a "true picture of the secluded, sober life of the north," while *Only a Fiddler* is

> remarkable for its strong drawn personal and national characteristics, founded upon his [Andersen's] own experience in early life. Perhaps there never was a more affecting picture of the hopeless attempts of a genius of second rate order to combat against and rise above poverty and adverse circumstances, than is given in the life of poor Christian, who dies at last, "only a fiddler."

Curiously, the article ignores the fairy tales and stories, which only two years earlier another critic had already adjudged Andersen's best-known works and those for which he would be best remembered in the future.[3]

A more expansive and higher caliber article of this kind appeared in 1858 as a chapter in a book by Charles B. Seymour titled *Self-Made Men.*[4] Seymour (1829–1869) moved from London to New York at age twenty to be a teacher but soon assumed the office of music and drama critic for the *New York Times*, where he remained from 1855 to 1869.[5] He was a regular at the Vault at Pfaff's, a beer cellar in lower Manhattan that served as a gathering place for New York's Bohemian community, which at that time included Walt Whitman, among many others.[6] *Self-Made Men* contains biographical sketches of sixty individuals, mostly Americans and Englishmen, who, like Andersen, "attained eminence in spite of adverse circumstances of birth and fortune."[7]

In the nearly ten pages of his article on Andersen, one of the longer ones in the book, Seymour recounts places and events from the autobiography that came to feature prominently in the American image of the poet: from the still medieval appearance of the Odense of his youth, to his rebuff of a bailiff about to strike him by referring to the presence of God, to his misplaced pride in his new, squeaky boots at his confirmation; on to his bumpkinly bumptious attempt to impress the celebrated—and scandalized—dancer Sophie Schall, his virtual adoption by some of Denmark's cultural and political elite, and, finally, the publications of his early and middle years. These writings include poems, plays, and opera libretti that receive an unexpected amount of attention in the general articles but very little, if any, elsewhere.

Regarding Andersen's literary work, Seymour writes, anticipating later commentators, "He is undoubtedly a man of genius, but his genius is more quaint than comprehensive. In fairy tales and brief stories he shines to best advantage. The brightness and genial fervor of his imagination, his poetical spirit and quaint humor, combined with unvarying kindliness, render these little works peculiarly delightful. They rank among the very best of their class, and are unquestionably of enduring value."[8] In the longer prose, surprisingly, Seymour finds Andersen "too descriptive, and too fond of elaboration. The wholeness of the art production is lost in the exaggeration of its details. In his books of travel there is a strong current of personal vanity, which, under Andersen's treatment, becomes a modest virtue. At first it is pleasant, but constant iteration makes it tedious."[9] On the whole, however, Seymour concludes that "[t]here is so much . . . that is excellent in every thing Mr. Andersen has written, that no one should deny himself the luxury of reading his smallest or his greatest work."[10] As if to demonstrate this point, he ends the article by printing extensive portions of the glowingly positive final two paragraphs of the autobiography.

One of Andersen's American commentators of the 1850s found more to say about him in the 1860s. In an article published in the *Independent* in 1861, Bayard Taylor drew on the same experiences that led to his book *Northern Travel* of 1857, which includes a chapter dealing in part with Copenhagen and Andersen.[11] While devoting most of his attention to Sweden and Norway in that volume, however, he concentrates here on Denmark and Andersen, adding substantially to his earlier impressions. Like other writers, he sees in Andersen an author who at once appeals to an international readership but reflects the character of his native land:

> Hans Christian Andersen is one of the few fortunate authors whose works are racy with the peculiar flavor of their native soil, yet harmonize with the natural taste of all other lands. The naïve simplicity of his style, the richness and quaintness of his fancy, and a minute delicacy of touch in his descriptive passages which reminds one of the pencil of [seventeenth-century Flemish artist David] Teniers, may be enjoyed by those most remote from the moors of Jutland, and the cliff-bound Baltic isles whence his themes are mostly drawn—yet doubly enjoyed by the few to whom the originals of his landscapes are familiar.[12]

Taylor then dilates at considerable length on his contention that "Denmark is rich in the natural elements of poetry," for example, surveying the mythico-historical and physical landscape of the country. Returning to Andersen, he continues,

> He who would truly enjoy Oehlenschläger and Heiberg and [versatile poet and critic Jens] Baggesen [1764–1826] and Andersen, must know Denmark. The latter, especially, although he has traveled much and has occasionally laid the scenes of his stories in foreign lands, is Danish, not only in the character of his mind, but in his most successful subjects. . . . The son of a poor shoemaker, a shy and persecuted factory-boy, a supernumerary on the stage, a charity scholar, he has worked his way steadily upward, through that tireless energy which is nothing less than a concentrated enthusiasm, until now he stands acknowledged as the first of living Danish authors—in fact, without a rival anywhere in his own special province of literature.

Taylor traces his introduction to Andersen's writings back to a sojourn in Germany in 1845:

> Shortly afterwards, Mary Howitt's translations of the "*Improvisatore*," "*O. T.*," and other works appeared. They were reprinted in this country, and became immediately popular. His "Story of My Life" [*sic*] was published in Boston in 1847. It is a charming autobiography, a little petulant, perhaps a little too free in the narration of his private hostilities, but as frank and picturesque as that of Benvenuto Cellini. I am rather surprised that it should have passed out of print so soon.

The relation of his conversation with Andersen goes well beyond that recorded in his book:[13]

> I was sitting at my window, the following afternoon, busily engaged in sketching the Nytorv [New Market], with its bronze statue of Christian IV. in the center, when some one knocked at the door. Without waiting for a summons, the door opened, and a tall, awkward, shambling figure entered. The first idea which occurred to me was: "Here is a man who is perfectly at home wherever he goes." . . . Presently we were seated face to face, and in a few minutes I knew his features as well as if I had seen them for years. He is nearly six feet high, but very loosely put together, large-jointed, angular, and ungainly in his movements. His head is thrown back in a way common to near-sighted persons, and he also has the peculiarity of partly closing the eyelids when looking at you. His features are as ill-assorted as his limbs: the eyes are gray and projecting; the nose large and not quite straight, the mouth broad, and the teeth irregular. His forehead is high and narrow, but well-developed at the temples, and his hair thin and sandy-gray. Yet the plainness of his face is attractive, through its

air of frankness, honesty, and kindness. . . . He has that winning and confiding way which not only encourages, but almost compels confidence in others. Such a man is not only unembarrassed himself, but his presence is an antidote to the embarrassment of others. This fact accounts for his personal popularity with all classes of men, from peasants to kings. He is a Knight of Da[n]nebrog, with the honorary titles of Professor and Doctor, yet it will never be possible to call him anything else than Hans Christian Andersen.[14]

Taylor not only reflected, but actively participated in the ongoing American discovery of the Nordic countries, which at least partly explains his keenness to portray Andersen as a representative of the Danish national character. Like many of his countrymen, he also saw the lands and literatures of the North as models for reinvigorating an American literature perceived as too long dependent on the "staid" conventions of the "overbearing" mother country. In contrast to Seymour, he celebrates Andersen's descriptive narrative style, thus joining the majority of his peers, although he extols its realistic qualities rather than any Tennysonian lyrical ethereality, as do some of his more Romantic contemporaries. The parallel he draws between the autobiographies of Andersen and Cellini respecting candor and picturesqueness is particularly striking in view of the Italian's great popularity with the Romantics. If perhaps influenced by his reading of Andersen's writings—Andersen was not always "unembarrassed" in the company of others—Taylor's portrait of the Dane nonetheless rests on personal acquaintance, however fleeting, which lends it a degree of credibility wanting in characterizations based exclusively on divinations inspired by the works.

Less than a month after Taylor's piece appeared, another traveler published a newspaper article containing remarks on Andersen that served as a prelude to a lengthy travelogue devoted in part to the Dane that came out two years later in a magazine.[15] That traveler was J. Ross Browne (1821–1875), an Irish-born writer and government agent whose books of travel and adventure at sea and in the American West influenced *Moby-Dick* and the Mark Twain of *Roughing It* and *Innocents Abroad.*[16] His "A Californian in Iceland," which came out in three parts in *Harper's New Monthly Magazine* in 1863, includes reminiscences of a conversation with Andersen that rank among the most vivid and interesting ever written by an American.[17] Browne wrote the earlier article while traveling in Europe for the *Sacramento Daily Union*, which was soon to number both Twain and Bret Harte among its contributors. Titled "Newspapers and Children's Stories," the piece involves Andersen, as paradoxical as it may sound, both peripherally and centrally.

Browne finds the German press behind the times and the German people ill-informed with regard to world affairs, but these drawbacks are for him somewhat offset by the absence of a low and depraved species of literature which has taken too strong a hold upon the reading public in the United States. No yellow-covered trash is popular in Germany. The most popular authors are generally the best. . . . Filthy writers, like some of the late French novelists, never take a very strong hold upon the mass of the German people. There must be something genuine and pure—something appealing to the higher sentiments—in any production issued in this country, to become extensively or permanently popular.[18]

The Germans' love of good writing and reading, according to Browne, is nowhere more apparent than in their books for children, with which nothing produced by Americans can compare: "It is a lamentable fact connected with American literature, that whilst we take a high rank in history, poetry and romance, and excel all other countries in entertaining works of travel, we have never yet produced a passably good book for children. I know of no American writer who can reasonably claim to have succeeded in this department of literature." Whatever one may think of this assertion—Hawthorne had written his stories for children by this time—Browne ascribes the alleged circumstance to the impact of frontier life on the American character: "It [literature for children] requires a peculiar quality of genius rarely to be found in a new country, where the prevailing traditions are of men, and the early struggles of men in carving out their fortunes in the wilderness, rather than those of fairies and the mystic spirits that hover around the monuments of by-gone ages." "There is some want of gentle playfulness in the American mind," he continues, "that seems to unfit it for this kind of writing. We have tracts enough and moral homilies enough in the shape of stories for children; but they are not genuine reading for children. There is something strained and unnatural in all these productions. The style is not adapted to children; it is neither simple nor genuine, but rather the puerile attempt of grown persons to be childish." Coming to Andersen, Browne writes,

> Let children read what they like best, provided it is unobjectionable in sentiment and moral, and they will soon acquire such a love for reading that it will not be difficult as their minds expand to lead them into the more practical walks of knowledge. I never could see the slightest objection to fairies, giants, talking cats and mice, wonderful genii, and the like; we enjoy them as grown people, and why should we not as children? I sincerely believe the stories of Hans Christian Andersen have done more for the cause of morals than all the juvenile tracts and libraries of useful reading for children ever issued by the American press. In this the Germans excel.

Browne is clearly one of the few writers of the time who find moral power in imaginative literature exemplified by the fairy tales of both Germany and Andersen. He closes by lamenting that Americans foreshorten the period of childhood, making their children prematurely old. Despite favoring American newspapers and the American form of government over their counterparts in Germany, he prefers the German educational system and, of course, German writing for children.

Browne's article offers an example of that critical reflection on one's country that often issues from a mind open to different, and possibly better ways of acting and thinking in other lands. Over the course of the article, it becomes apparent that he was neither a cultural jingoist nor, in the context of his time, a true moral rigorist. He faults American writing for children for its overt moralism and religiosity and welcomes the imaginative element of fairy tales still suspect in some quarters, freely acknowledging its appeal to adults, though he abhors the sensationalist writing of the day. It is in this connection that he makes the striking asseveration that Andersen's tales have better served the cause of morality than all the moralist writings published in the United States combined. Here, interestingly, a realist attributes greater moral force to the Romantic imagination than to the rationalist moral-religious mind.

One finds similar ideas in two articles published later in the 1860s in the *Round Table.* The first was written by Justin Winsor (1831–1897), a former editor of the *Crayon* who contributed poetry, translations, and criticism to several magazines and newspapers, eventually becoming librarian of the Boston Public and Harvard libraries and a leading figure in librarianship.[19] Titled simply "Boston," the article is essentially a lengthy review of recent children's books, including a multivolume collection of fairy tales containing works by Andersen and the Brothers Grimm. However, well over one-third of it is given over to a general discussion of children's literature in which Andersen serves as the touchstone. Winsor's central concern is whether authors should write down to children from an adult perspective or write in children's own language from within their peculiar perceptual and conceptual frame of reference:

> People talk of writing down to the capacity of the young as if it were an essential, which all presupposes that the child is only less adult than the adult himself. What Wordsworth meant in a restricted sense, "the child is father of the man," is proclaimed as a general predicate. There is, on the contrary, more than a grain of truth in what Landor says of children, that they are almost as different creatures from men and women as if they were never to become the one or the other—that they are as unlike, almost, as blossoms are unlike fruits.[20]

Winsor comes down on Landor's side of the question, citing Andersen in support of his contention:

> Andersen understood this when he said that to a young child its parent's language was hardly plainer than the signs of meaning which birds and animals

convey to their delicately sensitive perceptions. "Some children," he says, "cling to their infantile ways of thinking much longer than others, and it is the custom to call such children backward. People *may* say so!" But Hans Christian Andersen evidently thinks another thing or two. Instead of writing down, it may require more than ordinary power to write up to such.

Winsor goes on to attribute Andersen's success with children to his love of them:

> And we can well believe all the stories that are told of Andersen's genuine love of a frolicksome child when we look upon the frank, open countenance of his portraits, or hear of the cheery receptions that those get who visit him. He is kindly in temperament, and though not a father in blood, is more than one in sympathy. Critics may vex him, but children delight him. His very earnest, outspoken sincerity attracts them, and it is only the taint of a less spiritual mind than theirs that induces his catechizers to call this very trait by the harsher name of egotism.

Andersen was in fact not as uniformly enthusiastic in the company of children as portrayed here, but there is little doubt that his rumored antipathy to them was inaccurate.[21]

The second article published in the *Round Table* came out about a year and a half after the first under the title "Reading for Children."[22] Although unsigned, it—and the review of *The Will-o'-the-Wisps Are in Town* discussed in chapter 6—may also have been written by Justin Winsor, for it discloses much the same attitude toward children's literature as that expressed in the earlier piece and again uses Andersen as its point of reference.[23] The writer has a high opinion of both the interests and capabilities of young people: "Next to more pocket money and more license to go out in the evening than they can properly have, children want something to read which is bright without being silly, and sensible without being stupid and dull."[24] Younger children have limitations that place constraints on what teachers and writers can attempt, "but when a broader age is reached there is a fitter field for the deepest and most poetic natures than most people have dreamed."[25] However, the many well-meaning people who have written for youth have failed miserably, giving children "too largely a class of books which make of childhood an unhealthy monstrosity, while, at the same time, we ignored the qualities of fancy and exaggeration which have in childhood their natural and happy play."[26] This lack of success stems, on the one hand, from a moral-religious idealization of the young, who in reality "make mischief and prove the original Adam, and if this is to be a prosperous and healthy nation it must not make its children morally and mentally dyspeptic."[27] On the other hand, the failure derives from an acceptance of the "hard utilitarianism of the age," which "has tried to proscribe the whole class of fairy stories, and is in a great hurry to tell children that Santa Claus does not come down the chimney."[28] Such thinking ignores the true nature of children: "We are not all of us poets, surely; but we are more or less poetic in our young days. Children ask questions that check our tongues in very awe; they mingle the fanciful and the purely grotesque so oddly that every household keeps its own collection of juvenalia; they never reason but go by intuition directly to the root of things. And if they are not suffered to think that angels are around their pillows, they will certainly imagine bugaboos."[29]

The author pays Jacob Abbott his due, for he "has been for many years almost a monopolist in the department of juvenile books. . . . He has succeeded in interesting children, and his volumes while away an hour of at least one adult better than a great many newspapers."[30] Abbott's morality is sound, and his subject matter is largely both appealing and instructive. However, "he often bungles by trying to be too instructive, and his manner is sometimes execrable."[31] Following a couple of examples illustrative of these flaws, the writer holds up what he clearly feels to be proof of his contentions and an aspirational model for those who would avoid such ineptitude: "Very much better than all this drivel are the quaint, weird tales of dear old Hans Christian Andersen who has been so delightfully sketched by J. Ross Browne, and seems as unique as his wonderful tales. They are delicate vapor which the hot sun of mature life will soon enough raise from the heads of children; but they are natural mists, not heavy artificial smoke."[32]

These words mark the climax of the more discursive part of the article, although they occur approximately two-thirds of the way through the piece. Subsequently, the author criticizes certain children's magazines and some of their contributors—making an exception for Horace Scudder's *Riverside Magazine*, which "begins well" and contains a story, by Scudder, "which, like some of its successors, reminds one of Hans Christian Andersen himself."[33] He also challenges a "better class of authors" such as Louisa May Alcott, Longfellow, and Whittier to set themselves to the task of writing for a "waiting assemblage of younger and rounder faces," adding that "[i]t is not stooping to conquer."[34] For he adjures them, synecdochally, "Poet, do not be ignorant that in the little ones there is the very poetry of nature, yet clinging to them as the foam of the sea clung to Venus when she arose from the waves. Give children poetry, but let it be poetry for juveniles, not juvenile poetry."[35]

The author works with a contradictory, or at least very broad conception of childhood and juvenility, between which he appears to make no principal distinction. On the one hand, his "children" are old enough to desire money for "improper" evening activities away from home; on the other, their hearty and sound appreciation of literature "rest[s] on intuition which they cannot explain," and they are looked upon "as pure, as almost of another race."[36] What is unambiguous, however, is that he, like other writers discussed in these pages, ultimately idealizes them every bit as much as Jacob Abbott and his generation, only in a different way. Writing of the impact of contemporary socioeconomic changes on the American family, MacLeod cites the decisive fact, in the present context, that "children had entered upon a long process of separation from adult life. . . . A romantic view cherished children as children and gave childhood a value in and by itself, rather than as a preparatory school for adult life."[37] It may be that this privileged notion of childhood contributed to the increasingly common misapprehension that Andersen's tales had no relevance for mature readers, a misconception shared by most of the writers treated in the present chapter. For in the minds of individuals who nurtured it, something held so dear would have tended to repel intrusions from a sphere perceived as foreign, even inimical. We recall, in any case, that the "natural mists" of the stories are too "delicate" to survive the "hot sun" of adult life (i.e., that the stories indeed belong to childhood and not to maturity). The writer deals evenhandedly with Jacob Abbott, the incumbent dean of American children's literature, but it is evident that he considers him part of a bygone era and sees in Andersen the present and future of the field at large.

A few general articles appeared in the months following Andersen's death in August, 1875.[38] One of the earliest came out in the *Phrenological Journal* in September, but a passage toward the end makes clear that it was written some months earlier and was thus not intended as a tribute.[39] The article is divided into two parts, the first of which is a phrenological analysis of Andersen's character based on a reproduction of a photograph he presented to English critic Edmund W. Gosse in 1872.[40] The product of a now long since discredited pseudo-science, the study was perforce founded in large part on already formed opinions, but it is illuminating nevertheless.

The writer, who was perhaps *Journal* editor Orson Squire Fowler, in any event, an experienced phrenologist like him, reveals preconceptions about Andersen that are partly general and partly specific. In the first paragraph he states, "This face and head, although endowed with a certain masculine angularity, has a strikingly feminine appearance."[41] He then relates an incident involving a young lady of his acquaintance who, he says, looks enough like the picture of Andersen to be his daughter:

> Some twenty years ago, when this lady was a four-year-old child, she came up to the writer and gave him a certain confiding and inquiring look, which led him to remark to the mother, at the same time touching the child's forehead in the regions of observation and memory, "Oh, mamma, tell me another story!" The mother has often said that that one expression revealed the disposition and

intellectual tendency and confiding nature of the child more than any other statement could have done.[42]

Having thus ostensibly exemplified traits requisite to a storyteller, the author
writes, "This is a teacher's forehead, and what is it to be a teacher but to
have the power to acquire knowledge, remember it, and express it clearly
and happily?"[43]

The author sees a strong resemblance between Andersen's forehead and
that of Bayard Taylor, and it is perhaps his familiarity with the work of his
countryman as well as Andersen that leads him to continue, "Such a practical
and analytical intellect as this, so free from dogmatic speculation, can take
just views of the outward world; can appreciate nicely the inner life, and express both in such a manner as to make readers fascinated with the fullness
and fidelity of his descriptions; and when they have completed one of his stories or books, would naturally come back and say, 'Tell us another story.'"[44]
In various regions of Andersen's head, the writer identifies "remarkable
order" and high degrees of benevolence, veneration, politeness, firmness,
"Ideality and Sublimity," "Number and Tune," and a language that "is developed in such a manner as to indicate accuracy and smoothness of expression
rather than volubility. He talks right to the point, and expresses living facts
and living sympathies. His Language is not made up of verbose statements
and noisy adjectives, but he strikes right home to the root of the subject, at the
principles involved in the facts, and his memory is such that he holds all the
incidental circumstances in solution, and makes them available at pleasure."[45]
The author attributes great knowledge of human character to Andersen:

> He reads men intuitively, and adapts himself to all sorts and conditions of them
> with a readiness and a conformatory pliability which would astonish a person
> who should travel with him and notice the wisdom and skill indicated in his
> intercourse with others. He stands erect among men; he bends to children and
> people of weakness and simplicity, and those invite his confidence wherever he
> goes. Here is a strong character, but it is overlaid with geniality, sympathy, and
> tenderness.[46]

The second part of the article is an overview of Andersen's life and work,
which the author introduces as follows: "All the world has heard of Hans
Christian Andersen, the story-teller, poet, and traveler. Among the writers of
the day scarcely one stands more conspicuously related to the general reading public than the Danish author."[47] In connection with Andersen's youthful
employments, the author exhibits yet another preconception: "He learned the
trade of a joiner, but like most young men possessing gifts of authorship,
especially those of a romantic order, was a poor or unsteady workman, for he

scarcely earned enough at times to keep body and soul together."[48] The writer calls *The Improvisatore* one of Andersen's best-known works and includes the autobiography, "'Only a Fiddle'" [*sic*], and even *Ahasuerus* among his better known ones.[49] However, "[h]is 'Fairy Tales,' 'Picture-Book Without Pictures,' and other juvenile publications, have been and are still exceedingly popular. Perhaps there is scarcely a writer to-day who furnishes more agreeable stories for youth than M. Andersen."[50]

Whether peering at Andersen through the lens of his discipline, his reading of writing by and/or about him, or his experience in studying images of individuals—people of the nineteenth century were far more adept at divining character and personality from paintings and, later, portrait photography than we—the writer makes observations validated by contemporaries as well as later commentators. Andersen's effeminacy, indeed his purported, at least latent homosexuality, has assumed a prominent place in recent scholarship, if generally without compelling evidence or motivation beyond the related interest generated by Queer studies. As we have seen, moreover, even his earliest critics recognized his great powers of observation and description. Andersen was an intellectually inquisitive individual, but assuredly not one practiced or adroit in systematic speculation; his occasional forays into such, as in *Ahasuerus* and *To Be, or Not to Be?*, earned him almost universal, if not altogether justified, censure and even ridicule. More than once he expressed his faith in the Romantic-idealist trinity of the Good, the True, and the Beautiful. He was a curious combination of extrovert and introvert, but his pronounced sense of his own interiority did not result in characters as memorable as those of the leading novelists of the time but, rather, in the psychologically charged figures and objects of many of his fairy tales. The language of his novels could in fact be voluble, even florid, anything other than "right to the point." However, he possessed a mastery of language that is displayed most impressively perhaps in the descriptive passages of his novels and travel books, the subtle humor and irony of many of his tales, and the myriad poetic forms of his plays and libretti for the musical theater and opera. Though tested over and again by his critics and his native hypersensitivity, Andersen's was in fact a kindly nature, which is reflected not least of all in the sympathy for the poor and downtrodden evident in much of his work. That the writer for the *Journal* acknowledges this aspect of his character may be attributable at least in part to the reformist social and political impulses of the editors of the magazine.[51]

Before the year of Andersen's death was out, two of his most prolific and insightful American commentators published articles that both complement and supplement their other writings on him. Horace E. Scudder (1838–1902) was Andersen's greatest contemporary disciple and interpreter in the United States.[52] He was a member of the first generation of American children to grow up under the spell of the fairy tales, and the slender volumes of his own work in the genre show many traces of his mentor's influence. In the course of the 1860s, he began an increasingly warm correspondence with Andersen that led to the publication of numerous tales in the *Riverside Magazine for Young People*, most for the first time anywhere, as well as to the ten-volume Author's Edition. An article he published in 1861 may be credited with initiating American Andersen scholarship, which he then enriched with another contribution that appeared shortly before the one to be considered presently. In the meantime and thereafter, he also penned a number of articles of a more general nature. However, due to his epistolary friendship with Andersen, his extensive knowledge of the Dane's lifework, which probably exceeded that of any other individual in the United States, and his devotion particularly to the fairy tales, even his more popular writing discloses instances of critical insight.

The article in question came out under the title "Hans Christian Andersen" in the "Supplement" to the issue of *Harper's Weekly* for October 9, 1875, a section published irregularly that appears to have been reserved for topics of special interest.[53] Mott writes that "it is as a vigorous political journal of conservative tendencies that [the magazine] was most noteworthy," conceding it a "certain importance" from a literary point of view.[54] All the same, in the course of its run from 1857 to 1916, the periodical published serials by Bulwer-Lytton, Wilkie Collins, Charles Dickens, William Dean Howells, and Henry James; it also printed shorter prose and verse by the likes of James M. Barrie, Arthur Conan Doyle, Hamlin Garland, Henry James, and Rudyard Kipling, among many, many others. In addition to original literary work, the *Weekly* published book reviews as well as more essayistic reflections on literature and art such as George William Curtis's column "The Lounger," a sort of pendant to his writing from "The Easy Chair" in *Harper's New Monthly Magazine*. Scudder's piece on Andersen was thus not at all out of place in the *Weekly*. Highly successful for many years, the magazine estimated an impressive subscriber list of one hundred thousand in 1875.[55]

Scudder's article holds to the tradition of the critical biography, if writ small. Methodologically, it reflects the current positivistic notion of an integral relationship between an author's life and his literary work. Happily, Scudder was able to draw on Andersen's autobiography and commentary on his tales for examples of the relationship, such as the roof garden of his childhood home, which reappears in "The Snow Queen," and his squeaky confirmation boots, which metamorphosed into "The Red Shoes." He may himself have made a connection between stories Andersen heard as a child from women at the insane asylum where his grandmother worked and various superstitions that recur in the stories.

Scudder calls attention to early works that the vast majority of American critics ignored or were ignorant of. However, he posits a teleology according to which Andersen inexorably sloughed off one uncongenial poetic identity after the other before reaching his true artistic self—that is, his creative core as a teller of fairy tales. Few would challenge the validity of the telos per se, but Scudder thereby denies even the possibility of any other line of development and depreciates works of other kinds that have their own not inconsiderable value. To be sure, he writes, "The first result of his education was a book, *A Journey on Foot from the Holm Canal to the East Point of Amager*, which is much the same as if one were to publish a similar excursion from New York to Richmond on Staten Island. It is not read now, but its fantastic character foreshadowed peculiarities of ANDERSEN'S work afterward to be more temperately displayed," and "[u]nder the excitement of its issue and of his sense of freedom, ANDERSEN wrote a vaudeville, *Love on the Nicholas Tower* which was played, and still occasionally is given now, I believe. He still kept at his studies, and passed his second examination, and at Christmas in the same year brought out his first volume of poems."[56] However, Scudder continues, in provisional summary, "[Andersen] was restless with a pent-up nature, that burst forth now and then in a disorderly, irregular manner. He tried to conceal himself behind satire and mockery; he tried in vain to be something else than what he was."[57] Satire, albeit of a humoristic rather than sardonic sort, was in fact an essential element of Andersen's artistic makeup, as evidenced not least of all by many of his fairy tales and stories.

Scudder also misses the essential Andersen in his *Rambles in the Hartz Mountains*, a result of much literary activity "that was driven from him by necessity" (i.e., the necessity to keep body and soul together). "He was not yet free, and could not write freely."[58] "Still," Scudder proceeds, "in whatever he did there was a something which was his own, and not merely the reflection of other people's work; he gave a foretaste of certain qualities which were afterward to be found really characteristic of him, and from the beginning of his writing one could keep seeing the gayly dressed dolls and shimmer of light through calico that were his playthings in childhood."[59] According to Scudder, Andersen attained his poetic majority during his first stay in Italy: "He came of age, and a flood of poetic life burst forth in *The Improvisatore*. This book to many is too luscious and torrid; but it must be taken in connection with ANDERSEN'S life and nature, when it will be found that though the fall sunshine is somewhat glaring if we come into it out of the shade, it really envelops and bathes all that it touches."[60]

Finally, Scudder arrives at his rhetorical goal, though without demonstrating any true necessity for it: "Yet as an author he was still to produce certain writings which fix his place in literature and in popular affection far more surely than does *The Improvisatore*," works of which Andersen himself said, "'I would willingly have discontinued writing them, but they forced themselves from me.'"[61] In the course of composing his first volume of tales, Scudder opines, Andersen

> discovered . . . what, after all, must be counted as [his] chief contribution to literature—the delicious humor and fun which were to be disclosed by endowing ordinary and inanimate objects with imagined vitality. "The Steadfast Tin Soldier," "The Top and Ball," "The Shepherdess and Chimney-Sweep"—these give one the impression that he is looking at life through the reverse end of an opera-glass. The personalities are sharply and clearly defined, but every thing is on a most diminutive scale.[62]

Viewing the tales in historical context, Scudder concedes that some of Andersen's many imitators have been successful "in their way" and that "stories of this kind no longer have the charm of novelty."[63] However,

> [i]t was different then; and though other writers, like MUSAEUS and TIECK, had told fairy tales, no one had done just what ANDERSEN had done. The children captured the prize, and the elders were soon enjoying it with them. No Christmas-tree was grown unless some of this fruit hung from it, and every Christmas for years there came out one of these little volumes. They became the fashion, and actors declaimed the stories from the stage between the larger pieces. ANDERSEN himself was constantly called upon to tell the stories in circles of friends.[64]

Scudder offers the following overview of Andersen's lifework:

> He published something nearly every year up to the time of his death, and his collected writings are contained in some thirty volumes, of which the prose has nearly all been translated into English. His writings cover a tolerably wide range as regards the form in which they are cast, but the characteristics of all are much the same. The theatre plays . . . an important part in Denmark; and ANDERSEN has contributed a number of comedies and light vaudevilles which retain their place on the boards. His romances, besides *The Improvisatore*, are, *To Be or Not to Be*, *Only a Fiddler*, *The Two Baronesses*, and *O. T.* . . . .There are several volumes of poems also, and some of these, especially those of sentiment, have been favorites in Denmark. He has published several volumes of sketches of travels in Southern Europe and the East, under the title of *The Poet's Bazaar*; *Sweden, Spain, and Portugal*; *The Hartz Mountains, Switzerland, and England* [sic].[65]

On his many travels through Europe and his myriad visits to people of all ranks and walks of life, it was nevertheless his fairy tales that were the "open sesame."[66]

In the substantial remainder of the article, Scudder goes into his business connection and lengthy correspondence with Andersen. His subsequent study of Andersen's character draws on this experience as well as the autobiography, and it may be that the former helped him read between the lines of the latter:

> The *Wonder Story of my Life* [sic], which he wrote at different periods of his career, an autobiography of singular frankness, discloses constantly the character of the man. His failings lay all upon the surface. Any one could see that he was eager for praise, oversensitive to blame and ridicule, inclined to sentimentalize, and to wear his heart upon his sleeve. But when all this is said, there remains what never can be fully said, yet can be appreciated by those who read his autobiography and his writings; he carried with him through life an affectionate nature which was overflowing with sympathy and generous deeds; he entered into the estate of childhood, and remained there, drawing from it a wealth of poetry not before perceived; he was truly humble, and penetrated with a faith in God which was sometimes disturbed by intellectual speculations, but always rose fragrantly out of a nature that was incapable of spiritual skepticism. He was scrupulously exact in his dealings and in the performance of those little tasks which some treat lightly, thrusting them aside under the name of etiquette. His stories bear witness, too, to the purity of his life.[67]

Scudder follows Andersen into his later years, to his modest yet comfortable life in his two-room apartment in Copenhagen and the illumination held in his honor in Odense in 1867, closing with his recent death: "He was seventy years old when he died, August 4, 1875, and the affection of all classes was shown in the gathering at his funeral. The royal family were present, and the poor were there. His was a wide sympathy and a large soul, and yet it was the little child in him that led the multitudes who felt a personal interest and affection for him."[68]

Scudder's account of Andersen's life and work has its shortcomings, the aforementioned teleology with its implied diminishment chief among them. It would have been useful and self-consistent to give at least one example of how certain early writings anticipated later, more original works, for instance, how the lavish description of the part of Poesy's Temple devoted to Middle Eastern fairy tales in chapter 9 of *Journey on Foot* calls to mind the undersea palace in "The Little Mermaid." A separate study will show that actors were not the only nonliterary artists influenced by Andersen during the period in question. On the other hand, Scudder gives his readers a better impression of the extent and variety of the Dane's writing than most any other contemporary American.[69] He brings up the "vitality" of the inanimate objects depicted in the tales in other writings but expresses it in a different and equally striking way here. In his attempt to characterize the author, he resists the temptation to extrapolate absolutes from the evidence at his disposal, acknowledging a *je ne sais quoi* that his readers must account for themselves. One may choose to believe that, rather than passing his adulthood in an arrested state of development, Andersen possessed an exceedingly rare ability to draw on the recollection and inspiration of his childhood to create his fairy tales and stories. However, Scudder is accurate in his assertion that Andersen retained the faith in God of his youth, despite the questioning apparent in *Ahasuerus* and *To Be, or Not to Be?*. As a postlude to discussion of his article let it be said that the unobtrusive elegiac note of the last paragraph, which echoes one sounded in the introduction, suggests that the article was intended to be a tribute as well as an informative piece of lighter literary criticism.

Scudder's approximate equal in the prolificacy, if not the penetration of his writing on Andersen was Hjalmar Hjorth Boyesen (1848–1895).[70] Born and university educated in Norway, Boyesen emigrated to the United States at age twenty-one, where he became both a university professor and an uncommonly productive writer.[71] He held positions at Urbana and Cornell universities as an instructor of modern foreign languages before receiving an appointment at Columbia University, where he concluded his career as a full professor of Germanic languages and literatures. In the space of some twenty-five years—he died at the age of forty-seven—Boyesen penned eight novels, eight volumes of short stories, and eight other volumes that encompass children's books as well as literary scholarship in his fields of specialization. He was also a familiar fixture in periodicals, in which he published poems, essays, and reviews. Like many of his contemporaries, including in varying degrees both Andersen and Scudder, he began as a sentimentalist Romantic only to later embrace realism. He is known today mainly for his literary application of a Darwinism admitting of moral evolution and as a champion of realism and a forerunner of naturalism.

Bearing the ubiquitous title "Hans Christian Andersen," Boyesen's article appeared in *St. Nicholas* in December 1875.[72] *St. Nicholas* was one of the best and most successful children's magazines in the history of the genre in the United States. Running from 1873 to 1940, it had an estimated subscription list of forty thousand in 1875 and around seventy thousand for many years.[73] It was edited from its inception until 1905 by Mary Mapes Dodge and enjoyed the services of associate editor Frank Stockton for a time, both themselves major writers for children. The magazine published work by most everyone in the country who had a name in the field, from Louisa May Alcott, Frances Hodgson Burnett (*Little Lord Fauntleroy*), Edward Eggleston (*The Hoosier School-Boy*), and John T. Trowbridge (the Jack Hazard series for boys) to Bret Harte, William Dean Howells, Rudyard Kipling (*Mowgli*), A. A. Milne, Theodore Roosevelt, Robert Louis Stevenson, Mark Twain, and, not least of all, Scudder and Boyesen, among many others. Youthful contributors included William Faulkner, Ring Lardner, and Edna St. Vincent Millay.

Boyesen's article, like Scudder's, is a critical biography, though it is tailored in tone and content to younger readers—who, however, would seem to have had broader cultural horizons than their present-day counterparts. Boyesen displays mixed feelings toward Andersen the man, if not as markedly as in his later writings for adults. Similar to others, he observes a continuity between the Dane's childhood games of pretend and his fairy tales as well as his adult life (e.g., between his wish to be a fairy prince living in a palace and his later high regard for rank. At the same time, he defends Andersen against the accusation of snobbery, attributing his warm relationships with aristocrats to their support of him when he was in need and the butt of critics' ridicule. Boyesen is particularly repulsed by Andersen's lack of conventional manliness: "he was not a brave boy, he ran home to his mother"; "He was a regular girl's boy"; "he was never known to return a blow."[74] On the other hand, he gives examples of Andersen's great personal kindness.

Boyesen is also ambivalent toward Andersen's achievement as an artist. Much like Scudder, he finds that *Journey by Foot* was not a true reflection of Andersen's nature: "He had evidently learned from his rector in Slagelse that his own traits of character—his maidenly shyness and his readiness to weep over everything—had its ludicrous side, and in this book he shows himself as quite a different man. You hardly recognize the lachrymose, sentimental youth you knew at Slagelse; here he tries his best to make fun of everything."[75] The early dramatic adaptations of Sir Walter Scott's *The Bride of Lammermoor* and *Kenilworth* he attributes to pecuniary considerations rather than inner necessity. In the process, the native Norwegian has a little fun at the expense of Denmark, which had dominated Norway politically and culturally for more than four hundred years: "But the Danes are very fond of their own little country, and believe that there is no literature in the world equal to their own. Therefore, they ridiculed this attempt of Andersen's to introduce a foreign novel-writer upon their stage."[76]

Boyesen affirms the success of *The Mulatto*, which was indeed one of Andersen's most often performed plays, but then writes in general terms that his "great many dramas . . . had their day of success, but are now nearly forgotten."[77] He speaks well of *The Improvisatore*, which,

> although the hero . . . is an Italian and not a Dane, describes the author's own struggles and sufferings in his efforts to obtain recognition for himself as a poet. And if Andersen had not suffered so much, and been so sensitive to sufferings, he could hardly have described with such truthfulness the sufferings of another. The book is, at the same time, perfectly Italian in sentiment, and is a most beautiful account of the life, scenery, and traditions of that beautiful land.[78]

Aside from an explanation of the initials forming the title of *O. T.*, however, he writes only that that novel as well as *Only a Fiddler* are "both interesting narratives of popular life in Denmark."[79] He disposes of *The Two Baronesses*, along with the autobiography and *A Poet's Bazaar*, in a single sentence, and he totally ignores *Lucky Peer* and *To Be, or Not to Be?*, the latter of which he annihilated in a later writing.[80]

Again like Scudder, Boyesen reserves his greatest accolades for the fairy tales and stories. He characterizes Andersen's ultimate achievement as a "rise—not to fortune and power, but to what is far better than fortune and power—to a place in the hearts of all little boys and girls all over the wide world; for his stories are, perhaps, the only books except the Bible that have been translated, not only into English and French and German, but even into Japanese and Hindostanee, and all manner of strange languages."[81] Most interestingly, perhaps, he then immerses himself imaginatively in the well-spring of Andersen's creativity, at least that part of it that issues forth from his "child-heart":

> And at night, when the old Children's Poet sat at his table, and the student-lamp with the green shade threw a large ring of light around it, while a sort of green-ish dusk seemed to fill the rest of the room, then all these children came from all parts of the earth, and their curly heads and chubby faces thronged around their old poet,—for then he was writing a story for them, and they were eager to see what it might be. When he had written something which was very funny, all the little boys and girls laughed, and their bright laughter filled the room; but when the poet had gone to bed and was asleep, the laughter followed him in his dreams, and it grew and grew, rippling onward from land to land, until all the children in Germany, England, Asia and America laughed at the funny thing he had written. But if it was something sad, then their eyes grew big with tears, and the tear went from land to land as the laughter had done.[82]

Perhaps due to the nature of his audience, Boyesen makes no reference to the adult dimension of the tales, but he was well aware of it, writing elsewhere that the "'Wonder Stories' are the only books belonging to the pinafore period which are not discarded with advancing years; nay, which gain a new significance with maturing age. We read 'The Ugly Duckling' with the same delight at thirty that we did at ten, for we discover a new substratum of meaning which escaped our infantine eyes."[83] It was these stories that finally convinced Andersen's countrymen that they had been wrong about him: "Favorable criticism appeared in foreign journals, and Andersen was hailed everywhere as Denmark's greatest poet. The Danes themselves shook their heads doubtfully, and long refused to listen to the strange rumors from abroad, until at last the beautiful 'Wonder-Stories' began to appear, and they, too, had to open their eyes and acknowledge that they had been mistaken in their judgment."[84] Writing in conclusion of "The Ugly Duckling," Boyesen indulges in a bit of sentiment quite appropriate to his young readers and not at all out of place in what is essentially a commemorative piece by a young Andersen reader grown older: "That ugly duckling (I know it on the very best authority) was the poet himself. He suffered long among the hens and ducks, but at last he rose high above them, and now they all see that he was a swan—a great poet."[85]

In an article on Scandinavian literature published in the *Chautauquan*, Boyesen again articulates his appreciation and distaste for Andersen, expressing the latter with less restraint than in the piece written for children.[86] The *Chautauquan* was long the official organ of the Chautauqua Literary and Scientific Circle, the literary arm of a public education movement that commenced at Chautauqua Lake in western New York in 1874.[87] The Chautauqua consisted on the one hand of "summer courses of lectures and entertainments, usually under tents or in rude 'assembly halls'" at lakeside and, on the other, of "courses of systematic reading in history, literature, science, and art" pursued in the home.[88] By the time the article appeared, more than twenty thousand people all over the country were beginning the four-year course annually. Established in 1880, the *Chautauquan* was at first closely tied to the courses of study prescribed by the Circle and, following a period as a more general magazine, still colored by the Methodism of its founders, ultimately resumed its original function. According to Mott, it drew "into its net all—or nearly all—the big fish in the intellectual sea" in the country, including, in one issue, two future presidents, Theodore Roosevelt and Woodrow Wilson.[89] Claiming a subscription list of sixty-three thousand in 1888, the magazine's appeal gradually declined with that of the movement, and it was merged with the *Independent* in 1914.[90]

In the relevant passage of his article, Boyesen cites the year 1828 as one in which four great and twelve minor Danish poets passed their examination for admission to the University of Copenhagen. Thus,

> [t]he seed which Oehlenschläger had sown was beginning to sprout and bear fruit. One of the four, accounted great, was Hans Christian Andersen—the only Danish author who has ever rejoiced in a worldwide popularity. He had the misfortune to be of humble origin, a fact which his countrymen were slow to forgive him. He was ridiculed and persecuted by the critics and the wits of the town; and it was not until Europe and America re-echoed with his fame that his merits began to be recognized at home.[91]

For the resentful Norwegian, Andersen's flaws were at base those of all Danes: "For all that, he seems the very personification of the Danish national temperament. His childlike innocence and vanity, his hunger for praise, and his excessive sensibility are but slight exaggerations of the national character-istics"—traits that non-Norwegian writers of general interest articles also saw in Andersen.[92] In his final observations, Boyesen mixes praise and blame: "He had the courage to disregard all literary traditions and to write as he thought and spoke; and the refreshingly *naïve* and unsophisticated personal-ity that shone through the text of his simple 'Wonder-Tales' and 'Household Tales,' delighted all who did not know the original. In 'The Improvisatore,' and 'The Story of my Life,' where the author throws off all disguise and steps forward in his proper person, his somewhat overconscious *naiveté* is far less enjoyable."[93]

An article similar in ilk to the piece by Scudder and the longer one by Boyesen appeared in *Wide Awake* in August 1888.[94] *Wide Awake* was the most successful of a number of children's magazines published by Daniel Lothrop of Boston, who specialized in books for the young.[95] Initiated in 1875, it appealed to children of from around ten to eighteen years of age, the same demographic that *St. Nicholas* sought to reach, though it was somewhat more old-fashioned than its competitor insofar as "it was more inclined to give the children what was thought by their elders to be good for them in the way of instruction and entertainment than to consult their own tastes and pref-erences."[96] Its list of contributors is generally less impressive than that of *St. Nicholas* but nonetheless includes noted writers such as Edward Everett Hale, Louise Chandler Moulton (*Bed-Time Stories*), and Elizabeth Stuart Phelps (the Gypsy Brenton series), as well as Sarah Orne Jewett, James Whitcomb Riley, and Margaret Sidney, whose *Five Little Peppers and How They Grew* became especially popular. The magazine had a respectable circulation of twenty-five thousand in 1888 but was merged with *St. Nicholas* in 1893, the year after the publisher's death.[97]

The author of the piece was Oscar Fay Adams (1855–1919). Born in Worcester, Massachusetts, Adams graduated from Leicester Academy in Leicester, Massachusetts, and then from what is now the College of New Jersey, in Trenton.[98] After teaching classes in English literature for a time, he wrote and lectured widely on literature and architecture. The author of short stories and poetry, including hymn texts, as well as a biography of Jane Austen, he appears to have channeled most of his energy into editorial work, publishing anthologies of poetry; editions of Austen, William Morris, and Shakespeare; and handbooks or dictionaries of American and English authors, among much else. The year after the present article appeared, Adams included it in a volume titled *Dear Old Story-Tellers*, which also contains sketches of other writers popular with the young, from Homer and Æsop to La Fontaine, Daniel Defoe, and the German Friedrich de la Motte Fouqué, now best known for his fairy tale novella *Undine*.[99]

Adams's article bears the title "Hans Christian Andersen, 'The Goldsmith of the North,'" and in the initial paragraphs he indeed compares the two authors in terms of their common simplicity, or childlikeness of nature, and their excessive, though harmless, vanity. Thereafter, he proceeds along the lines of the critical biography, making observations that are generally less incisive and more laudatory than those of Scudder and Boyesen. Referring at the outset to Thackeray's comment on Goldsmith—"'To be the most beloved of English writers, what a distinction, that, for a man!'"—he writes, for example, "The story-teller of Copenhagen is perhaps dearer to the hearts of countless young readers than any other writer who ever lived. And what a distinction *that* is for any man to win!"[100]

It is unclear what sources Adams drew on for his information, but he is aware that Danes were long perplexed over Andersen's acclaim abroad, which he expresses and explains as follows:

> It must not, however, be imagined, because Andersen was so universally beloved by his countrymen, that they regarded him as the greatest glory of their literature. On the contrary the Danes have always been puzzled to account for the admiration with which he is regarded in other lands to the neglect of several other Danish writers whom they rightfully regard as superior to him. But the reason is not so far to seek. The simplicity of his style made translation comparatively easy. . . . Then, too, people who made acquaintance with his works in their childhood have never been able to forget their love for the teller of fairy tales, and have regarded his novels with much the same feeling of uncritical admiration. To the majority of readers Andersen is the only Danish writer, a state of things as unfair to Denmark's other great authors as harmful to the fame of Andersen himself.[101]

Additional, perhaps more decisive reasons were surely Americans' unfamiliarity with the Danish language and Danish literature, this despite the substantial number of works by Danes that were available in English translation.[102] In any case, Adams continues, "But even when the just claims of his contemporaries have been satisfied"—of which few other Americans were apparently aware—"much, very much, remains to be grateful for in the genius of Hans Andersen."[103]

Adams writes, however briefly, of works that typically escaped—and escape—Americans' ken:

> [Andersen] was twenty-three when his first work of any importance appeared, entitled *A Pedestrian Journey from Holmen's Canal to Amack.* Holmen's Canal is one of the principal features of Copenhagen, and Amack or Amager is an island connected with the city by long bridges, so the journey in question was not a long one. The book, which is mainly in rhyme and humorous in character,

met with sudden and unexpected success and in consequence his confidence in his own powers could never afterwards be shaken.[104]

The book is in fact written in prose, with occasional verse inlays, but it is indeed humorous, a satiric-ironic arabesque in the manner of E. T. A. Hoffmann and, indeed, caught the attention of the public. Adams writes further, "In 1829 a play of his called *Love on St. Nicholas's Tower* was acted with great success and the next year his first volume of poems appeared and became immediately popular."[105] The play owed most of its "success" to the large crowd of friends Andersen planted in the audience on opening night with the request to cheer enthusiastically and, later, to the impression of its reception he creates in his autobiography.[106] Critics were not as accommodating, and the play was performed only three times.[107] His *Poems* (*Digte*), however, was in fact well received. Adams also mentions Andersen's second collection of poetry, *Fantasies and Sketches* (*Phantasier og Skizzer*), and *Rambles in the Hartz Mountains* in passing.

Adams dwells longer on the Dane's first novel than on any of his other works:

> A year or two later, in 1834, he published what must be reckoned, all things considered, his greatest work, the famous *Improvisatore*. It is rarely that a man of one nationality enters so completely into the life of another people as does Andersen in this wonderful book. Madame de Staël ambitiously adds to her *Corinne* the sub-title "or Italy," but with far more truth might it be added to *The Improvisatore*. The book *is* Italy. Northman as he was by birth, Andersen was Italian by temperament, and the fervor, the excitability, the enthusiasm, the longing to impart to others the details of one's own life so characteristic of Italians, and to a less extent of other nations of the south of Europe, were part of his very nature. No wonder, then, that he could enter so fully into the heart of Italian life as he does in the brilliant pages of the wonderful *Improvisatore*.[108]

Significantly, Adams says not a word about the plot and characters of the novel, confining himself to the essence of Italy he feels it exudes. As chapter 2 shows, he was one with many contemporaries in his view of the "Italianness" of the work.

Given his introductory accentuation of Andersen's dearness to children, Adams has curiously little to say about the fairy tales and stories. Most of his pertinent remarks serve merely to introduce the phase of productivity that followed publication of *The Improvisatore*: "It was the grown-up public for which [Andersen] had written up to this time, but he was soon to gather about him another and much more extensive circle of readers, the children of Denmark at first, and later those of half the world. It was for these that he wrote in 1835 the first series of his *Eventyr* or *Fairy Tales* as we call them.

The collection thus begun he added to from time to time during a long course of years."[109] Andersen as a teller of tales and the tales themselves receive only 'the following comments: "No writer of his time has surpassed Andersen in the ability to gain the attention of children by story-telling. The sweet simplicity of these tales never fails to win their admiration. Himself as guileless as a little child he saw very clearly into child nature and children know him for one of themselves."[110] The sophistication of the tales was apparently lost on Adams. And in an instance of self-contradiction not at all unique in the United States, he appears to have at least momentarily allowed his understanding of them and their "guileless" author to color, by extension, his estimation of the other works.

Adams skims over the greater part of Andersen's productive life, from the mid-1830s to the early 1870s, in around three pages of the small format book, or little over a column of the magazine printing. All the same, he mentions the success of the dramas *Parting and Meeting* (*Skilles og mødes*, 1836) and *The Mulatto*, interesting and significant plays both, and writes of *In Sweden* and *Ole Lukoie* as follows:

> In 1851 *Pictures of Sweden* appeared which by an English critic has been considered as his most delightful work, the autobiography excepted. It is certainly a fascinating book, though it hardly deserves the rank the critic mentioned accords it. During these years he was continually producing dramas many of which were exceedingly popular. One of these, called *Ole Lukoie*, was a sort of wonder-comedy in which the adventures of the dream-god, who figures in more than one of his fairy tales, were narrated.[111]

In the autobiographies, Adams states, "it is easy enough to see the remarkable vanity of the man, but with this inordinate self-esteem was mingled so much of real gentleness and sweetness of temper that to judge harshly of Andersen because of his vanity becomes nearly impossible."[112] If less popular than his other novels, especially *Only a Fiddler*, *The Two Baronesses* is "very well worth reading for its pictures of Danish life and its masterly delineation of character."[113] As with Boyesen, *To Be, or Not to Be?* and *Lucky Peer* receive no mention.

Adams dedicates more than three pages of his article to an account of Andersen's final illness and public funeral. The latter he relates in considerable detail and with a reverence commensurate with the occasion, closing with the words,

> In spite of his love for splendor and show he never became forgetful of his own poor estate in early youth or ceased to have the warmest sympathy with the humblest person. His vanity, his self-esteem were in him the most amiable of foibles, the heart beneath was one of the tenderest and gentlest that ever beat. On

a laurel wreath from Berlin which lay upon his coffin was fastened this inscription, as touching as it is full of tender truth: "Thou art not dead, though thine eyes are closed. / In children's hearts thou shalt live forever."[114]

Despite the limitations of his article, determined at least in part by the nature of his intended readers, Adams provides a fairly comprehensive and insightful, if in parts rather pious overview of Andersen's life and work.

One of the more interesting, and most interestingly written articles on Andersen appeared in the *Critic* in 1895.[115] The piece presents itself as a review of H. Nisbet Bain's biography of Andersen, but only the final three sentences relate to the book per se. By far the greatest portion, which covers more than a column of the densely printed, two-column pages, reflects the reviewer's own animated personal and artistic response to Andersen, as prompted by Bain's book.[116] The review is anonymous, but both its content and style are reminiscent of Boyesen.[117]

Quoting Bain's motto, the reviewer writes,

The phrase of Amiel, "un esprit de femme dans un caractère d'enfant," exactly describes the curiously feminine and infantile character of the celebrated Dane who for fifty years enchanted all Europe with his fairy-tales and his follies. Never before, perhaps, had the world studied a figure so eccentrically compounded of genius and foolishness, common-sense and fantastic frippery, vanity and humility, shyness and audacious self-assertion—a being reminding one alternately of Molière's marvelous Sganarelles and Scapins, Cervantes's Don Quixote, or the birdlike creatures in the dreams and inventions of Aristophanes. A Midsummer Night's Dream of a man was this quaint cobbler's son.[118]

Much like Andersen himself, though without his deep-seated, compensatory need for self-promotion, the writer feels that Andersen's life was as extraordinary as any of his fairy tales:

There was something wonderful and fairy-like in it from the time it started in picturesque Odense until a nation rose in honor and erected a statue to the man still living, not long before his death. "Flowers know very well that I love them," he used to say. "Even if I were to stick a peg into the ground, I believe it would grow." He was a human moonstone, full of magical and phenomenal qualities that revealed themselves in whatever he did, whether cutting marvelous landscapes out of paper with a pair of scissors, or arranging queer little bouquets for those with whom he dined, or taking a darning-needle (at the suggestion of Thorvaldsen) and making of it a little masterpiece in prose.[119]

The reviewer writes imaginatively but confusingly about Andersen's tales and certain other works: "All he needed was to rake in the embers of faded old folktales and nursery rhymes, and they kindled into glowing rubies and garnets instinct with color and life. This kindling touch of his is in all his prose work, and there, too, his poetry is to be found, not in the formless epics and dramas *manqués* which he pertinaciously insisted on scribbling to the end of his life, and which were often greeted with uproarious ridicule."[120] It is certain that Andersen's "kindling touch" is also found in his original stories and tales, which comprise the vast majority of the total. However, if it is in *all* his prose, then why not in his "formless epics," which must mean his novels, and is it missing from his poetry?[121] To the second question one may wish to answer, "No," and respond to the first by saying that that touch is found there, too, if not as frequently as in the tales and stories.

Some of the writer's most interesting comments revolve around Andersen the man:

> Andersen's intellectual outfit . . . was of the most singular kind, and furnishes material for a most interesting psychological study. In his case not so much genius and madness as genius and idiocy were near allied: the partition between the two was in his individuality extremely thin, almost translucent. His conduct was generally idiotic, his creations were (in the charming words of old Vasari when he is describing the master-works of Michael Angelo) things divine. Nervous, excitable, self-conscious, self-important, sensitive in the extreme, his character closely resembles Racine's in some of its peculiarities, and Heine's in others. Like his own "Princess on a Pen [*sic*]," everything hurt him: he was born without an epidermis, he lived—and wriggled—in a hot blaze of public-ity, and he died with his doors wide open. No amount of harsh experience or bitter scourging from Heiberg or Molbeck [*sic*] toughened his tender feelings, or lessened the irritability of a temperament all nerves—and bleeding nerves at that. He was the Jenny Lind of the fairy-tale, who sang with matchless beauty in an ineloquent and unmelodious language as long as you listened, but stopped instantly, wounded unto death, if you talked or were inattentive.[122]

The discrepancy between Andersen's acceptance at home and abroad pro-vides fodder for the following observations:

> "They spat on the glow-worm just because it glowed," he said bitterly of his own countrymen; indeed, the way Danish criticism applied the *moxa* to his sensitive spine was both heroic and intolerable. All Europe rang with his praises except little Denmark, which obstinately through many years refused to honor the prophet who had lifted her out of obscurity. Andersen had actually become a worldwide celebrity when the King complacently informed him that he had seen his name in a French review! The delightful mixture of humor, sentiment and naïveté in his make-up crops out in his "Poet's Bazaar," his grotesquely beautiful tales, with their arabesque luxuriance and prettiness, and in those original works of travel in Sweden and Spain that are unlike any that have ever been written.[123]

Of Bain's work as such, we read "only" that his "biography of this almost uncanny man, so full of eccentricity, poetry, vanity and temper, is one of the most fascinating we have ever read. His observations on the English translations are excellent, and his knowledge of contemporary Danish literature is copious and exact. In his book, as in Dante's, 'Morti li morti, vivi parean vivi.'"[124]

The reviewer's basic opinions—his preference for the tales and the travel books over all of Andersen's other works and his sense of a dichotomy between artist and fool that distinguished the man—are in essence those of Scudder, Boyesen, and others. However, his comparison of Andersen to great figures of ancient and modern art, his characterization of Andersen's psyche as an antinomy between genius and idiocy, and the in part high poetry of his portrayal of the Dane and his tales—all these features, whatever their validity, combine to lift Andersen from time and place into the European cultural continuum of two and a half millennia. That is to say, they serve to make a virtually mythic figure of him. The writer's procedure was not widespread, but it is one more indication that in the years following his death Andersen was seen as a historical personage of considerable importance.

In a review that appeared in *Outlook* about two weeks after the previous one, the critic, as it were, "out-Bains" Bain.[125] "*Outlook*" was the new name given the *Christian Union* in 1893.[126] It was chosen to signal an editorial shift of emphasis from religion to public affairs and literature, though the liberal Protestantism of chief editor, sometime Congregational pastor, and theologian Lyman Abbott continued to determine the point of view and tone of the periodical. Responsibility for the literary and critical departments of the magazine belonged to associate editor H(amilton) W(right) Mabie (1846–1916). Having edited a volume of stories from the old Norse *Eddas* and anthologies containing numerous works by Andersen, he may well have written the review in question himself. During the year of its publication, according to *Rowell's*, *Outlook* had a circulation exceeding twenty thousand, though Mott states that it passed thirty thousand the year before.[127]

Unlike many observers, Bain does not rely exclusively on Andersen's autobiography for information about the author's life and character and thus adopts a skeptical attitude toward the positive image put forward in it. At the same time, he is not at all blind or indifferent to Andersen's better nature. The reviewer for *Outlook* acknowledges this side of the author in passing, but his introductory comments dominate the impression created by the notice:

> From posterity's standpoint it may be well for a man to work the best of himself into his books. Such an operation, however, does not always improve the actual man for daily companionship or make his biography a matter of congratulation to himself or to the world. This is emphatically the case in the biography

of Hans Christian Andersen, whose personality, we instinctively feel, must be worth while, but which proves instead mortifyingly disappointing. In place of the genuine man whom we had always pictured, we find a child, and a spoiled child.[128]

The reviewer overstates Bain's point when he writes, "Early in life the conviction that he was ill-used had so fastened itself upon him that he ever remained singularly unappreciative of the rare loyalty and sympathy *always* given him (no man ever had finer friends), and was self-centred [*sic*] to an unconscionable degree" [emphasis added]. It is true that Andersen had some fine friends and was hypersensitive to adverse criticism, which at times blinded him to the recognition he also received, but it is not as if he had no prejudiced and unfair critics at home. Indeed, the literary establishment in Denmark as a whole took its good time in discerning and acknowledging his true achievement and stature.

The writer also goes beyond Bain in his censure of the author's persistent attempts to succeed in the theater: "A dogged perseverance in both work and mood was one of his greatest characteristics; a good characteristic often, but with Andersen generally only an unfortunate one. In spite of repeated proofs that he could *never* succeed as a dramatic writer, he stubbornly persisted, taking a vast amount of time from work which he knew he could do well and in which he had already achieved a popular success" [emphasis added]. Bain makes no secret of his reservations toward Andersen the "man-child," but he also relates examples of Andersen's shrewdness, for example, in business and financial matters. Perhaps despite himself, he once speaks of Andersen as someone who took "an intense interest in the progress of humanity, saw more of the world than most men, and was always an acute observer with catholic tastes and cosmopolitan sympathies."[129] In this connection, the reviewer writes only that "[Andersen] never regarded men and things with a grown-up gaze; his enjoyment of novelty was essentially the child's; his comment never the man's."[130] However, he is one with Bain in his great admiration of the tales: "However much praise is given to 'Only a Fiddler,' and to parts of 'O. T.,' we must believe with Mr. Bain that Andersen's great achievement lay in his Fairy Tales, which represent an equal charm with Grimm's, but a greater originality. We rejoice for the many little people who with Andersen as companion have wandered through a most delight-fully fantastic world. Even though filled with everyday objects, a magician's wand is over the whole."

The final article to be discussed in this chapter is the entry on Andersen in the *Library of the World's Best Literature, Ancient and Modern*, a multi-volume bio-critical anthology that began publication in 1896.[131] The general editor was Charles Dudley Warner, who was able to draw on fifteen years of experience as editor of Houghton Mifflin's American Men of Letters series and edited both publications concurrently for several years. In his preface, Warner writes that the main purpose of the collection is "to present to American households a mass of good reading. But it goes much beyond this. For in selecting this reading it draws upon all literatures of all time and of every race, and thus becomes a conspectus of the thought and intellectual evolution of man from the beginning. Another and scarcely less important purpose is the interpretation of this literature in essays by scholars and authors competent to speak with authority."[132] The *Library* is indeed remarkable for the catholicity of its coverage, though in their attempt "to give . . . an idea of contemporary achievement and tendencies in all civilized countries" the editors felt justified in devoting the greatest amount of space to the literature of the United States and Great Britain.[133] Like others in the work, the chapter on Andersen comprises an introductory biographical-interpretive essay followed by texts, either in their entirety or in selection, specifically, "The Steadfast Tin Soldier," "The Teapot" ("Theepotten"), "The Ugly Duckling," the seventeenth evening from *Picture Book without Pictures*, "The Sweethearts," an excerpt from "The Snow Queen," "The Nightingale" ("Nattergalen"), and excerpts from the autobiography ("The Market Place at Odense," "The Andersen Jubilee at Odense") and *The Improvisatore* ("'Miserere' in the Sistine Chapel")—that is to say, generally "classical" early works from the 1830s and 1840s.[134]

The author of the essay on Andersen was scholar, journalist, and editor Benjamin W. Wells (1856–1923). Born and raised in Walpole, New Hampshire, Wells took both baccalaureate and doctoral degrees at Harvard and pursued additional study in Berlin.[135] A Fellow of Johns Hopkins University, he taught modern languages and literatures for a time at the University of the South, in Sewanee, Tennessee, and was a member of the staff of the *Churchman* in New York City. Among his major publications are *Modern German Literature* (1895), *Modern French Literature* (1897), and *A Century of French Fiction* (1898). He also contributed numerous articles to encyclopedias and journals dealing with German, French, and English literature and published editions of German and French texts.[136]

Wells's essay represents not so much an independent contribution to the understanding of Andersen's life and work as a codification of widely held current opinion, readily accessible in homes and libraries for decades after its publication and available, if less broadly, to the present day. He makes no secret of his view of Andersen's position in the world of letters, asserting at the beginning of the essay that "[t]he place of Hans Christian Andersen in literature is that of the 'Children's Poet,' though his best poetry is prose," and placing his main discussion of the tales in a prominent position at the end of the article.[137]

In the meantime, Wells touches briefly on the main stations in Andersen's life and many of his works, both major and minor. *Walking Tour* is a "fantastic arabesque, partly plagiarized and partly parodied from the German romanticists, but with a naïveté that might have disarmed criticism"; it was followed by a "volume of poems, the sentimental and rather mawkish 'Fantasies and Sketches,' product of a journey in Jutland and of a silly love affair"—the "silliness" of the typically chaste "affair" likely reflecting an extrapolation of Bain's patronizing portrayal of Andersen's infatuation with Riborg Voigt.[138] *Rambles in the Hartz Mountains* contains "some really admirable pages of description," though Andersen's subsequent return to the drama, inspired by its success, allegedly "failed once more."[139] It is unclear which play Wells had in mind here, for Andersen wrote four of them between 1831 and 1833, the years in which *Rambles* appeared and Andersen embarked on his first extended trip abroad, respectively. Whatever the case may have been, *The Bride of Lammermoor* (*Bruden fra Lammermoor*) and *The Raven, or The Test of Brotherhood* (*Ravnen eller Broderprøven*), both of which premiered in 1832, received mixed (i.e., partly positive) reviews.[140]

Wells writes of the salutary influence that Italy exerted on Andersen: "Italy had on him much the same clarifying effect that it had on Goethe; and his next book, the novel 'Improvisatore' (1835), achieved and deserved a European recognition. Within ten years the book was translated into six languages. It bears the mark of its date in its Romantic sentiments. There is indeed no firm character-drawing, here or in any of his novels; but the book still claims attention for its exquisite descriptions of Italian life and scenery."[141] *O. T.* "marks no advance on the 'Improvisatore,'" though *Only a Fiddler*, Andersen's "best romance," is "still charming for its autobiographical touches, its genuine humor, and its deep pathos."[142] Contrary to most reviewers, Wells calls *The Two Baronesses* a failure. Though ignoring *Lucky Peer*, which he may not have reckoned a novel, he writes objectively of *To Be, or Not to Be?* that it "reflects the religious speculations of his later years."[143]

Wells has nothing to say about the later travel books beyond terming *In Sweden* Andersen's "most exquisite" essay in the genre and *In Spain* "mediocre but successful"; *A Visit to Portugal* goes the way of *Lucky Peer*. He also omits any reference to the sizable body of poetry written after the early *Fantasies and Sketches*. For him, most of Andersen's work for the stage does not exist, though he does allude to the "considerable success" of the fairy dramas.[144] He also singles out *The King Dreams* (*Kongen drømmer*) and *The New Lying-In Room* (*Den nye Barselstue*) for mention but calls them Andersen's "last unsuccessful dramatic efforts," this, even though the former was in reality among his better accepted plays and the latter a decided success.[145] Wells includes two excerpts from the autobiography, but in his essay, he writes of it only that "[i]n the judgment of his friends and critics, [it] is strangely unjust, and [Andersen] never understood the limitations of his genius," perhaps thinking of the author's immoderate response to the criticism some of his works received.[146]

Andersen's character is for Wells "full of curious contrasts. Like the French fabulist, La Fontaine, he was a child all his life, and often a spoiled child; yet he joined to childlike simplicity no small share of worldly wisdom. Constant travel made him a shrewd observer of detail, but his self-absorption kept him from sympathy with the broad political aspirations of his generation."[147] Andersen's was indeed no politically astute mind, but he was keenly aware of related developments in the Europe of his time, most particularly when the events of 1848 and then 1864 involved his beloved Denmark in war with his cherished and highly esteemed Germany over Schleswig and Holstein.[148] His response was both artistic and emotional. In the revolutionary year 1848, very much in the spirit of his generation's aspirations, he began his creative, dramaturgical, and administrative activity with the Casino Theater, which for some time was avoided and even ridiculed by the country's elite.[149] Two years later, he released a volume of patriotic but conciliatory poems that earned him the enmity of some of his more chauvinistic countrymen.

It may strike one as odd, not to mention unnecessary, that Wells allots a paragraph to Andersen's gangling, unattractive appearance, drawing on Bain's rather condescending description of the author's attempts to compensate for it. On the other hand, it is altogether understandable that he perpetuates the interesting, if, in its undifferentiated formulation, inaccurate notion that the "Children's Poet" was not fond of children. He is basically right when he affirms that Andersen "always chafed a little at the modest fame of a writer for children," though he chafed more than a little early on and less as he grew older.[150] And in view of the extent and frequent success of his work in other genres, why would he not?

In keeping with his opening sentence, Wells reserves a lengthy portion of his essay for the tales, "those graceful fancies, which in their little domain still hold the first rank, and certainly gave the freest scope to Andersen's qualities, while they masked his faults and limitations"—perhaps an allusion to the shortcomings of Andersen's plot construction and delineation of character, which are most apparent in his novels.[151] The (planned) statue and the "magnificent" funeral given him by the state were great honors, but "his most enduring monument is that which his 'Wonder Tales' are still building all around the world."[152]

Wells credits Danish critic and scholar Georg Brandes as well as Boyesen for many of his comments on the style of the tales:

When not perverted by his translators, it is perhaps better suited than any other to the comprehension of children. His syntax and rhetoric are often faulty; and in the "Tales" he does not hesitate to take liberties even with German, if he can catch the vivid, darting imagery of juvenile fancy, the "ohs" and "ahs" of the nursery, its changing intonations, its fears, its smiles, its personal appeals, and its venerable devices to spur attention and kindle sympathy. Action, or imitation, takes the place of description. We hear the trumpeter's *taratantara* and "the pattering rain on the leaves, *rum dum dum, rum dum dum.*" The soldier "comes marching along, *left, right, left, right.*" No one puts himself so wholly in the child's place and looks at nature so wholly with his eyes as Andersen. "If you hold one of those burdock leaves before your little body it's just like an apron, and if you put it on your head it's almost as good as an umbrella, it's so big." Or he tells you that when the sun shone on the flax, the clouds watered it, "it was just as nice for it as it is for the little children to be washed and then get a kiss from mother: that makes them prettier; of course it does." And here, as Brandes remarks, every right-minded mamma stops and kisses the child, and their hearts are warmer for that day's tale. The starting-point of this art is personification. To the child's fancy the doll is as much alive as the cat, the broom as the bird, and even the letters in the copy-book can stretch themselves. On this foundation he builds myths that tease by a certain semblance of rationality,— elegiac, more often sentimental, but at their best, like normal children, without strained pathos or forced sympathy.[153]

"Such personification," Wells continues, "has obvious dramatic and lyric elements; but Andersen lacked the technique of poetic and dramatic art, and marred his prose descriptions, both in novels and books of travel, by an intrusive egotism and lyric exaggeration."[154] He then adjudges the *communis opinio* correct: "No doubt, therefore, the most permanent part of his work is that which popular instinct has selected, the 'Picture Book without Pictures,' the 'Tales and Stories'; and among these, those will last longest that have least of the lyric and most of the dramatic element."[155]

Wells, drawing on the work of others, goes significantly beyond the vast majority of Andersen's American commentators when he frames the orality of the tales as one of their most distinctive features and a key to their appeal. And he surpasses virtually all his peers in his emphasis on the verbal nature of Andersen's use of language in them, the prevalence of verb over adjective. These features lend a special distinction to what is probably the most comprehensive, if not original critical treatment of the Dane's lifework written in the United States during the nineteenth century. However, the Andersen who emerges from it is of much more modest proportions than the actual artist or even the Andersen who meets us in the pages of many an earlier review and article. In terms of recognition, this Andersen is essentially stripped of everything but the tales, which is to say, the lion's share of his work. Most of the poetry and plays might as well not have been written. The best of the novels are dated, and only a couple of the travel books still reward reading. To top it off, the tales and *Picture Book*, in which "the child speaks with all the naïveté of his nature," are presented as addressing a public that excludes everyone who has left childhood behind.[156]

How could such a state of affairs have arisen? The reasons can be subsumed perhaps at least in part under the notion of distance, understood in different ways. The geographic and historic cultural insularity of Great Britain and the United States meant that few British and even fewer American literati were conversant with Danish or Danish literature, which militated against the development of any continuity in the reception of Danish or any other Scandinavian literature. Bain was familiar with both. Though his biography was a signal event in the Anglo-American context, however, he wrote it from within a quasi-vacuum *and* from a temporal distance of some twenty-five years from the end of Andersen's creative life, which made his achievement a largely isolated event. Moreover, neither he nor his principal sources were free of bias that redounded greatly to Andersen's disadvantage.[157]

Perhaps the most significant kind of distance is suggested by the titles of a number of literary works that were published in 1896, the same year as Wells's essay: Ibsen's *John Gabriel Borkman*, Chekhov's *The Seagull*, Zola's *Rome*, Theodor Fontane's *Effi Briest*, Herman Bang's *Ida Brandt* (*Ludvigsbakke*), Joseph Conrad's *An Outcast of the Islands*, and Sarah Orne Jewett's *The Country of the Pointed Firs*. More sophisticated American readers might still have appreciated the local color of Andersen's novels. However, it was perhaps most pronounced in *To Be, or Not to Be?*, and neither the religious speculation conspicuous in it nor the Romantic-sentimentalist sensibility pervading the comparably local-colorist *Two Baronesses* and other works could appeal to a reading public increasingly attracted to the likes of an Ibsen or a Zola.

The conception of Andersen passed on by Wells corresponds essentially to the image prevalent in the United States and most of the rest of the world at present. Over the past few decades, international Andersen scholarship has brought this image more in line with the historical figure, but the work of scholars typically has depressingly little impact on the public at large.[158] Absent translations of the best poetry and plays and updated renderings of at least selected novels and travel books, for example, *The Two Baronesses* and *In Sweden*, the greatest part of Andersen's oeuvre will remain inaccessible even to cultivated readers of English and, thus, irretrievably lost to the past.[159] As I have written elsewhere, however, "Worldwide acknowledgment as the foremost figure in children's literature is a distinction of a kind few mortals can attain."[160] In the complete translation of Jean Hersholt from 1949, which

Hjørnager Pedersen maintains must be considered the standard rendering in English, this diminished but nonetheless eminently respectable Andersen is ever-present to English speakers, available to children and "children of larger growth"—as well as to adults per se—as a constant friend or as a perhaps surprisingly rewarding object of discovery.[161]

The authors of the critical general interest articles on Andersen include some of the best-known figures in the contemporary world of letters in the United States: Hjalmar Hjorth Boyesen, J. Ross Browne, Horace E. Scudder, and Bayard Taylor. Some of the publications in which their work appeared—the *Critic*, *Harper's Weekly*, the *Independent*, *Outlook*, and *St. Nicholas*, not to forget the prestigious *Library of the World's Best Literature, Ancient and Modern*—ranked among the best the country had to offer at the time. A significant number of the articles assume the form of a biographical sketch, but they as well as others also reveal varying degrees of critical engagement with the work.

The range of the writers' opinions on Andersen as a man is as great as that found in the reviews of the autobiography, and the nature of their sentiments is quite similar. Here, too, he is chastised for his vanity and conduct befitting a spoiled child, his excessive sensitivity and sentimentality. Boyesen is particularly hard on him for his lack of masculinity in the traditional sense, but others also label him effeminate by various names. If writing today, one of the authors would characterize his unique combination of genius and personal peculiarity as idiot savantism. On the other hand, Taylor and even Boyesen, both of whom benefited from firsthand acquaintance with Andersen, speak warmly of his personal kindness, and others make note of this and many other virtues, if perceived "only" in his writings. Among the chief of these is his sympathy for humanity, specifically his solidarity with the disadvantaged and downtrodden stemming from his own social origins. Similarly, some writers think of him as being distinctly Danish yet at the same time universal in his appeal, and one treats him as a figure of near mythic status.

Assessments of Andersen's work generally correspond to those found in the reviews but are broader in scope. *The Improvisatore* emerges as the most favored of the novels, though *Only a Fiddler* commands considerable respect. *The Two Baronesses* earns both plaudits and condemnation, while *O. T.* receives little notice, or appreciation. *Lucky Peer* remains totally ignored, but *To Be, or Not to Be?* is credited as a reflection of Andersen's late religious thought. Specific strengths and weaknesses go largely unnamed, though Andersen's descriptive ability, the Italian atmosphere of *The Improvisatore*, and the pathos of *Only a Fiddler* receive mention; Andersen's characterization is both praised and censured. Given their overall approval among reviewers, the travel books receive surprisingly little attention in these articles, though that little is quite positive. The poetry and plays, by contrast, have a no less surprisingly high profile. Authors mention an early collection of poems twice and advert to nine of the plays, some of them multiple times. Their awareness and opinions of these writings as well as a couple of lesser-known prose pieces may have been largely secondhand, but they at least demonstrate greater appreciation of the true extent of Andersen's lifework than do the review critics. The autobiography fares no better or worse than the man who wrote it and about the same as in the notices.

In light of the warm critical reception given the fairy tales and stories soon after their introduction in the United States, it is puzzling that the first article examined in the present chapter, which dates from as early as 1857, passes over them without so much as a word. This silence, however, is more than counterbalanced by the homage paid them and their creator by other writers, who underscore Andersen's position as the leading exponent of the form. As in the reviews, authors laud their imaginativeness, originality, and a hard-to-define "magic." Some suggest that despite—or precisely because of—their fanciful character, they are both more moral and more morally impactful than the customary literature written for the moral edification of children. A number recognize their appeal to adults as well as to the young, but, unlike most reviewers, the majority look at them exclusively in the context of children's literature.

NOTES

1. "Hans Christian Andersen, the Danish Poet," *Ballou's Pictorial Drawing-Room Companion*, October 17, 1857, 252.

2. "Hans Christian Andersen, the Danish Poet," 252.

3. See Richard Henry Stoddard, "Hans Christian Andersen," *National Magazine*, November 1855, 432.

4. Charles B. Seymour, "Hans Christian Andersen," in *Self-Made Men*, by Charles B. Seymour (New York: Harper & Brothers, 1858), 84–93.

5. "Seymour, Charles Bailey (1829–1869) Editor, Essayist, Music Critic, Theater Critic," The Vault at Pfaff's: An Archive of Art and Literature by the Bohemians of Antebellum New York, accessed October 27, 2015, https://pfaffs.web.lehigh.edu /node/54154.

6. See, for example, Johanna Levin, "The 'Vault at Pfaff's': Whitman, Bohemia, and the *Saturday Press*," in *Bohemia in America, 1858–1920*, by Johanna Levin (Stanford, CA: Stanford University Press, 2010), 13–69. Seymour was also the *Times* correspondent at the World Exposition in Paris in 1867, and he coedited the *New York Weekly Review* the same year. Also see note 5.

7. Seymour, *Self-Made Men*, unpaginated (v).

8. Seymour, "Hans Christian Andersen," 92.

9. Seymour, "Hans Christian Andersen," 92.

10. Seymour, "Hans Christian Andersen," 92.

11. Bayard Taylor, "Hans Christian Andersen," *Independent*, March 14, 1861, 1. See Bayard Taylor, "Journey to Gottenburg and Copenhagen," in *Northern Travel: Summer and Winter Pictures[;] Sweden, Denmark, and Lapland* (London: Sampson Low and Son, 1858 [1857]; New York: Putnam, 1858 [1857]), 222–34; Herbert Rowland, *More Than Meets the Eye: Hans Christian Andersen and Nineteenth-Century American Criticism* (Madison and Teaneck, NJ: Fairleigh Dickinson University Press, 2006), 115–16.

12. *Independent*, March 14, 1861, 1. Taylor is probably referring to David Teniers the Younger, the most celebrated of the four generations of painters bearing the same given and family names.

13. Taylor, *Northern Travel*, 232–33.

14. *Independent*, March 14, 1861, 1.

15. The full title of the article is "Ross Browne's Letters. [European Correspondence of the Union.] No. 11.—Newspapers and Children's Stories," *Sacramento Daily Union*, March 30, 1861, 1. Part of the article was reprinted under the title "Literature for Children in Germany and the United States" in the San Francisco *Daily Evening Bulletin*, April 3, 1861, 1.

16. See, for example, Joseph Csicsila, "J. Ross Browne," in *Nineteenth-Century American Fiction Writers*, ed. Kent P. Ljungquist, 57–64, vol. 202 of *Dictionary of Literary Biography* (Detroit: Gale Research, 1999).

17. See Rowland, *More Than Meets the Eye*, 116–18.

18. *Sacramento Daily Union*, March 30, 1861, 1.

19. "Boston," *Round Table*, December 2, 1865, 206. See Frank Luther Mott, *A History of American Magazines 1865–1885* (1938; repr., Cambridge, MA: Harvard University Press, 1966), 322; Joseph A. Borome, "The Life and Letters of Justin Winsor" (PhD diss., Columbia University, 1950), 52–59; Wayne Cutler and Michael H. Harris, eds., *Justin Winsor: Scholar-Librarian* (Littleton, CO: Libraries Unlimited, 1980), especially 17–56. Winsor signed his correspondences from Boston as "W.," which, according to a list of contributors published in the *Round Table*, could conceivably refer to one or the other of two additional Bostonians; *Round Table*, June 11, 1864, 401. However, the sources cited here as well as internal evidence place Winsor's authorship virtually beyond doubt.

20. *Round Table*, December 2, 1865, 206.

21. See, for example, Jens Andersen, *Hans Christian Andersen: A New Life*, trans. Tiina Nunnally (New York, Woodstock, and London: Overlook Duckworth, 2005), 221–22.

22. "Reading for Children," *Round Table*, May 18, 1867, 309–10.

23. See chapter 6, notes 117 and 119. Winsor's final correspondence from Boston was published in the issue of the *Round Table* for October 6, 1866. Thereafter, only three more contributions can be attributed to him with more or less certainty: a letter to the editor responding to an allegation of plagiarism in Whitman's *Leaves of Grass* made in an earlier reader letter, which is signed "W." ("'C.' on Walt Whitman,"

Round Table, February 16, 1867, 104); an anonymous article on the yearly report of the trustees of the Boston Public Library that at the very least reflects Winsor's early work for the institution, which led to his installment as superintendent ("The Experiment of Free Libraries," *Round Table*, December 14, 1867, 392–93; see Borome, "The Life and Letters of Justin Winsor," 79–85); and a tongue-in-cheek defense of women masquerading as a letter to the editor and signed "W." (*Round Table*, March 14, 1868, 166). Of course, it is entirely conceivable that Winsor continued to publish occasional pieces anonymously despite the heavy workload incurred by his new position. Another possible author is H(ermann) J(ackson) Warner (1831–1916), a Boston attorney who is also included on the *Round Table*'s list of contributors; *Round Table*, June 11, 1864, 401. Interestingly, Warner moved to Europe in 1869 due to poor health, living in Dresden, Germany, for the rest of his life, where he exchanged both visits and (inconsequential) letters with Andersen in 1871. See "Hermann Jackson Warner Photograph Collection," Massachusetts Historical Society, accessed December 9, 2016, http://www.masshist.org/collection-guides/view/fap032 (Warner took and collected many photographs during his extensive travels through Europe and Asia); *H. C. Andersens Dagbøger 1871–1872*, ed. Kirsten Weber, vol. 9 of *H. C. Andersens Dagbøger 1825–1875*, ed. Kåre Olsen and H. Topsøe-Jensen (Copenhagen: G • E • C Gads Forlag, 1975), 165; and Warner to Andersen, November 4, 1871, as well as Andersen to Warner, November 13, 1871, H. C. Andersen Centret / Hans Christian Andersen Center, last modified August 11, 2015, accessed December 9, 2016, http://andersen.sdu.dk/brevbase/person.html?pid=1066&breve=sendt&brevsor t=Afsender&sortorder=desc&start=0&limit250 and http://andersen.sdu.dk/brevbase /person.html?breve=modtaget&pid=1066, respectively.

24. *Round Table*, May 18, 1867, 309.
25. *Round Table*, May 18, 1867, 309.
26. *Round Table*, May 18, 1867, 309.
27. *Round Table*, May 18, 1867, 309.
28. *Round Table*, May 18, 1867, 309.
29. *Round Table*, May 18, 1867, 309.
30. *Round Table*, May 18, 1867, 309.
31. *Round Table*, May 18, 1867, 309.
32. *Round Table*, May 18, 1867, 309.
33. *Round Table*, May 18, 1867, 309.
34. *Round Table*, May 18, 1867, 310.
35. *Round Table*, May 18, 1867, 310.
36. *Round Table*, May 18, 1867, 310.

37. Anne Scott MacLeod, "Children's Literature in America from the Puritan Beginnings to 1870," in *Children's Literature: An Illustrated History*, ed. Peter Hunt (Oxford: Oxford University Press, 1995), 128.

38. See Herbert Rowland, "Chronological List of Primary Sources," in *More Than Meets the Eye: Hans Christian Andersen and Nineteenth-Century American Criticism*, by Herbert Rowland (Madison and Teaneck, NJ: Fairleigh Dickinson University Press, 2006), 250–51.

39. "Hans Christian Andersen, the Danish Author," *Phrenological Journal*, September 1875, 154–57. The penultimate sentence reads, "Although somewhat advanced in life, being just about seventy, he [Andersen] is yet industrious, furnishing American as well as European publications with delightful sketches of travel and stories drawn from domestic life" (157). The *Journal* claimed a subscription list of ten thousand for the year in question; see *Rowell's* for 1875, 157.

40. See, for example, Elias Bredsdorff, *Hans Christian Andersen: The Story of His Life and Work 1805–75* (London: Phaidon, 1975), 290.

41. *Phrenological Journal*, September 1875, 154.

42. *Phrenological Journal*, September 1875, 154.

43. *Phrenological Journal*, September 1875, 154.

44. *Phrenological Journal*, September 1875, 155.

45. *Phrenological Journal*, September 1875, 155, 156.

46. *Phrenological Journal*, September 1875, 156.

47. *Phrenological Journal*, September 1875, 156.

48. *Phrenological Journal*, September 1875, 156.

49. *Phrenological Journal*, September 1875, 157.

50. *Phrenological Journal*, September 1875, 157.

51. See "The Fowler Brothers," *The Cabinet of Phrenology and Crime* (blog), accessed November 9, 2015, http://phrenologyandcrime.com/2014/09/13/the-fowler-brothers/.

52. See Rowland, *More Than Meets the Eye,* 146–89.

53. Horace E. Scudder, "Hans Christian Andersen," "Supplement," *Harper's Weekly*, October 9, 1875, 830–32. An ad for the *Weekly* that appeared in the *Cultivator & Country Gentleman* and other periodicals several years later reads as follows: "Supplements will be given for the adequate delineation of important events, and from time to time Supplements will be devoted to specially selected literary productions, to striking features of American enterprise, or to foreign topics of worldwide interest"; *Cultivator & Country Gentleman*, January 5, 1888, 19.

54. Frank Luther Mott, *A History of American Magazines 1850–1865* (1938; repr., Cambridge, MA: Harvard University Press, 1966), 486–87. Mott adds that the *Weekly*'s "great fights for Lincoln, for the people of New York against Tammany, for Grant, for Cleveland, for the gold standard, and for Wilson are the achievements by which it deserves remembrance. Besides this, its record in text and picture of the events of sixty years make it a contemporaneous history of the highest value" (487). Also see Eugene Exman, "*Harper's Weekly* (1857–1900)," in *The House of Harper: One Hundred and Fifty Years of Publishing* (New York: Harper & Row, 1967), 80–93.

55. See *Rowell's* for 1875, 147.

56. *Harper's Weekly*, October 9, 1875, 830.

57. *Harper's Weekly*, October 9, 1875, 830.

58. *Harper's Weekly*, October 9, 1875, 831.

59. *Harper's Weekly*, October 9, 1875, 831.

60. *Harper's Weekly*, October 9, 1875, 831. That Scudder can then write, "Thenceforth, ANDERSEN'S life flowed brightly, and with no such violent contrasts as marked its earlier years," is likely due to an overreliance on the autobiography (831).

61. *Harper's Weekly*, October 9, 1875, 831.

62. *Harper's Weekly*, October 9, 1875, 831.

63. *Harper's Weekly*, October 9, 1875, 831.

64. *Harper's Weekly*, October 9, 1875, 831–32.

65. *Harper's Weekly*, October 9, 1875, 832.

66. *Harper's Weekly*, October 9, 1875, 832.

67. *Harper's Weekly*, October 9, 1875, 832.

68. *Harper's Weekly*, October 9, 1875, 832.

69. It is unclear why Scudder does not include *Lucky Peer*, which he shepherded through publication in *Scribner's Monthly,* among Andersen's romances. Perhaps its brevity and/or its partly discursive nature led him to think of it as something other than a romance, though romance, in the customary sense of a love story, is an integral part of the plot.

70. See the discussion of three relevant articles by Boyesen in Rowland, *More Than Meets the Eye*, 131–44.

71. See Robert S. Frederickson, "Hjalmar Hjorth Boyesen," in *American Realists and Naturalists*, ed. Donald Pizer and Earl N. Harbert, vol. 12 of *Dictionary of Literary Biography* (Detroit: Gale Research, 1982), 37–42.

72. Hjalmar Hjorth Boyesen, "Hans Christian Andersen," *St. Nicholas*, December 1875, 65–70.

73. See *Rowell's* for 1875, 157; Mott, *A History of American Magazines 1865–1885*, 501.

74. *St. Nicholas*, December 1875, 66, 67.

75. *St. Nicholas*, December 1875, 67.

76. *St. Nicholas*, December 1875, 67. Recent scholarship has shown that Andersen's libretti—for such his adaptations of Scott's novels were—fared better with the public and were more successful as artworks than contemporary critics allowed. See Jerome Mitchell, *The Walter Scott Operas: An Analysis of the Operas Based on the Works of Sir Walter Scott* (Tuscaloosa: University of Alabama Press, 1977), 127–36, 222–29, as well as Tove Barfoed Møller, "H. C. Andersens Scott-libretti i samtids- og nutidsbelysning," *Anderseniana*, 1996, 11–24; Erik Sønderholm, "Hans Christian Andersen als Opernlibrettist: Eine textkritische Untersuchung," *Anderseniana*, 1996, 25–48.

77. *St. Nicholas*, December 1875, 69.

78. *St. Nicholas*, December 1875, 68.

79. *St. Nicholas*, December 1875, 68.

80. For Boyesen's opinion of *To Be, or Not to Be?*, see Rowland, *More Than Meets the Eye*, 141.

81. *St. Nicholas*, December 1875, 65.

82. *St. Nicholas*, December 1875, 65.

83. Hjalmar Hjorth Boyesen, "An Acquaintance with Hans Christian Andersen," *Century*, March 1892, 785.

84. *St. Nicholas*, December 1875, 68–69.

85. *St. Nicholas*, December 1875, 70.

86. Hjalmar Hjorth Boyesen, "Scandinavian Literature. II. Denmark and Sweden," *Chautauquan*, March 1888, 335–37.

87. See Mott, *A History of American Magazines 1865–1885*, 173, 544–47. Founded in 1878, the Circle is currently the oldest continuous book club in the United States.

88. Mott, *A History of American Magazines 1865–1885*, 173.

89. Mott, *A History of American Magazines 1865–1885*, 545.

90. See *Rowell's* for 1888, 430.

91. *Chautauquan*, March 1888, 336.

92. *Chautauquan*, March 1888, 336.

93. *Chautauquan*, March 1888, 336.

94. Oscar Fay Adams, "Hans Christian Andersen, 'The Goldsmith of the North,'" *Wide Awake*, August 1888, 137–41.

95. See Mott, *A History of American Magazines 1865–1885*, 177, 508–9.

96. Mott, *A History of American Magazines 1865–1885*, 508.

97. See *Rowell's* for 1888, 216.

98. See, for example, *Marquis Who's Who in America*, 1908, s.v. "Adams, Oscar Fay."

99. Oscar Fay Adams, *Dear Old Story-Tellers: Twelve Portraits* (Boston: Lothrop, Lee & Shepard, 1889), 143–63. Quotations are from this printing of the piece, which, incidentally, is the longest of the volume.

100. Adams, *Dear Old Story-Tellers*, 143. Adams attributes the quotation to Washington Irving, but it actually occurs in Thackeray's *The English Humorists of the Eighteenth Century* and reads as follows: "To be the most beloved of English writers, what a title that is for a man!". See W[illiam] M[akepeace] Thackeray, *The English Humorists of the Eighteenth Century: A Series of Lectures Delivered in England, Scotland, and the United States of America* (London: Smith, Elder, 1853); quoted according to the German edition (Leipzig: Bernhard Tauchnitz, 1853), 282.

101. Adams, *Dear Old Story-Tellers*, 145–46.

102. For a bibliography of these renderings, see Elias Bredsdorff, *Danish Literature in English Translation, with a Special Hans Christian Andersen Supplement: A Bibliography* (Copenhagen: Ejnar Munksgaard, 1950), 25–117. The disparity between the number of translations and Americans' apparent ignorance of them suggests that the great majority experienced very limited distribution and critical discussion in the United States.

103. Adams, *Dear Old Story-Tellers*, 146.

104. Adams, *Dear Old Story-Tellers*, 153–54.

105. Adams, *Dear Old Story-Tellers*, 154.

106. See J. Andersen, *Hans Christian Andersen*, 128–30.

107. J. Andersen, *Hans Christian Andersen*, 128–30. Also see Arthur Aumont and Edgar Collin, *Det danske Nationalteater 1748–1889: En Statistisk Fremstilling af det Kongelige Teaters Historie fra Skuepladsens Aabning paa Kongens Nytorv 18. De-*

cember 1748 til Udgangen af Sæsonen 1888–89, 5 parts (Copenhagen: J. Jørgensen, 1896–1899), 2:1.

108. Adams, *Dear Old Story-Tellers*, 154–55.

109. Adams, *Dear Old Story-Tellers*, 155–56.

110. Adams, *Dear Old Story-Tellers*, 156.

111. Adams, *Dear Old Story-Tellers*, 158–59.

112. Adams, *Dear Old Story-Tellers*, 158.

113. Adams, *Dear Old Story-Tellers*, 158.

114. Adams, *Dear Old Story-Tellers*, 163.

115. Unsigned review of "Hans Christian Andersen," by R. Nisbet Bain, *Critic*, November 23, 1895, 339–40. According to *Rowell's* for 1896 (685), the magazine currently had a circulation of between four thousand and seventy-five hundred.

116. Bain is far more sober and much less allusive than the reviewer and, unlike him, has words of approval as well as criticism for the novels, even for *To Be, or Not to Be?* Though no admirer of Andersen's work for the stage, Bain acknowledges the success of certain plays and concedes that Andersen had the wherewithal to write presentable one-acters, if not full-length dramas. See Robert Nisbet Bain, *Hans Christian Andersen: A Biography* (New York: Dodd, Mead; London: Lawrence and Bullen, 1895), 334 and 237–38.

117. I have found no evidence that Boyesen reviewed for the *Critic*, which still maintained its anonymous reviewing policy in 1895, but in light of his widespread activity as a creative writer and critic it is not at all unthinkable. He published at least one article as well as a letter to the editor in the magazine. See "The New School in Norwegian Literature," *Critic*, May 7, 1887, 225–26; "An International Boswell," August 26, 1893, 142. Boyesen died the month before the review appeared, but his death was sudden, and the review could have already been in the hands of the magazine's editors.

118. *Critic*, November 23, 1895, 339. "Amiel" refers to the Swiss moral philosopher, poet, and critic Henri-Frédéric Amiel (1821–1881). The quoted line, which translates as "the mind of a woman in the character of a child," comes from the entry in Amiel's *Journal Intime* (Private Journal) for February 20, 1851. See *Amiel's Journal: The Journal Intime of Henri-Frédéric Amiel*, trans. Mrs. Humphry Ward (London and New York: Macmillan, 1891), 7. The passage serves as the motto for Bain's biography.

119. *Critic*, November 23, 1895, 339. Plans for the statue were in progress before Andersen's death, but it was not erected until 1887. It was ultimately created by August Saabye.

120. *Critic*, November 23, 1895, 339. Andersen's last novel, *Lucky Peer*, was published in 1871; his last works for the stage date from around the mid-1860s.

121. In a passage quoted below, it is evident that the reviewer thought highly of Andersen's travel books.

122. *Critic*, November 23, 1895, 339. Johan Ludvig Heiberg (1791–1860) was a highly influential Danish poet, playwright, and critic. Christian Molbech (1783–1857) was, among other things, a Danish historian, critic, and, for more than a decade, director of the Royal Theater.

123. *Critic*, November 23, 1895, 339–40.

124. *Critic*, November 23, 1895, 340. The quotation is from the *Divine Comedy: Purgatory*, 12:67, which reads in English, "Dead seemed the dead, living seemed the living"; "Commedia," Princeton Dante Project, accessed November 29, 2015, http://etcweb.princeton.edu/dante/index.html.

125. "The Holiday Books: The Season's Literature Reviewed and Illustrated," *Outlook*, December 7, 1895, 960.

126. See Mott, *A History of American Magazines 1865–1885*, 422.

127. See *Rowell's* for 1896, 689; Mott, *A History of American Magazines 1865–1885*, 429.

128. *Outlook*, December 7, 1895, 960.

129. Bain, *Hans Christian Andersen*, 303.

130. *Outlook*, December 7, 1895, 960.

131. "Hans Christian Andersen," in *Library of the World's Best Literature, Ancient and Modern*, ed. Charles Dudley Warner (New York: International Society, 1896), 1:500–539.

132. Warner, *Library of the World's Best Literature*, 1:xi.

133. Warner, *Library of the World's Best Literature*, 1:xiii.

134. The year 1896 also witnessed the appearance of W. H. De Puy's similar, but more modest *The University of Literature in Twenty Volumes: A Cyclopædia of Universal Literature, Presenting in Alphabetical Arrangement the Biography, Together with Critical Reviews and Extracts, of Eminent Writers of All Lands and All Ages* (New York: J. S. Barcus, 1896). The article on Andersen contains a brief and undistinguished survey of the life and work (the autobiography of 1847 "was continued by another hand down to the time of Andersen's death"); "The Dying Child"—one of the poems, all the same; an excerpt from the autobiography on Jenny Lind; and "The Ugly Duckling" ["The Ugly Little Duck"]. "Hans Christian Andersen," unpaginated.

135. "The Encyclopedia Americana (1920) / Wells, Benjamin Willis," Wikisource, last modified February 23, 2011, accessed December 4, 2015, https://en.wikisource.org/wiki/The_Encyclopedia_Americana_(1920)/Wells,_Benjamin_Willis.

136. See "Wells, Benjamin Willis," Internet Archive, accessed December 4, 2015, https://archive.org/index.php.

137. Warner, *Library of the World's Best Literature*, 1:500.

138. Warner, *Library of the World's Best Literature*, 1:500. At the end of his essay, Wells writes, "The 'Life of Hans Christian Andersen' by R. Nisbet Bain . . . is esteemed the best" (1:503). There are other indications of Wells's indebtedness to Bain.

139. Warner, *Library of the World's Best Literature*, 1:501.

140. See Anna Harwell Celenza, *Hans Christian Andersen and Music: "The Nightingale" Revealed* (Aldershot and Burlington, VT: Ashgate, 2005), 30–32. The other two plays were *The Ship* (*Skibet*; 1831) and *The Queen Sixteen Years of Age* (*Dronningen paa 16 Aar*; 1833).

141. Warner, *Library of the World's Best Literature*, 1:501.

142. Warner, *Library of the World's Best Literature*, 1:501.

143. Warner, *Library of the World's Best Literature*, 1:502.

144. Warner, *Library of the World's Best Literature*, 1:501.

145. *The King Dreams* went through fourteen performances, *The New Lying-In Room* sixty-one; see Aumont and Collin, *Det danske Nationalteater 1748–1889*, 2:1.

146. Warner, *Library of the World's Best Literature, Ancient and Modern*, 1:502.

147. Warner, *Library of the World's Best Literature, Ancient and Modern*, 1:502.

148. Here, "Germany" refers more specifically to Prussia and its allies (the German Confederation), which included tiny, but culturally highly influential Saxe-Weimar-Eisenach under the leadership of Andersen's close friend and supporter Hereditary Grand Duke Carl Alexander (1818–1901).

149. See Celenza, *Hans Christian Andersen and Music*, 166–67.

150. Warner, *Library of the World's Best Literature, Ancient and Modern*, 1:501.

151. Warner, *Library of the World's Best Literature, Ancient and Modern*, 1:501.

152. Warner, *Library of the World's Best Literature, Ancient and Modern*, 1:502.

153. Warner, *Library of the World's Best Literature, Ancient and Modern*, 1:502–3.

154. Warner, *Library of the World's Best Literature, Ancient and Modern*, 1:503.

155. Warner, *Library of the World's Best Literature, Ancient and Modern*, 1:503.

156. Warner, *Library of the World's Best Literature, Ancient and Modern*, 1:501.

157. Bain based his biography mainly on *H. C. Andersen og det Collinske Hus* (*H. C. Andersen and the Collin Family*), published by Andersen's friend Edvard Collin in 1882, and two collections of letters to and from the author edited by C. St. A. Bille and Nicholai Bøgh in 1877–1878 (Bain, *Hans Christian Andersen*, vi–vii). For reasons that need not concern us here, it eventually became evident that Collin's book was not the objective representation of Andersen that it purported to be. Jens Andersen writes,

[W]e notice right from the first pages that the book was written by a jurist. It is structured almost like a trial, in which documents and explanations are presented by an author who, in regard to his subject, is often more prosecutor than defender. . . . And here it becomes apparent that the defender is occasionally not only biased but also unreliable and downright dishonest in his documentation. His selection and abridgement of the letters from Hans Christian Andersen is extremely subjective and blatantly manipulative . . . [Andersen's] story belonged to [Collin], so to speak, for nearly fifty years, just as it had in the late 1870s when he blithely edited, abridged, added, and omitted whatever he liked. (J. Andersen, *Hans Christian Andersen*, 173–74)

Collin also determined which letters Bille and Bøgh could read and use in their collections (J. Andersen, *Hans Christian Andersen*, 171).

158. The articles and periodic bibliographies published in *Anderseniana* provide a very useful running account of scholarly work on Andersen (articles in Danish currently contain summaries in English and vice versa). Also informative are the dozens of papers, many of them written in English, that were presented at the four international conferences on Andersen held over the past some twenty-five years; see the introduction, note 1, of this study and "Conferences," H. C. Andersen Centret / Hans Christian Andersen Center, accessed February 28, 2017, http://andersen.sdu.dk /forskning/konference/index_e.html.

159. As indicated earlier, Frank Hugus published a new translation of *The Improvisatore* in 2018 (see chapter 2, note 3 of this volume). It should be added that Hersholt's translation of the tales includes both *Picture Book without Pictures* and, surprisingly enough, *Lucky Peer. In Spain, A Visit to Portugal*, and *A Poet's Bazaar* were newly translated by Grace Thornton in the 1970s and 1980s; see *A Visit to Spain and North Africa, 1862* (London: Peter Owen, 1975); *A Visit to Portugal, 1866* (London: Peter Owen, 1972); and *A Poet's Bazaar* (New York: M. Kesend, 1986). W. Glyn Jones published a new rendering of the autobiography as *The Fairy Tale of My Life* in 1954 (Copenhagen, London, and New York: Nyt Nordisk Forlag). Several scholars have recently written on Andersen's dramas, translations of several of which should be forthcoming.

160. Rowland, *More Than Meets the Eye*, 17.

161. See the introduction, p. 3 and note 5.

Conclusion

Americans of the nineteenth century became acquainted or reacquainted with Hans Christian Andersen and his work in two major ways: through the many editions published in England and the United States and the numerous individual fairy tales and extracts from longer texts printed in magazines and newspapers. They gained considerable insight into the works through the 238 reviews and critical general interest articles as well as a host of other writings that appeared in many of the same periodicals. The number of identifiable critics is small, but Hjalmar Hjorth Boyesen, John Neal, Horace E. Scudder, William Gilmore Simms, and Bayard Taylor, not to mention possibilities such as William Dean Howells, belong on any list of the better or best-known figures of their time. Many anonymous reviewers also demonstrated noteworthy expertise. The magazines addressed all levels of society, from youthful factory workers to the most sophisticated intelligentsia, though the majority targeted the educated and professional classes. If most were based in the Northeast, many had a national and, in some cases, international reach. General and religious magazines provided Andersen with his greatest exposure, many or most of the latter becoming more general over the course of the century. The newspapers were geographically and demographically much more broad based than the magazines, but many of them nonetheless offered their readers capable to expert commentaries on Andersen and his works. Both reserved much more space for literature than their modern-day counterparts. All together, they gave thousands upon thousands of their readers the opportunity to read and learn about Andersen and many of his writings.

Andersen's American reception occurred in several waves of varying size. Certain discontinuities exist between the two largest, which unfolded from 1845 to 1853 and from 1869 to 1871. Some reviewers of the later period were unaware of works that had been published and warmly greeted during the earlier phase, which may be attributable to a shift in journalistic generations and/or individual reading preferences. A number of critics were rather nonplussed by the first collections of stories and tales, though that was not at all the case with those who reviewed the editions of the early 1870s or, for that matter, even the 1860s. Their nonplus stemmed in large part from moral-religious concerns vis-à-vis the fairy tale as a means of educating children. Over the following two and a half decades, these concerns dissipated as changes in attitudes toward the function of the genre, the nature of childhood, and the edificatory role of literature took place. However, such breaches in continuity fade in the face of the uninterrupted currents of response to the perceived virtues and flaws of Andersen and his work that generally characterize his reception in the United States through the early 1870s and, in part, beyond. For more than half of the nineteenth century, the poet and his writings were a continual and significant presence in the review criticism of the country.

American critics commented on the novelty and originality, the simplicity and naturalness, and the imaginativeness and beauty of virtually all of Andersen's works, regardless of genre. They underscored his unusually acute descriptive ability, which they likewise discerned in all the forms he cultivated, even his autobiography and the stories and tales. Moreover, they sensed a poetic quality throughout his prose, both fiction and nonfiction, long and short. For many, his solidarity with the weak and poor transcended the boundaries of individual literary kinds.

Some of the reviewers' appreciation was genre specific. Andersen's first three novels came out in English translation in 1845 and determined Americans' view of the author for more than a year, at least until the individual collections of tales began to make their impression in 1846, and probably longer. At that time, as later, critics dwelled on the atmospheric density of the works, whether it was the Italianness of *The Improvisatore* or the Danishness of *O. T.*, *Only and Fiddler*, and *The Two Baronesses*. Incidentally, those who emphasized the "national" quality of the novels set in Denmark often implicitly challenged Longfellow's idealized conception of the North. If none used the terms "*Bildung*" or "bildungsroman," several were quite familiar with the phenomena themselves, for they singled out the role of art in the development of the individual as a major feature of the novels. Similarly, some reviewers noted the refining influence of the fairy tales and stories on the sensibilities and the moral-religious character of readers. For them, the morality of the tales resides integrally in their form and content, rather than in some external application, and achieves its effects indirectly. A couple remarked on the varieties of life with which Andersen invests his creatures and objects in accordance with their shapes or functions. A goodly number attributed an indescribable charm, or "magic," to the tales. Of course, these became Andersen's most popular and enduring works.

The history as well as the varying landscapes of the countries Andersen visited on his many journeys formed a central attraction for reviewers of the travelogues—as well as the novels and the autobiography. While the books themselves must be credited with much or most of their appeal, they were transplanted into fertile soil in the geographically isolated United States, where Melville's nautical adventure novels and the Twain of *The Innocents Abroad* could attain great popularity. Critics had favorable words for the humor and satire that come to the fore in these works, but they largely ignored their presence in the tales, and a couple dismissed them as entirely foreign to the poet's artistic makeup. Verdicts on the autobiographies and their author as an individual were very mixed, largely due to reservations to be mentioned shortly. The publication of two poems as texts in several hymnals, together with related editorial and critical comments, implies a very limited but positive reception of the poetry. Though one of the plays was deemed a failure at second hand, another met with respectful treatment in an original notice.

Most negative comments related to Andersen's work in individual genres. The plot construction and characterization in his novels earned him widespread censure, although a few early proponents of the romance approved of precisely these aspects of his art. Several reviewers of the autobiography responded tactfully to his vanity and oversensitivity to criticism, but a few condemned them in unusually harsh terms. Some regarded his relationship to the powerful as obsequious, treating it more or less politely but with poorly concealed or evident disdain. The travel books experienced no substantial criticism. Following initial quibbles, the stories and tales had the same good fortune.

American criticism of Andersen during our period reflects varying methodological and aesthetic assumptions. Commentary on the novels in particular discloses a positivistic reliance on Andersen's autobiography for a proper understanding of the works. John Neal is only the most prominent representative of the romantics who elevate the role of artistic genius in the creative process, while William Dean Howells or writers of his ilk call for a realistic depiction of life and society. All along, however, critics of varying persuasion reveal formalist expectations of the writer, which are most apparent in their strictures on the plot construction and character drawing in the novels.

Andersen's critics took part in the American discovery of Scandinavia during the nineteenth century. Partly for cultural-patriotic reasons they saw the Dane and the North in general as models for the revitalization of a specifically American literature too long tied to its original British moorings. In this connection, it was the perceived freshness, simplicity, and unaffectedness, a certain pristine quality of Andersen's work that most appealed to them. Many viewed him in part through the prism of Longfellow's ahistorical, idealized conception of Scandinavia, which derived ultimately from the Rousseauism of the previous century. However, they were nonetheless able to turn their understanding of him to real-world use.

They did so largely by evoking Andersen as the antithesis of the sensationalism that swept European and American literature and journalism from the early 1840s to the 1890s—that is, concurrently with the main stretches of his reception in the United States. It was primarily Andersen, the novelist, whom they called upon, but they did not forget either the traveler or the storyteller. Andersen participated willy-nilly in the debate between romantics and realists over the relative merits of the romance and the novel, generally commended by the former and condemned by the latter. His novels, which according to realist tenets were in fact romances, would probably have met with greater favor had they gained the attention of more reviewers during the first phase of his American reception. As the excursus in chapter 6 shows, "The Emperor's New Clothes" and *Picture Book without Pictures* were drawn into the mainstream of American history from the 1850s to the 1870s and positioned on opposing sides of the great national dispute and conflict.

At the end of the nineteenth century, Andersen stood in the American mind as a writer of fairy tales for children. However, a notable majority of the critics who read and reviewed collections of the works earlier in the century concluded that they had much to say to adults as well, and several contended that they were designed more, or specifically for the mature. Therefore, it is remarkable that, some 120 years after the last of these notices appeared, a Nordic scholar could still write, with a broader focus, that "[o]utside the North [Andersen's] literary reputation . . . is almost exclusively associated with his distinctiveness as an author of children's books. However, the tales he wrote for children can also be read by adults. At the same time, a very significant part of his stories and tales are intended exclusively for adults, although children can also read them. The last word in this discussion has yet to be said."[1] It is no less remarkable that within twelve years the author's prediction was strongly confirmed by the appearance of a volume titled *Hans Christian Andersen: Between Children's Literature and Adult Literature.* In it, scholars pursue issues reflected in titles such as "Hans Christian Andersen's Fairy Tales—Children's Literature?" and "Language for Children? An Examination of the Language and Intended Readership of the Fairy Tales"; one simply states, "For Adults Only."[2] While their treatments of these questions are largely more sophisticated, and more extensive, than those of the American reviewers, their conclusions are essentially the same. Thus, one may legitimately speculate that a comparison of modern attitudes toward

Andersen's other works with those of his nineteenth-century American critics would reveal wide areas of agreement.

In the course of this study, a number of possible reasons for the current view of Andersen's most popular works have been proposed. About one-quarter of his more or less realistic stories had little to no exposure in American book reviews, either escaping discussion altogether or considered in notices of only one or two collections. This factor, together with the eventual absence of the variously realistic novels from the review press, surely lowered Andersen's profile as a writer for adults. And even if readers enjoyed the most fantastic of the fairy tales, prevalent notions of masculinity and adulthood may well have prevented many of the men and some of the women from owning up to the fact.

However, the most salient reasons were most likely literary- and socio-historical in nature. From the nineteenth through the early twenty-first centuries, literature and the other arts have passed, in varying relationship to the movement of ideas and events, through the familiar, if ill-defined and vaguely contoured phases of romanticism, realism, naturalism, and modernism, followed by the even more nebulous postmodernism and its aftermath. Since around the middle of the nineteenth century, however, the modern notion and privileged position of childhood have remained comparatively constant. Even earlier in the century, the fairy tale began its descent from its lofty position as the centerpiece of romantic literary art into the nursery and the elementary school. For all the reasons cited—and there may well be more—the full range and sophistication of Andersen's stories and tales disappeared from public view. What remains is a number of excellent but nonetheless misleading works that enjoy abiding popularity.

As intimated in the introduction to this book, the international Andersen reception is so extensive that a thorough study of it would require a collaborative effort of scholars from many countries, which would surely result in a multi-volume work. However, even a survey of the research to date indicates that it assumes different forms and pursues diverse goals.[3] The majority of examinations consists of relatively short articles or, often, revised papers that appear in scholarly journals, conference proceedings, collections of essays by individual authors, and newspapers. Thus, most deal with discrete aspects of the reception. Moreover, writers understand the term "reception" in various ways. They have written, for example, on Andersen-inspired theatrical performances in Italy and productions of his tales in a miniature theater in Poland, together with the response to them in the press. One has treated "The Little Mermaid" as adapted in animated films in the United States, Australia, and Scandinavia, while another has investigated a retelling of "The Snow Queen" as a parable of the Spanish Republic and the notion of forgetfulness.

More traditional inquiries explore Andersen influences in the work of other authors, for instance, James Joyce, Thomas Mann, Anna Melikian, George Sand, and William Butler Yeats. The view of the Dane in the Russian press around 1900 and his role in the discussion of children's literature in Germany from roughly 1900 to 1950 have also come in for consideration. It should be noted that many of these publications examine phenomena of the twentieth and twenty-first centuries and that most center on the fairy tales and stories.

Fewer studies deal with the Andersen reception of an entire nation. These typically come out in lengthy articles, monographic numbers of periodicals, books, and other long forms. Surprisingly, perhaps, many share the limited scope of the short articles. Breitenstein and Rey-Henningsen follow Andersen on his physical and/or literary travels through Italy and Spain, respectively, while Trencsényi-Waldapfel looks at his spiritual presence in the work of Hungarian authors.[4] Like a lot of others, Høybye focuses on translations and translators as well as Andersen's personal contacts in his examinations of the French reception.[5] Very few writers address the critical assessment of Andersen in their respective countries of interest. In some instances, this is due simply to the absence of a substantial critical reception or the wartime destruction of libraries and archives.[6] In studies published before the advent of the internet, the general difficulty in uncovering related source material was likely the decisive factor.[7]

All the same, Bredsdorff, Åström, and Möller-Christensen were largely able to overcome this limitation in their investigations of the English, Swedish, and German receptions of 1954, 1972, and 1992, respectively.[8] Their studies represent at once the most extensive and substantive examinations of Andersen's critical reception conducted before the internet era.[9] An exhaustive comparison of their findings with those set forth in the present volume would go well beyond the scope of this book.[10] However, some related facts, impressions, and informed conjectures may prove illuminating.

The main period covered in the three earlier studies extends essentially from 1829 to 1852. It thus runs from Andersen's arrival on the international literary scene to around the midpoint of his career, when numerous collections of tales, his revised autobiographies, two novels, several travel books and sketches, nine plays, and a collection of poems still lay before him. Now, British critics published fifty-seven notices of his works between 1845 and 1848, an average of around fourteen per year.[11] However, they issued less than two a year from then until 1875, when reviewing of his writings reportedly came to an end in the country, and these failed to alter the already established image of the poet among Britons.[12] A similar situation prevailed in Sweden and Germany. Swedish and German commentators issued some 80 and 130 notices between 1829 and 1852 and between 1835 and 1850, an annual average of

3.3 and 8.1, respectively.[13] Although no relevant evidence has come to light, one is surely justified to assume that the number of reviews in these countries also decreased steeply after mid-century. The reasons for the decline of Andersen's popularity, like those for its rise, varied from one nation to the other, though the emergence of realism was common to all three. Whatever those factors were, the results were the same. A significant portion of Andersen's lifework, including writings that reflect his trend toward realism, appears to have received little or no critical scrutiny. By 1857, according to Bredsdorff, the English had pushed Andersen into the nursery and closed the door behind him, and the same was true of the Swedes and the Germans as well.[14]

The initial phase of Andersen's reception in the United States stretched from 1845 to 1853 and thus coincided with the final stages of his reception in Sweden and Germany and the sole period of his reception in England. During this time, American reviewers published 49 notices, an average of 5.4 per year, more than the Swedes but less than the Germans and far less than the English. While the Swedish and German critics issued their reviews over longer periods of time, they also wrote on a broader cross-section of Andersen's work, including poems and plays. This fact suggests a relative increase in the Americans' coverage of writings discussed in all three countries. In any case, the American reception went through three additional phases, the largest of which, running from 1869 to 1871, saw the appearance of 133 notices, an annual average of 44.3. This figure more than trebles the already impressive 14.2 per year that came out in England from 1845 to 1848. Following the publication of the Author's Edition, American reviewers created what is probably the most intense period of Andersen criticism to have occurred anywhere in the world. They also extended the vitality of his stories and tales among adults as well as children by around fifteen to twenty years, depending on the country in question.

Such data say little about the nature or quality of the nations' respective critical work. According to both Åström and Bredsdorff, Swedish and British reviewers were in aggregate kinder to Andersen than were their Danish counterparts, and the general tenor of the reviews considered by Möller-Christensen suggests that the same was also true of the Germans.[15] Andersen could have been content with the drift of American criticism as well. With the tone of his European neighbors' critiques in mind, however, he would not have anticipated or appreciated the sharpness of certain American critics' comments.

Åström writes that Swedish reviewers, unlike their Danish cousins, tended to base their opinions of Andersen's works on their content, ideas, and "heart" rather than aesthetic criteria.[16] Reading between the lines of his book, one may conclude that he had reservations toward the review criticism of his country during the time in question. Möller-Christensen emphasizes the literary-historical, sociocultural, and political underpinnings of the German reception.[17] Based on her findings, Germans saw in Andersen a "soothing" *Biedermeier* contrast to the politically oriented Young Germany movement, an incarnation of the romantic faith in genius, and a mythical representative of the romantics' notion of the relationship between art and life. Only when Andersen's ideality faded with the advance of realism and the rise of resentment stemming from the Three Years' War do German critics appear to have turned more uniformly to aesthetic considerations.

As stated in the introduction to this volume, British and American reviewers responded to Andersen in a similar fashion. During the mid-to-late 1840s, they critiqued the same works in the same order and at roughly the same time, though the Americans attended to them a few years longer. They both displayed considerable interest in matters of form and shared many of the same insights. Even in their misunderstandings of the Dane they at times revealed incisive parallels in their thinking. For example, one British writer labeled Andersen's imagination an antidote to the "machines of utilitarian inventions," while Charlotte Goodwyn wrote similarly but metaphorically of him as a prophet to the deliverer of man from a giant named Reality—both unaware of his commitment to technological progress.[18] British and American critics differed importantly in their attitudes toward the moral-religious and sociopolitical dimensions of Andersen's work, the Americans less concerned with the former and more so with the latter.

Andersen's fear of a transatlantic voyage kept him from visiting the United States.[19] He found the English Channel less daunting and crossed it twice, in 1847 and 1857. By the time of his second crossing, however, he was no longer the versatile, frequently and perceptively discussed author he had been during the first. He regained that distinction in the United States thanks to the good services of Horace Scudder and British critics' ignorance or unwillingness to take advantage of them.[20] American reviewers and other American writers gave Andersen renewed vigor in the critical and general press for a relatively brief but significant period and likely for the last time in any country.

NOTES

1. Ljudmila Brauda, "H. C. Andersens eventyr og historier 1850–70," in *Andersen og verden: Indlæg fra den Første Internationale H. C. Andersen-Konference 25.–31. august 1991*, ed. Johan de Mylius, Aage Jørgensen, and Viggo Hjørnager Pedersen (Odense: Odense Universitetsforlag, 1993), 83–84. My translation from the Swedish.

2. See chapter 6, note 6.

3. See the titles included in note 1 of the introduction.

4. See Jørgen Breitenstein, "H. C. Andersen og Italien," in *H. C. Andersen og Hans Kunst i Nyt Lys*, ed. Jørgen Breitenstein et al. (Odense: Odense Universitetsforlag, 1976), 31–51; Marisa Rey-Henningsen, "Spanien og H.C. Andersen," *Anderseniana*, 2005, 41–61; and Imre Trencsényi-Waldapfel, "H. C. Andersen in Ungarn," *Anderseniana* 6 (1966): 19–68.

5. See Poul Høybye, "H. C. Andersen og Frankrig," *Anderseniana*, 2nd ser., 2, no. 2 (1952): 136–206; Poul Høybye, *Andersen et la France* (Copenhagen: Munksgaard, 1960).

6. According to Rey-Henningsen's study, Spain exemplifies such an absence of reception. Brzozowska refers to the consequences of the two wars for Polish researchers. Zdydzislawa Brzozowska, "H. C. Andersen i Polen: Belyst ved værker udgivet in Polen i årene 1844–1960," *Anderseniana*, 1970, 94.

7. Among other reasons for the provisional nature of his study, for example, Høybye cites the impossibility of undertaking a complete examination of French, Belgian, Swiss, and Canadian magazines; Høybye, "H. C. Andersen og Frankrig," 136.

8. Elias Bredsdorff, "Den engelske kritiks behandling af H. C. Andersen," in *H. C. Andersen og England*, by Elias Bredsdorff (Copenhagen: Rosenkilde og Baggers Forlag, 1954), 428–88; Harald Åström, *H. C. Andersens genombrott i Sverige: Översättningarna och kritiken 1828–1852* (Odense: Andelsbogtrykkeriet, 1972); Ivy York Möller-Christensen, *Den gyldne trekant: H. C. Andersens gennembrud i Tyskland 1831–1850* (Odense: Odense Universitetsforlag, 1992). Bredsdorff and Åström also deal at length with the translations of Andersen's works into their respective languages of concern.

9. Bibliographies consulted for this book contain entries in languages that are inaccessible to the author, and it is therefore possible that some pertain to studies of Andersen's critical reception.

10. For a fuller, if far from comprehensive comparison of Andersen's critical reception in Sweden, Germany, England, and the United States, see Herbert Rowland, *More Than Meets the Eye: Hans Christian Andersen and Nineteenth-Century American Criticism* (Madison and Teaneck, NJ: Fairleigh Dickinson University Press, 2006), 201–8.

11. See Bredsdorff, *H. C. Andersen og England*, 467.

12. Bredsdorff, *H. C. Andersen og England*, 484, 482, and 467–68.

13. The numbers of reviews are drawn from Åström's notes and Möller-Christensen's bibliography: Åström, *H. C. Andersens genombrott i Sverige*, 159–67; Möller-Christensen, *Den gyldne trekant*, 310–81. Möller-Christensen's bibliography includes a list of forty-seven general and biographical articles but does not indicate whether they are critical in nature (382–87).

14. Bredsdorff, *H. C. Andersen og England*, 475.

15. See Åström, *H. C. Andersens genombrott i Sverige*, 153; Bredsdorff, *H. C. Andersen og England*, 484.

16. Åström, *H. C. Andersens genombrott i Sverige*, 153.

17. Möller-Christensen, *Den gyldne trekant*, 291–99.

18. See Bredsdorff, *H. C. Andersen og England*, 441.

19. See, for example, Erik Dal, "Hans Christian Andersen's Tales and America," *Scandinavian Studies* 40 (1968): 4–5.

20. The Author's Edition of the autobiography received one review, but otherwise British critics appear to have taken no note of Scudder's work; see chapter 5, note 6.

Chronological List of Primary Sources

Reviews, Articles, Announcements, and Ads

1845

Evening Post (*O. T., Only a Fiddler*), November 12, 2.

Hart, Samuel Nathan, Sr. Review of *Only a Fiddler* and *O. T. Southern Patriot*, December 30, 2.

New-York Commercial Advertiser (*The Improvisatore*), February 22, 3.

————. (*O. T., Only a Fiddler*), November, 13, 2.

North American and Daily Advertiser (*The Improvisatore*), April 4, 2.

Review of *Life in Italy: The Improvisatore. Broadway Journal*, April 12, 227.

————. *Ladies' National Magazine*, July, 36.

————. *Ladies' Repository* (Boston), May, 439.

Review of *Only a Fiddler!* ("Foreign Literature"). *North American*, October 30, 1.

Review of *Only a Fiddler* and *O. T. Anglo American*, November 22, 116.

————. *Gentleman's Magazine*, November, 508.

————. *Spectator* (London), August 30, 831–32.

Review of *The Improvisatore; or, Life in Italy. Daily National Intelligencer*, May 2, 1.

Simms, William Gilmore. Review of *Life in Italy: The Improvisatore. Southern and Western Magazine and Review*, September, 215.

1846

New-York Commercial Advertiser (*Wonderful Stories for Children*), April 4, 1.

New-York Spectator (*Wonderful Stories for Children*), April 8, 1.

Review of *A Poet's Bazaar. Spirit of the Times*, November 7, 441–42.

Review of *Only a Fiddler* and *O. T. Ladies' Repository* (Boston), January, 279.

Review of *The Nightingale, and Other Tales. Anglo American*, October 17, 605.

Review of *Wonderful Stories for Children. Churchman*, April 26, 27.

———. *Presbyterian*, April 11, 60.
———. *Spirit of the Times*, April 4, 72.

1847

Boston Recorder (*The True Story of My Life*), August 12, 127.
Christian Watchman (*The True Story of My Life*), August 13, 3.
Review of *The True Story of My Life*. *Boston Weekly Messenger*, August 11, 2.
———. *Christian Inquirer*, August 21, 180.
———. *Christian World*, August 14, 3.
———. *Young American's Magazine of Self-Improvement*, December, 364.
Review of *Wonderful Stories for Children*. *Mothers' Journal and Family Visitant*,
    February, 61.

1848

Christian Inquirer (*The Shoes of Fortune, and Other Tales*), May 6, 268.
Geraldine. Review of *The True Story of My Life*. *American Literary Magazine*, Janu-
    ary, 56–60.
———. *Christian Review*, March, 151.
Home Journal (*A Danish Story Book*), June 17, 2.
———. (*A Danish Story Book*), November 25, 2.
New York Evangelist (*A Danish Story Book*), June 15, 2.
New-York Commercial Advertiser (*A Christmas Greeting*), February 29, 2.
New-York Spectator (*A Christmas Greeting*), March 6, 1.
"A Page by Hans Christian Andersen." *Man in the Moon* 3, no. 15 (May[?] 1848[?]):
    143.
Review of *A Christmas Greeting*. *Christian Inquirer*, March 25, 93.
———. *Christian World*, March 4, 3.
Review of *A Danish Story Book*. *Boston Evening Transcript*, June 12, 1.
———. *Literary World*, July 1, 432.
Review of *A Picture Book without Pictures, and Other Stories*. *Christian Inquirer*,
    May 6, 120.
———. *Literary World*, May 6, 269.
———. *New York Evangelist*, June 15, 96.
Review of *Hans Andersen's Story Book*. *Literary World*, December 2, 873.
———. *Littell's Living Age*, December 16, 527.
Review of *The Dream of Little Tuk, and Other Tales*. *Boston Olive Branch*, March
    4, 3.
———. *Christian Inquirer*, June 17, 142.
———. *Christian Register*, May 20, 83.
———. *Christian World*, March 4, 3.

———. *Trumpet and Universalist Magazine*, March 4, 151.

Review of *The Shoes of Fortune, and Other Tales*. *Literary World*, May 6, 268.

———. *Presbyterian*, May 13, 80.

Review of *The Two Baronesses*. *Times* (London), December 26, 3.

"Topics of the Month" (*A Picture Book without Pictures*). *Holden's Dollar Magazine*, June, 384.

1849

Christian Inquirer (*Hans Andersen's Story Book*), December 15, 2.

Review of *A Picture Book without Pictures, and Other Stories*. *Christian Parlor Book*, January, 63.

Review of *The True Story of My Life* ("A Happy and Beautiful Life"). *Christian Register*, April 28, 1.

———. ("Hans Christian Andersen"). *Holden's Dollar Magazine*, July, 446–48.

———. *Salem Observer* (Salem, MA), July 14, 1.

1850

Review of *Wonderful Tales from Denmark*. *New-York Commercial Advertiser*, December 19, 2.

1851

Review of *The Story Teller* ("Holden's Review"). *Dollar Magazine*, June, 40.

Review of *Wonderful Tales from Denmark*. *Raleigh Register*, April 23, 1851, 2.

Sunday School Gazette (*The True Story of My Life*), January 4, 35.

1852

Leland, Charles Godfrey. "Authors and Books." *International Magazine*, April, 553.

Tennessean (*The True Story of My Life*), February 27, 2.

1853

Hillard, George Stillman. "Hans Christian Andersen." In *Six Months in Italy*, 2:440–43. Boston: Ticknor, Reed, and Fields.

Review of *A Poet's Day Dreams*. *Una*, July, 84–85.

1854

"You Have Heard of Them: Hans Christian Andersen." *Home Journal*, September 30, 1.

1857

American Publishers' Circular and Literary Gazette (*To Be, or Not to Be?*), February 7, 84; February 14, 102; June 27, 402; July 4, 421; July 11, 439, 441.

"Danish Authors: From Bayard Taylor's 'Correspondence to the New York Tribune.'" *American Publishers' Circular and Literary Gazette*, July 25, 466.

"Hans Christian Andersen, the Danish Poet." *Ballou's Pictorial Drawing-Room Companion*, October 17, 252.

Review of *To Be, or Not to Be? A Novel* (implicit). *Putnam's Monthly Magazine*, September, 411–12.

Review of *To Be, or Not to Be? A Novel. Athenæum*, June, 27, 815–16.

———. *Examiner*, June 27, 405.

———. *Literary Gazette*, June 13, 561–62.

———. *Lloyd's Weekly London Newspaper*, June 21, 8.

Rhode Island Schoolmaster (*To Be, or Not to Be? A Novel*), November, 285.

1858

Review of *Only a Fiddler! Ballou's Pictorial Drawing-Room Companion*, December 4, 352.

Seymour, Charles B. "Hans Christian Andersen." In *Self-Made Men*, 84–93. New York: Harper & Brothers, 1858.

Taylor, Bayard. "Journey to Gottenburg and Copenhagen." In *Northern Travel: Summer and Winter Pictures[;] Sweden, Denmark, and Lapland*, by Bayard Taylor, 222–34. London: Sampson Low and Son, 1858 [1857]; New York: Putnam, 1858 [1857].

1860

Godey's Lady's Book and Magazine (*The Sand-Hills of Jutland*), September, 274.

Morning Star (*The Sand-Hills of Jutland*), August 22, 8.

Neal, John. Review of *The Sand-Hills of Jutland. Portland Transcript*, July 21, 123.

Philadelphia Inquirer (*The Sand-Hills of Jutland*), July 4, 1.

Portland Transcript (*The Sand-Hills of Jutland*), July 14, 115.

Review. "Literary Intelligence: Poems in Prose" (*The Sand-Hills of Jutland*). *Providence Evening Press*, July 6, 2.

Review of *The Sand-Hills of Jutland. Boston Evening Transcript*, July 26, 1.
————. *Crayon*, September, 270.
————. *Daily Ohio State Journal*, October 26, 2.
————. *Eclectic Magazine*, August, 571–72.
————. *Evening Post*, September 20, 1.
————. *Independent*, August 16, 8.
————. *Ladies' Repository* (Boston), August, 104.
————. *Lady's Home Magazine*, September, 176–78 (From the *Home Journal*).
————. *Merchants' Magazine and Commercial Review*, August, 272.
————. *Methodist Quarterly Review*, October, 695.
————. *Monthly Journal of the American Unitarian Association*, October, 487.
————. *New-York Commercial Advertiser*, August 3, 1.
————. *Peterson's Magazine*, September, 237.
Sears, Edmund Hamilton. Review of *The Sand-Hills of Jutland. Monthly Religious Magazine and Independent Journal*, August, 143.
Vermont Phoenix (*The Sand-Hills of Jutland*), July 7, 2.

1861

Browne, J. Ross. ("Literature for Children in Germany and the United States"). *Daily Evening Bulletin*, April 3, 1.
————. "Newspapers and Children's Stories." *Sacramento Daily Union*, March 30, 1.
Taylor, Bayard. "Hans Christian Andersen." *Independent*, March 14, 1.

1863

Review of *The Ice-Maiden, and Other Tales. American Literary Gazette and Publishers' Circular*, May 1, 20.
————. *Independent*, August 13, 2.
————. *Peterson's Magazine*, April, 321.
————. *Press* (Philadelphia), February 26, 2.
————. *World*, April 18, 2.

1864

Godey's Lady's Book and Magazine (*The Ice-Maiden, and Other Tales*), February, 201.
Massachusetts Teacher and Journal of Home and School Education (*Bilderbuch ohne Bilder* [*Picture Book without Pictures*]), December, 404.
Review of an uncertain volume of tales ("Literary Notices"). *North American and United States Gazette*, December 20, 1.

Review of *The Danish Story Book; Little Rudy* ["The Ice Maiden"]*, and Other Stories*; *The Mud-King's Daughter, and Other Tales* ("Book Notices: Juvenile"). *American Literary Gazette and Publishers' Circular*, December 15, 114.

Review of *The Ice-Maiden, and Other Tales*. *Peterson's Magazine*, February 1864, 159.

1865

"Juvenile Works." *Springfield Weekly Republican*, December 16, 3.

K. E. "Hans Christian Andersen." *Boston Evening Transcript*, December 29, 1.

New Haven Daily Palladium (*Andersen's Tales*). December 23, 2.

Winsor, Justin. "Boston." *Round Table*, December 2, 206.

1867

"Hans Christian Andersen." *Arthur's Home Magazine*, September, 185.

"Reading for Children." *Round Table*, May 18, 309.

Review of *The Will-o'-the-Wisps Are in Town, and Other New Stories*. *Round Table*, April 6, 218.

1868

"Andersen, the Novelist." *Ripley Bee*, November 11, 1.

Farrar, Frederick Howard. "What the Moon Saw." *Fayetteville News*, May 19, 1.

———. *The Land We Love*, April, 493–94.

———. *Tarboro Southerner*, May 7, 1.

Review of *The Improvisatore*. *Galveston Daily News*, May 10, 2.

1869

American Literary Gazette and Publishers' Circular ("The Dying Child"), September 1, 254.

Boston Daily Advertiser (*The Two Baronesses*), October 2, 2.

———. (From the *Home Journal; The Two Baronesses*), December 18, 2.

Boston Journal (*The Improvisatore*), August 28, 3.

"Brief Mention" (*The Two Baronesses*). *Harper's New Monthly Magazine*, December, 144.

Clark, William J., Jr. Review of *The Improvisatore*. *Evening Telegraph*, September 11, 6.

Congregationalist and Boston Recorder (*The Two Baronesses*), October 14, 6.

"Editor's Book Table" (*The Improvisatore*). *Harper's New Monthly Magazine*, November, 925.

Independent (*The Two Baronesses*), October 14, 6.

Review of *The Improvisatore* and *The Two Baronesses: A Romance. Nation*, December 9, 514.

Review of *The Improvisatore. Advance*, October 14, 6.

———. *Albion*, September 25, 578.

———. *American Literary Gazette and Publishers' Circular*, September 1, 254.

———. *Brooklyn Daily Eagle*, September 8, 4.

———. *Christian Advocate*, September 30, 307.

———. *Maine Farmer*, September 25, 2.

———. *Pittsburgh Daily Commercial*, October 14, 3.

———. *Portland Transcript*, September 11, 186.

———. *Universe*, October 30, 145.

———. *Zion's Herald*, October 7, 473.

Review of *The Two Baronesses: A Romance. Albany Argus*, October 8, 2.

———. *Hartford Daily Courant*, October 18, 1.

———. *Daily Evening Bulletin*, November 13, 1.

———. *Detroit Free Press*, November 1, 3.

———. *Eclectic Magazine*, January, 119.

———. *Evening Telegraph*, November 26, 6.

———. *New York Evangelist*, October 14, 2.

———. *North American and United States Gazette*, October 28, 1.

———. *Portland Transcript*, October 6, 226.

———. *Presbyterian*, November 27, 7.

———. *Providence Evening Press*, October 5, 1.

———. *Sacramento Daily Union*, November 20, 2.

"The Worship of Children." *Spectator* (London), November 6, 10–12.

1870

Albion (*Wonder Stories Told for Children*). March 19, 185.

American Literary Gazette and Publishers' Circular (*In Spain and A Visit to Portugal*), May 16, 42.

American Presbyterian Review (*Wonder Stories Told for Children*), October, 768.

Boston Recorder (*O. T.*), June 23, 200.

Brooklyn Daily Eagle (*In Spain and A Visit to Portugal*), May 2, 2.

Clark, William J., Jr. "Literature: Review of New Books" [*O. T.: A Danish Romance*]. *Evening Telegraph*, July 1, 7.

Congregationalist and Boston Recorder (*In Spain and A Visit to Portugal*), May 5, 8.

Eclectic (*In Spain and A Visit to Portugal*), June, 763–64.

Evening Telegraph (*In Spain and A Visit to Portugal*), May 4, 6.

———. (*Only a Fiddler*), September 1, 7.

Liberal Christian (*Wonder Stories Told for Children*), April 2, 3.

Literary World (*Lucky Peer*), December, 107.
———. (*Only a Fiddler*), September, 61.
Maine Farmer (*In Spain and A Visit to Portugal*), May 28, 2.
Massachusetts Ploughman and New England Journal of Agriculture (*Only a Fiddler*), October 8, 3.
Monthly Review and Religious Magazine (*In Spain and A Visit to Portugal*), August, 192.
———. (*Wonder Stories Told for Children*), March, 310.
New York Evangelist (*Lucky Peer*), December 15, 5.
New-York Tribune (*Only a Fiddler*), August 18, 6.
"Notes on Books and Authors: *The Story of My Life.*" *Trade Circular and Publishers' Bulletin*, October 18, 9.
Review of "Hans Christian Andersen's Works." *Eclectic Magazine*, January, 118–19.
Review of *In Spain and A Visit to Portugal*. *Albany Evening Journal*, May 19, 2.
———. *American Quarterly Church Review*, July, 319.
———. *Christian Standard*, May 21, 365.
———. *Christian Union*, May 28, 343.
———. *Congregational Review*, September, 496.
———. *Eclectic Magazine*, June, 764.
———. *Evangelical Quarterly*, July, 484.
———. *Hours at Home*, July, 289.
———. *Liberal Christian*, May 28, 3.
———. *Phrenological Journal*, June, 437.
———. *Pittsburgh Weekly Gazette*, May 13, 2.
———. *Portland Transcript*, March 14, 50.
———. *Presbyterian*, May 14, 7.
———. *Southern Review*, July, 229–30.
———. *Sunday-School Times*, May 21, 333.
———. *Zion's Herald*, May 26, 245.
Review of *O. T.: A Danish Romance*. *Brooklyn Daily Eagle*, July 20, 1.
———. *Churchman*, July 23, 248.
———. *Daily Picayune*, July 17, 9.
———. *Golden Hours*, November, 574.
———. *Independent*, July 28, 6.
———. *Lowell Daily Citizen and News*, July 23, 2.
———. *New York Evangelist*, July 21, 8.
———. *North American and United States Gazette*, July 7, 1.
———. *Portland Transcript*, July 9, 114.
Review of *Only a Fiddler*. *Christian Union*, September 3, 34.
———. *Daily Evening Bulletin*, September 24, 1.
———. *Evening Post*, October 11, 1.
———. *North American and United States Gazette*, August 26, 1.
———. *Norwich Morning Bulletin*, October 12, 2.
———. *Portland Daily Press*, September 21, 1.
———. *Portland Transcript*, October 1, 210.

———. *Providence Evening Press*, September 29, 1.

———. *Zion's Herald*, October 20, 497.

Review of *The Improvisatore. Catholic World*, January, 575.

———. *Vermont Watchman & State Journal*, May 4, 1; May 11, 3.

Review of *The Two Baronesses: A Romance. American Presbyterian Review*, January, 193.

Review of *Wonder Stories Told for Children. Advance*, March 10, 6.

———. *Bangor Daily Whig and Courier*, March 15, 2.

———. *Christian Union*, March 12, 167.

———. *Congregationalist and Boston Recorder*, March 3, 6.

———. *Eclectic Magazine*, January, 118–19.

———. *New York Evangelist*, March 31, 8.

———. *North American and United States Gazette*, March 7, 1.

———. *Portland Transcript*, March 5, 386.

———. *Providence Evening Press*, February 28, 1.

———. *Sunday-School Times*, May 7, 301.

Revolution (*In Spain and A Visit to Portugal*), May 5, 286.

Vermont Watchman & State Journal (*O. T.*), August 31.

Zion's Herald (*The Two Baronesses*), January 6, 5.

1871

Advance (*Lucky Peer*), March 30, 6.

Albany Argus (*Stories and Tales*), March 21, 2.

American Literary Gazette and Publishers' Circular (*Lucky Peer*), February 1, 121.

———. (*Lucky Peer*), April 1, 231.

———. (*Pictures of Travel*), September 1, 257.

———. (*The Story of My Life*), April 15, 257.

Book Buyer (*Lucky Peer*), January 16, 17.

———. (*Lucky Peer*), March 15, 3, 16.

Boston Daily Advertiser (*A Poet's Bazaar*), June 20, 1.

———. (*Pictures of Travel*), September 11, 2.

Christian Standard (*Stories and Tales*), March 25, 93.

Christian Union (*Lucky Peer*), March 22, 192.

Congregationalist (*Pictures of Travel*), October 12, 6.

Daily Evening Bulletin (*Pictures of Travel*), October 7, 1.

———. (*Stories and Tales*), February 25, 1.

Daily Picayune (*A Poet's Bazaar*), June 11, 10.

Detroit Free Press (*Pictures of Travel*), October 29, 5.

Evening Telegraph (*Stories and Tales*), February 28, 6.

———. (*The Story of My Life*), April 18, 6.

Figaro (*The Story of My Life*), April 20, 6.

Golden Age (*Stories and Tales*), March 4, 1.

Herald of Health and Journal of Physical Culture (*The Story of My Life*), July, 42.

"Literary and Art Items" (poetry and plays), *Congregationalist*, September 28, 6.

"Literary Bulletin: *The Story of My Life*." *Trade Circular and Publishers' Bulletin*, February 1, 11.

Literary World (*The Story of My Life*), May, 188.

Memphis Daily Appeal (*The Story of My Life*), May 13, 7.

New England Homestead (*A Poet's Bazaar*), July, 60.

———. (*The Story of My Life*), July, 60.

New York Evangelist (*Pictures of Travel*), September 14, 6.

"Notes on Recent Publications" (*A Poet's Bazaar*). *Riverside Bulletin*, June 15, 23.

Portsmouth Journal of Literature and Politics (*A Poet's Bazaar*), June 17, 1.

———. (*Stories and Tales*), March 25, 1.

———. (*The Story of My Life*), May 6, 1.

Presbyterian (*Stories and Tales*), March 4, 7.

———. (*The Story of My Life*), August 5, 7.

Reformed Church Messenger (*Lucky Peer*), March 22, 8.

Religious Magazine and Monthly Review (*A Poet's Bazaar*), October, 388.

———. (*Pictures of Travel*), October, 387.

———. (*Stories and Tales*), April, 440.

———. (*The Story of My Life*), May, 544.

Review of *A Poet's Bazaar*. *Bangor Daily Whig & Courier*, June 8, 3.

———. *Christian Union*, June 28, 407.

———. *Daily Evening Bulletin*, June 17, 1871, 1.

———. *Detroit Free Press*, July 2, 5.

———. *Evening Post*, June 9, 1.

———. *Hall's Journal of Health*, July, 168.

———. *Harper's New Monthly Magazine*, September, 623.

———. *New-York Tribune*, June 2, 7.

———. *Overland Monthly*, January, 102–3.

———. *Portland Daily Press*, June 7, 1.

———. *Portland Transcript*, July 1, 59.

———. *Providence Evening Press*, June 20, 1.

———. *Sunday-School Times*, July 15, 445.

———. *Vermont Watchman & State Journal*, July 5, 1.

———. *Wood's Household Magazine*, February, 92.

Review of *O. T.: A Danish Romance*. *Moore's Rural New-Yorker*, April, 210.

Review of *Pictures of Travel*. *Capital*, December 23, 1.

———. *Christian Union*, September 20, 183.

———. *Churchman*, October 28, 348.

———. *College Courant*, September 16, 115.

———. *Democrat and Chronicle*, October 17, 2.

———. *Newport Mercury*, September 16, 2.

———. *North American and United States Gazette*, October 3, 1.

———. *Portland Transcript*, October 7, 218.

———. *Providence Evening Press*, September 26, 1.

———. *Trenton State Gazette*, October 9, 2.

Review of *Stories and Tales*. *Christian Union*, March 1, 135.

————. *College Courant*, April 1, 151.

————. *Hartford Daily Courant*, March 2, 1.

————. *Independent*, March 16, 6.

————. *Indianapolis News*, March 13, 3.

————. *Ladies' Repository* (Cincinnati), August, 153.

————. *Moore's Rural New-Yorker*, April 15, 240.

————. *Phrenological Journal*, April, 291.

————. *Portland Transcript*, March 18, 402.

————. *Press* (Chicago), April, 8.

Review of *The Story of My Life* ("Andersen's Autobiography"). *Aldine*, June, 100.

————. *Christian Standard*, May 13, 149.

————. *Christian Union*, April 26, 263.

————. *Churchman*, May 13, 156.

————. *Cleveland Morning Herald*, April 15, 5.

————. *College Courant*, May 6, 211.

————. *Congregational Review*, November, 577–78.

————. *Daily Evening Bulletin*, April 8, 1.

————. *Daily Picayune*, April 9, 7.

————. *Georgia Weekly Telegraph and Georgia Journal & Messenger*, April 18, 6.

————. *Harvard Advocate*, April 14, 74–75.

————. *National Sunday School Teacher*, September, 358.

————. *North American and United States Gazette*, April 14, 1.

————. *Peterson's Magazine*, September, 227.

————. *Phrenological Journal*, June, 435.

————. *Portland Transcript*, April 29, 34.

————. *Providence Evening Press*, June 20, 1.

————. *Riverside Bulletin*, March 15, 10.

————. *Sunday-School Times*, April 22, 253.

————. *Vermont Watchman & State Journal*, May 3, 1.

Review of *What the Moon Saw, and Other Tales*. *Tennessean*, November 29, 4.

Sunday-School Times (*Pictures of Travel*), September 23, 605.

Tennessean (*The Story of My Life*), April 16, 2.

Trade Circular and Publishers' Bulletin (*Pictures of Travel*), September 11, 11–12.

"Unexpected Pleasure, An" (*Ahasuerus*). *Pittsburgh Weekly Gazette*, November 27, 2.

Vermont Watchman & State Journal (*Pictures of Travel*), October 4, 2.

————. (*Stories and Tales*), March 15, 1.

1872

Christian Standard (*Pictures of Travel*), January 13, 13.

"The Invisible Web." *Ægis and Gazette*, September 14, 2.

————. *Indiana Progress*, November 21, 3.

————. *New Hampshire Sentinel*, October 24, 1.

Reading Times (*A Poet's Bazaar*), January 12, 2.
Review of *Pictures of Travel*. *Scribner's Monthly*, January, 8.

1873

Review of *Good Wishes for the Children*. *Boston Daily Advertiser*, December 24, 2.

1874

"Hans Christian Andersen: The Danish Story Teller." *Alexandria Gazette*, July 27, 1.
"The Scandinavian Drama." *Cincinnati Daily Gazette*, August 28, 3.

1875

Boyesen, Hjalmar Hjorth. "Hans Christian Andersen." *St. Nicholas*, December, 65–70.
"Hans Christian Andersen, the Danish Author." *Phrenological Journal*, September, 154–57.
Scudder, Horace E. "Hans Christian Andersen." "Supplement," *Harper's Weekly*, October 9, 830–32.

1876

"Hans Christian Andersen—*Only a Fiddler*." *Farmers' Home Journal*, September 14, 568.

1878

Goodwyn, Charlotte. "Something Lost." *Daily Picayune*, February 3, 11.

1882

Conway, Moncure Daniel. "The Wandering Jew and His Congenitors." *Methodist Quarterly Review*, July, 489–506.

1885

"Hans Christian Andersen." *Christian Union*, March 5, 20.
"Literary Notes and News." *Dial*, July, 81.

1886

Harrison, James A. "The Destruction of Rome: An Epilogue to Hans Christian Andersen" (*Picture Book without Pictures*). *Critic*, December 11, 287–88.

1887

"A Danish Critic of Modern Authors." *Literary World*, January, 3.
Review of *Fairy-Tales and Stories*. *Critic*, November 26, 272.

1888

Ad for *Harper's Weekly*. *Cultivator & Country Gentleman*, January 5, 19.
Adams, Oscar Fay. "Hans Christian Andersen, 'The Goldsmith of the North.'" *Wide Awake*, August, 137–41.
Boyesen, Hjalmar Hjorth. "Scandinavian Literature. II. Denmark and Sweden." *Chautauquan*, March, 335–37.

1889

Adams, Oscar Fay. "Hans Christian Andersen, 'The Goldsmith of the North.'" In *Dear Old Story-Tellers: Twelve Portraits*, 143–63. Boston: Lothrop, Lee & Shepard.

1891

Review of *The Improvisatore*. *Boston Herald*, June 23, 9.

1892

Boyesen, Hjalmar Hjorth. "An Acquaintance with Hans Christian Andersen." *Century*, March, 785.

Review of *The Improvisatore*. *Lebanon Courier and Semi-weekly Report*, October 26, 6.

1893

Review of *Tales from Hans Andersen*. *Lippincott's Monthly Magazine*, December, 770.

Review of *The Little Mermaid, and Other Stories*. *Detroit Free Press*, November 6, 3.

———. ("Books for the Young. II"). *Dial*, December 16, 400.

———. *Nation*, November 23, 398.

———. *New-York Tribune*, December 19, 8.

1894

"Books for the Young" (*Tales from Hans Andersen*). *Dial*, December 1, 339.

Review of *Fairy Tales*. *Inter Ocean*, December 1, 9.

1895

Gospel Voices: For Sunday-Schools, Church Services, Gospel and Evangelistic Meetings, Young People's Societies, Special Occasions, etc., ed. D. E. Dortch. Nashville, TN: South-Western Publishing House, no. 71.

"Personal Characteristics of Hans Christian Andersen." *Literary Digest*, August 17, 460–61.

Review of R. N. Bain, *Hans Christian Andersen*. *Critic*, November 23, 339–40.

———. *New-York Tribune*, November 16, 10.

———. "The Holiday Books: The Season's Literature Reviewed and Illustrated." *Outlook*, December 7, 955–66.

Review of *Stories and Fairy Tales* ("Holiday Books: Adventure, History and Fairy Tales for Young People"). *New-York Tribune*, November 20, 8.

1896

"Hans Christian Andersen." In *The University of Literature in Twenty Volumes: A Cyclopædia of Universal Literature, Presenting in Alphabetical Arrangement the Biography, Together with Critical Reviews and Extracts, of Eminent Writers of All Lands and All Ages*, edited by E. H. De Puy, vol. 1. New York: J. S. Barcus.

"Uncle Sam's Paradise." *Sunday Inter Ocean*, September 6, 36.

Wells, Benjamin W. "Hans Christian Andersen." In *Library of the World's Best Literature, Ancient and Modern*, edited by Charles Dudley Warner, 1:500–539. New York: International Society.

1897

Review of *Tales from Hans Andersen. Kansas City Journal*, October 11, 6.

1899

Review of *Fairy Tales from Hans Christian Andersen. Chicago Daily Tribune*, December 9, 10.

Ware, Ella Reeve. "Hans Christian Andersen, 'The Danish Boy.'" In *Talks about Authors and Their Work*, by Ella Reeve Ware, 41–51. Chicago: A. Flanagan.

Bibliography

Abbott, Lyman. Preface to *Plymouth Hymnal: For the Church[,] the Social Meeting[,] and the Home*, edited by Lyman Abbott, iii–v. New York: Outlook, 1893.

"About *Bangor Daily Whig & Courier* [Volume] (Bangor, Me.) 1834–1900." Chronicling America: Historic American Newspapers. Accessed July 11, 2015. http://chroniclingamerica.loc.gov/lccn/sn82015185/.

"About *Boston Weekly Messenger* [Volume] (Boston [Mass.]) 1833–1861." Chronicling America: Historic American Newspapers. Accessed April 5, 2016. http://chroniclingamerica.loc.gov/lccn/sn83021311/.

"About *Daily Ohio State Journal* [Volume] (Columbus [Ohio]) 1848–1865." Chronicling America: Historic American Newspapers. Accessed April 11, 2016. http://chroniclingamerica.loc.gov/lccn/sn84024216/.

"About *Kansas City Journal* [Volume] (Kansas City, Mo.) 1897–1928." Chronicling America: Historic American Newspapers. Accessed September 18, 2015. http://chroniclingamerica.loc.gov/lccn/sn86063615/.

"About the *Aegis and Gazette* [Volume] (Worcester, Mass.) 1866–1896." Chronicling America: Historic American Newspapers. Accessed April 18, 2016. http://chroniclingamerica.loc.gov/lccn/sn83020967/.

"About the *Capital* [Volume] (Washington City, D.C.) 1871–18??." Chronicling America: Historic American Newspapers. Accessed April 5, 2016. http://chroniclingamerica.loc.gov/lccn/sn82015845/.

"About the *Christian Advocate* [Volume] (New York [N.Y.]) 1866–1938." Chronicling America: Historic American Newspapers. Accessed April 20, 2015. https://chroniclingamerica.loc.gov/lccn/sn97066043/.

"About the *Christian World* [Volume] (Boston) 1843–1848." Chronicling America: Historic American Newspapers. Accessed May 30, 2015. http://chroniclingamerica.loc.gov/lccn/00221510/.

"About the *Congregationalist* [Microform Reel] (Boston) 1870–1901." Chronicling America: Historic American Newspapers. Accessed February 10, 2017. http://chroniclingamerica.loc.gov/lccn/sf89091700/.

"About the *New-York Evangelist* [Volume] (New York [N.Y.])." Chronicling America: Historic American Newspapers. Accessed April 22, 2015. http://chronicling america.loc.gov/lccn/sn85054545/.

"About the *Sunday-School Times* [Volume] (Philadelphia) 1859–1966." Chronicling America: Historic American Newspapers. Accessed April 23, 2015. http://chroni clingamerica.loc.gov/lccn/sn97067021/.

"About the *Weekly Messenger* [Volume] (Boston) 1811–1815." Chronicling America: Historic American Newspapers. Accessed April 5, 2016. http://chroniclingamerica .loc.gov/lccn/sn84045041/.

"About *Vermont Watchman and State Journal* [Volume] (Montpelier, Vt.) 1836–1883." Chronicling America: Historic American Newspapers. Accessed July 11, 2015. http://chroniclingamerica.loc.gov/lccn/sn84023200/.

Adams, Oscar Fay. *Dear Old Story-Tellers: Twelve Portraits.* Boston: Lothrop, Lee & Shepard, 1889.

Alphonso, Gwendoline. "Hearth and Soul: Economics and Culture in Partisan Conceptions of the Family in the Progressive Era, 1900–1920." *Studies in American Political Development* 24 (2010): 206–32.

Altick, Richard Daniel. *The Shows of London.* Cambridge, MA, and London: Harvard University Press, 1978.

American Periodicals Series Online. http://www.proquest.com/products-services /aps.html.

Amiel's Journal: The Journal Intime of Henri-Frédéric Amiel. Translated by Mrs. Humphry Ward. London and New York: Macmillan, 1891.

Andersen, Hans Christian. *Andersen: H. C. Andersens Samlede Værker.* Edited by Klaus P. Mortensen et al. 18 vols. Copenhagen: Danske Sprog- og Litteraturselskab / Gyldendal, 2003–2007. In the original Danish, the last two words of the title are not capitalized.

———. "Bemærkninger til 'Eventyr og Historier.' 1874." In *H. C. Andersens Samlede Skrifter*, 2nd ed., 15:305–19. Copenhagen: C. A. Reizel, 1880.

———. "The Celebration at Oberammergau." In *Pictures of Travel in Sweden, among the Hartz Mountains, and in Switzerland, with a Visit at Charles Dickens's House.* Author's ed., edited by Horace E. Scudder, 260–66. New York: Hurd and Houghton; Cambridge: Riverside Press, 1871.

———. *The Complete Andersen: All of the 168 Stories by Hans Christian Andersen.* Translated by Jean Hersholt. New York: Heritage Press, 1942–1947.

———. *The Fairy Tale of My Life.* Translated by W. Glyn Jones. Copenhagen, London, and New York: Nyt Nordisk Forlag, 1954.

———. *The Fairy Tale of My Life: An Autobiography.* New York: Cooper Square Press, 2000.

———. "Hans Christian Andersen: Et Besøg hos Charles Dickens i Sommeren 1857." H. C. Andersen Centret / Hans Christian Andersen Center. Last modified April 16, 2015. Accessed April 23, 2015. http://www.andersen.sdu.dk/vaerk/register /info_e.html?vid=716&oph=1.

———. *The Improvisatore: A Novel of Italy.* Translated by Frank Hugus. Minneapolis: University of Minnesota Press, 2018.

———. "Life in Italy: *The Improvisatore* Hardcover—December 31, 1844 by Hans Christian [Mary Howitt, Translator] Anderson [*sic*] (Author)." Accessed April 20, 2015. http://www.amazon.com/Italy-Christian-Howitt-Translator-Anderson /dp/B009OZM2QW.

———. *The Nightingale, and Other Tales.* Translated by Charles Boner. London: Joseph Cundall, 1846.

———. *A Poet's Bazaar.* Translated by Grace Thornton. New York: M. Kesend, 1986.

———. *The Sand-Hills of Jutland.* Translated by Mrs. Anne S. Bushby. London: Richard Bentley, 1860.

———. *Stories and Tales* (Advertisement), vii–xix. New York: Hurd and Houghton, and Cambridge, MA: Riverside Press, 1870.

———. *The Story of My Life.* Author's ed., edited by Horace E. Scudder. New York: Hurd and Houghton; Cambridge, MA: Riverside Press, 1871.

———. *To Be, or Not to Be? A Novel.* Translated by Mrs. [Anne S.] Bushby. London: Richard Bentley, 1857.

———. *The True Story of My Life: A Sketch.* Translated by Mary Howitt. Boston: James Munroe, 1847.

———. *The Two Baronesses: A Romance.* Author's ed., edited by Horace E. Scudder. Boston: Hurd and Houghton, 1869.

———. *A Visit to Portugal.* Author's ed., edited by Horace E. Scudder. New York: Hurd and Houghton; Cambridge: Riverside Press, 1870.

———. *A Visit to Portugal, 1866.* Translated by Grace Thornton. London: Peter Owen, 1972.

———. *A Visit to Spain and North Africa, 1862.* Translated by Grace Thornton. London: Peter Owen, 1975.

———. *What the Moon Saw, and Other Tales.* Translated by H. W. Dulcken. London: George Routledge and Sons, 1866 [1865].

———. *Wonderful Stories for Children.* Translated by Mary Howitt. London: Chapman & Hall, 1846.

Andersen, Jens. *Hans Christian Andersen: A New Life.* Translated by Tiina Nunnally. New York, Woodstock, and London: Overlook Duckworth, 2005.

Andersen og verden: Indlæg fra den Første Internationale H. C. Andersen-Konference 25.–31. august 1991. Edited by Johan de Mylius, Aage Jørgensen, and Viggo Hjørnager Pedersen. Odense: Odense Universitetsforlag, 1993.

Anderseniana. Edited by Ejnar Stig Askgaard. Odense: Odense Bys Museer, 1933–.

The Andersen-Scudder Letters. Edited by Jean Hersholt and Waldemar Westergaard. Berkeley and Los Angeles: University of California Press, 1949.

Anderson, George K. *The Legend of the Wandering Jew.* Providence, RI: Brown University Press, 1965.

Andrews, J. Cutler. *Pittsburgh's* Post-Gazette*: "The First Newspaper West of the Alleghenies."* Boston: Chapman & Grimes, 1936.

Angelo, Frank. *On Guard: A History of the* Detroit Free Press*.* Detroit: Detroit Free Press, 1981.

"Angus Reach." *Spartacus Educational.* Accessed December 1, 2016. http://spartacus -educational.com/Jreach.htm.

The Art of Poetry Written in French by the Sieur de Boileau; Made English. Early English Books Online: Text Creation Partnership. Accessed July 23, 2015. http:// quod.lib.umich.edu/cgi/t/text/text-idx?c=eebo;idno=A28571.

Åström, Harald. *H. C. Andersens genombrott i Sverige: Översättningarna och kritiken 1828–1852.* Odense: Andelsbogtrykkeriet, 1972.

Atchison, Ray M. "The *Land We Love:* A Southern Post-Bellum Magazine of Agriculture, Literature, and Military History." *North Carolina Historical Review* 37 (1960): 506–15.

Aumont, Arthur, and Edgar Collin. *Det danske Nationalteater 1748–1889: En Statistisk Fremstilling af det Kongelige Teaters Historie fra Skuepladsens Aabning paa Kongens Nytorv 18. December 1748 til Udgangen af Sæsonen 1888–89.* 5 parts. Copenhagen: J. Jørgensen, 1896–1899.

Ayer, N. W., and Son. *N. W. Ayer and Son's American Newspaper Annual.* Philadelphia: N. W. Ayer & Son, 1880–1920.

Baehr, Harry W., Jr. *The* New York Tribune *since the Civil War.* New York: Dodd, Mead, 1936.

Bain, Robert Nisbet. *Hans Christian Andersen: A Biography.* New York: Dodd, Mead; London: Lawrence and Bullen, 1895.

Baker, Paul R. *The Fortunate Pilgrims: Americans in Italy, 1800–1860.* Cambridge, MA: Harvard University Press, 1964.

Barnhart, Terry A. *Albert Taylor Bledsoe: Defender of the Old South and Architect of the Lost Cause.* Baton Rouge: Louisiana State University Press, 2011.

Barton, H. Arnold. "The Discovery of Norway Abroad." *Scandinavian Studies* 79 (2007): 25–40.

Bauschinger, Sigrid. *The Trumpet of Reform: German Literature in Nineteenth-Century New England.* Translated by Thomas Hansen. Columbia, SC: Camden House, 1999.

Baym, Nina. *Novels, Readers and Reviewers: Responses to Fiction in Antebellum America.* Ithaca, NY: Cornell University Press, 1984.

Bender, Thomas. *New York Intellect: A History of Intellectual Life in New York City, from 1750 to the Beginnings of Our Own Time.* New York: Knopf, 1987.

Bendroth, Margaret Lamberts. *A School of the Church: Andover Newton across Two Centuries.* Grand Rapids, MI, and Cambridge: Eerdmans, 2008.

Benson, Adolph B. "The Beginning of American Interest in Scandinavian Literature." *Scandinavian Studies and Notes* 8 (1925): 133–41.

———. "Henry Wheaton's Writings on Scandinavia." *Journal of English and Germanic Philology* 29 (1930): 546–61.

Bernd, Clifford Albrecht. *Poetic Realism in Scandinavia and Central Europe 1820–1895.* Columbia, SC: Camden House, 1995.

Binding, Paul. *Hans Christian Andersen: European Witness.* New Haven, CT: Yale University Press, 2014.

Bird, Robert Montgomery. *Sheppard Lee: Written by Himself.* 2 vols. New York: Harper & Brothers, 1836.

Blamirez, David. "The Adventures of Baron Munchhausen." In *Telling Tales: The Impact of Germany on English Children's Books 1780–1918*, 9–22. Cambridge and London: Open Book Publishers, 2009.

Bloom, Robert L. "Morton McMichael's *North American*." *Pennsylvania Magazine of History and Biography*, April 1953, 164–80.

Boles, John. "Jacob Abbott and the Rollo Books: New England Culture for Children." *Journal of Popular Culture* 6 (1973): 507–28.

Booth, John. "A Comparative Study of Four Major Non-denominational, Evangelical, American Hymnals in Current Use." PhD diss., New Orleans Baptist Theological Seminary, 1986.

Borome, Joseph A. "The Life and Letters of Justin Winsor." PhD diss., Columbia University, 1950.

Bostrup, Lise. "H. C. Andersens bouts rimés—sjove digte i en glemt genre." *Anderseniana*, 2015, 5–32.

Bowman, S. M., and R. B. Irwin. *Sherman and His Campaigns: A Military Biography.* New York: Charles B. Richardson, 1865.

Brauda, Ljudmila. "H. C. Andersens eventyr og historier 1850–70." In *Andersen og verden: Indlæg fra den Første Internationale H. C. Andersen-Konference 25.–31. august 1991*, edited by Johan de Mylius, Aage Jørgensen, and Viggo Hjørnager Pedersen, 75–84. Odense: Odense Universitetsforlag, 1993.

Bredsdorff, Elias. *Danish Literature in English Translation, with a Special Hans Christian Andersen Supplement: A Bibliography.* Copenhagen: Ejnar Munksgaard, 1950.

———. "Den engelske kritiks behandling af H. C. Andersen." In *H. C. Andersen og England*, by Elias Bredsdorff. Copenhagen: Rosenkilde og Baggers Forlag, 1954.

———. *H. C. Andersen og Charles Dickens, et venskab og dets opløsning.* Copenhagen: Rosenkilde and Bagger, 1951.

———. *H. C. Andersen og England.* Copenhagen: Rosenkilde og Baggers Forlag, 1954.

———. *Hans Christian Andersen: The Story of His Life and Work 1805–75.* London: Phaidon, 1975.

Breitenstein, Jørgen. "H. C. Andersen og Italien." In *H. C. Andersen og Hans Kunst i Nyt Lys*, edited by Jørgen Breitenstein et al., 31–51. Odense: Odense Universitetsforlag, 1976.

Bridges, Peter. *Donn Piatt: Gadfly of the Gilded Age.* Kent, OH: Kent State University Press, 2012.

"Brief Histories of Printing Companies Cited in This Survey." Print Worcester: Documenting Worcester's Printing Industry. Accessed April 18, 2016. https://www.wpi.edu/academics/library/collections/printworcester/histories_worcester.html.

Brøndsted, Mogens. "Modtagelse." In *"At være eller ikke være": Roman i tre Dele*, by H. C. Andersen, edited by Erik Dal and Mogens Brøndsted, 242–44. Copenhagen: Det Danske Sprog- og Litteraturselskab / Borgen, 2001.

———. "Modtagelse." In *Improvisatoren: Original Roman i to Dele*, by H. C. Andersen, edited by Mogens Brøndsted, 307–10. Copenhagen: Det Danske Sprog- og Litteraturselskab / Borgen, 1987.

————. "Modtagelse." In *Kun en Spillemand: Original Roman i tre Dele*, by H. C. Andersen, edited by Mogens Brøndsted, 290–92. Copenhagen: Det Danske Sprog- og Litteraturselskab / Borgen, 1988.

————. "Modtagelse." In *O. T.: Original Roman i to Dele*, by H. C. Andersen, edited by Mogens Brøndsted, 268. Copenhagen: Det Danske Sprog- og Litteraturselskab / Borgen, 1987.

Brzozowska, Zdydzislawa. "H. C. Andersen i Polen: Belyst ved værker udgivet in Polen i årene 1844–1960." *Anderseniana*, 1970, 88–113.

Bülow, E[duard] v[on]. "Das Novellenbuch: Fortsetzung" [continuation]. *Heidelberger Jahrbücher der Literatur* 43 (1837): 673–88.

————. "So ist der Lauf der Welt." In *Das Novellenbuch, oder hundert Novellen: nach alten italienischen, spanischen, französischen, lateinischen, englischen und deutschen bearbeitet*, edited by Eduard von Bülow, 4:40–44. Leipzig: F. A. Brockhaus, 1836.

Bushby, Anne. *Poems by the Late Anne S. Bushby*. London: Richard Bentley & Son, 1876.

Carey, Edward. *George William Curtis*. Boston and New York: Houghton Mifflin, 1894.

Celenza, Anna Harwell. *Hans Christian Andersen and Music: "The Nightingale" Revealed*. Aldershot and Burlington, VT: Ashgate, 2005.

Chadwick, French Ensor. *The Relations of the United States and Spain: Diplomacy*. New York: Scribner, 1909.

Chamberlin, Joseph Edgar. *The* Boston Transcript*: A History of Its First Hundred Years*. Boston and New York: Houghton Mifflin, 1930.

"The Charleston Book: A Miscellany in Prose and Verse." Simms Initiatives, University of South Carolina. Accessed March 29, 2016. http://simms.library.sc.edu/view_item.php?item=132071.

"*Christian Inquirer*." WorldCat. Accessed June 2, 2015. http://www.worldcat.org/title/christian-inquirer/oclc/8371032.

"The *Christian Register* (1821–1957)." Unitarian Christian Journals: Yesterday and Today. Accessed June 9, 2015. http://www.americanunitarian.org/journals.htm.

Chronicling America: Historic American Newspapers. http://chroniclingamerica.loc.gov.

"Clark, Jr., William J. (1839–1889)." Philadelphia Sketch Club. Accessed April 20, 2015. sketchclub.org/art-collection/archives/.

Cohoon, Lorinda B. *Serialized Citizenships: Periodicals, Books, and American Boys*. Lanham, MD: Scarecrow Press, 2006.

"Commedia." Princeton Dante Project. Accessed November 29, 2015. http://etcweb.princeton.edu/dante/index.html.

"Conferences." H. C. Andersen Centret / Hans Christian Andersen Center. Accessed February 28, 2017. http://andersen.sdu.dk/forskning/konference/index_e.html.

Cook, C. A. *United States Newspaper Directory*. Rev. ed. Chicago: C. A. Cook, 1881.

Courtney, William Prideaux. "Mitford, John (1781–1859)." In *Dictionary of National Biography, 1885–1900*. Last modified November 12, 2012. Accessed April 21, 2015. http://en.wikisource.org/wiki/Mitford,_John_(1781–1859)_(DNB00).

Crane, Oliver. "Timothy Dwight Sprague." In *Record of the Class of 1845 of Yale College*, 182–84. New York: Jenkins & Thomas, 1881.

Csicsila, Joseph. "J. Ross Browne." In *Nineteenth-Century American Fiction Writers*, edited by Kent P. Ljungquist, 57–64. Vol. 202 of *Dictionary of Literary Biography*. Detroit: Gale Research, 1999.

Curran, Eileen. "Biographies of Some Obscure Contributors to 19th-Century Periodicals: Charles Beckwith(-Lohmeyer)." Victoria Research Web. Accessed August 22, 2016. http://victorianresearch.org/Obscure_contributors.html.

Cutler, Wayne, and Michael H. Harris, eds. *Justin Winsor: Scholar-Librarian*. Littleton, CO: Libraries Unlimited, 1980.

"The Cyclopædia of American Biography/Gilder, Richard Watson." Wikisource. Last modified November 18, 2011. Accessed April 23, 2015. http://en.wikisource.org/w/index.php?title=The_Cyclop%C3%A6dia_of_American_Biography/Gilder,_Richard_Watson&oldid=3519470.

Dal, Erik. "Hans Christian Andersen's Tales and America." *Scandinavian Studies* 40 (1968): 1–25.

———. "Jødiske elementer in H. C. Andersens skrifter." In *Andersen og verden: Indlæg fra den Første Internationale H. C. Andersen-Konference 25.–31. august 1991*, edited by Johan de Mylius, Aage Jørgensen, and Viggo Hjørnager Pedersen, 444–52. Odense: Odense Universitetsforlag, 1993.

———. "Modtagelsen." In *Lykke-Peer*, by H. C. Andersen, edited by Erik Dal, 101–3. Copenhagen: Det Danske Sprog- og Litteraturselskab / Borgen, 2000.

———. "Romanens modtagelse." In *De to Baronesser*, by H. C. Andersen, edited by Erik Dal. Copenhagen: Det Danske Sprog- og Litteraturselskab / Borgen, 1997.

"Daniel H. Hill." Office of the Chancellor: UA Presidents and Chancellors. Accessed May 17, 2016. https://chancellor.uark.edu/presidents-chancellors/daniel-h-hill.php.

"Daniel Whedon (1808–1885)." Christian Heritage Fellowship. Accessed April 23, 2015. http://christianheritagefellowship.com/daniel-whedon-1808-1885/.

"The Danish Lutheran Publishing House of Blair, Nebraska." Danish American Archive and Library: Center for Research and Education. Accessed August 5, 2018. http://danishamericanarchive.com/danish-lutheran-publishing-house-blair-nebraska/.

"Davis, Paulina Kellogg Wright." *American National Biography Online*. Accessed December 4, 2016. http://www.anb.org/articles/15/15-00166.html.

Denning, Michael. *Mechanic Accents: Dime Novels and Working-Class Culture in America*. London: Verso, 1987.

"Destruction of Rome, The: Herman Grimm (1886) on the Development of the Rione Ludovisi." Archivio Digitale Boncompagni Ludovisi: Toward a History of the Boncompagni Ludovisi and Their Palace Ludovisi. Accessed October 6, 2016. https://villaludovisi.org.

Detering, Heinrich. "Hans Christian Andersen, poète inconnu." In *(Re)lire Andersen: Modernité de l'œuvre*, edited by Marc Auchet, 257–77. Paris: Klincksieck, 2007.

Dickens, Charles. "Frauds on the Fairies." *Household Words*, October 1853, 97–100.

During, Simon. *Modern Enchantments: The Cultural Power of Secular Magic*. Cambridge, MA: Harvard University Press, 2002.

"Edmund Hamilton Sears." In *Dictionary of Unitarian and Universalist Biography.* Accessed December 2, 2016. http://uudb.org/articles/edmundhamiltonsears.html.

"Edward Lloyd: Victorian Newspaper Proprietor, Publisher and Entrepreneur." EdwardLloyd.org. Accessed April 22, 2015. https://www.edwardlloyd.org.

Egge, Albert E. "Scandinavian Studies in the United States." *Modern Language Notes* 3 (1888): 66–68.

Ehrlich, Heyward. "Charles Frederick Briggs." In *Antebellum Writers in New York*, 2nd ser., edited by Kent P. Ljungquist, 48–60. Vol. 250 of *Dictionary of Literary Biography.* Detroit: Gale Research, 2002.

"Eliza C. Allen (1803–1848)." In *Portraits of American Women in Religion That Appeared in Print before 1861.* LibraryCompany.org. Accessed July 25, 2015. http://www.librarycompany.org/women/portraits_religion/allen.htm.

Endres, Kathleen L., and Therese L. Lueck. *Women's Periodicals in the United States: Consumer Magazines.* Westport, CT, and London: Greenwood, 1995.

"The Evangelical Hymnal." *Missionary Herald*, January 1885, 46.

Exman, Eugene. "*Harper's Weekly* (1857–1900)." In *The House of Harper: One Hundred and Fifty Years of Publishing*, by Eugene Exman, 80–93. New York: Harper & Row, 1967.

———. *The House of Harper: One Hundred and Fifty Years of Publishing.* New York: Harper & Row, 1967.

Eyal, Yonatan. *The Young America Movement and the Transformation of the Democratic Party 1828–1861.* Cambridge: Cambridge University Press, 2007.

Felix, Antonia, et al. *The Post's New York: Celebrating 200 Years of New York City through the Pages and Pictures of the* New York Post. New York: HarperResource, 2001.

"F H Farrar Civil War (Confederate): Confederate Army." Fold 3 Ancestry. Last modified November 9, 2014. Accessed August 15, 2018. https://www.fold3.com/page/636154877-f-h-farrar.

Flom, George T. *A History of Scandinavian Studies in American Universities.* Iowa Studies in Language and Literature 11. Iowa City: State University of Iowa, 1907.

———. "A Sketch of Scandinavian Study in American Universities." *Publications of the Society for the Advancement of Scandinavian Study* 1 (1911): 15–16.

Florio, Caryl. "Introductory Note." In *Children's Hymns, with Tunes: A Book for Use in the Sunday School*, edited by Caryl Florio, 2. New York and Chicago: Biglow & Main, 1885.

Fowler, H. "A Tribute to the Memory of Charles W. Holden." *Holden's Dollar Magazine*, January 1850, 33–38.

"The Fowler Brothers." *The Cabinet of Phrenology and Crime* (blog). Accessed November 9, 2015. http://phrenologyandcrime.com/2014/09/13/the-fowler-brothers/.

Frederickson, Robert S. "Hjalmar Hjorth Boyesen." In *American Realists and Naturalists*, edited by Donald Pizer and Earl N. Harbert, 37–42. Vol. 12 of *Dictionary of Literary Biography.* Detroit: Gale Research, 1982.

Freeman, Mara. "Tree Lore: Elder." Order of Bards, Ovates & Druids. Accessed December 29, 2016. http://www.druidry.org/library/trees/tree-lore-elder.

Friis, Niels. *Det Kongelige Theater: Vor Nationale Scene i Fortid og Nutid.* Copenhagen: H. Hagerup, 1943.

Fryckstedt, Monica Correa. "Geraldine Jewsbury's *Athenaeum* Reviews: A Mirror of Mid-Victorian Attitudes to Fiction." *Victorian Periodicals Review* 23 (1990): 13–25.

"Geneology." *Virginia Magazine of History and Biography* 9 (1902): 323.

"Geraldine." "The Cavern of Waneonda." *American Literary Magazine*, February 1848, 106–11.

Goethe, Johann Wolfgang von. "Didactic Poetry: 1827." In *Essays on Art and Literature*, edited by John Geary, translated by Ellen and Ernst von Nardroff, 194–95. New York: Suhrkamp, 1983.

Goodman, Susan, and Carl Dawson. *William Dean Howells: A Writer's Life.* Berkeley, Los Angeles, and London: University of California Press, 2005.

Graff, Gerald. *Professing Literature: An Institutional History.* Chicago and London: University of Chicago Press, 1987.

Griffin, Joseph, ed. *History of the Press of Maine.* Brunswick, ME: J. Griffin, 1872.

Grimm, Herman. *The Destruction of Rome: A Letter.* Boston: Cupples, Upham, 1886.

Grønbech, Bo. *H. C. Andersen: Levnedsløb-Digtning-Personlighed.* Copenhagen: Nyt Nordisk Forlag Arnold Busck, 1971.

———. *Hans Christian Andersen.* Boston: Twayne, 1980.

Gross, John. *The Rise and Fall of the Man of Letters: English Literary Life since 1800.* Chicago: Ivan R. Dee, 1969.

Guild, Caroline Snowden. *Hymns for Mothers and Children.* 2nd ser. Boston: Walker and Fuller, 1866.

Guilds, John C. *Simms: A Literary Life.* Fayetteville: University of Arkansas Press, 1992.

"H. C. ANDERSEN: DIGTE - 1024 TITLER." H. C. Andersen Centret / Hans Christian Andersen Center. Last modified August 11, 2015. Accessed August 5, 2018. http://andersen.sdu.dk/rundtom/borge/danmark.html.

"H. C. ANDERSEN: EVENTYRSAMLINGER - 38 TITLER." H. C. Andersen Centret / Hans Christian Andersen Center. Last modified December 29, 2011. Accessed August 3, 2015. http://www.andersen.sdu.dk/vaerk/register/esamling.html.

H. C. Andersen: Old Problems and New Readings. Edited by Steven P. Sondrup. Odense and Provo: Hans Christian Andersen Center, University of Southern Denmark Press, and Brigham Young University, 2004.

H. C. Andersens Dagbøger 1871–1872, edited by Kirsten Weber. Vol. 9 of *H. C. Andersens Dagbøger 1825–1875*, edited by Kåre Olsen and H. Topsøe-Jensen. Copenhagen: G • E • C Gads Forlag, 1975.

"Hale, John." In *Appletons' Cyclopædia of American Biography*, vol. 3, edited by John Fiske and James Grant Wilson, 30–33. New York: D. Appleton, 1888.

Hall, Charles Cuthbert, and Sigismond Lasar. Preface to *The Evangelical Hymnal with Tunes*, edited by Charles Cuthbert Hall and Sigismond Lasar, iii–v. New York: A. S. Barnes, 1880.

Hall, Fitzedward. "Recent Biographies of Lessing." *Nation*, December 4, 1879, 390–91.

Hamilton, Holman. *Prologue to Conflict: The Crisis and Compromise of 1850.* 1964. Reprint, Lexington: University Press of Kentucky, 2005.

Handesten, Lars. "Modtagelsen." In *En Digters Bazar*, by H. C. Andersen, edited by Finn Gredal Jensen, Lars Handesten, Gunilla Hermansson, and Klaus P. Mortensen, 387–93. Copenhagen: Det Danske Sprog- og Litteraturselskab / Borgen, 2006.

"Hans Christian Andersen." In *Library of the World's Best Literature, Ancient and Modern*, edited by Charles Dudley Warner, 1:500–539. New York: International Society, 1896.

Hans Christian Andersen, a Poet in Time: Papers from the Second International Hans Christian Andersen Conference 29 July to 2 August 1996. Edited by Johan de Mylius, Aage Jørgensen, and Viggo Hjørnager Pedersen. Odense: Odense University Press, 1999.

Hans Christian Andersen: Between Children's Literature and Adult Literature: Papers from the Fourth International Hans Christian Andersen Conference 1 August to 5 August 2005. Edited by Johan de Mylius, Aage Jørgensen, and Viggo Hjørnager Pedersen. Odense: Hans Christian Andersen Center, University of Southern Denmark, 2005.

"Hans Christian Andersen—FAQ: Stage Performances." H. C. Andersen Centret / Hans Christian Andersen Center. Last modified August 24, 2010. Accessed April 23, 2015. http://www.andersen.sdu.dk/rundtom/faq/index_e.html?emne=scene.

"Hans Christian Andersen: Shadow Pictures." Praesens. Accessed August 1, 2018. http://www.praesens.at/praesens2013/?p=2031.

Harper, J. Henry. *The House of Harper: A Century of Publishing in Franklin Square.* New York and London: Harper Brothers, 1912.

Harrison, Caskie. "Obituary. Fitzedward Hall, C.E., M.A., D.C.L., L.L.D." *Modern Language Notes* 16 (1901): 184–91.

"Harrison, James Albert: 1848–1911." In *Lives of Mississippi Authors, 1817–1967*, edited by James B. Lloyd. Jackson: University Press of Mississippi, 1981.

Harrison, Kimberly, and Richard Fantina, eds. *Victorian Sensations: Essays on a Scandalous Genre.* Columbus: Ohio State University Press, 2006.

Hartmann, Regina. "Selbst- und Fremdbild von Deutschland: Heinrich Heines 'Harzreise' (1826) und Hans Christian Andersens 'Schattenbilder von einer Reise in den Harz [. . .].'" *Wirkendes Wort* 51 (2001): 183–94.

Harvard Advocate. Accessed December 3, 2016. http://theharvardadvocate.com/about.

Haveman, Heather A. *Magazines and the Making of America: Modernization, Community, and Print Culture, 1741–1860.* Princeton, NJ, and Oxford: Princeton University Press, 2015.

"Hawley, Joseph Roswell (1826–1905)." In *Biographical Directory of the United States Congress 1774–Present.* Accessed April 1, 2016. http://bioguide.congress.gov/scripts/biodisplay.pl?index=H000377.

Hawthorne, Nathaniel. "P.'s Correspondence." In *Mosses from an Old Manse*, by Nathaniel Hawthorne. London: Wiley & Putnam, 1846.

"Hermann Jackson Warner Photograph Collection." Massachusetts Historical Society. Accessed December 9, 2016. http://www.masshist.org/collection-guides/view/fap032.

Hilen, Andrew. *Longfellow and Scandinavia: A Study of the Poet's Relationship with the Northern Languages and Literatures.* New Haven, CT: Yale University Press, 1947.

Hillard, George Stillman. "Hans Christian Andersen." In *Six Months in Italy*, by George Stillman Hillard. Vol. 2. Boston: Ticknor, Reed, and Fields, 1853.

———. *The Relation of the Poet to His Age: A Discourse Delivered before the Phi Beta Kappa Society of Harvard University on Thursday, August 24, 1843.* Boston: Charles C. Little and James Brown, 1843.

Hilton, Timothy. *The Pre-Raphaelites.* London: Thames and Hudson, 1970.

"History (1870 Fast Facts)." United States Census Bureau. Accessed May 4, 2015. https://www.census.gov/history/www/through_the_decades/fast_facts/1870_fast_facts.html.

Hjørnager Pedersen, Viggo. "Anne Bushby, Translator of Hans Christian Andersen." *Nordic Journal of English Studies* 3 (2004): 159–72.

———. *Ugly Ducklings? Studies in the English Translations of Hans Christian Andersen's Tales and Stories.* Odense: University Press of Southern Denmark, 2004.

Holk, Iben. "'At være eller ikke være': Roman i tre Dele (1857)." Epoke—Danske Romaner før 1900. Last modified November 1, 2012. Accessed July 30, 2018. https://www.e-poke.dk/andersen_atvaere_1.php.

———. "*Improvisatoren* (1835)." Epoke—Danske Romaner før 1900. Last modified August 3, 2004. Accessed July 20, 2018. https://www.e-poke.dk/andersen_imp_1-2.php.

———. "*Kun en Spillemand: Original Roman i tre Dele* (1837)." Epoke—Danske Romaner før 1900. Last modified January 11, 2005. Accessed April 21, 2015. http://www.e-poke.dk/andersen_kun_1.php.

———. "*O. T.: Original Roman i to Deele* (1836)." Epoke—Danske Romaner før 1900. Last modified August 30, 2004. Accessed March 28, 2016. http://www.e-poke.dk/andersen_ot_1.php.

Holman, J. K. *Wagner's Ring: A Listener's Companion & Concordance.* Pompton Plains, NJ: Amadeus, 1996.

Hostrup Jessen, Paula. *Brothers, Very Far Away and Other Poems.* Edited by Sven H. Rossel. Seattle: Mermaid Press, 1991.

Howe, Charles A. "Moncure Conway." In *Dictionary of Unitarian & Universalist Biography.* Last modified August 31, 2004. Accessed April 23, 2015. http://uudb.org/articles/moncureconway.html.

Howells, William Dean. *Selected Literary Criticism, 1898–1920.* Edited by Ulrich Halfmann, Donald Pizer, and Ronald Gottesman. 3 vols. Bloomington: Indiana University Press, 1993.

Hows, John William Stanhope. *The Ladies' Reader: Designed for the Use of Ladies' Schools and Family.* Philadelphia: E. H. Butler, 1860.

Howitt, Mary. *Mary Howitt: An Autobiography.* Edited by Margaret Howitt. London: Isbister, 1889.

Høybye, Poul. *Andersen et la France.* Copenhagen: Munksgaard, 1960.

———. "H. C. Andersen og Frankrig." *Anderseniana*, 2nd ser., 2, no. 2 (1952): 136–206.

Hudspeth, Robert N. *Ellery Channing.* Twayne's United States Authors Series 223. New York: Twayne, 1973.

Hughes, Winifred. *The Maniac in the Cellar: Sensation Novels of the 1860s.* Princeton, NJ: Princeton University Press, 1980.

Hugus, Frank. "En genvurdering af to dramaer af H. C. Andersen." *Anderseniana,* 2000, 53–69.

———. Introduction to *The Improvisatore: A Novel of Italy,* by Hans Christian Andersen, translated by Frank Hugus, ix–xii. Minneapolis: University of Minnesota Press, 2018.

Hurd, D. Hamilton. *History of Worcester County, Massachusetts with Biographical Sketches of Many of Its Pioneers and Prominent Men.* 2 vols. Philadelphia: J. W. Lewis, 1889.

"I Danmark er jeg født." H. C. Andersens Centret / Hans Christian Andersen Center. Last modified August 11, 2015. Accessed August 5, 2018. http://andersen.sdu.dk /rundtom/borge/danmark.html.

Internet Broadway Database. Accessed December 4, 2016. https://www.ibdb.com/.

Jørgensen, Aage. "H. C. Andersen i Europas spejl." *Anderseniana,* 1995, 22–24.

———. *H. C. Andersen—Litteraturen 1875–1968: En Bibliografi.* Aarhus: Akademisk Boghandel, 1970.

———. *H. C. Andersen—Litteraturen 1969–1994: En Bibliografi.* Odense: H. C. Andersens Hus, 1995.

———. *H. C. Andersen—Litteraturen 1995–2006: En Bibliografi.* Odense: Odense Bys Museer, 2006.

"John B. Gough (1817–1886): The Temperance Orator as Revivalist." TeachUS History.org. Accessed April 19, 2016. http://www.teachushistory.org/second -great-awakening-age-reform/approaches/john-b-gough-1817–1886-temperance -orator-revivalist.

"John Neal." *Lady's Home Magazine,* September 1860, 190.

Juan Manuel, Don. *Count Lucanor; or, The Fifty Pleasant Stories of Patronio.* Translated by James York. London: Gibbings, 1868.

Juergens, George W. *Joseph Pulitzer and the New York World.* Princeton, NJ: Princeton University Press, 1966.

"Justification." Episcopal Church. Accessed August 24, 2016. http://www.episcopal church.org/library/glossary/justification.

Kaplan, Richard L. *Politics and the American Press: The Rise of Objectivity, 1865–1920.* Cambridge: Cambridge University Press, 2002.

Karcher, Carolyn L. *The First Woman in the Republic: A Cultural Biography of Lydia Maria Child.* Durham, NC: Duke University Press, 1994.

"Keene Congregational (Unitarian) Society of Keene, NH." Access Genealogy: A Free Genealogy Resource. Accessed June 9, 2015. http://www.accessgenealogy. com/new-hampshire/keene-congregational-unitarian-society-of-keene-nh.htm.

Keigwin, R. P., trans. *Seven Poems by Hans Christian Andersen, Syv Digte af H. C. Andersen.* 2nd ed. Odense: Hans Christian Andersen's House, 1970.

Kemble, Edward C. *A History of California Newspapers 1846–1858.* Los Gatos, CA: Talisman, 1962.

King, William L. *The Newspaper Press of Charleston, S.C.: A Chronological and Biographical History, Embracing a Period of One Hundred and Forty Years.* Charleston, SC: Edward Perry, 1872.

Knight, Stephen. *The Mysteries of the Cities: Urban Crime Fiction in the Nineteenth Century.* Jefferson, NC, and London: McFarland, 2012.

Kofoed. Niels. "Hans Christian Andersen and the European Literary Tradition." In *Hans Christian Andersen: Danish Writer and Citizen of the World*, edited by Sven Hakon Rossel, 209–56. Amsterdam and New York: Rodopi, 1996.

Kohlenbach, Margarete. "*Lucinde* 1799. Novel by Friedrich Schlegel." In *Encyclopedia of the Romantic Era, 1760–1850*, 2 vols., edited by Christopher John Murray, 2:698–99. London: Routledge, 2004.

Kotzin, Michael C. *Dickens and the Fairy Tale.* Bowling Green, OH: Bowling Green University Popular Press, 1972.

Lanes, Selma G. *Down the Rabbit Hole: Adventures and Misadventures in the Realm of Children's Literature.* New York: Atheneum, 1972.

Langsted, Jørn. "H. C. Andersens 'Hyldemoer,' 1851: En dramaturgisk analyse." *Anderseniana*, 1968, 234–62.

Lawrence, Vera Brodsky. *Strong on Music: The New York Music Scene in the Days of George Templeton Strong.* 3 vols. Chicago: University of Chicago Press, 1988.

Lease, Benjamin. *That Wild Fellow John Neal and the American Literary Revolution.* Chicago and London: University of Chicago Press, 1972.

Lehmann-Haupt, Hellmut, et al. *The Book in America: A History of the Making and Selling of Books in the United States.* 2nd ed. New York: R. R. Bowker, 1952.

Lehuu, Isabelle. *Carnival on the Page: Popular Print Media in Antebellum America.* Chapel Hill: University of North Carolina Press, 2000.

Levin, Johanna. "The 'Vault at Pfaff's': Whitman, Bohemia, and the *Saturday Press.*" In *Bohemia in America, 1858–1920*, by Johanna Levin. Stanford, CA: Stanford University Press, 2010.

"Literacy." Our World in Data. Accessed May 2, 2015. http://ourworldindata.org /data/education-knowledge/literacy/#note-1.

"The *Literary World*." OCLC WorldCat. Accessed July 28, 2015. http://www.world cat.org/title/literary-world/oclc/17880978.

"Longest-Running Broadway Shows." Broadway League. Accessed March 14, 2017. https://www.broadwayleague.com/research/statistics-broadway-nyc/.

Lundskær-Nielsen, Tom. "Language for Children? An Examination of the Language and Intended Readership of the Fairy Tales." In *Hans Christian Andersen: Between Children's Literature and Adult Literature: Papers from the Fourth International Hans Christian Andersen Conference 1 August to 5 August 2005*, edited by Johan de Mylius, Aage Jørgensen, and Viggo Hjørnager Pedersen, 466–77. Odense: Hans Christian Andersen Center, University of Southern Denmark, 2005.

"Mackenzie, Robert Shelton (1809–1880)." The Vault at Pfaff's: An Archive of Art and Literature by the Bohemians of Antebellum New York. Accessed April 20, 2015. http://digital.lib.lehigh.edu/pfaffs/p117/.

MacLeod, Anne Scott. "Children's Literature in America from the Puritan Beginnings to 1870." In *Children's Literature: An Illustrated History*, edited by Peter Hunt, 102–29. Oxford: Oxford University Press, 1995.

Madsen, Annette. "*Count Lucanor* by Don Juan Manuel as Inspiration for Hans Christian Andersen and Other European Writers." In *Hans Christian Andersen, a Poet in Time: Papers from the Second International Hans Christian Andersen Conference 29 July to 2 August 1996*, edited by Johan de Mylius, Aage Jørgensen, and Viggo Hjørnager Pedersen, 173–76. Odense: Odense University Press, 1999.

Marker, Frederick P. *Hans Christian Andersen and the Romantic Theatre: A Study of Stage Practices in the Prenaturalistic Scandinavian Theatre.* Toronto: University of Toronto Press, 1971.

Marquis Who's Who in America. 1908, s.v. "Adams, Oscar Fay."

Martin, E. S. "New Departures and Old Ways." *Ladies' Repository* (Cincinnati), February 1874, 99–103.

Mason, Julian. "The *Land We Love*." In *NCpedia.* Accessed May 12, 2016. http://ncpedia.org/land-we-love.

"Matthew 21:16." Bible Hub. Accessed April 22, 2016. http://biblehub.com/matthew/21-16.htm.

McDonough, James Lee. *William Tecumseh Sherman: In the Service of My Country: A Life.* New York and London: Norton, 2016.

McGill, Frederick T., Jr. *Channing of Concord: A Life of William Ellery Channing II.* New Brunswick, NJ: Rutgers University Press, 1967.

McHenry, Robert, ed. *Famous American Women: A Biographical Dictionary from Colonial Times to the Present.* New York: Dover, 1980.

Miller, Perry. *The Raven and the Whale: The War of Words and Wits in the Era of Poe and Melville.* 1956. Reprint, Westport, CT: Greenwood, 1973.

Milne, Gordon. *George William Curtis & the Genteel Tradition.* Bloomington: Indiana University Press, 1956.

Mitchell, Jerome. *The Walter Scott Operas: An Analysis of the Operas Based on the Works of Sir Walter Scott.* Tuscaloosa: University of Alabama Press, 1977.

Møller, Tove Barfoed. "H. C. Andersen og teatret." *Anderseniana*, 1998, 7–20.

———. "H. C. Andersens Scott-libretti i samtids- og nutidsbelysning." *Anderseniana*, 1996, 11–24.

———. *Teaterdigteren H. C. Andersen og "Meer end Perler og Guld": En dramaturgisk-musikalsk undersøgelse.* Odense: Odense Universitetsforlag, 1995.

Möller-Christensen, Ivy York. *Den gyldne trekant: H. C. Andersens gennembrud i Tyskland 1831–1850.* Odense: Odense Universitetsforlag, 1992.

Montluzin, Emily Lorraine de. "The *Gentleman's Magazine*: A Short History." Attributions of Authorship in the *Gentleman's Magazine*, 1731–1868: An Electronic Union List. Last modified March 13, 2003. Accessed April 21, 2015. bsuva.org/bsuva/gm2/GMintro.html#history.

Mortensen, Klaus. "The Poetry of Chance: On Hans Christian Andersen's 'Picture Book without Pictures.'" *Fabula* 46 (2005): 55–66.

Mott, Frank Luther. *American Journalism, a History: 1690–1960.* 3rd ed. New York: Macmillan, 1962.

———. *A History of American Magazines 1741–1850.* 1930. Reprint, Cambridge, MA: Harvard University Press, 1957.

———. *A History of American Magazines 1850–1865.* 1938. Reprint, Cambridge, MA: Harvard University Press, 1966.

———. *A History of American Magazines 1865–1885.* 1938. Reprint, Cambridge, MA: Harvard University Press, 1966.

———. *A History of American Magazines 1885–1905.* Cambridge, MA: Harvard University Press, 1957.

Murray, James R. "Publishers Preface." In *Heavenward: A Choice Selection of Sacred Songs, Adapted to the Wants of Sunday Schools, Praise Meetings, and the Home Circle,* edited by James R. Murray. Cleveland: Brainard, 1877.

Mylius, Johan de. "Et stykke, der gav hus." *Anderseniana,* 1996, 59–78.

———. "H. C. Andersen og politik." In *Myte og Roman: H. C. Andersens romaner mellem romantik og realisme: En traditionshistorisk undersøgelse.* Copenhagen: Gyldendal, 1981.

———. "Hans Christian Andersen—on the Wave of Liberalism." In *Hans Christian Andersen, a Poet in Time: Papers from the Second International Hans Christian Andersen Conference 29 July to 2 August 1996,* edited by Johan de Mylius, Aage Jørgensen, and Viggo Hjørnager Pedersen, 109–24. Odense: Odense University Press, 1999.

———. *Myte og Roman: H. C. Andersens romaner mellem romantik og realisme: En traditionshistorisk undersøgelse.* Copenhagen: Gyldendal, 1981.

———. "Øjeblikket—en anskuelsesform hos H. C. Andersen." In *Andersen og verden: Indlæg fra den Første Internationale H. C. Andersen-Konference 25.–31. august 1991,* edited by Johan de Mylius, Aage Jørgensen, and Viggo Hjørnager Pedersen, 57–74. Odense: Odense Universitetsforlag, 1993.

———. "Religious Views in Hans Christian Andersen's Works—and Their Literary Implications." *Orbis Litterarum* 62 (2007): 23–38.

"*The Mysteries of Paris,* by Eugène Sue." *New World,* October 14, 1843, 446.

The Mysteries of Paris, by Eugène Sue. Openlibrary.org. Accessed April 20, 2015. https://archive.org/stream/mysteriesofpari00suee#page/n5/node/2up.

Nagashima, Yoichi. "For Adults Only." In *Hans Christian Andersen: Between Children's Literature and Adult Literature: Papers from the Fourth International Hans Christian Andersen Conference 1 August to 5 August 2005,* edited by Johan de Mylius, Aage Jørgensen, and Viggo Hjørnager Pedersen, 369–73. Odense: Hans Christian Andersen Center, University of Southern Denmark, 2005.

Nakamura, Masahiro. *Visions of Order in William Gilmore Simms: Southern Conservatism and the Other American Romance.* Columbia: University of South Carolina Press, 2009.

Nevins, Allan. *The Evening Post: A Century of Journalism.* New York: Boni and Liveright, 1922.

New International Encyclopedia. 2nd ed., s.v. "Kock . . . Charles Paul de."

"Newspapers." In *Encyclopedia of Chicago.* Accessed May 19, 2016. http://www.encyclopedia.chicagohistory.org/pages/889.html.

Nielsen, Erling, and Flemming Hovmann, eds. *Kommentar.* Vol. 7 of *H. C. Andersens Eventyr*, edited by Erik Dal et al. Copenhagen: C. A. Reitzels Forlag, 1990.

"Notes for Dorsey GARDNER." Rash's Surname Index. Accessed April 21, 2015. www.pennock.ws/surnames/nti/nti142837.html.

"Obituary: Charles Rudolph Rode." *American Literary Gazette and Publishers' Circular*, March 1, 1865, 238.

O'Brien, David J. *Isaac Hecker: An American Catholic.* New York and Mahwah, NJ: Paulist Press, 1992.

Ohl, J. F. Preface to *School and Parish Hymnal: With Tunes*, compiled and edited by J. F. Ohl, 3–6. Philadelphia: G. W. Frederick, 1892.

"The Oldest US Newspaper in Continuous Publication." ConnecticutHistory.org. Accessed April 1, 2016. http://connecticuthistory.org/the-oldest-newspaper-in-continuous-publication/.

Øster, Anette. "Hans Christian Andersen's Fairy Tales—Children's Literature?" In *Hans Christian Andersen: Between Children's Literature and Adult Literature: Papers from the Fourth International Hans Christian Andersen Conference 1 August to 5 August 2005*, edited by Johan de Mylius, Aage Jørgensen, and Viggo Hjørnager Pedersen, 398–408. Odense: Hans Christian Andersen Center, University of Southern Denmark, 2005.

"Oversigt digte—poems." H. C. Andersen Centret / Hans Christian Andersen Center. Accessed August 5, 2018. http://www.hcandersen-homepage.dk/?page_id=4978.

Palfrey, Francis W. "Memoir of the Hon. George Stillman Hillard, LL.D." *Proceedings of the Massachusetts Historical Society* 19 (1881–1882): 339–48.

"Parke Godwin." In *American Literary Critics and Scholars, 1850–1880*, edited by John W. Rathbun and Monica M. Grecu, 82–86. Vol. 64 of *Dictionary of Literary Biography*. Detroit: Gale Research, 1988.

"Parke Godwin." In *Antebellum Writers in New York*, 2nd ser., edited by Kent P. Ljungquist, 142–47. Vol. 250 of *Dictionary of Literary Biography*. Detroit: Gale Research, 2002.

Parks, Edd Winfield. *William Gilmore Simms as Literary Critic.* Athens: University of Georgia Press, 1961.

"The Passion Play in Oberammergau in 1870." *Harper's New Monthly Magazine*, January 1871, 174–86.

Peebles, J. M. *Immortality and Our Employments in the Hereafter.* Boston: Colby and Rich, 1880.

Pennell, Elizabeth Robins. *Charles Godfrey Leland: A Biography.* 2 vols. Boston: Houghton Mifflin, 1906.

Perman, Michael. *Emancipation and Reconstruction 1862–1879.* Arlington Heights, IL: Harlan Davidson, 1987.

Phillips, Christopher N. *The Hymnal: A Reading History.* Baltimore: Johns Hopkins University Press, 2018.

Pickard, Samuel T. *Life and Letters of John Greenleaf Whittier.* 2 vols. Boston and New York: Houghton, Mifflin and Company, Cambridge, MA: Riverside Press, 1895.

Pochmann, Henry A. *German Culture in America: Philosophical and Literary Influences 1600–1900.* Madison, WI: University of Wisconsin Press, 1961.

Pollak, Gustav. "The *Nation* and Its Contributors." In *Fifty Years of American Idealism: The New York* Nation *1865–1915: Selections and Comments*, edited by Gustav Pollak, 3–83. Boston and New York: Houghton Mifflin, 1915.

Potts, J. H. *The Golden Dawn; or, Light on the Great Future: In This Life, through the Dark Valley, and in the Life Eternal, as Seen in the Best Thoughts of Over Three Hundred Leading Authors and Scholars.* Philadelphia: P. W. Ziegler, 1883.

"The Press." Historical New Orleans. Accessed December 5, 2016. http://www.storyvilledistrictnola.com/newspapers.html.

Proceedings of the American Antiquarian Society, n.s., 25 (1915): 498–501.

Reese, William J. "The Origins of Progressive Education." *History of Education Quarterly* 41 (2001): 1–24.

Rey-Henningsen, Marisa. "Spanien og H. C. Andersen." *Anderseniana*, 2005, 41–61.

Reynolds, David. *Beneath the American Renaissance: The Subversive Imagination in the Age of Emerson and Melville.* New York: Knopf, 1988.

———. Introduction to *The Quaker City, or The Monks of Monk Hall*, by George Lippard. Amherst: University of Massachusetts Press, 1995.

Rindom, Erik. "H. C. Andersen og Ahasverus: En litterærhistorisk Studie ved Andersen-Jubilæet." *Gads Danske Magasin* 24 (1930): 171–92.

"Robert G. Valentine Family Papers." Massachusetts Historical Society: Collection Guides. Accessed June 2, 2015. http://www.masshist.org/collection-guides/view/fa0383.

"Robert Shelton Mackenzie." Virtual American Biographies. Accessed April 20, 2015. http://famousamericans.net/robertsheltonmackenzie/.

Rowell, George P. *George P. Rowell & Co.'s American Newspaper Directory.* New York: Rowell, 1869–1909.

Rowland, Herbert. "The Author's Edition of H. C. Andersen's Works: An American-Danish Collaboration." *Orbis Litterarum* 60 (2005): 449–76.

———. "Chronological List of Primary Sources." In *More Than Meets the Eye: Hans Christian Andersen and Nineteenth-Century American Criticism*, by Herbert Rowland. Madison and Teaneck, NJ: Fairleigh Dickinson University Press, 2006.

———. "The Image of H. C. Andersen in American Magazines during the Author's Lifetime." In *H. C. Andersen: Old Problems and New Readings*, edited by Steven P. Sondrup, 175–98. Odense and Provo: University of Southern Denmark Press and Brigham Young University, 2004.

———. *More Than Meets the Eye: Hans Christian Andersen and Nineteenth-Century American Criticism.* Madison and Teaneck, NJ: Fairleigh Dickinson University Press, 2006.

Ruskin, John. "Arrows of the Chace." In *The Works of John Ruskin*, edited by E. T. Cook and Alexander Wedderburn, 34:455–622. London: George Allen, 1908.

———. Introduction to *German Popular Stories*, edited by Edgar Taylor, v–xiv. London: John Camden Hotten, 1868.

Sanborn, Kate. *The Rainbow Calendar.* Boston and New York: Houghton Mifflin, 1889.

Scharf, John Thomas, and Thompson Westcott. *A History of Philadelphia 1609–1884*. 3 vols. Philadelphia: L. H. Everts, 1884.

———. "The *North American and United States Gazette*." In *A History of Philadelphia 1609–1884*, by John Thomas Scharf and Thompson Westcott, 3:1970–73. Philadelphia: L. H. Everts, 1884.

Schoolcraft, Henry Rowe. "The Enchanted Moccasins: A Maskego Tale." In *Algic Researches, Comprising Inquiries Respecting the Mental Characteristics of the North American Indians*, by Henry Rowe Schoolcraft, 1:226–32. 2 vols. New York: Harper & Brothers, 1839.

Schovsbo, Henrik. "Modtagelsen." In *I Spanien*, by H. C. Andersen, edited by Erik Dal and Henrik Schovsbo, 241–42. Copenhagen: Det Danske Sprog- og Litteraturselskab / Borgen, 2004.

Schudson, Michael. *Discovering the News: A Social History of American Newspapers*. New York: Basic Books, 1978.

Scudder, Horace E. "Advertisement." In *Stories and Tales*, by Hans Christian Andersen. Author's ed., edited by Horace E. Scudder, vii–xix. Boston and New York: Hurd and Houghton, 1871.

———. "Advertisement." In *The Story of My Life*, by Hans Christian Andersen. Author's ed., edited by Horace E. Scudder, iii. New York: Hurd and Houghton, 1871.

———. "Advertisement." In *Wonder Stories Told for Children*, by Hans Christian Andersen. Author's ed., edited by Horace E. Scudder, n.p. New York: Hurd and Houghton, 1870.

Sears, Donald A. *John Neal*. Boston: Twayne, 1978.

"Sermon Structures: Text-Application." Concordia Theology. Accessed June 10, 2015. http://concordiatheology.org/sermon-structs/.

Seymour, Charles B. "Hans Christian Andersen." In *Self-Made Men*, by Charles B. Seymour, 84–93. New York: Harper & Brothers, 1858.

———. *Self-Made Men*. New York: Harper & Brothers, 1858.

"Seymour, Charles Bailey (1829–1869) Editor, Essayist, Music Critic, Theater Critic." The Vault at Pfaff's: An Archive of Art and Literature by the Bohemians of Antebellum New York. Accessed October 27, 2015. https://pfaffs.web.lehigh.edu/node/54154.

Sheppard, Si. *The Partisan Press: A History of Media Bias in the United States*. Jefferson, NC, and London: McFarland, 2008.

Shields, David S. Foreword to *William Gilmore Simms's Unfinished Civil War: Consequences for a Southern Man of Letters*, edited by David Moltke-Hansen, ix–xix. Columbia: University of South Carolina Press, 2013.

Shore, Dan. "The Emergence of Danish National Opera, 1779–1846." PhD diss., City University of New York, 2008.

Shorney, George H., Jr. "The History of Hope Publishing Company and Its Divisions and Affiliates." In *Dictionary-Handbook to Hymns for the Living Church*, edited by Donald P. Hustad, 1–21. Carol Stream, IL: Hope Publishing, 1978.

Shumaker, Arthur W. *A History of Indiana Literature: With Emphasis on the Authors of Imaginative Works Who Commenced Writing Prior to World War II*. [Indianapolis]: Indiana Historical Bureau, 1962.

Simon, Janice. "Consuming Pictures: The *Aldine: The Art Journal of America* and the Art of Self-Promotion." *American Transcendental Quarterly* 12 (1998): 220–45.

Smith, Troy Wellington. "From Autonomy to Dependency: The Aesthetics of Andersen's First Novelistic Trilogy." *Anderseniana*, 2017, 33–57.

"Søgning i Brevbasen." H. C. Andersen Centret / Hans Christian Andersen Center. Last modified August 11, 2015. Accessed December 9, 2016. http://andersen.sdu.dk/brevbase/find/.

Sønderholm, Erik. "Hans Christian Andersen als Opernlibrettist: Eine textkritische Untersuchung." *Anderseniana*, 1996, 25–48.

"The Southwestern Company." In *The Tennessee Encyclopedia of History and Culture*. Last modified January 1, 2010. Accessed December 13, 2016. http://tennessee encyclopedia.net/entry.php?rec=1237.

Southwick, Albert B. *150 Years of Worcester: 1848–1998.* Worcester, MA: Chandler House, 1998.

Stoddard, Richard Henry. "Hans Christian Andersen." *National Magazine*, November 1855, 428–33.

Streeby, Shelley. *American Sensations: Class, Empire, and the Production of Popular Culture.* Berkeley: University of California Press, 2002.

Sue, Eugène. *The Mysteries of Paris: A Novel.* Translated by Charles H. Town. New York: Harper & Brothers, 1843.

———. *The Mysteries of Paris: A Romance of the Rich and Poor.* Translated by Henry C. Deming. New York: J. Winchester, 1844.

Svane, Marie-Louise. "Experimente mit dem orientalischen Blickwinkel in H. C. Andersens 'Eines Dichters Basar.'" In *Romantik im Norden*, edited by Annegret Heitmann and Hanne Roswall Laursen, 175–89. Würzburg: Königshausen & Neumann, 2010.

Taylor, Bayard. "Journey to Gottenburg and Copenhagen." In *Northern Travel: Summer and Winter Pictures[;] Sweden, Denmark, and Lapland*, by Bayard Taylor, 222–34. London: Sampson Low and Son, 1858 [1857]; New York: Putnam, 1858 [1857].

———. *Northern Travel: Summer and Winter Pictures[;] Sweden, Denmark, and Lapland.* London: Sampson Low and Son, 1858 [1857]; New York: Putnam, 1858 [1857].

Tebbel, John. *The Creation of an Industry 1630 to 1865.* Vol. 1 of *A History of Book Publishing in the United States.* 4 vols. New York and London: R. R. Bowker, 1972.

———. *The Expansion of an Industry 1865–1919.* Vol. 2 of *A History of Book Publishing in the United States.* 4 vols. New York and London: R. R. Bowker, 1975.

Thackeray, William Makepeace. *The English Humorists of the Eighteenth Century: A Series of Lectures Delivered in England, Scotland, and the United States of America.* Leipzig: Bernhard Tauchnitz, 1853.

Tholle, Johannes. "Hyldebusken." In *Danske Studier for Universitetsjubilæets Danske Samfund*, edited by Gunnar Knudsen and Ejnar Thomsen, 1–38. Copenhagen: Gyldendalske Boghandel Nordisk Forlag, 1944.

Thomas, Emory M. *Robert E. Lee: A Biography.* New York and London: Norton, 1995.

Thomas, Owen C. *Theological Questions: Analysis and Argument.* Wilton, CT: Morehouse-Barlow, 1983.

Thompson, Denys. "A Hundred Years of the Higher Journalism." TheFossils.org. Accessed April 22, 2015. http://www.thefossils.org/horvat/higher/higher.htm.

Thompson, G. R., and Eric Carl Link. *Neutral Ground: New Traditionalism and the American Romance Controversy.* Baton Rouge: Louisiana State University Press, 1999.

Thomsen, Bjarne Thorup. "Connecting Cultures: Hans Christian Andersen as a Travel Writer." *Northern Studies* 39 (2005): 51–69.

———. "Contesting the Novel: Andersen and the Challenges of Criticism, with Particular Reference to 'De to Baronesser.'" *Scandinavica* 46 (2007): 175–94.

"The Timetable Year by Year." H. C. Andersen Centret / Hans Christian Andersen Center. Last modified October 8, 2013. Accessed April 23, 2015. http://www.andersen.sdu.dk/liv/tidstavle/vis_e.html.

Tomlinson, David. "Simms's Monthly Magazine: The *Southern and Western Monthly Magazine and Review.*" *Southern Literary Journal* 8 (1975): 95–125.

Topsøe-Jensen, Helge. "Inledning." In *Mit Livs Eventyr*, by Hans Christian Andersen, edited by Helge Topsøe-Jensen, 1:8–23. 2 vols. Copenhagen: Gyldendal, 1951.

Trencsényi-Waldapfel, Imre. "H. C. Andersen in Ungarn." *Anderseniana* 6 (1966): 19–68.

Turner, Katherine. "Critical Reception to 1900." In *Samuel Johnson in Context*, edited by Jack Lynch, 45–53. Cambridge: Cambridge University Press, 2012.

"The *Una*: American Periodicals." In *Encyclopædia Britannica.* Accessed August 9, 2015. http://www.britannica.com/topic/The-Una.

Vogel, Stanley M. *German Literary Influences on the American Transcendentalists.* New Haven, CT: Yale University Press, 1955.

Wamberg, Niels Birger. *H. C. Andersen og Heiberg: Åndsfrænder og Åndsfjender.* Copenhagen: Politiken, 1971.

Warner, Charles Dudley, ed. *Library of the World's Best Literature, Ancient and Modern.* Vol. 1. New York: International Society, 1896.

Wasowicz, Laura. "A Small Masterpiece and Its Illustrator Are Re-discovered!" *Past Is Present: The American Antiquarian Society Blog*, December 1, 2010. http://pastispresent.org/2010/curatorscorner/a-small-masterpiece-and-its-illustrator-are-re-discovered/comment-page-1/.

Watson, J. Madison. *Independent Fifth Reader.* New York, Chicago, and New Orleans: A. S. Barnes, 1876.

Watts, Edward, and David J. Carlson, eds. *John Neal and Nineteenth-Century American Literature and Culture.* Lewisburg, PA: Bucknell University Press, 2012.

Webb, Henry E. *In Search of Christian Unity: A History of the Restoration Movement.* Cincinnati: Standard, 1990.

Weber, Jennifer L. *Copperheads: The Rise and Fall of Lincoln's Opponents in the North.* New York: Oxford University Press, 2006.

"Wells, Benjamin Willis." Internet Archive. Accessed December 4, 2015. https://archive.org/index.php.

Wennerscheid, Sophie. "Haben oder Nichthaben: Zur Zirkulation der Werte in H. C. Andersens *'At være eller ikke være.'*" In *Wechselkurse des Vertrauens: Zur Konzeptualisierung von Ökonomie und Vertrauen im nordischen Idealismus*, edited by Klaus Müller-Wille and Joachim Schiedermair, 69–87. Tübingen and Basel: A. Francke Verlag, 2013.

Widmer, Edward L. *Young America: The Flowering of Democracy in New York City.* New York and Oxford: Oxford University Press, 1999.

Willard, Frances E. *Writing Out My Heart: Selections from the Journal of Frances E. Willard, 1855–1896.* Edited by Carolyn De Swarte Gifford. Urbana and Chicago: University of Illinois Press, 1995.

"William Ellery Channing." PoemHunter.com. Accessed October 27, 2016. http://www.poemhunter.com/william-ellery-channing/biography/.

Wilpert, Gero von. *Sachwörterbuch der Literatur.* 8th ed. Stuttgart: Kröner Verlag, 2001.

Wimsatt, Mary Ann. *The Major Fiction of William Gilmore Simms: Cultural Traditions and Literary Form.* Baton Rouge and London: Louisiana State University Press, 1989.

Woodring, Carl. *Victorian Samplers: William and Mary Howitt.* Lawrence: University of Kansas Press, 1952.

Woods, Robert. "The Population of Britain in the Nineteenth Century." In *British Population History: From the Black Death to the Present Day*, edited by Michael Anderson, 281–357. Cambridge: Cambridge University Press, 1996.

Wullschlager, Jackie. *Hans Christian Andersen: The Life of a Storyteller.* New York: Knopf, 2001.

Yates, Norris W. *William T. Porter and the* Spirit of the Times*: A Study of the BIG BEAR School of Humor.* Baton Rouge: Louisiana State University Press, 1957.

Young American's Magazine of Self-Improvement, edited by George W. Light, vol. 1. Boston: Charles H. Pierce, 1847. Accessed June 2, 2015. https://books.google.com/books?id=REFAAAAAYAAJ&pg=PA371&lpg=PA371&dq=%22Young+American's+Magazine+of+Self-Improvement+%22&source=bl&ots=GtS8R3NpcS&sig=hddxDCd4qDh7RO4yUjcQGXu8Nts&hl=en&sa=X&ei=ACpuVe-3J4fvtQX2koKICw&ved=0CCAQ6AEwAA#v=onepage&q=%22Young%20American's%20Magazine%20of%20Self-Improvement%20%22&f=false.

"*Zion's Herald*." World Public Library. Accessed April 21, 2015. www.netlibrary.net/articles/Zion's_Herald.

Index of Works by
Hans Christian Andersen

Individual Stories

Index

Abbott, Jacob, 192, 201, 275–76
Abbott, Lyman, 147n19, 293
Adams, Oscar Fay, 287–91, 306n100
Advance, 47, 48, 217
Ægis and Gazette, 20, 21, 230–34, 261n201
Aesop, 188, 193, 202, 219, 287
Albany Evening Journal, 20
Albion, 40, 41–42, 44, 189
Alcott, Louisa May, 58, 223, 275
Aldine, 17, 176–77
Aldrich, Thomas Bailey, 106
Alger, Horatio, 29, 155, 178
Allen, Eliza C., 187–88
American Literary Gazette and Publishers' Circular, 18, 37, 87n67, 88n72, 208, 210, 211, 212
American Literary Magazine, 161
American Presbyterian Review, 18, 72
American Quarterly Church Review, 103–104
Andersen's American reception in an international context, 1, 4, 315–318
Andersen's method of writing fairy tales, 251n44
Andersen's works' relevance to U. S. history, 224–34, 248, 259n174
Anglo American, 189

Art in relation to religion and morality, 61, 63–64, 76, 80, 125–26, 188, 189, 198, 201–202, 247–48, 250n23, 258–59n164, 273, 312
Author's Edition of Andersen's works, 8–9, 12–13, 14, 23, 35, 38, 40, 41, 42, 44, 47, 50, 51, 54, 57, 66, 78, 80, 88, 91, 102, 105, 106, 108, 112, 117, 118, 120, 125, 127n18, 141, 153, 154, 168, 178n3, 178n6, 179n13, 216, 217, 223, 224, 230, 249, 264n227, 279, 317, 320n20

Ballou's Pictorial Drawing-Room Companion, 17, 268
Bacon, Elizabeth A., 202
Bacon, Henry, 28, 202
Bain, R. Nisbet, 237, 291, 293, 294, 296, 297, 299, 307n116, 307n118, 308n138, 309n157
Bang, Herman, 62, 299
Bangor Daily Whig, 20, 114, 219
Barrie, James M., 238
Beckwith(-Lohmeyer), Charles, 65, 69, 95n194, 110
Beecher, Henry Ward, 53, 58, 146n13
Bigelow, Avis A., 235–36, 263nn225–26

About the Author

Herbert Rowland was born and attended school in Little Rock, Arkansas, and received a BA with High Honors in English and German from the University of Arkansas. He continued his study of German literature at the University of Tübingen and, on returning to the United States, earned MA and PhD degrees in German from the University of Oregon. Following two years as a high school teacher in Oregon, he taught first at Eastern Washington University and then at Purdue University, from which he retired as an emeritus professor of German. Rowland's research has dealt mainly with German literature of the late eighteenth and early nineteenth centuries. More recently, he has written on the literary relations among Denmark, Germany, and the United States, principally as they relate to Hans Christian Andersen. He has authored six books and some three dozen articles and book chapters, among other scholarly publications.

CRIMINAL JUSTICE IN IRELAND